COMING OF AGE

Coming of Age

Constructing and Controlling Youth in Munich, 1942–1973

Martin Kalb

berghahn

NEW YORK · OXFORD

www.berghahnbooks.com

Published in 2016 by

Berghahn Books

www.berghahnbooks.com

Library of Congress Cataloging-in-Publication Data

Names: Kalb, Martin, author.
Title: Coming of age : constructing and controlling youth in Munich, 1942–
   1973 / Martin Kalb.
Description: New York : Berghahn Books, 2016. | Includes bibliographical
   references and index.
Identifiers: LCCN 2015041483 (print) | LCCN 2015046187 (ebook) | ISBN
   9781785331534 (hardback : alk. paper) | ISBN 9781785331541 (ebook)
Subjects: LCSH: Juvenile delinquency—Germany—Munich—History—20th
   century. | Youth—Political activity—Germany—Munich—History—20th
   century. | Munich (Germany) —History—20th century.
Classification: LCC HV9160.M8 K35 2016 (print) | LCC HV9160.M8 (ebook) |
   DDC 364.360943/3640904—dc23
LC record available at http://lccn.loc.gov/2015041483

British Library Cataloguing in Publication Data

A catalogue record for this book is available from the British Library

ISBN 978-1-78533-153-4 hardback
ISBN 978-1-78533-154-1 ebook

To Jen, with love

Contents

Illustrations

Preface

"At least you are off the street!" I heard this undoubtedly sarcastic re-
mark numerous times when talking to my dad in Germany while being
in graduate school here in the United States. As a phrase now part of
many family conversations it speaks to the continuing support and interest of my parents in my work and doings (thank you for that!); but it
also alludes to a much larger discourse regarding widespread perceptions of youth: lingering, loitering, and smoking youngsters standing
on street corners wasting time. To think about such attitudes, to hear
widespread understandings of youth and reflect on its history, all of
that reminded me that youth remains only an access point into much
broader conversations around law and order, appropriate behaviors,
and societal norms.

I had stumbled upon such discussions surrounding youth in the immediate post–World War II period on a snowy winter day in Northern
Arizona. I had spent much time looking through newspapers on mi-
crofilm in the library, namely consulting *Die Süddeutsche Zeitung,* the
only major publication I could access for Bavaria. At the time I was interested in complexities surrounding denazification and re-education.
One headline from September 1946, however, caught my attention and
eventually shifted my focus towards discussing images of youth in Munich. It read, "Bavarian Problems: Youth–Food–Export." I wondered,
how could the state of youth be as important as economic recovery and
access to food?

To try answering this question became an incredible journey, one
I could only complete due to the assistance and kindness of many
along the way. My original interest fell on fertile ground within and
outside academia, as many encouraged me to pursue this study early
on. Friends and colleagues alike looked at early ideas, drafts, and conference papers, thus helping this project to move forward. I had the

luxury to dedicate much time to this study based on funding from my home institution and several grants. Yet I am also fortunate to have friends and family in Germany, kind enough to open their doors and homes. Such helpfulness allowed me to afford long research stays in Munich while living in comfortable and welcoming environments. The latter was vital because completing any scholarly project can become a rather lonely endeavor. The actual research process relied on the help of many individuals, including archivists and their patience when answering endless questions. I experienced many moments of such kindness, at times from complete strangers: people sat down with me for several hours to share their stories about growing up in Munich, others simply forwarded me a whole set of primary documents prior to being available elsewhere. One gentleman happily greeted me each morning as I made my way into the reading room of the *Hauptstaatsarchiv* archive in Munich for yet another day of research. In the United States I could build on the help of my dissertation advisors and readers, their suggestions and critiques. Later the questions of students helped me rethink elements of my work, or reminded me about the importance of my study overall. Throughout all of this time the patience and kindness of my ever-supporting wife was vital: without her support and continuing encouragement this book would simply not exist. Then there were numerous readers, the comments of anonymous reviewers, and the help of editors at Berghahn Books that eventually helped me turn a potentially promising manuscript into a coherent publication. As I write this, that journey comes to a conclusion, and I thus look back at numerous open doors and arms of both friends and strangers, many of them simply intrigued by the research, all of them young at one point, and kind enough to share their knowledge and advice, or time and homes. Thank you for such help, support, memories, and stories, and for giving me the opportunity to complete research meant to shed new light onto images of youth as Munich came of age.

Martin Kalb
Bridgewater, VA, 2015

Introduction

The message to the Bavarian president was clear: juvenile delinquency is a major problem in Munich. During his visit to the Bavarian capital in spring 1947 local officials again emphasized their concerns regarding the devastating state of the young: wandering and homeless youth, unwilling to work, and an explosion of sexually transmitted diseases, namely amongst female youth, threatened Munich's recovery.[1] In June 1946 the mayor of Munich had already stressed the need to make juvenile delinquency a priority.[2] Extensive media coverage had also called attention to the fact that "unorganized and unsupervised youth is a problem that cannot be overlooked."[3] Major local newspapers like *Der Münchner Merkur* had even inaugurated a segment primarily dedicated to the problem of youth by November 1946.[4] For adult contemporaries, a supposedly widespread delinquent youth remained a major problem within Munich and allegedly endangered the city's recovery and future.

My study challenges such pervasive constructions or representations of youth as delinquent, and indicates that those in power repeatedly created these threatening images of young people according to their needs. Such an interpretation builds mainly on Michel Foucault's discussion regarding the benefits of illegality, a framework that is in the center of this volume. As Foucault noted in *Discipline and Punish* several decades ago, "the establishment of a delinquency ... has in fact a number of advantages."[5] When taking such benefits into consideration, it is easily apparent how constructions of youth as delinquent provided postwar authorities with options to control society. First, constructing delinquency, and with that a deviant Other, helped mark norms or standards for a society trying to regain stability and normality. If black-marketeering youngsters are deviant, then hard-working adults must be the desired norm. Second, the existence of juvenile deviancy legitimized the being of certain institutions. In fact, shortly after World War II the Youth Welfare Office in Munich pointed to the state of the young to justify and legitimize its quick denazification, re-creation, and overall efforts in disciplining youth. Finally, to physically and symbolically wrestle with such marked ills of society as embodied by juvenile delinquents ultimately increased the power and influence of various institutions. After all, if an institution is successful in dealing with threats to society during times of confusion, then it will gain more legitimacy and authority from those trying to return to normality. Most contemporaries defined such normality as the rule of law, a communal effort to rebuild and recover, and the eventual resurgence of a healthy German national identity.[6] Supervising juvenile delinquency provided the leeway and justification for those in power to expand various mechanisms of social control, which, overall, limited the freedoms not only of the young but also of broader groups in postwar society.

Age plays only a minor role when analyzing postwar constructions of youth. Historically, scholars have understood youth as the phase between childhood and adulthood.[7] Yet postwar representations of youth as delinquent or deviant, I believe, need to be understood more as a broad idea or fluid state. This reading is in line with scholarship seeing youth as a construct only partially connected to age;[8] it also builds on a larger awareness regarding representations of youth as hope and threat.[9] My study solemnly focuses on images of youth as delinquent given its prominence in Munich at the time. I am also not interested in generational cohorts or subcultures. Instead, my discussion concentrates on images or constructs of juvenile delinquency in Munich as a way to access larger conversations.

Such an analysis needs to acknowledge gendered dynamics once describing constructs of male and female youth. Given long-standing terminology, a potential lack of sources, and an underlying bias, male youth continues to dominate many studies. Young females, on the other hand, have been largely ignored. This silence has indeed limited discussions around gendered dynamics, frameworks, and stereotypes, leaving the experiences of young females largely uncovered. *Coming of Age* acknowledges complex dynamics between male and female youth and also exposes that for young females gender and sexuality, *plus* age, mattered. Notions of respectability, traditional gender mores, and sexuality are indeed "all important yet unmentionable" when analyzing female youth, as demonstrated by several scholars.[10] Male youngsters, on the other hand, had comparatively more freedoms, a situation apparent once putting constructs of male and female youth in conversation with each other. Mechanisms of control eventually take shape, as Michel Foucault highlighted in a different context, "through useful and public discourses,"[11] a dynamic apparent in numerous circumstances and beyond Nazi Germany.[12]

With such discussions in mind I ultimately argue that the misery of the young in the postwar period became a microcosm or communication channel for larger conversations. Put differently, youth became the discursive space for discussions about postwar society, future objectives, and contemporary threats. The destitution of youth signified the hardship of society, while allusions to youth could also embody the hope for a quick recovery and a bright future. In fact, talking about youth was not only a way to discuss the young but also became a strategy to revisit, reframe, and rewrite history. In this sense, understanding youth as a construction carrying social meanings is helpful when trying to decipher postwar conversations and norms.

In order to access these conversations I emphasize the importance of representations of youth at a particular juncture in Modern German history, generally defined as the immediate postwar period. In Munich this timeframe arguably began in 1942 with the first aerial bombing targeting the Bavarian capital in August of that year.[13] Whereas a conception of war had been present in different forms on Munich's streets and households beforehand, this event made the city's landscape and topography a real place of war. It thus set the stage for subsequent disorder, destruction, and disillusionment cutting across an only imaginative *Stunde Null* or zero hour.[14] My analysis concludes in 1973. Then local authorities had finally let go of using protests and *the student* to their advantage. Throughout this time period I trace six images of male and female youth in particular and analyze the re-creation, continuation, and alteration of the moral fabric emerging within post–World War II Munich: *the delinquent boy* and *the sexually deviant girl* appeared in the immediate postwar period, or crisis years[15] (1942–1949), and supposedly challenged the rebuilding process. During the time of economic recovery of the miracle years (1949–1962),[16] so-called *Halbstarke* semistrong male rowdies and the newly emerging female *teenager* stepped into the limelight to question traditional norms, gender mores, and overall productivity. The Schwabing riots in 1962 then triggered the rise of the protest years in Munich (1962–1973), defined by *the student* and *the Gammler,* the latter a bumming around youngster hanging out primarily in the bohemian quarter of Schwabing. At that time, to follow historian Konrad Jarausch, *the student* was the most antagonistic image of youth.[17] All of these images of youth have subsisted within the historical record and have a complex history. *Jugendliche Verwahrlosung* or juvenile delinquency amongst male and female youth, for instance, has been described in numerous contexts within

German history prior to World War II. Historian Detlev Peukert most notably engaged with *Halbstarke* working-class youth in Imperial Germany and the Weimar Republic;[18] other scholarship centered on "wild youth" in urban environments during the depression and National Socialism.[19] Constructs of youth as delinquent are thus present in unstable times, making them an excellent avenue for accessing particular conversations tied to the re-creation of societal norms, morals, structures, and institutions.

Reactions to such images of youth repeatedly brought Munich into a state of panic. As captured most notably by cultural theorist Stanley Cohen, societies can slip into hysteria or paranoia once circumstances or groups of people "become defined as a threat to societal values."[20] Cohen focused on the mods and rockers phenomenon in Britain in the 1960s to capture the creation of deviancy and the moral outrage nourished by the media. His framework showed how this panic emerged, and helped describe the exaggerated nature of juvenile delinquency. Fellow cultural theorist Stuart Hall traced such panics and episodes, and ultimately exposed state responses in more detail.[21] My analysis builds on these accounts by illustrating the constructed nature and overall benefits of these moral panics.[22] The inevitably complex process of constructing and controlling youth was not a conspiracy of authorities. It was rather a product of historical precedent, contemporary exigencies, conflicting motives of diverse actors, and the genuinely new circumstances of postwar Germany and the world in which it existed. As noted above, authorities have been constructing youth as deviant in the past.[23] Periods of actual and perceived instability for adult authorities, including war and postwar environments, often provided the context for such conversations. Those constructing and eventually controlling youth, described by scholars like Anthony Platt in similar contexts as "child-savers,"[24] then work under different premises, reaching from a genuine concern for the well-being of youth to more ambiguous motivations and mere self-interest. In Munich, such groups included local institutions, the U.S. Military Government, specific individuals, and many others hoping to secure their power. All of them formed a rather surprising coalition fighting against a perceived threat to society.

My proposed arguments and findings are in conversation with a complex scholarship that has come a long way, and has increasingly moved away from focusing on generations or age cohorts.[25] Such generational frameworks help capture larger trends, yet continue to build on random markers and age ranges, male protagonists, and upper-class sources. The work of scholars like Philippe Ariès, John Gillis, and

Pierre Bourdieu, on the other hand, originally paved the way when discussing youth beyond the restrictive category of age.[26] As cultural historian Richard Ivan Jobs wrote more recently when discussing youth in post–World War II France, "youth served as a common denominator that crossed boundaries of class, gender, race, and region."[27] Germanist Jaimey Fisher takes it a step further and describes youth as a discursive space, an opening to deal with the Nazi past.[28] Although Jobs and Fisher both touch on efforts to regulate behaviors of youth, their discussions of concise mechanisms of control remain limited given their overall emphases. Similar trends are apparent when surveying the historiography focusing on youth in the 1950s and 1960s, although some discussions take on youth culture, Americanization, and protests.[29] Kaspar Maase and Uta Poiger most notably engaged with such conversations yet again limit themselves to descriptive discussions of youth culture within Cold War environments.[30] A widespread reliance on high culture due to a broader geographical focus further speaks to the need for sensible and manageable local case studies that trace images of young people within their local, daily, historical, and topographical contexts. Cultural and social historian Jennifer Evans moved towards this approach in her recent publication *Life Among the Ruins* (2011), utilizing cityscapes as a way to analyze such conversations. *Coming of Age* follows in these footsteps, now with the objective to gather empirical evidence for tracing connections between constructing and controlling youth in Munich.

The city of Munich is an excellent microcosm for achieving these objectives. Located on the elevated plains of Southern Bavaria, this metropolis has always been among the largest urban spaces within the region. Like Berlin, it became an important cultural and industrial center during industrialization; unlike Berlin, it did not have a special status during the Cold War, thus making a focus on youth in this space all the more interesting.[31] Munich dealt with traditional fears of urban environments and modernity, especially because inhabitants of agrarian, conservative, and deeply Catholic backgrounds and mindsets surround the city. This location and environment along with other cultural, regional, and economic factors arguably limited the public display of sex and sexuality in interwar Munich, unlike in a more openminded and liberal Berlin. As the site of Adolf Hitler's failed Beer Hall Putsch of 1923, and with the first Nazi concentration camp Dachau nearby, the former capital of the Nazi movement continues to carry a difficult past. The Americans eventually occupied Munich in April 1945. Soon the city became a vibrant cultural hub and important economic center—along with Frankfurt am Main and Stuttgart—that kept its political composition as a social democratic beacon within a heavily conservative Bavarian state. Until the currency reform in 1948 and the ensuing economic miracle, however, Munich struggled economically given the widespread destruction and refugee crisis. An increased Americanization visible in the rise of popular youth culture and postwar prosperity demonstrated how times increasingly changed thereafter. As early as 1962 Munich then experienced the first supposed student protests, as protestors rioted in the city's bohemian Schwabing district. Six years later Munich mourned the death of a student and a journalist during the protests of 1968. For these reasons the Bavarian capital offers an abundance of materials for historians working on youth, while also being a sensible and manageable case study for mapping local variations and tracing larger postwar trends, all while keeping youth's relations to topography and cityscape in mind.

The historical record offers countless ways to trace, analyze, and discuss images of youth. As historian John Gillis put it, scholars must "capture the voices and faces of the young, as well as those of the adults who claim to speak in their name."[32] The latter is of key importance for my approach because I examine social constructions of youth. After all, to scrutinize the historical record based on the construction of deviant behaviors at a specific conjuncture in history is in the center of *Coming of Age*. I consulted traditional materials in archives throughout Munich, including governmental documents and newspapers. I also relied on popular culture—music, movies, youth magazines—oral histories, city spaces, and other materials. The actual young did increasingly participate in the construction of youth, an aspect that becomes apparent in this study. After all, as noted by one scholar, "'Youth' is not constructed or otherwise acted upon through the pure subjection and passivity of young people: they have clearly participated in the processes of differentiation, and their creation of youth cultures speaks to their ongoing negotiations with the multiplicity of their social identities."[33] Shortly after World War II, local authorities and larger dynamics extremely restricted the power of young people, and only as the new Germany came of age did the voices of young people assist with more force in the configuration of discourses.

Since I present a social microhistory my methodology or use of sources favors a bottom-up approach. As visible in the use of evidence, I move beyond the voices of the powerful. Instead, this analysis places itself within the larger tradition of a history of everyday life (*Alltagsgeschichte*) as I focus on images of youth and the silenced voices of the young. This approach falls in line with an emphasis on those traditionally left behind, to align with the framework laid out by historian

Alf Lüdtke several decades ago. As he put it, *Alltagsgeschichte* concentrates on "the life and survival of those who have remained largely anonymous in history."[34] More recently, historians have built on this approach and kept it alive. As illustrated in that context, historians of *Alltagsgeschichte* "dwell on historical actors' stories, told in the language of everyday life, while nonetheless subjecting their myths (and our own analysis as well) to critical scrutiny, attempting to disclose their contradictions and to identify their human consequences. These acts of criticism and translation 'respect' everyday life in all its contradictions by recounting stories and incidents, yet we criticize and translate these stories patiently not only in order to understand but also to undermine them."[35] *Coming of Age* follows this tradition because it highlights the stories of the disenfranchised; plus, my study investigates and expose dynamics surrounding constructions of youth in everyday Munich. "The model of subaltern studies, with its emphasis on writing history from the margins of power, of trying to hear the voices unrecorded by mainstream histories,"[36] also helps make sense of the sources. The voices of the actual young, male and female, play a key role in my attempt to illustrate life on street corners, in bars, and other supposedly deviant spaces. My focus on a specific urban space, neighborhoods, or the topography at large allows me to shed light onto daily experiences and demonstrates how such helped frame constructs of youth—a different perspective compared to more recent studies trying to take on whole nation-states.[37] Such an emphasis also exposes lingering stereotypes of youth—defined along simplistic binaries as hope and threat—as I ask about the benefits of such constructs, frameworks, or discourses.[38] In effect I read documents along and against the grain in an attempt to expose underlying debates and broader objectives and build on the moralized language apparent in the sources and question its validity and benefits. As a result, this monograph is less interested in simply describing youth but more so in asking *how* and *why* certain descriptions, representations, and images of youth have been useful. Answering this question, I contend, tells us much about dynamics between constructing and controlling youth, everyday life, and the coming of age of Munich as one space with a young West German democracy.

To focus on the postwar period as a way to expose these dynamics is sensible given the surprising limitations of scholarship tied to youth for that time period and broader transformations within Munich's history. Whereas the Nazi era has seen extensive research, the crisis years have experienced little discussion beyond political and occasional economic histories. Apart from a couple of local case studies focusing on youth,[39]

most research highlights the 1950s and beyond, apparent in the si-
lences within a more recent overview.[40] Such an emphasis devalues
continuations and previous discussions surrounding youth; it also
aligns the importance of young people primarily with a rise of popular
culture and protest movements. In contrast, I believe that the exposure
of hidden continuities apparent in daily life within seemingly distinct
periods allows scholars to see such underlining currents. For example, the crisis years in Munich began with the first aerial bombings in
1942 and not with the end of World War II. Throughout this period
mechanisms of social control against youth remained very much in-
tact. Whereas this aspect underlines larger continuities between Nazi
rule and postwar setups, it also allows for comparative discussions
with the situation across the inner-German border. In fact, traditional
mechanisms of social control in place against youth during Nazi rule
lingered well into the postwar period; they were also in many instances
not fundamentally different from mechanisms in place in East Germany.[41] In that way, the coming of age of a postwar society, as it played
out on the streets of Munich, ultimately provides an excellent physical
and metaphorical space for tracing social constructions of youth and
opens up future possibilities for more fully exposing potential similarities regarding mechanisms of control against youth. In Munich, at
least, circumstances changed slowly and the city did not move toward
a more open society until the early 1970s. Finally, this coming of age
epoch marks a fundamental shift within the city's history, apparent
once focusing on images of youth. Confusion increased throughout
the final years of World War II as destruction set in; soon authorities
pushed for reconstruction, and hoped for a quick return to normality.
Once the situation stabilized towards the end of the 1940s, protecting
and defending such normality—increasingly defined along prosperity,
stability, and traditional values—became the key objective of adult
authorities. My focus on discussions surrounding youth brings these
trends to the forefront, in a time when Munich and West Germany as
a whole slowly transitioned into adulthood.

Distinctions between social constructs and the actual young are
grounded in the original language, documents, and discussions. The
terms *youth* or *the young* (*die Jugend*) refers to youth as a social construct; the actual young are described as exactly that, or simply as
youngsters (*Jugendliche*), male (*Jungen*) or female (*Mädchen*). Specific
constructions of youth like *the delinquent boy* are rooted in a German
original, in this case, *der verwahrloste Junge*. Such vocabulary appeared repeatedly in that exact jargon in the historical record and contemporary discussions, and thereby helped me in identifying certain

images of youth. I provide literal translations while I leave the original term in place if its use is in line with a broader scholarly consensus; I also mark constructs or images of youth in italics throughout the text to make it easier for the reader.[42] Gender dynamics embedded within semantics are worth mentioning as well, especially given that male and female identities matured in conversation with each other. In Munich, *the delinquent boy* steps into the limelight along with his female counterpart, the well-researched *sexually deviant girl*, also known as *Veronika Dankeschön* or *Fräulein*. The *Halbstarke* finds his match in *the teenager* during the 1950s, as both are defined in the context of an emerging youth culture and increased Americanization. Such dynamics are apparent for *the student* and *the Gammler* as well, although both constructions pay comparably less attention to still prevalent traditional gender norms. This characteristic is visible in the language because the male student (*der Student*) becomes a broader phrase, which, at times, also works as an umbrella term accommodating young female protestors. Such semantics already underscore the importance of gender mores when determining contemporary conceptions of normality. Clear distinctions also underscore that this is neither a history of a specific generation, nor age cohort or young people; it is also not a subcultural history of those who identified as *Halbstarke* in an attempt to resist existing societal norms. Although such elements informed discussions and alerted me again and again to specific images of youth, neither of these approaches captures the main point of this analysis: a variety of powerful adult contemporaries constructed youth as deviant in order to have reasons to control the young and society.

I organized this book along three main parts, each section tracing, defining, and characterizing overriding constructs of youth before indicating how those representations became tools of social control. Part I sketches the rise of *the delinquent boy* and *the sexually deviant girl* in the so-called crisis years (1942–1949). Here I outline how contemporaries constructed delinquency as homelessness, black marketeering, an apolitical mindset, and sexual deviancy due to fraternization. Not surprisingly, by spring 1946 local U.S. and German authorities began actively targeting youth, a process that reached its climax in a large-scale raid in October 1947. Part II then focuses on the miracle years (1949–1962). During these long 1950s the return to normality defined as economic stability shifted constructions of youth only slightly. *The Halbstarke* semistrong male rowdy and *the teenager* embodied a threat against established values and norms. Americanization of German high culture supposedly ignited a wasteful lifestyle and a rebellious character while so-called teenager clubs moved young girls into unsupervised and thus dangerous spaces. Local authorities together with an increasingly powerful commercial sector symbolically wrestled with such constructs, and based on that, I assert, these groups were able to establish an apolitical young consumer that was of little danger for existing norms. Part III then introduces *the student* and *the Gammler* during the protest years (1962–1973), both constructs emerging in the public sphere in Munich as early as 1962. In this section I demonstrate how open clashes with law enforcement outlined a shift because the increasing power of young people now more actively helped in reshaping existing representations of youth. Authorities, on the other hand, needed to come up with more subtle ways to control youth, an aspect apparent in the rise of undercover missions and the use of spatial planning. In the conclusion I ultimately highlight larger consequences of my analysis; I also comment on the continuing power of constructing youth as a threat in Munich and beyond, thereby demonstrating that talking about youth is still more than simply discussing young people.

Notes

1. "Verwahrloste Großstadtjugend—ein Problem unserer Zeit," *Die Süddeutsche Zeitung,* 31 May 1947.
2. Sozialpädagogische Sammlung Archiv Munich (SozipädAM), Mayor Karl Scharnagl (15 June 1946). See also: Mayor Karl Scharnagl (*Appell an die Münchner Schuljugend, bei der Schutträumung zu helfen; April 11, 1946*), quoted in Richard Bauer, *Ruinen-Jahre: Bilder aus dem zerstörten München 1945–1949* (Munich, 1983), 33.
3. "Bayerische Probleme: Jugend—Ernährung—Export," *Die Süddeutsche Zeitung,* 13 September 1946.
4. "Die Jungen," *Der Münchner Merkur,* November 15, 1946–March 18, 1947.
5. Michel Foucault, *Discipline and Punish: The Birth of the Prison,* 2d ed, trans. Alan Sheridan (New York, 1995), 278.
6. Stefan Berger, *The Search for Normality: National Identity and Historical Consciousness in Germany since 1800* (New York, 1997); Hanna Schissler, ed., *The Miracle Years: A Cultural History of West Germany, 1949–1968* (Princeton, 2001). See also: Jürgen Link, *Versuch über den Normalismus: Wie Normalität produziert wird,* 3r ed. (Göttingen, 2006).
7. See, for instance: Gill Jones, *Youth* (Malden, 2007).
8. See, for example: Mark Ruff, *The Wayward Flock: Catholic Youth in Postwar Germany, 1945–1965* (Chapel Hill, 2005); Richard Ivan Jobs, *Riding the New Wave: Youth and the Rejuvenation of France after the Second World War* (Stanford, 2007); Jaimey Fisher, *Disciplining Germany: Youth, Reeducation, and Reconstruction After the Second World War* (Detroit, 2007); Susan Whitney, *Mobilizing Youth: Communists and Catholics in Interwar*

France (Durham, 2009); Philip Jost Janssen, "Jugend und Jugendbilder in der frühen Bundesrepublik: Kontexte, Diskurse, Umfragen" (Ph.D. diss., Zentrum für Historische Sozialforschung Cologne, 2010).

9. Jobs, *Riding the New Wave*.
10. Mary Jo Maynes, Brigitte Søland, and Christina Benninghaus, eds, *Secret Gardens, Satanic Mills: Placing Girls in European History, 1750–1960* (Bloomington, 2005), 7.
11. Michel Foucault, *History of Sexuality, Volume 1: An Introduction*, trans. Robert Hurley (New York, 1978), 25.
12. Annette Timm, "Sex with a Purpose: Prostitution, Venereal Disease and Militarized Masculinity in the Third Reich," *Journal of the History of Sexuality* 11, no. 1/2 (2002): 223–55, here 225.
13. Hans-Günter Richardi, *Bomber über München: Der Luftkrieg von 1939 bis 1945 dargestellt am Beispiel der "Hauptstadt der Bewegung"* (Munich, 1992), 97.
14. See, for instance: Martin Broszat, Klaus-Dietmar Henke, and Hans Woller, eds, *Von Stalingrad zur Währungsreform: Zur Sozialgeschichte des Umbruchs in Deutschland*, 3rd ed. (Munich, 1990), Introduction.
15. Elizabeth Heineman, "The Hour of the Woman: Memories of Germany's 'Crisis Years' and West German National Identity," *American Historical Review* 101, no. 2 (1996): 356–95.
16. Schissler, *The Miracle Years*.
17. The definition of the protest years refers to the period between 1962 and 1973. It partially builds on the definition "dynamic times" by Konrad Jarausch. Konrad H. Jarausch, *After Hitler: Recivilizing Germans, 1945–1995* (New York, 2006), 16.
18. Detlev Peukert, "Die Halbstarken: Protestverhalten von Arbeiterjugendlichen zwischen Wilhelminischem Kaiserreich und Ära Adenauer," *Zeitschrift für Pädagogik* 30 (1984): 533–48; Detlev Peukert, *Jugend zwischen Krieg und Krise: Lebenswelten von Arbeiterjungen in der Weimarer Republik* (Cologne, 1987).
19. Alfons Kenkmann, *Wilde Jugend: Lebenswelt großstädtischer Jugendlicher zwischen Weltwirtschaftskrise, Nationalsozialismus und Währungsreform* (Essen, 1996).
20. Stanley Cohen, *Folk Devils and Moral Panics: The Creation of the Mods and Rockers*, 3rd ed. (London/ New York, 2002), 1. In the United States, James Gilbert described similar trends as "cycles of outrage." See: James Gilbert, *A Cycle of Outrage: America's Reaction to the Juvenile Delinquent in the 1950s* (Oxford, 1986). See also: Alan France, *Understanding Youth in Late Modernity* (Buckingham: 2007), 1–5; Jones, *Youth*, 182. More recently historian Frank Biess has illustrated the usefulness of this framework. See: Frank Biess, "Moral Panic in Postwar Germany: The Abduction of Young Germans into the Foreign Legion and French Colonialism in the 1950s," *The Journal of Modern History* 84, no. 4 (2012): 789–832.
21. Stuart Hall, et al., *Policing the Crisis: Mugging, the State, and Law and Order* (New York, 1978).
22. Foucault, *Discipline and Punish*, 278.

23. Peukert, "Die Halbstarken"; Thomas Koeber, Rolf-Peter Janz, and Frank Trommler, eds, *Mit uns zieht die neue Zeit: Der Mythos Jugend* (Frankfurt am Main, 1985).
24. Anthony Platt, *The Child Savers: The Invention of Delinquency* (Newark, 2009).
25. Wilhelm Dilthey, "Novalis," *Preußischer Jahrbücher* 15, no. 6 (Berlin, 1865): 596–650; Karl Mannheim, "Das Problem der Generationen," in *Wissenssoziologie: Auswahl aus dem Werk*, ed. Kurt H. Wolff, 509–565, 2nd ed. (Neuwied/ Darmstadt, 1970); Ulrich Hermann, "Das Konzept der 'Generation,'" in *Jugendpolitik in der Nachkriegszeit*, ed. Ulrich Hermann (Weinheim, 1993); Bernd Weisbrod, "Generation und Generationalität in der Neueren Geschichte," *Aus Politik und Zeitgeschichte* 8 (2005): 3–9.
26. Philippe Ariès, *Centuries of Childhood: A Social History of Family Life* (New York, 1962); John Gillis, *Youth and History: Tradition and Change in European Age Relations 1770–Present* (New York/ London, 1974); Pierre Bourdieu, "Youth Is Just a Word," in *Sociology in Question*, trans. Richard Nice (London, 1993), 94–102.
27. Jobs, *Riding the New Wave*, 3.
28. Fisher, *Disciplining Germany*.
29. See, for example: Henning Wrage, "Neue Jugend: Einleitung," in *Handbuch Nachkriegskultur: Literatur, Sachbuch und Film in Deutschland (1945–1962)*, ed. Elena Agazzi and Erhard H. Schütz (Berlin, 2013), 641–65; Detlef Siegfried, *Time Is on My Side: Konsum und Politik in der westdeutschen Jugendkultur der 60er Jahre* (Göttingen, 2008).
30. Kaspar Maase, *Bravo Amerika: Erkundungen zur Jugendkultur der Bundesrepublik in den fünfziger Jahren* (Hamburg, 1992); Uta G. Poiger, *Jazz, Rock, and Rebels: Cold War Politics and American Culture in a Divided Germany* (Berkeley, 2000).
31. Studies engaging with youth in West Germany generally focus on Berlin. See namely: Poiger, *Jazz, Rock, and Rebels*; Jennifer Evans, *Life Among the Ruins: Cityscape and Sexuality in Cold War Berlin* (New York, 2011).
32. Gillis, *Youth and History*, xi.
33. Joe Austin and Michael Nevin Willard, "Introduction: Angels of History, Demons of Culture," in *Generations of Youth: Youth Culture and History in Twentieth Century America*, ed. Joe Austin and Michael Nevin Willard (New York, 1998), 1–20, here 6.
34. Alf Lüdtke, ed., *The History of Everyday Life: Reconstructing Historical Experiences and Ways of Life*, trans. William Templer (Princeton, 1995), 4.
35. Paul Steege et al., "The History of Everyday Life: A Second Chapter," *Journal of Modern History* 80, no. 2 (2008): 358–78, here 378.
36. Maynes, Søland, and Benninghaus, *Secret Gardens, Satanic Mills*, 15.
37. Fisher, *Disciplining Germany;* Jobs, *Riding the New Wave;* Whitney, *Mobilizing Youth*.
38. Foucault, *Discipline and Punish*, 278.
39. Kenkmann, *Wilde Jugend;* Frank Kebbedies, *Außer Kontrolle: Jugendkriminalitätspolitik in der NS-Zeit und der frühen Nachkriegszeit* (Essen, 2000).
40. Heinz-Hermann Krüger, "Vom Punk zum Emo: Ein Überblick über die Entwicklung und die aktuelle Kartographie jugendkultureller Stile," in

inter-cool 3.0: Jugend, Bild, Medien: Ein Kompendium zur aktuellen Jugend-kulturforschung, ed. Birgit Richard and Heinz-Hermann Krüger (Munich, 2010), 13–41, here 15.

41. See namely: Barbara Hille and Walter Jaide, eds, *DDR-Jugend: Politisches Bewußtsein und Lebensalltag* (Opladen, 1991); Dorothee Wierling, *Geboren im Jahr Eins: Der Jahrgang 1949 in der DDR: Versuch einer Kollektivbiographie* (Berlin, 2002); Mark Fenemore, *Sex, Thugs and Rock 'N' Roll: Teenage Rebels in Cold-War East Germany* (New York, 2007); Wiebke Janssen, *Halbstarke in der DDR: Verfolgung und Kriminalisierung einer Jugendkultur* (Berlin, 2010).

42. I do not italicize references to constructs of youth within original quotes.

PART I

DELINQUENCY IN
THE CRISIS YEARS, 1942–1949

CHAPTER I

Constructing *the Delinquent Boy* and *the Sexually Deviant Girl*

In the summer of 1947, the Munich Youth Exhibit welcomed its guests with a large banner reading, "The worst in Germany, worse than a lack of food, [and] overcrowding ... is the psychological state of youth."[1] Upon entering the first tent of the exhibit, visitors saw "the misery of the young" depicted in various photographs. Numerous statistics and charts supported the notion that juvenile delinquency posed a major problem in Munich.[2] Visitors then learned about solutions: local youth organizations showed how to lure youth off the streets; state institutions including the Youth Welfare Office provided information on dealing with disruptors. Concerned contemporaries could leave the exhibit without worry: the misery and delinquency of youth was under control, and with that society on the right path towards recovery and stability.

The Youth Exhibit captured a widespread and highly moralized postwar discourse and functioned as a magnet for engaging with broader issues. Equating misery with deviancy, the exhibit exemplified an obsession with juvenile delinquency in the Bavarian capital during the so-called crisis years. According to popular sentiments, National Socialism, the war, and postwar destitution had led young people of both sexes towards a life of homelessness, black marketeering, and sexual deviancy. Like ruins and rubble, juvenile delinquency became a visual reminder of defeat, destruction, and disorder; its existence jeopardized social order and postwar recovery. Organizing the young within institutions, on the other hand, painted a positive picture of the current state of affairs and the city's future. As a result, and even though authorities condemned the strict hierarchies of the Hitler Youth, the general public supported those willing to rebuild the young through traditional institutionalization, watchful guidance, and rigorous law enforcement.

The construction of juvenile wrongdoing had benefits. Whereas it is apparent that some youngsters participated in illegal endeavors given postwar circumstances, local officials generally exaggerated the extent of deviancy to frame a broader consensus. Once exploring benefits of illegality,[3] to follow Michel Foucault, it becomes clear that the construction of delinquency offered a variety of traditional powers a way to reorganize society. Authorities from across the political spectrum were mainly interested in restoring security, stability, social order, and traditional morality. Actually, first post-1945 Bavarian President Fritz Schäffer from the conservative party called on Christian morals and the power of the Bavarian *Heimat* or homeland as the foundation for recovery.[4] His social democratic successor, Wilhelm Hoegner, noted in his 1946 inauguration speech, "A whole world is out of balance and must return to order."[5] Authorities relied on pre-1914 sentiments when marking norms across party lines as law and order, recovery, and stability. They defined this return to a state of normality in a way that delegitimized the horrors of National Socialism and the instability of the Weimar years. Understood as the future, youth proved a powerful rhetorical space for such discussions.

As the Youth Exhibit demonstrates, it was fortunate that delinquency already had a solution: more intervention by adult authorities. Anxious to prove their ability to create order and ensure recovery, those responsible for controlling youth had an interest in spotting juvenile delinquency. Given such overlapping intentions, representations of youth increasingly became disconnected from reality. In fact, while there was a real youth crisis—as there might be in many societies at any given moment—it was consistently exaggerated for self-serving purposes. Instead of portraying youth as victims of war, authorities increasingly depicted young males in particular as work-shy vagabonds and disruptors. Females, on the other hand, were tied to sexual misbehaviors, especially after the U.S. arrival. This connection between postwar delinquencies defined as juvenile behavioral problems called for state action, thereby making youth a powerful tool and an excellent excuse for expanding mechanisms of social control.

The first part of *Coming of Age* focuses on the construction of male and female youth in the immediate postwar period, defined as the crisis years. It presents *the delinquent boy* (*der verwahrloste Junge*) and *the sexually deviant girl*, also known as *Veronika Dankeschön* or *Fräulein*, as a case in point for the rhetorical construction and normalization of masculinity, femininity, and authority. No strangers in German history,[6] both images of youth emerged in the postwar period in new forms. After all, male adult-dominated societies discriminate against *the sexually deviant girl* because of her gender and sexuality.[7] To add on to such conversations by focusing also on age is in the center of the following discussion. Keeping the historical context of the crisis years in mind is important, as youngsters actually had reason to complain. Many had lost their families, homes, and youth to National Socialism and war. Yet supported by a broad consensus that there had to be a larger problem, a whole array of contemporaries scrambling for post-war power fostered the image of male and female deviancy as active delinquency to advance their own ends and agendas.

Creating *the Delinquent Boy*

The crisis years beginning with the first aerial bombings in summer 1942 were devastating for many in Munich, including the young. The first heavy aerial bombing occurred in late August 1942 and marked, according to historian Hans-Günter Richardi, a shift for the situation in Munich.[8] Prior to 29 August citizens had visited a local exhibit to learn about potential bombings. With the massive attack that night, however, the situation changed and the Bavarian capital now became a regular target. Soon U.S. planes bombed during the day and the British at night. By the end of the war Munich had endured more than seventy bombings, destroying about 90 percent of the old city center.[9] The increasing and visible destruction of the cityscape brought the war more directly into the Bavarian capital and gradually destabilized society. In fact, residents began to pillage even if that could result in being shot by authorities.[10] Young people originally experienced these events as scary yet exciting since the cityscape increasingly became an unmonitored playground in which many began to collect shrapnel or wandered around in destroyed buildings.[11] Parents and authorities eventually sent some children to the countryside, away from the bombs, thus further disrupting a perceived normality and stability in Munich.

The months following Germany's defeat at Stalingrad increased instability in Munich.[12] Most notably, thousands poured into the city.[13] By late 1944, a young boy from Munich described the scene as he recalled seeing ragged soldiers dragging themselves home from the East: "They told us that the war was lost and asked for civilian clothes. Many of them were wounded, amputated, bandaged. After the soldiers came masses of refugees. They were frightening to us because they told sto-

ries about atrocities by Russians and Czechs. We did not know anything about the miseries of these refugees and were hesitant to believe
them."[14] In such disorder countless youngsters had been separated
from their families or loved ones as well. Contemporary photographs
by Heidi and Georg Fruhstorfer from 1945, for example, captured the
ordeal as thousands of young refugees poured into the city from all
directions.[15] Amongst them, according to some officials, "hundreds of
thousands of such youngsters" just in Bavaria;[16] other sources stated
that in the U.S. Zone of Occupation alone homeless youngsters living
on streets ranged from ten thousand to eighty thousand.[17] Up to one
hundred thousand wayward youngsters supposedly roamed around in
the three western zones of occupation.[18] Whereas reliable data for this
period remains difficult to obtain, it is undeniable that war, misery,
and the loss of family had left the young in a visible state of destitution
and trauma.

Given the lack of food and coal, the young had to play a key role in
scavenging for resources. Apart from looking for loved ones in a ruined
cityscape, they traveled long distances to the countryside alongside
adults or by themselves hoping to find food. This sudden visibility of
the young was striking and became a clear symbol of Germany's larger
decay: during Nazism and the early years of war, the young spent their
days at school and in supervised youth organizations, like the Hitler
Youth; beginning by 1942, and certainly by the end of the war, however, a lack of adequate facilities, ongoing processes of denazification,
and missing parental and state supervision kept schools and youth
groups closed. These restrictions left many youngsters on the streets
and in other unsupervised city spaces. Local authorities and the public
at large perceived and described this increased visibility of the young
as abnormal. According to one local commentator, "The metropolis
is playing the role of a dam against vagabonding youngsters, whose
numbers have risen based on different economic and personal circumstances. Being at home nowhere has created emotional nomads."[19]
Such voices saw it as a sign of disorder or a rupture within normality
because previously youth had been organized in specific institutions,
and even along clear ranks, and the young certainly did not roam
around without any adult supervision or guidance.

Reaching Munich on 30 April 1945, U.S. soldiers, on the other hand,
recognized young Germans as victims of World War II. Although originally advised to see male youth in particular as potential fanatic Nazi
fighters, American GIs witnessed the dire situation of youth and quickly
changed their conceptions.[20] Soon nonfraternization measures excluded small children, however defined, and U.S. authorities allowed

soldiers to officially socialize with the young.[21] Most did so by giving out candy. With death around every ruined corner of this overcrowded city, narratives of victimization increasingly came to the forefront. In Munich and elsewhere, contemporaries already discussed the impact of bombings and the war. American understandings of an indoctrinated German youth fitted into such frameworks. For adult Germans at the time such descriptions were beneficial: many insinuated how a few Nazis had seduced an innocent, young nation, and these claims ultimately allowed more Germans to present and construct themselves as victims. Moreover, descriptions of youth as a metaphor for the future automatically shifted debates away from the past. As Germanist Jaimey Fisher explains, discussions about youth as victims served as a platform "onto which to displace and with which to distract from, the wider challenges of coming to terms with Germany's burdensome past."[22]

Within several months, however, increased stabilization of administrative structures shifted the way the public constructed male youngsters from victims to criminals. Some schools and youth groups reopened in fall 1945. Most importantly, local authorities needed workers of all ages to clear the rubble within the city, providing employment for youth. Aware of such opportunities, contemporaries increasingly saw living on the street as an active choice. Those young persons who were homeless or wandering around became known as unwilling, resistant, and deviant. Various prejudices and speculations regarding the motives for homelessness played a key role in constructing such behaviors as deviancy. Instead of portraying youth simply as passive victims of National Socialism and war, descriptions now included assumptions about why male youngsters choose to live on the streets. Anton Buckel's description of Munich youth in his 1948 Ph.D. dissertation epitomizes how easily the marks of destitution became moralized into signs of deviancy:

> This group of people mostly wears blackened U.S. uniforms, miserable footwear. Around the neck there is often a bright cloth. Even during the coldest winters there is in principle no hat, no jacket, no gloves, no underwear, and often not even a shirt. The young have distinctively overlong hair not to be found within other milieus, not even amongst other young people. Face and neck are mostly clean, like the hair, because the young spend their nights frequently in bunkers where they are deloused. Worth noting is the fact that a majority of their bodies shows scabs and rashes. The hands are disgustingly black from daily endeavors. The fingers are "decorated" by five to eight millimeter long scruffy nails. The gaze is restless and distrustful, always scenting danger, at times bold and presumptuous. The face is glaringly pale. The gait slow, sagging. The whole stature seems—even though young—senile.[23]

A variety of other contemporary voices painted a similar picture,[24] thereby increasingly setting the tone for criminalizing homelessness among the young.

Metropolitan spaces like Munich played a key role in sustaining and spreading such sentiments. In urban environments people mingled and saw the supposed state of society: homelessness, destitution, deviancy. Traditional antiurban sentiments so prevalent in Munich's conservative surroundings exacerbated this effect, characterizing urban public spaces and those spending their time there as delinquent. According to widespread interpretations outlined by historian Jennifer Evans, youngsters at home in dark alleys, train stations, or gloomy restaurants would necessarily mingle with a variety of criminals, foreigners, and other shady characters.[25] As Anton Buckel observed in Munich shortly after World War II, "The central train station is a major space for sin and delinquency. Any morally unwavering individual meets disgusting young deviants at 5:30 A.M. as they roam a snack bar to get their breakfast."[26] Others noted an increased appearance of "homeless, destitute individuals, vagabonds, pillagers, thieves" in the city's public spaces.[27] For those constructing youth, homelessness hence became an active choice amongst youth, not a state grounded in postwar destitution and destruction, and such misbehaviors were now also inherently tied to specific locations.

Yet unlike the Foucauldian heterotopic sites described by Jennifer Evans when discussing postwar Berlin,[28] discussions surrounding homosexuality took a backseat when framing male delinquency in Munich. Local scholars did mention fears in regard to sexual deviancy amongst males.[29] Anton Buckel describes such only briefly, noting, "masturbation among the young is threatening but not a hopeless cause. Unrestrained homosexuality, on the other hand, and even more terrible sexual perversions are truly threatening."[30] Some anecdotal evidence and random statistics repeatedly sustained his and similar views regarding alleged sexually abnormal behaviors. However, unlike in Berlin, such fears rarely influenced larger conversations. As a result, contemporaries did not tie delinquency in Munich to a homosexual subculture so widespread in 1920s Berlin. Instead, male sexual deviancy rarely came up in discussions. Those commentators, like Anton Buckel, who debated homosexuality linked it to vagrancy and a lack of resources. In this sense, the limited discussion of sexual deviancy amongst males apparent in Munich actually helped frame homelessness as willful vagrancy, even resistance to order.

Overall, shifts in the construction of youth soon appeared in the media. The newspaper *Die Süddeutsche Zeitung*, for example, introduced twenty-one-year-old Fritz J. by noting how he "supposedly worked for several different farmers in the area of Ingolstadt."[31] The paper implied that Fritz should have stayed there to fulfill his role for a society in need. Instead, he ran away to Munich. There, the police picked him up during a raid and sent him to prison for fourteen days. This odyssey, like other similar stories, was partially blamed on the dire situation after the war; yet the boy was also clearly held responsible for running away in order to sustain a questionable lifestyle. In fact, publications increasingly referred to vagabondage instead of homelessness, depicting life on the street as a lifestyle choice, not a necessity. Reminiscent of 1920s rhetoric, this interpretation more and more dismissed postwar circumstances. Instead, commentators even put vagabondage in the same category as theft and murder, characterizing all three behaviors as *jugendliche Verwahrlosung* or juvenile delinquency.[32]

Structured around traditionally gendered understandings of male youth as disciplined workers and future providers, contemporaries demonized those unwilling to participate in the reconstruction process by portraying them as individual pleasure-seekers. City officials in particular saw the youth as wasting time. Signs set up by the city of Munich reading "Youth! Help rebuild!" in April 1946[33] did not change the situation. *Die Süddeutsche Zeitung* noted that at this rate the rubble symbolizing destruction would not be cleared for the next six to eight years.[34] Then, in June 1946, the city ran out of money and could not pay its regular workers. In response to such scarcities Mayor Karl Scharnagl put forward a proclamation aimed specifically at male youth. He stated, "All our efforts are in vain if the whole population does not support these measures and if the young do not implement them the way we propose."[35] *Die Süddeutsche Zeitung* picked up this call three days later arguing, "In this context there has been no effort [by the young] so far; but especially with regard to the youth who could inspire and serve the public good regarding reconstruction—where is it?"[36] Deputy Mayor Thomas Wimmer linked common perceptions regarding individualistic endeavors of the young with their unwillingness to work. In his view, "At this point it would be much desired if everyone would work together; this is better than seeing how every afternoon hundreds of youngsters spend their time at the Isar river, while others work; there is not much the youth does concerning clearing the rubble. Something has to be done so that at least over the summer the young help."[37] This connection completed negative portrayals of male youth: they enjoyed themselves swimming instead of helping to rebuild the city, and with that kind of behavior endangered the reconstruction process, which jeopardized the overall recovery of Munich. Soon shortages of help-

ing hands became a morally charged discussion. Even though unemployment rates are difficult to assess, by 1947 the employment office
indicated that there were forty-six thousand job openings in Munich.[38]
Local companies frequently complained about a lack of workers, and
at the outskirts of the Bavarian capital farmers desperately looked for
helping hands. Where were the young when it came to bringing Munich back from abyss? An upset citizen noted with outrage that "young
and strong boys" spend time at the movie theaters instead of working.[39]
In contrast to the legendary *Trümmerfrau,* or woman of the rubble, attempts to frame *Trümmerjungen,* or rubble boys, seemed fruitless.

Black marketeering, supposedly sustained by male youngsters, deepened anxieties and seemingly explained male reluctance to work. In
operation since the early 1940s, the existence of a black market signified Munich's dire situation. Similar to circumstances in many other
cities throughout Germany and beyond, food shortages had become
visible during the war and often continued after the U.S. arrival.[40] In
May 1945, food rations sank below one thousand calories per day per
person.[41] Once authorities tried to stabilize the economic situation by
bringing food into the city, the existence of a broad underground economy jeopardized their attempts. In September 1946, *Die Süddeutsche
Zeitung* noted how more than a third of the food arriving at Munich's
central train station would never make it to local businesses. Instead,
individuals and groups stole and hoarded massive amounts of valuables, at times robbing entire trains. The produce then reappeared on
the black market, where law-abiding citizens had to pay outrageous
prices to primarily young entrepreneurs.[42] Black marketeering tied to
male youngsters increased widespread fears regarding economic stability, moral order, and recovery. Authorities felt that it showed how
youngsters preferred to work for their own benefit, rather than helping
rebuild the city.

By 1946, speculations about the work habits of the young not only
framed delinquency but also defined the broader debates about Munich's economic and moral future. Similar to circumstances in other
major cities,[43] the black market in Munich subverted a recovering yet
fragile economic system. The German currency, the Reichsmark, had
long lost its purchasing power and value, making cigarettes, coffee,
chocolate, and ration cards the main currencies. While the black market undercut attempts by local officials to provide food for reasonable
prices, those who had access to scarce produce could make a fortune
selling it informally. Certain groups began hoarding, organizing, and
stealing.[44] As one Munich official noted, it was "only the willingness of

local farmers to fulfill requirements regarding food that guaranteed sufficient rations for the city."[45]

There is indeed some evidence that mainly male youngsters became experts in trading, organizing, and black marketeering. Some roamed around hoping to find Camels, Lucky Strikes, and Chesterfields while others began collecting stumps of cigarettes. If an American GI emptied his ashtray he could be sure that he just made the day of several youngsters. Jacob C., for example, loitered in front of an American bar in downtown Munich before caught by the local police for picking up stumps of cigarettes.[46] Many older Germans saw the act of picking up stumps of cigarettes as a symbolic willingness of young Germans to bow down and surrender before an occupation force; *Die Süddeutsche Zeitung* noted how "youngsters solicit cigarettes out of the mouths of U.S. soldiers."[47] That some GIs willingly gave youngsters valuables once approached did not matter. Instead, in a society run by the older generation, the young as the future of society were under scrutiny. Adults supposedly knew that illegal trade was only a temporary solution. Yet local authorities feared that youngsters growing up with no other moral referents would continue to actively subvert a slowly recovering and fragile economy.

Parents did not always help the situation. They faced devastating times, and many relied on the ingenuity of their children. According to one male youngster, "This was the time when I started stealing coal from a nearby train depot. There were steam engines, and magnificent hard coal. I filled my pockets and was not even yelled at for making my clothes dirty. Instead my mom sewed me a bag so that I could carry more."[48] He recalled seeing a poster showing the well-known *Kohlenklau* or Coal Thief. This character became a warning sign displayed throughout this period and intended to keep people from stealing coal. The encouragement of his parents, however, seemed enough to dismiss any moral quandary for this youngster, keeping authorities wondering how individuals like him should ever learn right from wrong.

The participation of the young in illegal trades was also seen as devaluing the honest, hard work of adults. Whereas honorable adult citizens went to work for little money, young black marketeers benefited from an illegal environment. This binary appeared repeatedly by early 1946 as scholars and the media reported on youngsters who stopped working in regular jobs in order to make more money on the black market. According to this interpretation, such behaviors "underlined the tempting and dangerous downward-pulling effect the black market and illicit trade had on the young mind."[49] Writing about the morale in postwar society, a local newspaper juxtaposed hard work with black marketeering: "There are people who get up at 5 A.M. every morning, have a long commute to their work, only to toil for twenty-five Reichsmark. And then there are people who spent double of that amount at the black market for their daily need of cigarettes."[50] Numerous anecdotes discussing youngsters' unwillingness to work sustained these storylines. One paper, for instance, quoted a male youngster stating, "I do not want to go to [and work for] the farmer—why did I get an education? I'd rather work on the black market, then I can at least help out my mother."[51] The conclusion, according to Der Münchner Merkur, was simple: "There is a direct path from black marketeering to stealing, all eventually ending in juvenile detention."[52]

By early 1946, a widespread public consensus constructed work ethic dichotomies in which age proved definitive. Adults working regular jobs and helping clear the rubble became the norm; young people seeking individual pleasure, wandering around all day, and profiting from the black market defined an ill or problem of society. Such dynamics outline, to follow historian Stefan Mörchen, that the black market provided one basis for creating moral categories, as those associating with this deviant space became the abnormal Other.[53] In Munich, contemporary social commentator and journalist Werner Friedmann sketched out such newly forming moral paradigms in relation to youth. He concluded that we adults "have to exemplify a moral being to them [the young] through our own life."[54] Youth, who attended the black market and participated in illegal actions, jeopardized this crucial role of adults as role models. Blaming the parents and society at large became a way to initiate discussions about broader issues. In this sense, demonizing youth helped officials to establish norms of hard work for parents and society at large.

In addition to such dynamics, authorities saw male youth not only as disciplined workers but also future political leaders. Shortly after the war women had little influence in politics. Reassigned to kitchen, children, and church, their role in clearing the rubble was enough of a deviation from traditional norms. Die Neue Zeitung captured contemporary sentiments, while hinting at the sexually deviant girl. It printed a letter stating, "Before women go political, they should measure their honor against their moral barometers. The number of those afflicted with venereal disease is climbing to pyramidal heights. Women are sacrificing their beauty and integrity to the material desire for consumer goods and food."[55] Whereas a rebuttal occurred later on in the same newspaper,[56] this understanding was widespread and made male youth the prime targets for initiating new democratic processes.

Yet shortly after the end of National Socialism many male youngsters remained reserved in regard to traditional political structures.
This supposed lack of political participation became another highly
moralized discourse in early 1946. German and U.S. officials felt that
local residents needed democratic experiences prior to casting their
votes. Since Military Governor Lucius D. Clay had called for spring
elections in fall 1945, numerous societal forces began encouraging participation in new democratic processes. Authorities saw male youth in
particular as Germany's future leaders, and debates consequently focused on this demographic. In January 1946, *Die Süddeutsche Zeitung*
speculated about the "lost vote" of the young.[57] Numerous discussions
in the media followed similar storylines, even though it became clear
that elections in several Bavarian counties and municipalities showed
high turnout rates. Yet the media and the general public had noticed
a lack of party membership amongst youngsters and simply equated
this trend with a disinterest in politics and democracy overall. Some
publications like the satirical magazine *Der Simpl* wondered about the
political morals of the young altogether. In one issue *Der Simpl* showed
an image of a male youngster from the front with a sign reading "democracy"; once he turned around, the sign showed the word "reaction-
ism." Titled "German Democracy," the caption read, "A nice kid from
the front but not from the back!"[58] The young did indeed come of age
during the Nazi era, which partially explains such depictions. At the
same time, these representations tell more about underlining adult
fears regarding the democratic reorganization of the city. And, such
depictions ultimately helped tie supposed apolitical or reactionist behaviors amongst male youth to delinquency.

The limits of such contemporary readings are apparent in a postwar
surge in youth newspapers, giving some of the actual young a voice
and room for an alternative interpretation. In Munich, it was mostly
Der Pinguin and *Der Ruf*. Although generally run by adults, these plat-
forms provided a rare venue for more nuanced discussions of young
people's relation to politics. In fact, in March 1947 *Der Ruf* published
a powerful "testimony of a young German."[59] The author discussed
religious beliefs, antimilitary sentiments, and a deep distrust of na-
tionalism; he also warned his readers about political intolerance and
problematized the rightful detachment of the youth from traditional
political processes. In his view, current elites were "old and used."[60]
"One should get used to the fact that, once heard, the youth will put
forward new words and independent thoughts,"[61] he warned and pre-
dicted. That surely had to sound threatening to adults and the emerging
political system. According to historian Manfred Burschka, the youth

press "was—in clear rejection of an apolitical youth culture—political, but did not try to indoctrinate. As a counter piece to the National Socialist youth press it provided a political reorientation towards democracy."[62] Burschka concludes, "The youth press refutes the thesis of a 'silent generation.'"[63] Moreover, many youngsters took matters in their own hands. Shortly after the war, groups from Munich traveled to the French-German border promoting a European community. As one young participant recalled years later, "this idea of a unified Europe drew large crowds of youngsters." For him, being political was "an emotional event"[64] disconnected from traditional party structures. The editor of the student newspaper *Das Steckenpferd*, Klaus Heller, even promoted international cooperation at International Youth Days, especially "once political parties fail."[65] However, even though the International Youth Days were promoted as events about youth, such venues took place without the young. *Der Simpl* noted this paradox showing a room filled with adults playing with model trains, bikes, and games. The young looked through the cracked door, only to be told, "Children, get lost! Youngsters are not allowed in here!"[66] Such aspects underline that male youngsters hoped to participate, but on their own terms. Adult contemporaries interested in established formats saw party affiliation as participation in democratic processes; the young had a different view. One male youngster noted, "As long as the older generation does not take these [our] political attempts seriously, there is no ground for attacking the young for their disinterest, black marketeering, and such."[67] For him political parties were stuck in old and non-democratic worldviews with hierarchies still dominated by old elites. To an emerging liberal German state rebuilding society on the basis of conservative values, this approach cast the young as a threat to political stability and represented a traditional party system as the norm for West German democracy.

By early 1946 *the delinquent boy*, a specific image of male juvenile deviancy, appeared more clearly within the media in Munich: he was vagrant by choice, worked on the black market, and cared little about politics. The media sustained these readings. Local newspapers featured articles that showed photographs of homeless youngsters standing under a sign warning against theft.[68] The satirical magazine *Der Simpl* featured three young males on its cover, two of them smoking, while one is holding a bottle of alcohol. In the background, adults are waiting in line for their rations. The caption reads, "Whatever Santa Claus. I paid five packs of Americans [cigarettes] for this"[69] [Figure 1.1]. Even the newspaper of the U.S. military government, *Die Neue Zeitung*, disseminated this new image of juvenile delinquency,[70] as did

Figure 1.1 The satirical magazine *Der Simpl* portrays male youth in one of their supposed post–World War II habitats, the black market. The caption reads: "Whatever Santa Claus. I paid five packs of Americans [cigarettes] for this." (*Der Simpl*, December 1947, no. 24). Courtesy of Universitätsbibliothek Heidelberg.

the series "The Young" (*Die Jungen*) in *Der Münchner Merkur.*[71] Soon
the delinquent boy was seemingly everywhere: there was "a sixteen-year
old boy captured without identification at Munich's central station,"[72]
the police caught "a well-dressed" young man on the black market,[73]
and various male youngsters were trying to break into buildings.[74] *The
delinquent boy* personified societal ills: he lived on the street, did not
contribute through work, and was unwilling to take a leadership role
in postwar Munich.

This figure similarly suffused scholarly debate. Anton Buckel's descriptions mentioned earlier did so in vivid ways;[75] others made similar
claims. Edeltraut Lauter's 1946 dissertation provided a status report
that depicted postwar youth in Munich as a genuine threat to Germany's social order, aligning homelessness and black marketeering with
broader debates.[76] Gundelinde Reithmeier painted a similar picture of
"astray and unwilling youngsters,"[77] further describing *the delinquent
boy* and influencing scholarship up until today.

Statistics only outwardly sustained such understandings. Since the
Youth Welfare Office responsible for surveying problem youth was
partially destroyed and lacked personnel, the first official statistics
published in Munich's statistical yearbook did not resume until 1948.
Historian Daniela Zahner suggests that statistics regarding juveniles
remain questionable until at least 1950.[78] The scarce data available was
based on verdicts. Homelessness and theft dominated these numbers.
In 1945, for instance, there were 183 cases of theft, 169 of them by
male youngsters; a year later there were 346 cases, with 306 of them
committed by male youngsters. Whereas such crimes decreased slowly
as early as 1947, homelessness increased in the same timeframe.[79] Definitions throughout such statistics remain vague suggesting that local
institutions also simply linked vagrant youth to crime. The use of deviancy as a blanket term increased numbers by including absences from
school, visits to the black market, or loitering on street corners. Broadly
defined categories like "waywardness" (*Verwahrlosung*) and "wildness"
(*Verwilderung*) consequently saw the highest increase during the crisis
years. Sociologist Curt Bondy thus noted in 1945, "Never before in
history have there been so many criminals, delinquents and neurotics.
There will be still more after the war. The underlying psychic state
of mind of many of them is waywardness."[80] Cultural historian Hermann Glaser rightfully resists such interpretations and highlights how
"broadly the concept of 'degeneracy' was understood. Very often, it referred only to a special form of the art of survival."[81] Nonetheless, delinquency became the synonym for abnormal behavior, turning crime
rates into moral statistics. In fact, authorities paid lots of attention to

youth, which also inflated numbers. The media, local authorities, and scholarly publications relied on this flawed data and broad definitions. Such circumstances then led to higher reported crime rates, marking what sociologist Stanley Cohen has titled "the interplay between deviation and reaction,"[82] and turning *the delinquent boy* into a folk devil challenging the creation of postwar norms.

Creating *the Sexually Deviant Girl*

According to Anton Buckel, sharing what he saw in Munich in the immediate postwar period, "Apart from male delinquents there are also hordes of girls at our main train station and in shady restaurants. Behind many ruins some go about their business as prostitutes and the next morning such 'ladies' complete transactions at restaurant tables ... with adolescent youngsters."[83] Similar to *the delinquent boy,* an image of female youth thus emerged in the crisis years: *the sexually deviant girl (sexuell verwahrloste Mädchen),* also known as *Veronika Dankeschön* or *Fräulein.* Like her male counterpart, she endangered efforts of recovery. Contemporaries blamed her for jeopardizing the crucial role of women during this period, as young females in particular needed to help clear the rubble, find a German husband, and reproduce for Germany's future. Fraternizing with U.S. soldiers, enjoying an extravagant lifestyle, or simply being too sexual, on the other hand, ran against these higher purposes. Furthermore, interracial relationships challenged categories of race, and the spread of venereal diseases endangered the health of the nation. Constructed as abnormal, such females became known as sexually deviant, a characterization that ultimately helped in defining norms for the immediate postwar period.

The widely described "hour of the woman"[84] also began before 1945. Initially, females had had an assigned role within National Socialist doctrine: they were the "mothers of the state."[85] The war, however, increasingly disrupted such responsibilities. More and more men left their families to fight in battle, a development that created labor shortages at the home front. While forced labor helped decrease such scarcities, high-ranking Nazi officials soon realized that this would not be enough. In summer 1943 it was clear, to follow scholarly discussions, that "girl or woman ... : everyone must participate."[86] One young woman in Munich, for instance, recalled becoming a conductor on cable cars;[87] a child wrote in her diary how by summer 1943 "a young female teacher barely nineteen or twenty years old ... [had to] ... teach second and third grade. Each class has about seventy students."[88] The described individual was one among roughly 500,000 additional women that had been mobilized by the end of 1943.[89] By then high-ranking Nazi officials like Hermann Göring had acknowledged that women would not only be brood mares but also had to be workhorses.[90]

State authorities and contemporaries soon vilified those failing to comply. In Munich, as elsewhere, postings did not merely remind females of their obligations but also emphasized moral standards: "Every German woman has the duty towards those fighting on the front to keep her distance from foreigners. The German woman also needs to abstain from false appearances—for the sake of her honor."[91] In addition, sexualized references increasingly degraded those women who behaved outside accepted norms: contemporaries described women seen with foreign workers as sexually immoral or saw those dressing or behaving provocatively, however defined, as prostitutes—an analysis in line with historian Annette Timm's discussion of similar dynamics in Berlin.[92] According to historian Robert Gellately, "young women who went out alone or with different men, others who seemed to know many men, but had no regular work, all had to worry about accusations that they were secretly working as prostitutes."[93] During the early crisis years Nazi authorities arrested women simply because they were homeless, without work, or perceived as sexual outsiders carrying venereal diseases.

Such perceptions of women only increased with the end of the war. Many men had been killed in action, were still imprisoned, or mentally and physically unable to take their traditional role in postwar society. *Die Süddeutsche Zeitung* noted, for example, that there were eighty men for one hundred women.[94] The population census for Bavaria from 1946 paints a similar picture. That year Munich counted 715,147 inhabitants: 341,538 males and 410,429 females.[95] This discrepancy pushed women into the center of the family, even though gender mores and morality had shifted little. Instead, men technically remained providers and protectors. After all, the hour of the woman marked a deviation from norms only because of the wartime emergency. Women needed to help overcome this disorder by working for the benefit of all, before eventually returning to their rightful place at the stove.

The arrival of U.S. troops introduced even more areas of contention because the presence of powerful foreign occupiers, some of them African Americans, brought disruptions of normality and historical anxieties increasingly to the forefront. Although fears of rape rarely materialized in Munich,[96] German honor was violated in a different way. Instead of being forcefully taken, contemporaries experiencing the arrival of U.S. forces documented how young females gave themselves away willingly. According to a local priest describing the American arrival, "immoral girls and women welcomed U.S. troops with flowers, hugs, and kisses, and took them home at night;"[97] other sources speak about the "exultation specifically within womanhood who immorally pushed themselves towards the armored vehicle of the Americans."[98] One seventeen-year-old boy described his moment of shock when he saw "our single women ... fall around the neck of the Americans."[99] These observations underlined how in the immediate postwar period female behaviors—captured in discussions surrounding their bodies—became a microcosm for broader topics of contention. Many contemporary voices perceived German women as traitors, especially once they saw U.S.-German relations through the prism of material benefits and prostitution. Vivid descriptions further emphasized female behavior as an affront to German honor. According to a pastor from a Munich suburb, "since the arrival of the Americans, local women and girls mingle with U.S. soldiers and socialize within sight of children and youngsters even in between the graves [of a local cemetery] and on the grass."[100] Whereas prostitution near religious sites or children was a crime, the location for such sexual deviancy underlined how German women desacralized male suffering. Such behavior painted a shameful picture of the German nation and honor. According to contemporary sentiments, "German soldiers fought for six years, the German women only for five minutes."[101] Once U.S. soldiers arrived, bystanders believed that young women simply walked away from their important role in recovery, stabbed their countrymen in the back, and ran off with American GIs.

Discussions about fraternization between American soldiers and German girls continued long after American arrival. Such debates sustained previous U.S. fears regarding the treacherous character of young and unmarried German women or *Fräuleins*.[102] Actually, in September 1944 American authorities had proclaimed an antifraternization policy, which prohibited fraternization between Americans and Germans from shaking hands to spending time in their homes. During combat, problems with fraternization remained at a minimum. Once Germany surrendered, however, fraternization became a much more substantial concern. According to U.S. Military Governor General Lucius D. Clay, "the only fraternization that really interests the soldiers is going on with the pretty German girl, who is very much in evidence." He continued, "Frankly, I do not know the answer to this problem as yet."[103] One youngster noticed that—compared to male youth—girls had "better chances" to acquire valuables because they had "a secret."[104] A girl experiencing the arrival of U.S. troops in Munich underlined the downside of not fraternizing: "once the smell of coffee and other good stuff came from their room ... we were the 'dumb ones,' however, because we did not get anything."[105] Fraternization had clear benefits, and measures to prevent U.S. soldiers and German girls from socializing could do little to foil such affiliations given widespread destitution in the crisis years.

As these interactions took center stage and female delinquency became increasingly tied to notions of sexual deviancy or prostitution, discussions centered on possible motives for such misbehaviors. The satirical magazine *Der Simpl* captured the perceived reasons for liaisons when showing the image of two lovers on its cover. The caption read, "'Sylvia, do you feel my impulse and vehement romantic desires exhumed in me by nature?' 'Yes, Bobby, I have been hungry for a while too!'"[106] For contemporaries quickly judging such relationships it were material desires that undoubtedly jeopardized the cohesion of German families. Young and attractive females fraternized with U.S. soldiers to gain access to chocolate and other valuables rather than dating Germans and working for a living. The complicated nature of such relationships, on the other hand, and the fluid borderlines between love, prostitution, and even rape, did not matter. Instead, fraternization was equated with prostitution, making it, according to historian Timothy Gilfoyle, an "allegorical threat to the nation"[107] and, to follow Foucault, a useful public discourse.[108]

Yet a more concise analysis of causes illustrates the diversity of motivations for such relationships. In many ways overwhelmed by being abroad and preferred, young GIs showed a clear interest in local girls. One U.S. soldier was blunt when noting in 1946 how the "bulging, fat, overfed, [and] lonely" American soldier was "standing on a street corner in Germany" with three things on his mind: "(1) To find a German woman and sleep with her. (2) To buy and steal.... (3) To go home."[109] German girls, on the other hand, were often interested in the warmth and comfort of a male counterpart, especially given the ongoing devastation of the crisis years. One young woman commented on the appreciation Americans showed towards them: "They were generous, complimentary and thoughtful in such a casual way, which was a totally different behavior pattern than that of German men."[110] That they always looked and smelled good certainly helped. A lack of German men had further limited marriage choices, especially given that those available for marriage dealt with the consequences of a horrific war. As historian Perry Biddiscombe summarizes, "The outlook was particularly bleak for girls just out of school, who complained that there were 'no men [for them] to get."'[111] The women's magazine *Constanze* asked, "which woman, in view of such oppressive statistical surplus of female marriage partners can still ask, What is the man like? rather than simply, Where, where is the man?"[112] Of course, material gains brought additional advantages when dating an American. Those who had an American boyfriend or acquaintance had access to cigarettes, coffee, and chocolate. As one youngster observed about one such relationship, "She had quickly realized that humans don't need morals to eat and that life is way better on the side of the winners. Being an 'American whore' was a little infamous, but filling."[113] All of these motivations shifted and overlapped, reaching from purely sexual interests to desire for economic security, to romantic and real love.

At the same time, such circumstances emasculated German men. More physically and mentally healthy American soldiers could easily provide for German women while local men lacked such advantages, pushing them into the role of disgruntled bystanders. Their masculinity was under attack, a situation that made them question their overall position within postwar society as providers, protectors, and procreators. In their view, women had become more independent during war times, and now U.S. soldiers had fully replaced German men as providers and protectors. For contemporaries favoring traditional gender roles, these aspects had to be concerning. The study by contemporary anthropologist Hilde Thurnwald discusses the difficulties of families in the immediate postwar period. She focuses on the situation in Berlin, a space increasingly overshadowed by growing tensions given nearby Soviet presence. Nonetheless, Thurnwald provides some striking examples of male fears apparent in Munich as well. In her view, sacrifice, suffering, and domesticity remained vital in order to overcome current problems.[114] As historian Hermann Glaser rightfully noted, scholars like Thurnwald saw

> The housewife as guardian of the home and loving, nurturing, healing center of the family [who] should undertake without gratification, the reproductive labor of giving birth to the new generation, socializing them into accepted morality. The man, however, ... as the head of the household ..., should receive compensation for all the authority that society had either taken away from him or denied him through industrialization, technology, destruction of property, power and influence, and, at that time also through Fascism, war, defeat, and the division of the German Reich.[115]

In this sense, the devaluation of German masculinity had begun long before the end of the war, yet increased due to the hour of woman. Not surprisingly, Thurnwald, among others, saw those fraternizing with foreign soldiers, while abandoning their duties towards German men, in the context of previous challenges to more traditional family structures.[116] These interpretations made such trends symbols for abnormal times and a threat to family life and society.

Unable to compete with, let alone challenge American occupiers, local men became more and more disheartened, and some spoke up. In fact in early September 1946 handwritten posts demonizing German females willing to give up their honor for a couple of cigarettes and some chocolate appeared throughout Munich. Local authorities also confiscated a poem, laying out the situation according to returning German soldiers. It concluded, "We have neither cigarettes nor butter, yet the foreigner has coffee and sugar. And if he brings chocolate, then no one cares about skin color."[117] Some men even wanted to "beat them" and "cut the hair ... of these American whores."[118] In another instance a posting portrayed a suffering German soldier captioned, "All this to allow women to be whores?"[119] Even the faraway *New York Times* reported on such instances on the streets of Munich. In an article titled "SS Remnants Warn German Women," it described how locals complained about females ignoring the sacrifices of so many. "Oh God, if it would be up to us, you would pay for it,"[120] one posting stated at the Max-Weber Platz square. A young male caught for hanging up such posters explained the larger motivations behind his action: "We were angry about the fact that the girls of fourteen or so, who always used to talk to us, refuse to have anything to do with us now."[121] Sexual and material envy plus the inability to compete with U.S. materialism, vigor, and masculinity upset contemporaries and fueled the anger against young women.

As apparent in some of these postings, attempts to recast racial categories also played a role within discussions about female youth. With the arrival of U.S. soldiers, many locals in Munich saw individuals with a distinctly different skin color often for the first time. Of course previous discourses had ingrained racial stereotypes in Germany's collective memory, making these parts of a larger identity. Germany's imperial doings in Africa had left marks in publications at home; during the Weimar years, conservative authorities had demonized jazz for its black roots, an idea they shared with National Socialist ideology later on. Throughout Nazi rule such discrimination resulted in the sterilization of numerous so-called occupation children. Most of them had been born during the occupation of the Rhineland by African-French soldiers following World War I, an event widely understood as yet another humiliation and insult by the French. National Socialist propaganda also specifically demonized African American soldiers. The newspaper *Münchner Neuste Nachrichten,* for instance, reported that the U.S. Air Force employed African American pilots and encouraged them to unleash their "congenital hatred for the white race and its cultural achievements."[122] According to the subsequent article, such motivations clearly betrayed a "level of moral degeneration that must fill every true European with disgust."[123] These plus other stereotypes linked a fear of black men to sexuality and created what historian Lutz Niethammer has called an "expectation of rape."[124]

African American soldiers stationed in Munich, on the other hand, enjoyed themselves, and in that way worried contemporary adults all the more. Often experiencing a nonsegregated environment for the first time, they could move around and go in almost every store without problems. Children came up to them "intrigued by and curious about their otherness," as recalled by one youngster.[125] To them, African Americans were exceptionally friendly, and were more likely to give chocolate and candy. Adult bystanders became concerned when they witnessed such casual engagements, especially when seeing young girls and African American GIs interact in a friendly and seemingly carefree manner. Fearing for gender mores and morality, while also desiring clear racial categories, local German authorities and many contemporaries tried to find ways to limit encounters. But to openly condemn relations between German women and African American soldiers was difficult, especially given power structures and Germany's recent past. Based on this, a more nuanced and subversive criticism emerged. Instead of employing deliberately racist statements, contemporaries referred to immorality and deviancy as characteristics to construct and frame females in particular as a threat to moral and social order. One way to do so was connected to the role of women within society. After World War II, women remained guardians of family and nation. Their position as mothers, homemakers, and wives gave them special roles and responsibilities in society. But when women crossed national boundaries in sexual relations, it became acceptable to critique them as sexually immoral. According to historian Timothy Schroer, "women who engaged in sexual relations across the color line were by definition immoral and could even run the risk of somehow ceasing to be fully white."[126] This understanding made interracial liaisons a space for recasting racial categories. As Schroer continues, African American GIs worked "as a foil to Germans' self-definition as white."[127] Racially mixed children or "Other Germans" broke such categories visibly, as apparent, for example, in *Der Simpl*. This satirical magazine portrayed a young woman following her African American husband with their child. The depiction of the father and the child did not hide racial stereotypes and a perceived Otherness. The suggested notion that she would follow him to Africa played with preconceived and widespread readings of race: the image shows the father sitting in the jungle, almost completely naked while smoking a cigarette, as his formerly German family arrives.[128] The youth magazine *Der Pinguin* asked more directly, "what will happen to the children of the Fräuleins?"[129] In this sense, to again build on Schroer, accusations about "immorality often served as a euphemism" employed to describe interracial relations between German women and African American GIs;[130] it also indicated how such relations not only jeopardized German families but also traditional categories of race.

Demonizing German girls became a more direct and common way to deal with the situation. Many contemporaries called females fraternizing with GIs "chocolate girls" or "chocolate whores."[131] Such characteristics underlined their desires for candy and other material goods while insinuating prostitution; references to chocolate also carried blatant racist characteristics. Terms like "chocolate prostitution"[132] captured such aspects openly and illustrated a focus on interracial liaisons. In Munich, expressions like *Ami-Flitscherl* encapsulated similar aspects and gave deviant behaviors local meanings.[133] It seemed as if public opinion sustained these emerging encounters or constructs. Whereas contemporary polls paint a complicated picture, the "sponsorship affect" of existing surveys leaves additional room for doubt.[134] Moreover, comments by various institutions left little uncertainty regarding the creation of evidence. In fact, the Bavarian Ministry of the Interior blatantly stated "that girls are more prone to immorality than boys. They also seem to feel constraints regarding local men while many are tempted by the adventure of spending time with foreign soldiers."[135] According to Biddiscombe, "fraternization was only the latest in a long line of sins to which women are supposedly prone."[136] As a result, young unmarried women in particular had little power to resist these stereotypes. They faced discrimination based on their age, gender, and sexuality, allowing for little room to even discuss, let alone question, the morals and norms of a male-dominated German society. Poems like,

> How did you do it when you were away?
> Did you not have girls and women by night and by day?
> So shut up and be quite still
> Every girl can do what she will[137]

seemed misplaced and had little use to most young girls, who had never even been married to a German soldier.

The term *Veronika Dankeschön* became another way to define and characterize sexual deviancy while referring to a growing concern: a rise in venereal diseases. *Veronika Dankeschön* made her first appearance in a cartoon published in the American Army newspaper *Stars and Stripes*.[138] Embodying female delinquency, her initials V and D stood for venereal disease. Her last name *Dankeschön* or Thank You signaled gratitude.[139] According to contemporary sentiments such appreciation worked both ways: American GIs were thankful for the company of German females and sexual relations, and German girls were grateful for chocolate, coffee, cigarettes, and other valuables. For U.S. and German authorities, on the other hand, the spread of venereal diseases was a nightmare. Whereas the U.S. Army had to deal with these issues prior to its arrival in Germany,[140] local Munich officials panicked, especially since *Veronika Dankeschön* not only endangered herself—in the immediate postwar period she also threatened social order and stability, as German authorities saw the health and reproduction of the nation endangered.[141] In this sense, discussions about venereal disease were connected to the individual but also became a showcase for broader debates about the health and reproductive qualities of a newly forming German society.

Veronika Dankeschön was not the first personification of female sexual deviancy. The German abbreviation *hwG* (*häufig wechselnde Geschlechtspartner*), a label for those with constantly changing sexual partners, had been present well before *Veronika's* arrival. As outlined by historian Robert Gellately when discussing the early crisis years, authorities simply arrested some women because they were homeless after a divorce; others were seen as outsiders or even as asocials because they supposedly or actually suffered from a venereal disease.[142] Inconsistencies and contradictions within Nazi morality had exhumed such fears. Since it was the duty of women to bear children, Nazi ideology favored what has been described a "state-organized sexual promiscuity."[143] Ideally children would be born within an 'Aryan' marriage. However, the collapse of traditional social structures as well as a growing deficit of males increasingly limited such possibilities, especially during the crisis years. This fact contested contemporary ideologies on various levels. According to Nazi sentiments,

> We must hope that these women, who lost their husbands in the war and/ or have no future marriage prospects, will have something like a marital relationship with preferably one man, thereby producing and raising as many children as possible.... For the sake of our future we must promote a veritable cult of motherhood.... In special circumstances, a man

should be allowed to enter into a permanent married relationship with a woman other than his spouse.[144]

However, as historian Michael Kater points out, by 1944, "park benches and adjoining lawns" at the outskirts of Munich had become "notoriously occupied by soldiers and their teenage consorts" and "every spot was littered with condoms."[145] Such incidents underlined the dissolution of morals during the early crisis years and resulted in "illegal pregnancies" and "venereal diseases,"[146] a discourse that ultimately continued across 1945.

Again, a variety of observations suggested a surge in venereal disease shortly after the war. In August 1945, the official Munich city chronicles revealed a severe increase in sexually transmitted diseases.[147] Two years later a conservative state representative simply noted, "Today, each group arriving in Munich or Bavaria brings a multitude of youngsters along…. Ninety percent of them that are picked up at raids are people, not born here, non-Bavarian vagabonds and roaming youngsters, and fifty percent of females have sexually transmitted diseases."[148] After six months of occupation and about three months of limited or tolerated fraternization, a survey asked U.S. soldiers about a wide array of issues, including how much time they actually spent with Germans in the course of a week. Such socializing included broad categories like "talking" and contacts "other than those of purely conversational nature."[149] Not surprisingly, the survey report concluded that few associated with older Germans or men of their own age; however, 56 percent had spent time with German girls, 25 percent more than ten hours a week.[150] A different U.S. Army report from November 1947 simply played around with numbers only to state that 2.5 million Germans knew at least one American very well.[151] Again, no indication was made what "knowing" an American exactly meant. Yet for contemporaries such results were sufficient evidence to indicate that most U.S. soldiers had sexual relations with German girls. Soon such broad definitions of sexual deviancy helped produce high numbers, as pollsters carelessly applied terms like "roaming" to young girls in particular. In 1946, the Munich police registered 2,576 "roaming girls."[152] "What is roaming?" asked one state representative several years later. He explained, "If the military police observes a girl that is clearly waiting, then such actions can be defined as roaming, but not if a woman or a girl is, for instance, coming home from work."[153] Moreover, insinuations or broad references to valuables like chocolate or cigarettes linked certain behaviors to prostitution and provided even local Munich scholars with avenues to extend a problem. According to Gundeline Reithmeier, for example, "a noticeable rise in moral delinquency within girls" was apparent, but "crime rates do not capture such facts though because they are not criminal actions."[154] Such evidence highlights how broad definitions artificially increased numbers and helped manufacture juvenile delinquency.

This reading and analysis does not deny the existence of relations between young German females and American GIs. As apparent in the historical record, a fair number fraternized with U.S. soldiers. However, not everyone seen with an American GI was having sexual relations or carried a venereal disease. Yet at the height of a growing panic gripping Munich and its conservative and Catholic surroundings such generalizations became ubiquitous, especially because—unlike in Cold War frontline Berlin—conflict and instability were supposed to have ended in the Bavarian capital by 1945. Soon authorities replaced probable cause as the main reasoning for arresting suspected girls with references to or suspicions of inappropriate behaviors. Take the story of Elisabeth: captured and searched, the seventeen-year-old girl had various amounts of valuables in her pockets, namely coffee, chocolate, cigarettes. Though she claimed in court that she worked for the U.S. Military Government in Munich, the judge and the journalist writing the article did not believe her. Instead, the mere fact that she possessed American products was sufficient evidence for sentencing her to one year of probation.[155]

Publications and commentators soon linked such supposed misbehaviors with presumed appearance. Newspapers described *the sexually deviant girl* as wearing "make-up"[156] or having a "badly rouged" face.[157] Various symbols like nylon stockings or a line painted on the back of legs to mimic such valued legwear hinted at Americanization and thereby further connected girls to sexual promiscuity and prostitution. Soon contemporaries did not hold back:

> The *Mädchen*: "girls," red lips, red nails, red toe nails, American shoes, high heels, … bright sweaters, red coats, bright colored headscarves, … gifts from half a dozen hands, all from Joe, Jimmy, Charles and Joe again, and George, sent with cigarettes and gum, Chanel no. 5 and care-packets, each week a special delivery, with hopes for marriage and chances to marry.[158]

After a while, newspapers did not merely catch up with emerging fears but increasingly spearheaded conversations. In January 1946, *Der Münchner Stadtanzeiger* referred to the rise of sexually transmitted diseases as a "pandemic."[159] By August, *Die Süddeutsche Zeitung* already asked, "Who is 'Veronika Dankeschön'?"[160] Explaining the roots of this term, the article stated that in the first half of 1945 a total of 566 girls out of 1,173 suspects were diagnosed with sexually transmitted diseases. The fact that half of those girls were under twenty underscored the danger. Apart from the expenses to help such individuals, the article also underlined an inherent promiscuity supposedly present in all young girls.[161] In spring 1946, the media were full of similar stories discussing sexual deviancy. One American newspaper described how hitchhikers raised rates of venereal diseases and how U.S. soldiers are innocent prey: "Typical autobahn girl technique is to stand along the highway a few miles outside of a large city and solicit rides. She generally carries a small, almost empty suitcase. She lets the soldier know, usually through innuendo, that she is not a prude and then begins her request for food, cigarettes and candy."[162] Soon references to the current situation of the young generally included wayward girls with venereal diseases, captured near the central train station, within sight of U.S. barracks, or close to food depositories. Loitering, unwillingness to work, a lack of identification papers, or the simple suspicion of carrying sexually transmitted diseases thus became sufficient to justify arrests.

Specific stories often gave sexual immorality—seen as a deviation from accepted norms—face and context. Nineteen-year-old Margarete M., for instance, was one of those supposedly sexually deviant girls. In October 1946, authorities "hauled [her] out of a room" that was located in the American barracks as she spent time with a "colored soldier." After spending fourteen days in prison for "trespassing," she "again became acquainted with a colored soldier and was picked up within the barracks" thereafter. Instead of complying with her sentence and working in the Youth Labor Camp Dachau, she left Munich for a little while only to return a couple months later. Next, she was seen "in suspicious company and ambiguous circumstances" around Christmas. Again sentenced to fourteen days in prison, Margarete then "trespassed" onto U.S. property and was caught in "an infamous restaurant." "This time, she did not get off so easily but was sentenced to a four-month prison term."[163]

As the image or portrait of *the sexually deviant girl* took shape, the media also employed another widespread construct: the *Trümmerfrau*. This well-known image showed women clearing the rubble after the war.[164] Although women of all ages did so, images predominately showed older women. Age consequently became a defining category and a way to exclude young females. Moreover, contemporaries constructed the *Trümmerfrau* as a "de-sexualized, family-oriented, and hard-working"[165] mother. These characteristics made her the complete opposite of fraternizing and sexually deviant girls. A binary evolved, and it underscored how sexual relations with GIs were considered abnormal. Young females enjoying themselves instead of helping out were not simply the "wayward sister of the *Trümmerfrau*"[166] but a deviant and threatening Other that jeopardized postwar recovery. She faced excessive demonization while the *Trümmerfrau* became an almost mythical embodiment of Germany's postwar struggle from rubble to renewal, to riches.

Scholars sustained these increasingly looming fears. Although primarily focusing on male youth, Anton Buckel referred to "fallen girls" when talking about "vagabonds, beggars, thieves, and forgers." He also stated that the morals of women and girls have declined "due to materialism and sexualism."[167] For Buckel the situation was clear: prostitution happened in certain city spaces and youngsters were part of it. Other scholars agreed with such sentiments and equally linked girls and soldiers to deviant spaces like coffee shops and movie theatres. Elisabeth Lauter added how the current situation "primarily enhances sexual errors of girls."[168] Only her references to the domestic role of girls and women illustrated that girls were less threatening than boys. Medical studies also demonized females by projecting "an extraordinary danger for youth."[169] An early postwar dissertation on sexually transmitted diseases indicated continuities regarding social constructions of female deviancy while underlining that a fight against prostitution would not be sufficient to deal with venereal diseases.[170] Overall, most agreed with Anton Buckel who claimed, "Sexual deviancy was only the beginning for a variety of immoral and criminal behaviors."[171]

Anecdotes again exemplified sexual deviancy by following similar narratives and familiar patterns. A study discussing the reorganization of various welfare offices laid out its broad features when noting,

> We encounter an alarming number of girls, whose weakness in character, a lack of control, and bad company have led them to unrestrained sexual devotion—more often than not for material gains and sometimes even employed by their parents to make money. They repeatedly come to the hospital once infected with sexual diseases. Exceedingly worrisome is that some are of elementary-school age.[172]

"That was the future of Germany!" noted well-known author and social commentator Hans Magnus Enzensberger in this context: "A drunk, pimpled American soldier and a German girl walking the streets."[173] One contemporary publication summarized the story of any female youngster in several photos. In the first image an innocent-looking girl is sitting on the steps outside of an office building. The image underlines her destitution, loss, and potential unemployment in the crisis years. The next photo of this sequence shows her sleeping on a bench,

Figure 1.2 The 1948 publication *Ein Neuer Anfang* (*A New Beginning*) tells the story of juvenile delinquency in Munich. The caption reads: "Welfare: The Fate of a Young Person." Courtesy of Stadtarchiv München.

identifying that she was homeless. She is then portrayed talking to men, smoking a cigarette, and drinking beer—her moral decline. Such a deviant lifestyle eventually led her into the arms of two policemen. Her story and this morality tale ended in prison[174] [Figure 1.2]. For contemporary readers, authorities, and a concerned overall adult public interested in law and order, traditional morals, and recovery, the message and course of action was clear.

Notes

Parts of this section have appeared under the title "'The Youth is Is a Threat!' Controlling the Delinquent Boy in Post-WWII Munich," in the *Journal of the History of Childhood and Youth* in 2013. It is reprinted here with the permission of the publisher.

1. "Not und Hoffnung in Bildern," *Die Süddeutsche Zeitung,* 5 August 1947.
2. "Ausstellung über Jugendnot," *Die Süddeutsche Zeitung,* 19 July 1947.

3. Foucault, *Discipline and Punish*, 278.
4. Peter Jacob Kock, ed., *Der Bayerische Landtag 1946–1986. Band I. Chronik* (Bamberg, 1986), 23.
5. Peter Jacob Kock, ed., *Der Bayerische Landtag 1946–1986. Band II. Protokolle* (Bamberg, 1986), 11.
6. Detlev Peukert, *Grenzen der Sozialdisziplinierung: Aufstieg und Krise der deutschen Jugendfürsorge von 1878 bis 1932* (Cologne, 1986). See also: Michael Mitterauer, *A History of Youth*, trans. Graeme Dunphy (Oxford, 1992). Lutz Roth indicates that after 1945 the "concept of youth" has returned with all its negative connotations. Lutz Roth, *Die Erfindung des Jugendlichen* (Munich, 1983), 138.
7. On broader discussions see, for example: Cesare Lombroso and Guglielmo Ferrero, *Das Weib als Verbrecherin und Prostitutierte: Anthropologische Studien* (Hamburg, 1894); Sybille Krafft, *Zucht und Unzucht: Prostitution und Sittenpolizei im München der Jahrhundertwende* (Munich, 1996); Annette F. Timm, *The Politics of Fertility in Twentieth-Century Berlin* (Cambridge, 2010).
8. Richardi, *Bomber über München*, 79.
9. Ibid., 97.
10. Eva Berthold and Norbert Matern, *München im Bombenkrieg* (Düsseldorf, 1983), 34.
11. Ibid., 50–51. See also: Angelika Baumann, ed. *Verdunkeltes München: Die Nationalsozialistische Gewaltherrschaft, ihr Ende und ihre Folgen. Geschichtswettbewerb 1985/1986* (Munich, 1995).
12. Josef Falter, *Chronik des Polizeipräsidiums München*, 2n ed (Munich, 1995), 78; Ian Kershaw, *The 'Hitler Myth': Image and Reality in the Third Reich* (Oxford, 1987), 195. See also: Broszat, Henke, and Woller, eds., *Von Stalingrad zur Währungsreform*, Introduction.
13. Angela Fox, "Flüchtlinge und Vertriebene nach 1945 in München," *Xenopolis* (2005): 307–15; Josef Nussbaumer, "Wirtschaftliche und soziale Entwicklung der Stadt München, 1945–1990," *Münchner Wirtschaftschronik* (1994): I/223–I/224.
14. Daniel Beckh, "Mohren, Zigaretten und Kinderspiele," in *Münchner Nachkriegsjahre. 1945–1946–1947–1948–1949–1950. Lesebuch zur Geschichte des Münchner Alltags: Geschichtswettbewerb 1995/96*, ed. Angelika Baumann (Munich, 1997), 57–63, here 57.
15. Heidi und Georg Fruhstorfer, *Hurra, wir leben noch! München nach 1945* (Munich, 2003). A large collection of these photos are at the BayStaBiM, accessible online at https://www.bsb-muenchen.de/ literatursuche/spezial bestaende/bilder, [last accessed 11 March 2015].
16. BayHStAM, Minn 807039, quoted in Daniela Zahner, *Jugendfürsorge in Bayern im Nachkriegsjahrzehnt 1945–1955/56* (Munich, 2006), 51. See also: BayHStAM, Staatskanzlei 113776.
17. Zahner, *Jugendfürsorge in Bayern*, 51.
18. Benno Hafeneger, *Alle Arbeit für Deutschland: Arbeit, Jugendarbeit und Erziehung in der Weimarer Republik, unter dem Nationalsozialismus und in der Nachkriegszeit* (Cologne, 1988), 178. Beate Wagner speaks of 1,555,000

homeless youngsters (between fourteen and twenty-four years of age) living in West Germany by 1949. Beate Wagner, *Jugendliche Lebenswelten nach 1945: Sozialistische Jugendarbeit zwischen Selbstdeutung und Reeducation* (Opladen, 1995), 52. See also: Ulrich Chaussy, "Jugend," in *Die Geschichte der Bundesrepublik Deutschland: Gesellschaft,* ed. Wolfgang Benz (Frankfurt am Main, 1989), 207–42, here 207.

19. Gundelinde Reithmeier, *Verwahrlosung und Kriminalität der Jugendlichen in München in den Nachkriegsjahren 1945–1947* (Munich, 1948), 30.

20. Discussions in the United States regarding the future of German youth were widespread. See, for instance: Herbert Lewin, "Problems of Re-Educating Fascist Youth," *Journal of Educational Sociology* 19, no. 7 (1946): 452–58.

21. Earl Frederick Ziemke, *The U.S. Army in the Occupation of Germany 1944–1946* (Washington, DC, 1975), 323. At this point surveys had indicated that nonfraternization rules were "fairly well observed except in the case of small children." Ibid.

22. Fisher, *Disciplining Germany,* 2.

23. Anton Buckel, "Der verwahrloste Großstadtjugendliche und seine Erziehung in der Arbeitserziehungsanstalt" (Ph.D. diss., Ludwig-Maximilians University Munich, 1948), 9–10.

24. Edeltraut Lauter, "Krieg und Jugendkriminalität der Stadt München 1939–1946" (Ph.D. diss., Ludwig-Maximilians University Munich, 1947); Reithmeier, *Verwahrlosung und Kriminalität der Jugendlichen.*

25. Evans, *Life Among the Ruins,* 103.

26. Buckel, "Der verwahrloste Großstadtjugendliche," 36.

27. Franz Obermaier and Josef Mauerer, *Aus Trümmern wächst das neue Leben: Eine Chronik für Stadt und Land* (Munich, 1949), 41.

28. Evans, *Life Among the Ruins,* 103–4.

29. Lauter, "Krieg und Jugendkriminalität," 69; Reithmeier, *Verwahrlosung und Kriminalität der Jugendlichen,* 51.

30. Buckel, "Der verwahrloste Großstadtjugendliche," 110.

31. "Junge Vagabunden werden erzogen," *Die Süddeutsche Zeitung,* 8 February 1947.

32. Contemporary commentators sustained such interpretations. See, for instance: Reithmeier, *Verwahrlosung und Kriminalität der Jugendlichen,* 27; Buckel, "Der verwahrloste Großstadtjugendliche," 25–27.

33. "Appell an die Münchner Schuljugend, bei der Schutträumung mitzuhelfen," 11 April 1946, quoted in Bauer, *Ruinen-Jahre,* 33. See also: "Schuttaktion geht weiter!" *Die Süddeutsche Zeitung,* 10 September 1946.

34. "Wie lange dauert die Schutträumung?" *Die Süddeutsche Zeitung,* 7 May 1946.

35. SozipädAM, Karl Scharnagl, "Jugend!" (15 June 1946).

36. "Ein Kubikmeter Schutt kostet zwölf Mark," *Die Süddeutsche Zeitung,* 18 June 1946.

37. "Finanzierung der Schutträumung," *Die Süddeutsche Zeitung,* 25 June 1946.

38. Nussbaumer, "Wirtschaftliche und soziale Entwicklung der Stadt München," I/228.

Constructing the Delinquent Boy and the Sexually Deviant Girl   47

39. "Hier spricht der Leser," *Die Süddeutsche Zeitung*, 16 April 1946. See also: "Die Jungen: Zwei von vielen," *Der Münchner Merkur*, 6 December 1946; "Lehrlinge gesucht!" *Der Münchner Merkur*, 31 January 1947.
40. Obermaier and Mauerer, *Aus Trümmern wächst das neue Leben*, 46. See also: Hans Dollinger, ed., *München im 20. Jahrhundert: Eine Chronik der Stadt von 1900 bis 2000*. 2nd ed. (Munich, 2001), 174.
41. See, for example: Friedrich Prinz, ed., *Trümmerzeit in München: Kultur und Gesellschaft einer deutschen Großstadt im Aufbruch 1945–1949* (Munich, 1984).
42. "Kaloriengebiete sind bevorzugt," *Die Süddeutsche Zeitung*, 10 September 1946; "Der Bauch der Großstadt," *Die Süddeutsche Zeitung*, 25 June 1946.
43. See namely: Stefan Mörchen, "'Echte Kriminelle' und 'zeitbedingte Rechtsbrecher': Schwarzer Markt und Konstruktion des Kriminellen in der Nachkriegszeit," *Werkstatt Geschichte* (2006): 57–76; Paul Steege, *Black Market, Cold War: Everyday Life in Berlin, 1946–1949* (Cambridge, 2007); Malte Zierenberg, *Stadt der Schieber: Der Berliner Schwarzmarkt 1939–1950* (Göttingen, 2008).
44. Margot Fuchs, "'Zucker, wer hat? Öl, wer kauft?' Ernährungslage und Schwarzmarkt in München 1945–1948," in Prinz, ed., *Trümmerzeit in München*, 312–19.
45. Obermaier and Mauerer, *Aus Trümmern wächst das neue Leben*, 73.
46. Reithmeier, *Verwahrlosung und Kriminalität*, 19.
47. "In München fällt auf," *Die Süddeutsche Zeitung*, 9 November 1945. See also: "Kippenaufkleber," *Der Simpl*, no. 5 (1946); Fuchs, "'Zucker, wer hat? Öl, wer kauft?'" 318.
48. Beckh, "'Mohren, Zigarren und Kinderspiele'," 60.
49. Reithmeier, *Verwahrlosung und Kriminalität der Jugendlichen*, 29.
50. "Über den Anstand," *Die Süddeutsche Zeitung*, 10 May 1946.
51. "Jugend will nicht arbeiten," *Der Münchner Merkur*, 28 February 1947. See also: "Chancen für alle, die arbeiten wollen," *Der Pinguin*, no. 10 (1946).
52. "Jugend will nicht arbeiten," *Der Münchner Merkur*, 28 February 1947.
53. Mörchen, "'Echte Kriminelle' und 'zeitbedingte Rechtsbrecher'," 70.
54. "Über den Anstand," *Die Süddeutsche Zeitung*, 10 May 1946.
55. *Die Neue Zeitung*, 10 December 1945, quoted in Perry Biddiscombe, "Dangerous Liaisons: The Anti-Fraternization Movement in U.S. Occupation Zones in Germany and Austria, 1945–1949," *Journal of Social History* 34, no. 3 (2001): 611–47, here 614. See also: "Women and Politics," *Die Neue Zeitung* (10 December 1945–1 March 1946).
56. *Die Neue Zeitung*, 18 January 1946, quoted in Biddiscombe, "Dangerous Liaisons," 614.
57. "Verlorene Stimme," *Die Süddeutsche Zeitung*, 29 January 1946. See also: "Wir Jungen und die Wahlen," *Die Süddeutsche Zeitung*, 1 February 1946; "Gebrannte Kinder: Die Scheu der Jugend vor dem Parteibuch," *Die Süddeutsche Zeitung*, 3 May 1946; "Jugend und Wahlen," *Die Süddeutsche Zeitung*, 24 May 1946; "Gefährlich Logik," *Die Süddeutsche Zeitung*, 30 November 1946.
58. "Deutsche Demokratie," *Der Simpl*, no. 6 (1946).

59. "Bekenntnis eines deutschen Studenten," *Der Ruf*, 15 March 1947. See also: "Warum schweigt die Jugend?" *Der Ruf*, 1 September 1946.

60. "Bekenntnis eines deutschen Studenten," *Der Ruf*, 15 March 1947.

61. Ibid.

62. Manfred Burschka, "Re-education und Jugendöffentlichkeit: Orientierung und Selbstverständnis deutscher Nachkriegsjugend in der Jugendpresse, 1945–1948: Ein Beitrag zur politischen Kultur der Nachkriegszeit" (Ph.D. diss., Georg-August-University Göttingen, 1987), 235.

63. Ibid., 237.

64. Josef Hederer (*1927), interview by author, tape recording, Munich, 5 August 2009. Widespread participation in the local youth parliament fostered by the U.S. military government also underlines the involvement of youth. "Das Stadtparlament der Jugend," *Der Münchner Merkur*, 27 December 1946; Staatsarchiv Munich (StAM), Bürgermeister & Rat, Nr. 2552.

65. "Fünf Punkte zur Diskussion," *Das Steckenpferd*, (July 1947). See also: "Das Steckenpferd. Münchner Schülerzeitschrift," *Der Pinguin*, no. 4 (1947); "Antworten," *Der Pinguin*, no. 8 (1947); Evan Torner, "'Das Steckenpferd' und die Jugendzeitschriften der fünfziger Jahre," in *Handbuch Nachkriegskultur*, 652–55.

66. "Zweites Internationales Jugendtreffen in den Augen der Jugend," *Der Simpl*, no. 11 (1948).

67. "Die Jungen: Gleicher Lohn für gleiche Leistung!" *Der Münchner Merkur*, 24 January 1947. See also: "Worte und Taten. Eine Stimme der Jugend," *Die Süddeutsche Zeitung*, 28 December 1946; "Fordert die Zeit alte oder junge Politiker?" *Der Münchner Merkur*, 2 January 1948; "Jugend gegen Parteien," *Der Münchner Merkur*, 2 January 1948.

68. "Fünfzehnjährige um Mitternacht," *Die Süddeutsche Zeitung*, 23 August 1946.

69. *Der Simpl*, [cover page], no. 24 (Dec. 1947).

70. "Junge Menschen über ihre Not," *Die Neue Zeitung*, 1 April 1946. See also: Henry J. Kellermann, *The Present Status of German Youth* (Washington, DC, 1946).

71. *Der Münchner Merkur*, 1 October 1946; 15 November 1946; 29 November 1946.

72. "Verwahrloste Großstadtjugend: Ein Problem unserer Zeit," *Die Süddeutsche Zeitung*, 31 May 1947. See also: "Fünfzehnjährige um Mitternacht," *Die Süddeutsche Zeitung*, 23 August 1946; "Streunende Jugend: Eine bedrohliche Nachkriegserscheinung," *Die Süddeutsche Zeitung*, 10 September 1946.

73. "Verwahrloste Großstadtjugend: Ein Problem unserer Zeit," *Die Süddeutsche Zeitung*, 31 May 1947.

74. *Ibid.*

75. Buckel, "Der verwahrloste Großstadtjugendliche," 9–10.

76. Lauter, "Krieg und Jugendkriminalität," 8.

77. Reithmeier, *Verwahrlosung und Kriminalität der Jugendlichen*, 73.

78. Zahner, *Jugendfürsorge in Bayern*, 21.

79. Ibid., 53 and 51–52. On other statistics surfacing during this period see

BayHStAM, Staatskanzlei 13776; BayHStAM, Ministerium des Inneren 92087. Early data relied on cases from various courts in Munich. See: Lauter, "Krieg und Jugendkriminalität," 13; Reithmeier, *Verwahrlosung und Kriminalität der Jugendlichen*, 7–17, passim. See also: MonM, 4° Mon 3831: Kurt Seelmann, "Das Halbstarken-Problem in München" (1957).

80. Curt Bondy, "A Psychological Interpretation of Waywardness," *Journal of Criminal Law and Criminology* 36, no. 1 (1945): 3–10, here 3. Bondy later also proposed measures to deal with waywardness. See: Curt Bondy, "The Youth Village: A Plan for the Reeducation of the Uprooted," *Journal of Criminal Law and Criminology* 37, no. 1 (1946): 49.

81. Hermann Glaser, *Rubble Years: The Cultural Roots of Postwar Germany 1945–1948* (New York, 1986), 154.

82. Cohen, *Folk Devils and Moral Panics,* 25. See also: Stuart Hall, Chas Critcher, Tony Jefferson, John Clarke, and Brian Roberts, *Policing the Crisis: Mugging, the State, and Law and Order* (New York, 1978).

83. Buckel, "Der verwahrloste Großstadtjugendliche," 28.

84. Heineman, "The Hour of the Woman."

85. Ute Benz, ed., *Frauen im Nationalsozialismus: Dokumente und Zeugnisse* (Munich, 1993). See also: Elaine Martin, *Gender, Patriarchy, and Fascism in the Third Reich: The Response of Women Writers* (Detroit, 1993); Matthew Stibbe, *Women in the Third Reich* (Oxford, 2003).

86. Klaus-Jörg Ruhl, *Unsere verlorenen Jahre: Frauenalltag in Kriegs- und Nachkriegszeit 1939–1949 in Berichten, Dokumenten und Bildern* (Neuwied/Darmstadt, 1985), 61.

87. Christel Letzke, "Die Familie gab uns immer wieder Kraft," in *Jugendbilder: Kindheit und Jugend in München. Geschichtswettbewerb 1987*, ed. Landeshauptstadt München (Munich, 1995), 108–15, here 114.

88. Diary of Helene Marschler, quoted in Berthold and Matern, *München im Bombenkrieg*, 44.

89. Michael Burleigh and Wolfgang Wippermann, *The Racial State: Germany 1933–1945* (Cambridge, 1991), 264. See also: Marita A. Panzer, "'Volksmütter,'" in *Frauenleben in Bayern von der Jahrhundertwende bis zur Trümmerzeit*, ed. Sybille Krafft (Munich, 1993) 234–319, here 281–82.

90. Hermann Göring, in ibid., 266.

91. Ruhl, *Unsere verlorenen Jahre*, 81.

92. Annette Timm, "The Ambivalent Outsider: Prostitution, Promiscuity and VD Control in Nazi Berlin," in *Social Outsiders in the Third Reich*, eds. Robert Gellately and Nathan Stoltzfus (Princeton, 2001); Timm, "Sex with a Purpose," here namely 225. See also: Timm, *The Politics of Fertility in Twentieth-Century Berlin*, 2–3.

93. Robert Gellately, *Backing Hitler: Consent and Coercion in Nazi Germany* (Oxford, 2001), 112.

94. "Auf 80 Männer 100 Frauen," *Die Süddeutsche Zeitung*, 14 December 1945. Other sources reference that there were only 100 men for 269 women (twenty-five- to thirty-year-olds). Karin Sommer, "'Überleben im Chaos.' Frauen in der Trümmerzeit 1945–1948," in Krafft, ed., *Frauenleben in Bayern*, 320–62, here 341.

95. Statistisches Amt der Stadt München, ed., *Statistisches Handbuch der Stadt München* (1954), quoted in Krauss, "... es geschahen Dinge, die Wunder ersetzten," in Prinz, ed., *Trümmerzeit in München*, 282 and 420.

96. Arrival reports by church officials include a couple of references to rape in Munich. Peter Pfister, ed., *Das Ende des Zweiten Weltkriegs im Erzbistum München und Freising: Die Kriegs- und Einmarschberichte im Archiv des Erzbistums München und Freising* (Regensburg, 2005), 353, 244, and 241–42. Defining rape can be difficult in such circumstances. Some sources do, for example, discuss "molestation."' Ibid., 535.

97. Ibid., 239.

98. Ibid., 79. See also: ibid., 287.

99. Institut für Bayerische Geschichte, Universität München, Sammlung 'Trümmerbriefe,' Brief Nr. 37, quoted in Johannes Kleinschmidt, *Do Not Fraternize: Die schwierigen Anfänge deutsch-amerikanischer Freundschaft, 1944–1949* (Trier, 1997), 154.

100. Pfister, ed., *Das Ende des Zweiten Weltkriegs*, 242.

101. Biddiscombe, "Dangerous Liaisons," 615. See also: Christoph Boyer and Hans Woller, "Hat die deutsche Frau versagt? Die neue Freiheit der deutschen Frau in der Trümmerzeit 1945," *Journal für Geschichte* 2 (1983): 32–36, here, 36.

102. Susanne zur Nieden, "Geschichten vom 'Fräulein,'" *Feministische Studien* 13, no. 2 (1995): 25–33.

103. Lucius D. Clay made these comments on 29 June 1945, towards John J. McCloy. See: Lucius D. Clay, *The Papers of General Clay*, vol. 1, ed. Jean Smith (Bloomington, 1974), 42.

104. Rudolf Woerl, "Die Teestunde," 24–25, here 24, in *Münchner Nachkriegsgeschichte*.

105. Yiengst, "Frauenhaushalt," 146, in *Jugendbilder*.

106. *Der Simpl*, [coverpage], no. 11 (1948).

107. Timothy Gilfoyle, "Prostitutes in History: From Parables of Pornography to Metaphors of Modernity," *American Historical Review* 104, no. 1 (1999): 117–41, here 122.

108. Foucault, *The History of Sexuality*, 25.

109. "Conquering a Conquering Complex," *Newsweek*, 6 May 1946.

110. Elfrieda Shukert and Barbara Scibetta, *War Brides of World War II* (Novato, 1988), 129.

111. Biddiscombe, "Dangerous Liaisons," 613. See also: Hilde Thurnwald, *Gegenwartsprobleme Berliner Familien: Eine soziologische Untersuchung an 498 Familien* (Berlin, 1948), 139.

112. "Zwei Frauen? Mir Reicht's!," *Constanze*, no. 20 (1948), quoted in Dagmar Herzog, *Sex after Fascism: Memory and Morality in Twentieth-Century Germany* (Princeton, 2005), 68. See also: "Ein Königreich für einen Mann," *Constanze*, no. 7 (1948); Angela Delille and Andrea Grohn, eds, *Perlonzeit: Wie die Frauen ihr Wirtschaftswunder erlebten* (Berlin, 1985).

113. Beckh, "'Mohren,' Zigarren und Kinderspiele," 58.

114. Thurnwald, *Gegenwartsprobleme Berliner Familien*.

115. Glaser, *Rubble Years*, 52.

116. Thurnwald, *Gegenwartsproblem Berliner Familien*, 211. Hilde Thurnwald speaks about the "irreplaceability" (*Unersetztlichkeit*) of the traditional family as a societal institution. Ibid., 227.

117. *Beschlagnahmter Anschlag gegen 'Amibräute'* (1945), quoted in Bauer, *Ruinen-Jahre*, 29.

118. Wolfram Selig, et al., eds., *Chronik der Stadt München 1945–1948* (Munich, 1980), 78. See also: Julian Bach, *America's Germany: An Account of the Occupation* (New York, 1946), 82; Sonja Hosseinzadeh, ed., *Nur Trümmerfrauen und Amiliebchen? Stuttgarterinnen in der Nachkriegszeit: Ein geschichtliches Lesebuch* (Tübingen, 1998), 93–104.

119. *Konfiziertes Plakat* (1946), quoted in Bauer, *Ruinen-Jahre*, 30. See also: Sommer, "'Überleben im Chaos,' 343, in *Frauenleben in Bayern*.

120. "SS Remnants Warn German Women; Bavaria Underground Placards Threaten Reprisals for Any Fraternizing With Yanks," *New York Times*, 30 September 1945. See also: Petra Goedde, *GIs and Germans: Culture, Gender, and Foreign Relations, 1945–1949* (New Haven, 2003), 113.

121. Bach, *America's Germany*, 80.

122. *Münchner Neuste Nachrichten*, quoted in David Clay Large, "Capital of the Anti-Movement? Munich and the End of World War II," Paper presented at the conference Germany and Versailles: Seventy-Five Years After, Berkeley, CA, 28 April 28–1 May 1995, 8. See also: Kurt Preis, *München unterm Hakenkreuz: Die Hauptstadt der Bewegung: Zwischen Pracht und Trümmern* (Munich, 1980).

123. *Münchner Neuste Nachrichten*, quoted in Large, "Capital of the Anti-Movement?"

124. Lutz Niethammer, "Privat-Wirtschaft. Erinnerungsfragmente einer anderen Umerziehung," in *"Hinterher merkt man, dass es richtig war, dass es schiefgegangen ist": Nachkriegserfahrungen im Ruhrgebiet*, ed. Lutz Niethammer (Berlin, 1983), 17–105, here 22 and 28.

125. Beckh, "'Mohren,' Zigarren und Kinderspiele," 58.

126. Timothy L. Schroer, *Recasting Race after WWII: Germans and African Americans in American-Occupied Germany* (Boulder, 2007), 84.

127. Ibid., 41.

128. "Hausangestellte im Aulsand dringend gesucht," *Der Simpl*, no. 13 (1948). See also: Tina Campt, *Other Germans: Black Germans and the Politics of Race, Gender, and Memory in the Third Reich* (Ann Arbor, 2004).

129. "Was wird aus den Kinder der Fräuleins?" *Der Pinguin*, no. 8 (1949).

130. Schroer, *Recasting Race after World War II*, 96. See also: Maria Höhn, *GIs and Fräuleins: The German-American Encounter in 1950s West Germany* (Chapel Hill, 2002).

131. Doris Foitzik, "Sittlich verwahrlost!' Disziplinierung und Diskriminierung geschlechtskranker Mädchen in der Nachkriegszeit am Beispiel Hamburg," *1999. Zeitschrift für Sozialgeschichte des 20. und 21. Jahrhunderts* no. 1 (1997): 68–82, here 68. Other derogatory terms included, for instance, *Ami-Hure* (American whore) or *Amiliebchen* (American lover/darling).

132. Karin Sommer, "In der 'Raubtierwelt' der Trümmerzeit: Jugendliche im Zonendeutschland," in *'Schön ist die Jugendzeit...?' Das Leben junger*

Leute in Bayern 1899–2001, ed. Harald Parigger, Bernhard Schoßig, and Evamaria Brockhoff (Augsburg, 1994), 63–65, here 64.

133. Annegret Braun and Norbert Göttler, eds., *Nach der 'Stunde Null' II: Historische Nahaufnahmen aus den Gemeinden des Landkreises Dachau 1945 bis 1949* (Munich, 2013), 40; Heinz Staudinger, *Weilheimer Schulgeschichten, 1939–1952, Band 1* (Norderstedt, 2010), 107.

134. Leo Crespi, "The Influence of Military Government Sponsorship in German Opinion Polling," *International Journal of Opinion and Attitude Research* 4 (1950): 151–78, here 172; Kleinschmidt, *Do Not Fraternize*, 158; Biddiscombe, "Dangerous Liaisons," 626–27. See also: Ute Frevert, *Women in German History: Form Bourgeois Emancipation to Sexual Liberation* (Oxford, 1988).

135. BayHStAM, Ministerium des Inneren 79902, quoted in Zahner, *Jugendfürsorge in Bayern*, 60.

136. Biddiscombe, "Dangerous Liaisons," 633.

137. Klaus-Dietmar Henke, "Fraternization," in *Die amerikanische Besetzung Deutschlands*, ed. Klaus-Dietmar Henke (Munich, 1995), 185–204, here 199. See also: Luise Drasdo, "Kein Dank für Veronika Dankeschön," *Sozial Extra. Zeitschrift für soziale Arbeit* 10, no. 4 (1986): 34–38, here 38.

138. Goedde, *GIs and Germans*, 93–94. See also: "Drifting Frauleins Pose Problems," *Stars and Stripes*, 20 July 1946.

139. Drasdo, "Kein Dank für Veronika Dankeschön." Tamara Domentat calls *Veronika Dankeschön* a "derogatory term" (*Schmähbegriff*). Tamara Domentat, *"Hallo Fräulein!" Deutsche Frauen und amerikanische Soldaten* (Berlin, 1998), 155.

140. Mary Louise Roberts, "The Price of Discretion: Prostitution, Venereal Disease, and the American Military in France, 1944–1946," *American Historical Review* 115. no. 4 (Oct. 2010): 1002–30.

141. Timm, *The Politics of Fertility in Twentieth Century Berlin.*

142. Gellately, *Backing Hitler*, 111–16, namely 112.

143. Marc Hillel, *Die Invasion der Be-Freier: Die GIs in Europa 1942–1947* (Hamburg, 1983), 176. Although partly questionable in regard to his overall approach, Marc Hillel provides some valuable insights.

144. Martin Bormann has documented these sentiments after a talk with Adolf Hitler on 29 January 1944. See: Hans Adolf Jacobsen and Werner Jochmann, *Ausgewählte Dokumente zur Geschichte des Nationalsozialismus 1933–1945* (Bielefeld, 1961). See also: Glaser, *Rubble Years*, 48.

145. Michael Kater, *Hitler Youth* (Cambridge, 2004), 111. These encounters took place in Dachau, near Munich.

146. Panzer, "'Volksmütter,'" 250, in *Frauenleben in Bayern*.

147. Selig et al., *Chronik der Stadt München*, 69.

148. Conservative State Representative Maria Deku (CSU), (30 October 1947), ABL, StBBd, II/1, no. 31, 116, quoted in Zahner, *Jugendfürsorge in Bayern*, 55–56.

149. Quoted in Samuel Andrew Stouffer, *The American Soldier*, vol. 2 (Princeton, 1949), 569. A survey from August 1945 noted: 57 percent state that almost all fraternize; 51 percent of those longer in Germany say they had contact with German girls. Ibid.

150. Ibid.

151. Ziemke, *The U.S. Army in the Occupation of Germany*, 327. See also: Kleinschmidt, *Do Not Fraternize*, 145 and 146.

152. Sommer, "In der 'Raubtierwelt' der Trümmerzeit," 64.

153. Conservative State Representative Franz Michel (CSU), (10 June 1948), ABL, StBBd, II/2, no. 5, 1568, quoted in Zahner, *Jugendfürsorge in Bayern*, 56.

154. Reithmeier, *Verwahrlosung und Kriminalität der Jugendlichen*, 44.

155. "Vor dem Richter," *Die Süddeutsche Zeitung*, 22 February 1946.

156. "Die Jungen—Nur ein Mädchen," *Der Münchner Merkur*, 21 March 1946. See also: "Geschlechtsmoral im Abstieg," *Die Neue Zeitung*, 8 November 1945; "Das Mädchen Elisabeth," *Die Süddeutsche Zeitung*, 22 February 1946; "Girls in der Retorte," *Die Süddeutsche Zeitung*, 30 May 1946.

157. "Fünfzehnjährige um Mitternacht," *Die Süddeutsche Zeitung*, 23 August 1946.

158. Hans Rühmelin, "Fischer, Kurt J., US-Zone, 1947, *So lebten wir... ein Querschnitt durch 1947* (1947): 3–27, here 4.

159. "Bekämpfung von Geschlechtskrankheiten," *Der Münchner Stadtanzeiger*, 16 January 1946.

160. "Wer ist 'Veronika Dankeschön?,'" *Die Süddeutsche Zeitung*, 13 August 1946. There were only a couple of rare voices underlining how broad generalizations demonized young girls. According to one article, "the lipstick that so greatly offends the elderly is often merely a symptom for a feeling of deceit." "Die Jungen: Nur ein Mädchen," *Der Münchner Merkur*, 21 March 1946.

161. "Wer ist 'Veronika Dankeschön?,'" *Die Süddeutsche Zeitung*, 13 August 1946.

162. "Autobahn-Girl Hitch Hikers Threaten to Raise VD Rate," *Stars and Stripes*, 12 July 1946.

163. "Jugendverwahrlosung: Ein Problem unserer Zeit," *Die Süddeutsche Zeitung*, 31 May 1947.

164. Hosseinzadeh, *Nur Trümmerfrauen und Amiliebchen?* 93–104; Maria Höhn, "Frau im Haus und Girl im *Spiegel*: Discourse on Women in the Interregnum Period of 1945–1949 and the Question of German Identity," *Central European History* 26, no. 1 (1993): 57–90, here 64.

165. Annette Brauerhoch, *'Fräulein' und GIs: Geschichte und Filmgeschichte* (Frankfurt am Main/ Basel, 2006), 11.

166. Raingard Esser, "'Language No Obstacle': War Brides in the German Press, 1945–49," *Women's History Review* 12, no. 4 (Jan., 2003): 577–606, here 577. See also: Hosseinzadeh, ed., *Nur Trümmerfrauen und Ami-Liebchen*; Trude Unruh, ed., *Trümmerfrauen: Biografien einer betrogenen Generation* (Essen, 1987).

167. Buckel, "Der verwahrloste Großstadtjugendliche," 25 and 27.

168. Lauter, "Krieg und Jugendkriminalität," 37 and 41. See also: Reithmeier, *Verwahrlosung und Kriminalität der Jugendlichen*, 33 and 38.

169. Erich Langer and Wilhelm Brandt, *Geschlechts-Krankheiten bei Kinder und Jugendlichen* (Berlin, 1948), 7.

170. Josef Schmid, "Kann eine wirksame Bekämpfung der Geschlechtskrank-
     heiten auf die Dauer ohne Meldepflicht erfolgen?" (Ph.D. diss., Ludwig-
     Maximilians University Munich, 1945), 16.
171. Buckel, "Der verwahrloste Großstadtjugendliche," 29.
172. Landeshauptstadt München, ed., *Ein Neuer Anfang im Wohlfahrts-, Ju-
     gend- und Gesundheitswesen* (Munich, 1948), 53. See also: Thurnwald,
     Gegenwartsproblem Berliner Familien, 146.
173. Hans Magnus Enzensberger, *Europa in Ruinen: Augenzeugenberichte aus
     den Jahren 1944–1948* (Frankfurt am Main, 1990), 208.
174. Landeshauptstadt München, ed. *Ein Neuer Anfang,* [no page number].

CHAPTER 2

Controlling Juvenile Delinquents in the Crisis Years

"An unorganized and unsupervised youth is a problem that cannot be taken lightly."[1] This sentiment appeared in *Die Süddeutsche Zeitung* in fall 1946. It captured attempts to defend the state, morality, and social order. The article also quoted a local U.S. official arguing in favor of institutionalization in schools, youth organizations, and the Youth Welfare Office as a way to deal with *the delinquent boy* and *the sexually deviant girl*. Both images embodied abnormal behaviors and had turned into discursive spaces and signifiers for wrongdoing. These constructs had their benefits[2] and now also became valuable tools of social control for those defending Munich's recovery and future.

Moving forward against such youth during a complex transition period was a complicated endeavor; yet growing fears among the general public increasingly united authorities against juvenile delinquency and provided the leeway for contemporaries to draw on traditional means of control. Such an interpretation sustains claims regarding continuities in German history across 1945, especially widespread within *Alltagsgeschichte*. As the evidence suggests, the situation for the young changed little during the crisis years. Take the story of Albert O. and his sister. Born in 1928, Albert had spent time in juvenile detention during the Nazi period. Briefly liberated by U.S. troops from the concentration camp in Dachau, he was eventually penalized for a variety of minor property crimes. Authorities at Dachau prison sent his sixteen-year-old sister to juvenile detention for, according to the official language, "constantly changing sexual partners."[3] These measures against Albert, his sister, and many other youngsters built on widespread public support, and were grounded in the constructed meaning of juvenile delinquency. Once faced with these perceived threats in a time of crisis, local authorities willingly and forcefully clamped down on the young, starting with efforts to reinstitutionalize youth and later taking much more direct actions. According to authorities, reopening schools and youth organizations would get the young off the streets and would help the recovery of society; the Youth Welfare Office would deal with those unwilling to conform. By fall 1945 and early spring 1946, however, such measures appeared increasingly inadequate, as juvenile delinquency seemed rampant. Finding itself in a state of panic and hysteria, authorities in Munich began favoring a more thorough use of existing institutions; they also relied on new measures grounded in a widespread postwar consensus. Soon more intrusive policies and measures helped fight juvenile delinquency in order to save society and Munich's future. In October 1947 a large-scale raid swept through Munich and Bavaria for twenty-four hours, making it the climax of authoritative responses. It would ultimately take until the stabilization of the German economy following the currency reform in June 1948 before juvenile delinquency became detached from broader fears regarding Munich's recovery and future.

Authorities fighting against youth consisted of many diverse groups and displayed and acted upon a shared "restoration-of-order" attitude. Their outlook was based around the noble sacrifices of the "rubble women" and what was supposed to become a similar contribution of the "reconstruction generation." Forming, in some ways, an improbable and very practical coalition that came together for the sole purpose of defending recovery, many journalists, social commentators, experts, as well as a variety of public voices pushed for opposition against delinquency. Cardinal Michael von Faulhaber and conservative politician Alois Hundhammer, for instance, became important voices in favor of a faith-based education and corporal punishment as ways to fight juvenile deviancy. Since democratic processes developed from the ground up, the coalition fighting delinquency consisted also of the local military administration and the city government. In Munich, this alliance included the city council as well as mayors Karl Scharnagl and Thomas Wimmer. City Schools Inspector Anton Fingerle and the Director of the Youth Welfare Office Elisabeth Bamberger also played important roles. On the streets of Munich it was primarily the newly organized city police, led by Police Chief Franz-Xaver Pitzer, which initially dealt with youngsters. The overall excellent coordination between the U.S. Military Government and local German officials on this particular topic is striking given "two utterly different perspectives"[4] on education as such. This aspect only highlights the perceived common-sense reaction in line with German and American ideals once dealing with juvenile delinquency. That this unlikely coalition had initially helped construct youth as a threat outlines inherent connections between constructed meanings and social control.

Fighting an Uphill Battle

At the beginning of the crisis years, attempts to control youth were secondary. With the constant increase of daily bombings, a rise in the amount of refugees, and the growing lack of basic necessities, Nazi authorities and contemporaries had little time to discipline youth. Waning institutional structures like schools, the Hitler Youth, and the Youth Welfare Office tried to stay afloat as much as possible, pushing male youngsters, if anything, as a last stand against approaching enemy forces. Nazi authorities had formed the *Volkssturm* or people's army by fall 1944, consisting of every available male age sixteen to sixty. In Munich, "a couple of seventeen-year-old *Hitlerjungen* shot twice onto approaching Americans."[5] Elsewhere such fanatic attempts to prevent or at least participate in an ever-likely downfall swept many youngsters into horrific situations. Bernhard Wicki's movie *Die Brücke* (1959) paints a realistic picture of the futility of such circumstances. The late occupation of Munich shortly before the end of World War II, however, allowed most youngsters to do their best to avoid tragic situations, especially during the last weeks of the war.

Shortly after U.S. arrival in Munich and in response to previous experiences and standardized policies, Americans strictly controlled daily life. Authorities proclaimed curfews, which initially prohibited locals to be away from their residence between 7 P.M. and 6 A.M. Yet those ended within a couple of weeks and officials simply monitored and patrolled certain city spaces. Train stations, bars, and other potentially deviant areas saw much supervision early on, namely to prevent a feared guerilla warfare by Nazi groups like the Werwulf (Werewolf). In Munich Werwolf activities did not materialize.[6] Instead, the allied victory was complete, making curfews and extensive controls of daily life for security reasons increasingly obsolete.[7]

Within a short amount of time, American and German authorities focused on sexual deviancy. Again grounded in previous experiences when liberating or occupying various locations,[8] U.S. officials set up warning signs aimed at their own men. One of such signs read, "V.D.— Big Army Problem";[9] another one stated, "You'd better be without VD."[10] Furthermore, as an official U.S. report put it, "All possible measures were taken to further an educational program on the prevention of venereal diseases."[11] This effort included lectures and movies for GIs on sexual morality, even demonstrations with infected patients. With limited success, the emphasis shifted towards German girls. By summer 1945, American officials created so-called prophylactic stations to treat those carrying sexually transmitted diseases. Initially set up only for American soldiers and personnel, these facilities soon opened their doors to *the sexually deviant girl*. The city of Munich set up its own hospitals focusing primarily on venereal disease, and the U.S. Military Government provided penicillin, a drug until then not widely available in Germany. To its relief, *Der Münchner Stadtanzeiger* commented that the Military Government now "took this danger seriously and worked together with local German institutions to fight this pandemic. Directives requiring reports of the contraction of venereal disease are indicative of the realistic view which the Army has heretofore taken of this problem."[12] By March 1946 there were ninety-eight special clinics for patients with venereal diseases and twenty-eight diagnostic centers throughout the U.S. Zone of Occupation.[13] In that sense, opposition to fraternization and fears regarding *Veronika Dankeschön* "created an unusual alliance between those reactionary Germans and the American military government," as historian Petra Goedde has put it.[14] Gaining control over the female body thus does not only signify the overall power of U.S. and German officials but also highlights a rather straightforward coordination between authorities against supposed female misbehaviors [Figure 2.1].

Although penicillin brought quick relief to most patients, authorities remained concerned. Numerous patients returned various times after an initial treatment. Whereas this fact sustained claims regarding rampant sexual deviancy, local German officials felt they were losing more than just the fight against venereal diseases. Seeing sexually transmitted diseases as part of female immorality, they felt that the state was losing the war against immorality altogether. In times of recovery, loss of control was deemed extremely dangerous. It was consequently not surprising that the introduction of penicillin was not seen as a victory in the battle against societal ills.[15]

As local officials tried to step up their efforts they also began employing a variety of existing laws still in place from the Nazi period or from before. Apart from regulating areas around U.S. barracks, hoping to spot female deviants, the "Law for Combating Sexually Transmitted Diseases"[16] provided a valuable vantage point to actively control *the sexually deviant girl*. Enacted in 1927, it had remained in place after 1945. At the time, comments one historian, this law "did not simply hope to limit infections; it also utilized discussions of hygiene, welfare, and education" to fight venereal diseases.[17] Applicable to both sexes,

Figure 2.1 An American GI and German Fräuleins on the streets of Munich, 1948.
Courtesy of Georg Fruhstorfer/Bayerische Staatsbibliothek München/Bildarchiv.

conceptions of loose female morals made this law an excellent tool in the fight against *the sexually deviant girl* in particular. According to paragraph four of this regulation, authorities could force those "who carry sexually-transmitted diseases or *are suspect of such* [emphasis added]" to be tested.[18] If authorities determined that a girl carried a venereal disease, then she faced various charges, including youth arrest. Apart from this measure, laws in place to limit prostitution offered another way to target female youngsters. Whereas prostitution was not illegal in Germany, the German criminal code prohibited prostitution "publicly and in a conspicuous manner" or "in a manner offensive to individuals or the public;"[19] the law also specifically forbade prostitution near churches and all places frequented by the young, hence offering additional frames for supervision. Finally, paragraph 175, originally included in the German penal code in 1871, prohibited coitus-like behavior among men. Whereas homosexuality was not a prime concern of authorities in Munich, the broad application of this law could provide an avenue for criminalizing sexual deviancy among male youngsters, if desired. As outlined by historian Dagmar Herzog, "Supporters of the paragraph strongly emphasized the need to protect youth and repeatedly invoked the belief that male homosexuality was a contagious condition that would spread ineluctably unless forceful punitive action was taken." According to her, some authorities believed young delinquents loitering around train stations to be "vulnerable to conversion via seduction ... [and these voices] explicitly named [that] as *the* reason for retaining Paragraph 175."[20] Hence, shortly after the war contemporaries had little problems in finding the legal basis to control real and imagined sexual deviancy in Munich.

However, local authorities rarely had the capabilities to implement existing laws, especially without American assistance and support. These limitations are apparent in the context of the black market. As a threat to the food supply, and as the supposed habitat of *the delinquent boy*, black markets had been part of city life for several years. Located at the central train station, the German Museum, and certain streets throughout the city, several restaurants and bars also became places for such semilegal activities.[21] In an attempt to regain control, local authorities soon began observing these spaces more closely. Yet according to one police report from summer 1945, those trading in such spaces did not mind the police: "The threshold to participate in illegal activities is so high that some even set up little booths with umbrellas and all, laying out their products."[22] Early raids helped little because black marketeers soon recognized policemen and warned other participants, dealers, or bystanders. Besides, raids were not always safe for law enforcement because some marketeers attacked a usually outnumbered and ill-equipped police force. In fact, during an early raid, forty-five policemen experienced exactly that as they tried to clamp down on a black market in downtown Munich:

> Right at the arrival a mob ... jumped the police car, stopped it, and took it over. Officers were kicked off, surrounded, and attacked. Only with major difficulties were the police able to arrest fourteen and free the injured driver. Stones flew and the officers rushed away.... The eight arrested individuals ultimately jumped off the car and escaped.[23]

In general, those caught rarely faced charges because it was difficult to prove their participation in illegal activities. As a result, the local police felt increasingly helpless in safeguarding recovery, as it had neither the capabilities nor the legal backing to step in against black marketeering youth.

Newly installed Police Chief Franz-Xaver Pitzer eventually spoke up about such inabilities. Like many before him, he utilized the misery of youth to give his call more authority. Based on the slogan "all decent individuals to the front in the fight against indecency,"[24] he called for stricter measures including the arming of the local police. The U.S. Military Government declined to supply weapons until October 1945;[25] it did, however, allow an increase in forces. This concession allowed Pitzer to set up a "special unit for combat against black-marketeering."[26] It consisted of thirty-two officers and relied on the newly passed "Law for the Fight against the Black Market."[27] Although this law remained only briefly on the books due to its inadequate legal grounding, the police arrested 650 black marketeers, some of them male youngsters.[28] At that point it became apparent that only a solid legal basis and powerful law enforcement could control youth.

Institutionalization: Schools, Youth Groups, and the Youth Welfare Office

Given the chaotic situation shortly after the war, rebuilding traditional institutions for the young turned out to be a sensible starting point when fighting delinquency. Schools would house youngsters during the day, and teach them about their role as productive citizens. Afterwards, they would be under the supervision of their parents or other legal guardians. Those without such afternoon support could go to traditional youth groups, or would receive the help of the Youth Welfare Office. Authorities thus primarily rebuilt these three institutions to get youth off the streets and back into a supervised environment.

More and more throughout the crisis years, and certainly at the time of U.S. arrival, local schools lay in shambles, and little changed for the first months of occupation. War and postwar struggles had significantly disturbed schooling. After years of Nazi education, elementary schools had closed and many children had been sent to the countryside once the war intensified.[29] By early 1945, a lack of coal had briefly terminated instructing for those still in schools.[30] During the final weeks of the Nazi regime schooling and education had not been on the mind of local residents and faltering Nazi authorities. The U.S. arrival did

not change much. At first, schooling and education were not priorities
for American authorities. Instead, U.S. officials confiscated buildings
for their own use, including schools.[31] By summer 1945, some U.S.
policies regarding schooling began to emerge although confusion remained for months to come.[32] Originally released in April 1945, Directive JCS 1067 to the Commander in Chief of U.S. forces in Germany
then noted, "All educational institutions within your zone except those
previously re-established by Allied authority will be closed." It inaugurated "a coordinated system of control over German education" in an
attempt to completely eliminate Nazi and militaristic doctrines. This
directive also permitted "the reopening of elementary, middle and vo-
cational schools at the earliest possible date after Nazi personnel has
been eliminated."[33] Another directive later on translated such abstract
measures into precise administrative rules, stressing denazification
and the necessity for military control at all levels.[34] By summer 1945,
American officials started to implement JCS 1067. Part of a larger
process, they began with the denazification of teachers. But replacing
those deemed unsuitable, finding new textbooks, and dealing with a
lack of facilities took time. For example, 21 percent of all school buildings had been destroyed, and the occupation force seized 255 facilities
for its own purposes.[35]

Apart from such problems facing a youth crisis also increasingly
changed priorities. Although U.S. authorities made an attempt to de-
nazify schools, a quick reopening was soon deemed of higher importance. Compared to German officials, the Americans saw such quick
steps as emergency measures, with more reform to follow later. For
many Germans, on the other hand, quick denazification was not the
beginning but the end of educational reform as a whole. Working together in order to reestablish some kind of "orderly schooling even if
only getting the kids off the streets to prevent delinquency"[36] became a
common ground, as one scholar rightfully noted later on; references to
a supposed rise in juvenile delinquency turned into one way to justify
the quick reorganization of schools. In August 1945, officials formed
a committee for schools within the city council. There, local authorities connected "worries about the psychological and mental future of
our people and our city … to worries about education and schooling
of our youth."[37] On 3 September, all between the ages of six to fourteen started to register for schools. Two weeks later, several elementary
schools opened their doors. Middle schools and secondary schools followed, as the Munich school system took shape again.[38] By early 1946
growing fears of *the delinquent boy* and *the sexually deviant girl* had
contributed significantly to the reopening of seventy-seven elementary

schools in Munich,[39] despite questions about their readiness to accept students.

This rapid reorganization brought problems. Most notably, the denazification demanded by JCS 1067 had limited the availability of teachers. In Munich's elementary schools 400 teachers taught 52,201 children making one teacher responsible for about 130 students.[40] Most educators were categorized as National Socialists, and those rehired often followed outdated teaching methods. City Schools Inspector Anton Fingerle called upon certified teachers to "adopt a new and tolerant attitude,"[41] advice that assumed such changes can simply happen overnight. Plus, his comments seemed of little use without the infrastructure to provide preparation and help. Books were either widely unavailable, soaked with National Socialist narratives and doctrines, or grounded in outdated nineteenth-century teaching ideas. Moreover, children had to bring their own paper to school. As late as the summer of 1946, 70 percent of students in Munich had no notebooks, and 90 percent did not own a jacket to keep them warm while in school.[42] Facilities were inadequate and most at least partially destroyed. Students were squeezed into large classes restricting the quality of learning. One student remembered how she attended a school that was in ruin with cardboard covering the windows. During the winter months a little round iron stove could not fully heat the room although most students brought coal. Without shoes or jackets she and her classmates were shivering and their ink froze.[43] Another individual remembered how the children "sat in school in their coats, and between classes they did a little sport, so that they did not get too cold."[44] Schools during the crisis years were hardly appropriate environments for learning.

Broader ignorance about these issues or the inability to deal with them due to a lack of funds could explain these shortcomings, yet neither was the case for Munich. Local officials, most notably City Schools Inspector Anton Fingerle, were well informed about the situation. They did little in response. For them, such problems were secondary given the looming threat of juvenile delinquency. Institutionalization, not learning, was a priority and deemed the basis for quick recovery. According to Munich's school office, "even the formal opening of a school ... had to be seen as progress."[45] The same office later deliberately stated that the main objective for schooling was first, to get the young "off the streets," and second, "to return them to a regulated and orderly mental and intellectual occupation."[46] Authorities hoped that once schools reopened children and youngsters would return to their assigned roles within society. Institutionalization as control—not learning—was consequently the priority of schooling and the reason why authorities rushed towards reopening schools.

Officials could rely on the support of the public, which made these choices easier. Newspapers captured such sentiments when reporting on the problems with schools but emphasizing their necessity in times of crises. In late 1945, *Die Süddeutsche Zeitung* aligned the opening of schools with Munich's hopeful future and complete recovery.[47] Other public voices sustained such calls for society's return to order[48] while local church officials hoped to influence future educational models.[49] Such conversations took center stage particularly in Munich. Whereas the reintroduction of corporal punishment and numerous other disagreements resulted in conflicts between conservatives, liberals, social democrats, and the U.S. Military Government,[50] awareness regarding *the delinquent boy* and *the sexually deviant girl* brought even the latter onto the same page.[51] After all, rebuilding and reopening institutions of education was a way to get youth off the streets and as such signified Munich's recovery and success of occupation policies.

The re-creation of youth groups followed a similar mindset and pattern, initially spearheaded by American authorities. By October 1945, a report by the U.S. Military Government had outlined, "formal education, as such in the narrow sense of the term, will only partially solve the tremendous problem of what to do with defeated German youth, to give them hope, to form them into decent citizens, and, from a very practical point of view, to keep them 'out of mischief.'"[52] "The Report on the United States Education Mission to Germany" presented in 1946 made similar suggestions.[53] After all, the Hitler Youth had indicated the power of after-school programs, though such setups could not remerge after denazification. As a result, no new youth group took shape in the first two months after U.S. arrival, leaving a "vacuum" in Munich, as one contemporary described it.[54] The first new youth organizations then reappeared in the summer—at the time mostly Catholic youth groups.[55] By fall 1945 and once aware of the increasing need for afternoon supervision, U.S. authorities made a more coordinated effort to reorganize youth organizations. Beginning in October 1945, the US Forces, European Theater (USFET) set up a synchronized process according to which each county had to create so-called youth committees. Organizations interested in reviving a former or creating a new youth group had to get official permission from these committees. The board of youth committees faced final approval by the local military governor.[56] Following this arrangement, numerous youth groups sprouted throughout Munich in the following months. The first was the Youth Club Munich-South for Girls, which was licensed in July

1946;[57] others like the Boy Scouts St. Georg, the Young Socialists, the Falcons, or the Free German Youth soon followed. Most important became local chapters of the Bavarian Youth Ring and the City Youth Ring Munich, both supported by Anton Fingerle, who made them a quasi-municipal organization and a semi-official arm of the city of Munich.[58]

The Youth Ring emerged in reaction to U.S. efforts, demonstrating the desire of German officials to control their young, especially once the Americans got involved more directly. Spreading from Northern Germany, the U.S. Army had long developed a program aimed at German youngsters. It had originated in the Enclave of Bremen in summer 1945, where a grassroots effort within the Seventh U.S. Army had resulted in open facilities for the young and certain youth groups. By September 1945, according to a contemporary publication, it "instituted the first broad program of German Youth activities" beyond Bremen.[59] Increasingly rooted in the desire to help the young and fight against delinquency as personified by *the delinquent boy* and *the sexually deviant girl*, the so-called German Youth Activities Program (GYA) spread throughout the U.S. Zone of Occupation, and eventually arrived in Munich.[60] There, as elsewhere, local German authorities needed U.S. help. According to U.S. officials, "social workers [in Munich] were aiding 13,000 children in the city. Over 3,000 orphan children were being cared for in homes maintained by the youth office funds and 10,000 others were being visited regularly by the organization's nurses."[61] Another report concluded, "The enormity of this problem ultimately foiled military government's intention of retaining only a directive responsibility for youth activities and welfare."[62] Soon U.S. authorities strengthened their efforts to help. Interested in controlling youth and re-educating the young, a directive from April 1946 outlined exact measures: "Getting the young off the streets" and into U.S. monitored formats was crucial to rebuilding German society.[63] Apart from limiting the possibilities of juvenile delinquency, it gave U.S. officials prime authority over German youth. Hoping to plant the seed of democracy in the young, youth work within the GYA became an important area for U.S. policies of re-education. Boys and girls would be off the streets and learn about democracy by playing sports, discussing various contemporary issues, or simply learning about the United States. As summarized by a U.S. official report, American policies were "motivated by the wish to use youth organizations as an additional means of re-education and control."[64]

Whereas the U.S. military government spent sixty million Deutsche Marks on the GYA by 1950,[65] German city officials equally concerned with *the delinquent boy* and *the sexually deviant girl* had mixed feelings about American involvement. Although they supported youth groups as a mechanism to deal with delinquency, they heavily criticized the setup of the GYA. Youngsters did not have a membership card but could show up whenever they wanted. U.S. groups were also more democratic, apparent in the fact that youngsters could lead groups themselves. Traditional youth workers "could simply not empathize with such setups and mindsets," remarked one contemporary.[66] Furthermore, most U.S. youth groups were coeducational.[67] In Munich, division along lines of gender had been well established for decades. To allow both sexes to visit the same group was a slap in the face to those hoping to stabilize society, return boys and girls to their traditional roles, and recover quickly. Traditional fears of Americanization played a role as well[68] and became ways to question the subservient German part in such setups. It indicated that getting youth off the streets *and* under German control was what ultimately mattered most to local German authorities.

With schools and youth groups more and more in place, the reorganization of the Youth Welfare Office became the final puzzle piece regarding the institutionalization of youth. Traditionally the prime institution for controlling wayward youngsters, it had been embedded within a National Socialist system. To resurrect its power meant another step towards stability. The expanded function of the local Youth Welfare Office within a society fearing disruptions was clear: dealing with juvenile delinquency, youngsters unwilling to work, and numerous other groups threatening postwar recovery. Those in charge considered young refugees from the Soviet sector in the East as part of the homeless and thus delinquent youth, at least until their fate was exploited for propagandistic purposes in an emerging Cold War paradigm. Of course, the local Youth Welfare Office was also concerned with alarming numbers of *sexually deviant girls*. According to contemporaries, these girls were "morally weak, unsupervised, seduced [into deviancy] by bad company, and unscrupulous in their sexual activity, often for material benefits."[69] Though initially targeted by the U.S. Military Government and treated in various hospitals, the Youth Welfare Office increasingly helped in such undertakings, making this institution, in many ways, the final stand in the fight against juvenile delinquency.

The complicated resurrection process of the Youth Welfare Office began in July 1945. According to a U.S. report, the first youth offices "were established by the military government and staffed by Germans to supervise and to provide care for orphaned, needy, and delinquent

German youth."[70] American and German local officials again coordinated their efforts to accelerate the reorganization of this institution. But adequate facilities and personnel were rare: buildings had been destroyed or U.S. authorities had seized them, while properly trained personnel were in short supply. A strict denazification process further amplified these problems: most youth workers had been employed by the National Socialist People's Welfare or other National Socialist organizations, which limited the pool of personnel. According to one local publication analyzing the reconstruction of this institution by the late 1940s, "the lack of personnel became a major problem in the attempt to combat juvenile vagabondage."[71] The fact that the Youth Welfare Office did not play a major role during National Socialism exacerbated the situation. During Nazi rule, the National Socialist People's Welfare had been responsible for welfare and youth. As a strictly hierarchical National Socialist organization, it had merely used the Youth Welfare Office as an executive body. This role had not only tarnished the legitimacy and credibility of the Youth Welfare Office after the war but had also forced it to undergo something like a rebirth after 1945. To gather documentation and set up its former administrational apparatus took time, and as late as the summer of 1946, the Bavarian Ministry of the Interior underlined that qualified workers were still in short supply.[72]

Legally speaking, the Youth Welfare Office relied on the Reich Youth Welfare Law (RJWG). Influenced by the devastating situation for the young after World War I, the RJWG had been passed in June 1922 to become the first attempt in Germany to coordinate regulations regarding youth. The law established youth welfare offices as separate institutions and provided administrative procedures once self-help, personal responsibility, and charity failed. During National Socialist rule the RJWG remained in place but the Youth Welfare Office lost its power. Instead, a law passed in February 1939 installed a strict hierarchical structure apparent in organizations like the National Socialist People's Welfare and the Hitler Youth. The Youth Welfare Office was merely used for executing policies. After 1945, the RJWG remained in place. The U.S. Military Government only banned certain National Socialist elements and language from existing laws, leaving various restrictive measures in place or at least up to the interpretation of local officials.[73] These continuities led to questions and uncertainties regarding the application of laws but at the same time gave local officials a lot of authority concerning the implementation of measures.

By the end of 1945, the Youth Welfare Office slowly began to deal with juvenile delinquency. As organizational structures partially returned, youth offices began cooperating with a variety of other institutions. The police were obliged to inform the youth office when picking up youngsters, and a variety of welfare institutions provided additional assistance. In fact, the local Youth Welfare Office in Munich worked closely with religious welfare organizations like the Caritas and the Innere Mission. Both groups helped significantly regarding financial assistance; they also increased the ability of the Youth Welfare Office to fulfill its duty towards urban youngsters.[74] The Youth Welfare Office had not established itself in all quarters of town and would lack personnel and financial means for quite a while, even with such assistance. Not surprisingly, in spring 1946, Director of the Youth Welfare Office Elisabeth Bamberger sent a letter to the mayor asking for additional measures in the fight against delinquency. In her correspondence she conveniently employed constructed images of youth as a way to give her argument more credibility, sway, and authority. Bamberger discussed, for instance, the need for additional measures by referencing dancing and fraternizing between GIs and young females.[75] With most inhabitants of Munich by now aware of the threat posed by juvenile delinquency, Bamberger could rely on a growing consensus and widespread support among authorities and the general public for new and more stringent policies, now increasingly reaching beyond institutionalization.

New Policies 1946–1947

In response to Bamberger and others, the Bavarian Ministry of the Interior put forward specific policies to enforce conformity among youth. "The Plan about Taken and Proposed Measures Regarding the Youth Between the Age of Fifteen and Twenty-Two," proposed on 1 April 1946, outlined the limits of existing policies and proposed a variety of additional measures. Such measures were aimed at "the wandering or wayward youth," "delinquent women and girls older than eighteen," "the male youngsters unwilling or not used to work," and it repeated earlier policing suggestions. The plan also included three specific proposals aimed at *the delinquent boy* and *the sexually deviant girl*. The first ordinance referred to "the protection of homeless juveniles," defined as youngsters under the age of eighteen, "who are without a permanent place of residence and who are not under the supervision of grown-up relatives." Framed in the language of providing protection, youth welfare offices would now "comprise the task, to accustom juveniles again to a regular mode of life and to settle them down." These measures included detainment "in order to investigate their personal

circumstances" as well as "support" and "care" for them. "All authorities" had "the duty to immediately report homeless juveniles." A second ordinance specifically focused on bringing "demoralized women
and girls into custody," defined as females older than eighteen, "whose
conduct is conducive to the spreading of venereal disease and who are
thus a danger to public health, or who are otherwise demoralized."
This broad definition provided the basis for the institutionalization of
females for up to two years, with room for even longer sentences. In
cases of those married or under age, parents or husbands "will have
to be informed of the resolution without delay." While this measure
undeniably criminalized virtually all girls and women suspected of
abnormal behaviors, it was mostly aimed against fraternization and
the spread of venereal diseases. Ordinance number three then referred
to "education by work," a euphemism to describe corrective actions
against "Juveniles up to the age of 25, who as the result of the war have
lost the habit of work" and needed "to reaccustom to a settled mode
of living and regular work." The ordinance goes on noting, "juveniles,
who have been assigned to work by the Labor Office" but "who have
repeatedly shirked their duty of work" were to "be committed to institutions for education by work." Such prison or detention sentences
would last at least three months and continue, "Until the objective has
been attained."[76] All proposals aimed at reintegrating male and female
youth into the work force, in that way making them productive members of society, stabilizing postwar order, and securing their masculinity and femininity for Munich's recovery.

The quick passage of the blueprint as ordinance no. 73, no. 74, and
no. 75 on 5 April 1946 demonstrated a widespread postwar consensus.[77] Irritated by loitering, vagrant, fraternizing, and work-shy youngsters, the general public was happy to see authorities act. Newspapers
had captured popular sentiments and opinions, and had repeatedly
called for additional actions in the form of raids to clean up the city.[78]
Besides, the measures had the support of the Office of the U.S. Military
Government for Bavaria. Official correspondence documents that its
local headquarters had "no objection to the enactment" of the ordinances aimed to deal with juvenile delinquency.[79] Less concerned in
some regards, the Americans had only stepped in once local German
officials had tried to limit their influence. This situation had emerged
in the context of expanded censorship for movies regarding children
and youngsters. Then the U.S. Military Government for Bavaria had
opposed the proposal suggesting that forcing juveniles to be "accompanied by adults would seem a more practical solution than an attempt
to place films in certain categories."[80] As a result, however, widespread

fear of *the delinquent boy* and *the sexually deviant girl* gave authorities the leverage to move forward against supposed misbehaviors while facing little if any political resistance.

With all three measures in place, authorities had gained substantial prerogatives by early 1946. At first, officials posted announcements calling on those younger than twenty-five years of age to participate in the reconstruction effort; they also briefly expanded attempts to limit female access to U.S. facilities. An article in the news magazine *Der Spiegel* later recalled failed attempts to distribute special passes for young females to get access to U.S. bases.[81] With little success, authorities relied on ordinance no. 73, no. 74, and no. 75 to create a stringent system of control in line with pre-1945 measures. The police arrested young males seen near the black market or just on the streets at an "abnormal" time; female youngsters faced charges once spotted near U.S. facilities or simply caught with chocolate and candy. In this sense, all juveniles perceived as behaving inappropriately in public had to fear criminalization. Once arrested, the police handed supposed delinquents over to the Youth Welfare Office or to medical facilities set up to check young females for venereal diseases. Various institutions also housed those not picked up by parents or legal guardians. A lack of facilities initiated a brief discussion but seemed not to bother authorities too much. According to a local newspaper, officials sent "youngsters unwilling to work and off track" or simply "without adequate identification or work permit" to a former refugee site in the suburb of Munich-Pasing.[82] There, youngsters spent their time without actual opportunities for work or rehabilitation.[83]

The general public was by and large in favor of this crackdown against youth. As noted earlier, newspapers had repeatedly called for additional raids to clean up the city. According to one publication, the central train station was widely seen as "deviant and dirty and would not leave a welcoming impression of the city for newly arriving visitors. The restaurant at the station is the center for black marketeers and hookers."[84] In an anonymous letter to *Die Süddeutsche Zeitung*, an unknown organization even threatened to take care of black marketeers "with iron and steel," killing them if necessary.[85] In Munich, some institutions had also created lists of women with venereal diseases to help control *the sexually deviant girl*.[86] Signs and postings demonizing female fraternization indicated that, as noted by historian Perry Biddiscombe in a similar context, there "was certainly no shortage of jealous and quarrelsome young men willing to 'police' women." He continues, "One thing the repatriates had counted on was returning to a domestic order of stability and contentment, and some of them were willing to take steps to 'recreate' this condition, however much it may have always been a romantic fiction."[87]

Although a general consensus is apparent, some opposition is worth mentioning. Local German authorities, for example, complained about the costs of additional forces;[88] other institutions wondered about privacy issues regarding record keeping.[89] Most important was the response of actual youngsters. With limited possibilities to fight back, many resisted by escaping once imprisoned. Whereas this behavior merely sustained ingrained constructions of juvenile delinquency, it at least helps dismantle the supposed passivity of youth. Take the example of Karl H., a twenty-one-year-old Munich native. Described as "typical in his appearance," he was supposedly unwilling to work. In his view, "There is no need for it, unless one gets to work for the Americans, they have always something going on." Whereas Karl did not feel that prison camps would help him, the director of the facility, a psychologist, believed in the betterment of the young. He admitted, however, that it would be difficult to teach the young how to find their role in society without adequate clothes and shoes.[90] It was thus not surprising that many youngsters like Karl avoided these facilities, well aware that they did not actually help them.

Even though youth camps and juvenile detention centers within the city filled up quickly, local Police Chief Franz-Xaver Pitzer was not pleased. In his view, the young remained a threat as long as the police had limited authority. By early 1947, he called for more "radical measures in the fight against crime."[91] In *Die Süddeutsche Zeitung*, Pitzer demanded the reintroduction and passage of even stricter laws; he further insisted on measures that would allow authorities to keep young delinquents imprisoned for longer periods of time: "If barbed wire surrounding such objects is taken down, then most of the youngsters will run away. As the police chief I can only advise against that."[92] Pitzer noted that he was aware that Germany was now democratic. Nonetheless, he questioned whether Munich had to be a "Mecca for immoral and loitering youngsters."[93] Such sentiments fell on fertile ground. According to an internal correspondence dated 28 May 1947, the Bavarian minister wanted "to check up on possibilities" of tightening existing laws.[94] The U.S. military government similarly expressed alarm at the "apparent failure of German police agencies ... to successfully enforce" existing laws; it also seemed concerned about shortcomings in correctly handling "homeless, vagrant, and wandering youth."[95] The use of these broad terms underlined the harmony between the U.S. military government and German authorities when it came to dealing with juvenile delinquency. By September 1947, local U.S. officials advised the city police "to determine to what extent such a problem exists" and ensure "that every possible means be used to correct conditions;" it also recommended the "control of public spaces of assembly, particularly railroad stations in the approximately twenty-five Stadtkreise [municipalities] of Bavaria."[96] Calls for stricter retributions against "roamers, those unwilling to work, those black-marketeers without identification, prostitutes" and others now underscored the need for stricter actions[97] [Figure 2.2]. By early fall 1947 additional means of social control appeared to be in the making.

Yet the newly adopted Bavarian Constitution posed limits to existent and proposed policies. Enunciating civil liberties in a newly formed democracy, a Bavarian state representative was curious about the constitutionality of the existing ordinances.[98] Whereas ordinance no. 73 was grounded in article 126 (3) of the Bavarian Constitution,[99] skepticism regarding ordinance no. 74 and no. 75 remained. Both measures applied to those over the age of eighteen and hence included individuals not technically considered youngsters. In this sense, the Bavarian Constitution only legitimized and institutionalized the denial of civil liberties to those perceived as youth, meaning individuals under the age of eighteen. Soon the U.S. military government and the Bavarian State Parliament became concerned as well and formally joined the call for the revocation of these two ordinances. On 10 October 1947, the U.S. military government then stated that ordinance no. 74 and no. 75 "did not align with the Bavarian Constitution" because youngsters were not brought in front of a judge as outlined by Article 102 (2) of the state constitution.[100] The Bavarian government agreed.

Although this decision led to the annulment of ordinance no. 74 and no. 75, it did not mark the end of many existing restrictions, or even the end of measures against young people. U.S. military government and local officials had merely noticed a lack of constitutionality regarding age. They could still rely on ordinance no. 73, which targeted those perceived as youth. As has been pointed out by historian Daniela Zahner, "The extensive power of the youth welfare offices grounded in ordinance no. 73 led to an increased and almost mechanical referral of homeless and 'astray' youngsters into institutions for the protection of youth in 1946 and 1947."[101] The use of this decree in combination with raids illustrated that city officials, the state, and the military government were still willing to persecute any deviation from the norm by the young.

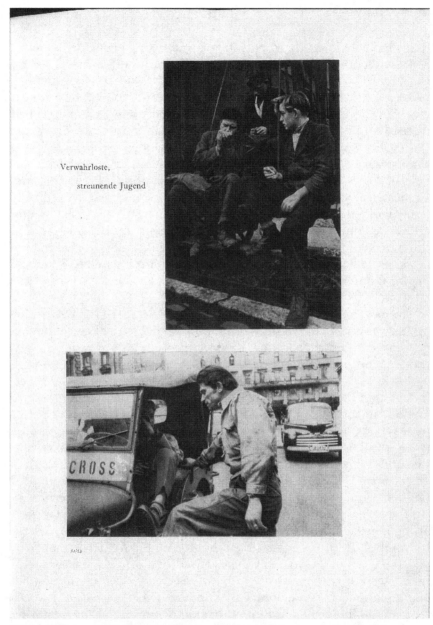

Figure 2.2 Juvenile delinquency amongst male youth is supposedly easy to spot on the streets of post–World War II Munich, as apparent in this photo. The caption simply reads: "Delinquent, Roaming Youth." Courtesy of Stadtarchiv München.

Raids

Raids had long been the key strategy for targeting young delinquents. As described by numerous historians, the local authorities relied on raids to arrest black marketeers, to crack down on certain establishments, and to move forward against prostitution.[102] Within this context crackdowns explicitly aimed against supposed young delinquents had increased dramatically since their widespread appearance in spring 1946. On 9 September 1947, for instance, the local police held a raid against young people at the central train station. According to an article in *Die Süddeutsche Zeitung*, officials arrested "18 children and youngsters." Six of them were "relapse roamers" and sent immediately to a "work education camp."[103] Four days later, the same newspaper underlined how other raids throughout previous weeks made the central train station look more "tidy."[104] Such attempts even made national news, as Police Chief Franz-Xaver Pitzer shared his delight regarding local attempts to remove the stain of Munich as a "Mecca of the underworld."[105]

The most ambitious raid occurred on 28 October 1947. Then, the US military government, youth welfare offices, and the police conducted a twenty-four-hour coordinated and large-scale raid throughout Bavaria. According to a directive by the Bavarian Ministry of the Interior, all institutions were required to work together and to repeat their efforts within their assigned areas at various times throughout the day. The document noted, "In order to avoid the fragmentation of police forces, raids need to focus on specific spaces frequently occupied by the young."[106] These spaces included the black market, certain restaurants and bars, movie theaters, and even institutions providing shelter for homeless youth at night. Authorities prepared and coordinated raids in Munich as well. As noted by the local military government, "in the cities, youth were picked up at the Bahnhofs [train stations], at the movies, in the streets, and in restaurants."[107] Officials particularly linked the urban environment of Munich to juvenile delinquency, and the city not surprisingly experienced one of the most extensive raids. According to an article in *Die Süddeutsche Zeitung*, more than one thousand policemen and two hundred detectives participated in the raid in Munich, 95 percent of them undercover.[108] Prior to moving forward, authorities made preparations to deal with the expected prisoners. They would catalogue captured young men and women to later determine their status. For those deemed to be delinquent, however defined, or found to be without a legal guardian, a government camp in the city of Augsburg and various local facilities had been prepared. As reported by the media, all major organizations concerned with the young, including Director of the Youth Welfare Office Elisabeth Bamberger, had supported the growing availability of such camps.[109]

Young individuals sent to prison camps had a terrible experience. Squeezed into inadequate facilities, these sites provided little help to youngsters.[110] Officials had faced a shortage of housing and consequently had to keep the young in rundown prisons. Many supposed delinquents resisted attempts by authorities to harness their movements within this appalling environment; others fled only to be picked up again and returned to the same or a different facility.[111] Whereas some officials seemed amazed about such constant recidivism, they do not appear to have considered why the young resisted. Adults often mistrusted youth in general, yet particularly at this point in time given widespread hysteria grounded in descriptions of juvenile delinquency. As a result, once caught, resilient behaviors amongst the young merely strengthened dominant understandings of juvenile delinquency. In addition, authorities saw the inability of camps to provide a closed environment as an indication that temptations were simply too high and fences too low, an understanding that illuminates continuities with Nazi regulations and behaviors; it also warrants a comparison to mechanisms in place in East Germany at the time. In any case, in the view of local officials in Munich, the recent annulment of ordinance no. 74 and 75 had restricted their ability to complete their work.

The twenty-four-hour raid occurring in October 1947 in Munich was a failure. According to *Die Süddeutsche Zeitung*, authorities captured about three hundred individuals, only fifty of them youngsters.[112] Many of them had to be released within a short amount of time. This included a thirteen-year-old boy who was on his way to bring his aunt some fruit. The *Munich City Chronicle* referred to 309 individuals caught in Munich with only fifty of them youngsters.[113] According to the numbers of the Bavarian State Ministry, police captured a total of 1,586 young people between twelve and eighteen throughout the whole state of Bavaria. Most of them came from Upper Bavaria. For Munich, the Bavarian government had comparatively higher numbers. It noted that officials had arrested 318 youngsters.[114] That authorities could not legally hold them but might still have counted them as arrests partially explains such divergences in numbers. Either way, authorities caught fewer youngsters than anticipated. Facing such meager results, officials pointed to each other's supposed inabilities. The U.S. military government blamed this failure on inadequate preparation and bad

timing. According to an American report that accused German officials, "the date of the raid was bad because a) the weather was bad, b)
it was not on a weekend, when the most youth are to be seen in public, c) it did not include Wednesday night, a traditional 'dance night'
in most areas, d) raids should be conducted more frequently and on
unannounced dates."[115] Yet subsequent raids did not bring different
results. A lack of preparation was thus not the main reason for the
disappointment.[116]

Given this study's focus on discourses concerned with youth, the
lack of actual delinquents is not surprising. Blown out of proportion
and exaggerated as a postwar problem, juvenile delinquency was never
about crime. Instead, it had become an almost mystical symbol embodying a variety of societal fears: disorder, disillusionment, immorality, and destitution. Male and female youth purportedly jeopardized
recovery by destabilizing the creation of norms and questioning a postwar consensus. Whereas some youngsters fit in this framework, most
did not. Once authorities specifically looked for *the delinquent boy*
and *the sexually deviant girl*, reality ruined their illusions. Discussions
about youth had led to the construction of a perceived and exaggerated
threat that did simply not exist to the extent imagined.

As the German economy lurched towards recovery, a modicum of
normalcy returned to the streets of Munich, and the threat of male and
female delinquency faded from view. In June 1948, the Deutsche Mark
replaced the virtually worthless Reichsmark, and economic conditions
began to improve. With a stable currency, traditional businesses were
able to fulfill the needs of the local population, and the black market slowly disappeared along with its supposed youthful facilitators.
Whereas this economic shift marked only the beginning of recovery
and unprecedented postwar progress, it was sufficient to push *the delinquent boy* and *the sexually deviant girl* as symbols of disorder out
of the limelight by 1949. Like his supposed home, the black market
located amongst ruins and rubble, he disappeared almost overnight;[117]
she similarly vanished once American presence and authority dwin-
dled in Munich and beyond.

Until that point local officials and U.S. authorities had widely employed fear over juvenile delinquency to control society. Deemed as a
threat to recovery, officials hastened the rebuilding process of institutions, expanded measures to control society, and employed large-scale
raids against numerous abnormal behaviors. The need to recover often
became a pretense for broad actions and a constant justification to

move forward against those unable or unwilling to conform. In the end, such choices shaped Munich as it slowly came of age. While discussions about youth thus became a microcosm for broader debates, references to societal fears turned out to be valuable tools of social control. The connection between constructing and controlling played out during the crisis years and onto the backs of the young. Some adult contemporaries had clearly benefited from the existence of both images. As demonstrated in this section, the emerging postwar liberal state remained wedded to highly conservative notions of governance and wanted to control those who refused to conform. To achieve that it relied on a broad postwar consensus that portrayed a society in disorder. Pointing to *the delinquent boy* and *the sexually deviant girl* became one beneficial route to normalization because it justified intrusive, interventionist measures. This approach seemed successful given that postwar destitution left the actual young little room to contribute to discussions framing and defining youth.

On a broader level, the crisis years remain an almost mythical period in German history. Most historians describe these rubble years simply as an interlude or new beginning; popular conceptions embedded within Germany's collective memory frame a heroic story. The latter reading became apparent when the Federal Republic turned sixty in 2009. As portrayed by various popular magazines, West Germany's postwar history—unlike the history of East Germany—was a Cinderella story: rising out of the ashes, hard-working and disciplined Germans overcame many odds.[118] They cleared the rubble and rebuilt cities, thus setting the stage for unprecedented economic recovery in the 1950s. As outlined throughout part I, prominent symbols like the *Trümmerfrau* personified this storyline, and eventually trumped other recollections of the crisis years. *The delinquent boy* and *the sexually deviant girl* ultimately disappeared from Germany's memory.

A focus on social constructions of youth helps complicate these interpretations. In fact, it becomes apparent that the year 1945 was not a new beginning, especially for the young. Whereas new opportunities emerged due to the arrival of the Americans, young people were still not only picked up when misbehaving but also when actually or supposedly deviating from very traditional norms. Many were sent to camps, which were at least partially reminiscent of detention facilities during the Nazi period and the war; they were also similar to setups in East Germany, a fact that simply did not fit into understandings of a new, liberal, and democratic West Germany, defined by the adult image of the hard-working *Trümmerfrau*.

Notes

1. "Bayerische Probleme: Jugend-Ernährung-Export," *Die Süddeutsche Zeitung*, 13 September 1946.
2. Foucault, *Discipline and Punish*, 278.
3. Reithmeier, *Verwahrlosung und Kriminalität der Jugendlichen*, 21.
4. James F. Tent, *Mission on the Rhine: Reeducation and Denazification in American-Occupied Germany* (Chicago, 1982), 3.
5. Pfister, *Das Ende des Zweiten Weltkriegs*, 167.
6. Local reports from Munich refer only to a couple of instances potentially involving Werwolf activities. Ibid., 309. See also: Herbert Schott, "Gefahr für die Demokratie? Die Angst der Amerikaner vor Edelweisspiraten und Werwölfen in Bayern 1945/46," 595–607, in *Ingolstadt im Nationalsozialismus: Eine Studie*, ed. Stadtarchiv Ingolstadt (Ingolstadt, 1995).
7. Selig et al., eds., *Chronik der Stadt München*, 43.
8. For discussions in France see namely: Roberts, "The Price of Discretion."
9. Hillel, *Invasion der Be-freier*, 187.
10. Annette Timm, "'Think It Over!'—Soldiers, Veronikas and Venereal Diseases in Occupied Berlin," 50–56, here 53, in *Es begann mit einem Kuss: Deutsch-alliierte Beziehungen nach 1945*, ed. Florian Weiss (Berlin, 2005).
11. James Synder, *The Establishment and Operations of the United States Constabulary*, 3 (October 1945–June 1947). Historical Sub-Section—United States Constabulary, 1947, 168, quoted in Kleinschmidt, *Do Not Fraternize*, 194.
12. "Bekämpfung von Geschlechtskrankheiten," *Der Münchner Stadtanzeiger*, 16 January 1946.
13. The city of Munich set up the German hospital. It was located in the former Hansaheim. See: Selig et al., *Chronik der Stadt München*, 69.
14. Petra Goedde, "From Villains to Victims: Fraternization and the Feminization of Germany, 1945–1947," *Diplomatic History* 23, no. 1 (1999): 1–20, here 13.
15. On relapses (*Rückfälle*) due to an easy cure see: Zahner, *Jugendfürsorge in Bayern*, 57–58. See also Allan Brandt, *No Magic Bullet: A Social History of Venereal Disease in the United States since 1880* (Oxford, 1987), 161–82.
16. Gesetz zur Bekämpfung der Geschlechtskrankheiten, Reichsgesetzblatt 1, 1927, 61.
17. Kurt Holm, *Die Bekämpfung der Geschlechtskrankheiten in Hamburg: Erfahrungen seit dem Inkrafttreten des neuen Gesetzes am 1. Oktober 1927* (Berlin, 1933), 1. See also Michaela Freund-Widder, *Frauen unter Kontrolle: Prostitution und ihre staatliche Bekämpfung in Hamburg vom Ende des Kaiserreichs bis zu den Anfängen der Bundesrepublik* (Münster, 2003), 81–82.
18. Gesetz zur Bekämpfung der Geschlechtskrankheiten, Reichsgesetzblatt 1, 1927, 61.
19. Schroer, *Recasting Race after WWII*, 98.
20. Herzog, *Sex After Fascism*, 93 and 94. See also: "Eine Million Delike," *Der Spiegel*, 29 November 1950; Wilhelm Ellinghaus, "Verfassungsmässigkeit des Paragraphen 175 RsTGB," *Kriminalistik* 8, no. 3 (1954): 61–63.

21. Such locations included, for instance, the German Museum (Deutsches Museum), the train station in Pasing (a quarter of Munich), streets like the Hirtenstraße, and the temporary facility for displaced persons in the Simmernschule school. Fuchs, "'Zucker, wer hat? Öl, wer kauft?," 115.

22. Ibid., 113. See also: Rümelin, Hans, ed., *So lebten wir...ein Querschnitt durch 1947* (Stuttgart, 1997), 7. In one part of town black marketeers even set up their own bike patrol and warning system. See: Fuchs, "'Zucker, wer hat? Öl, wer kauft?,'" 115.

23. StadtAM, BUR 1722, quoted in Fuchs, "'Zucker, wer hat? Öl, wer kauft?,'" 116.

24. Hans Wacker, "Münchner Kommunalpolitik nach 1945: Nachlaßverwaltung oder demokratische Erneuerung?" 39–59, here 55, in *Trümmerzeit in München*.

25. Falter, *Chronik des Polizeipräsidiums München*, 98.

26. Selig, et al., *Chronik der Stadt München*, 92. See also: Obermaier and Mauerer, *Aus Trümmern wächst das neue Leben*, 73.

27. Gesetz zur Bekämpfung des Schwarzmarktes, Obermaier and Mauerer, *Aus Trümmern wächst das neue Leben*, 73.

28. Selig et al., *Chronik der Stadt München*, 92. The time period for these arrests was 1 September to 19 October.

29. Ibid., 31. See also: Dollinger, *München im 20. Jahrhundert*, 172–73.

30. Selig et al., *Chronik der Stadt München*, 23. See also: Winfried Müller, *Schulpolitik in Bayern im Spannungsfeld von Kultusbürokratie und Besatzungsmacht, 1945–1949* (Munich, 1995), 88–89; Karl-Ernst Bungenstab, *Umerziehung zur Demokratie! Re-education-Politik im Bildungswesen der US-Zone 1945–1949* (Düsseldorf, 1970); Max Liedtke, ed., *Handbuch der Geschichte des Bayerischen Bildungswesens, Volume 3: Geschichte der Schule in Bayern: Von 1918–1990* (Bad Heilbrunn, 1997).

31. Until 3 May 1947, U.S. officials seized 1,700 buildings within Munich's city limits. Beyond that point, an authorization from the headquarters in Frankfurt am Main was necessary. Selig et al., *Chronik der Stadt München*, 262. Attempts to avoid or protest against ongoing confiscations achieved little. See, for instance: StadtAM, Schulamt 8366.

32. Tent, *Mission on the Rhine*, 111.

33. Directive to Commander-in-Chief of United States Forces of Occupation Regarding the Military Government of Germany; April 1945 (JCS 1067), accessible at http://usa.usembassy.de/etexts/ga3-450426.pdf, [last accessed 27 February 2015]. See also: John Gimbel, *The American Occupation of Germany. Politics and Military 1945–1949* (Stanford, 1968), 2.

34. The USEFET directive was released on 7 August 1945. See: Leonhard Froese and Viktor von Blumenthal, *Bildungspolitik und Bildungsreform: Amtliche Texte und Dokumente zur Bildungspolitik im Deutschland der Besatzungszonen, der Bundesrepublik Deutschland und der Deutschen Demokratischen Republik* (Munich, 1969), 75–83.

35. StadtAM, Schulamt 8005, quoted in Müller, *Schulpolitik in Bayern*, 57. See also: Jürgen Fleischer-Schumann, *Das Bildungs- und Erziehungswesen in München 1945–1976: Die Ära Anton Fingerle* (Munich, 1987), 9–15.

36. Müller, *Schulpolitik in Bayern*, 89.

37. StadtAM, Schulamt 8366.
38. On 3 September 1945 registration for school year 1945/46 began, includ-
    ing all between six and fourteen years of age. Selig et al, *Chronik der Stadt
    München*, 74. On 4 October 1945, all institutions like Oberschulen for girls
    resumed. Ibid., 86. On 26 January 1946, there were seventy-seven *Volks-
    schulen*, eight *Hilfsschulen*, and one *Schwerbehinderten Schule* in Munich;
    these broke down into 1,157 classes with a total of 54,290 students. See
    StadtAM, Schulamt 8353. See also: Fleischer-Schumann, *Das Bildungs-
    und Erziehungswesen in München*, 9–15.
39. StadtAM, Schulamt 8353.
40. BayHStAM, MK 61318, referenced in Müller, *Schulpolitik in Bayern*, 92.
41. StadtAM, Schulamt 8366. See also: Anton Fingerle, "Zur Schulreform in
    Deutschland," *Europa Archiv* 1 (1946): 303–7.
42. BayHStAM, MK 61318, referenced in Müller, *Schulpolitik in Bayern*, 92.
    See also: Landeshauptstadt München, ed., *Zur Geschichte der Erziehung in
    München: Lesebuch zur Geschichte des Münchner Alltags. Geschichtswett-
    bewerb 1997/98* (Munich, 2001); Fleischer-Schumann, *Das Bildungs- und
    Erziehungswesen in München*.
43. Christine Pelkofer, "Rückkehr in die zerstörte Stadt," 160, in *Jugendbilder*.
    See also: Johannes Timmermann, "Schule und Jugend in der Trümmer-
    zeit," 168–72, here 169, in *Trümmerzeit in München*.
44. Josefa Halbinger, *Josefa Halbinger, Jahrgang 1900: Lebensgeschichte eines
    Münchner Arbeiterkindes*, ed. Carlamaria Heim, 2 ed (Munich, 1990), 110.
45. StadtAM, Schulamt 8353. See also: StadtAM, Schulamt, 8366.
46. StadtAM, Schulamt 8353.
47. "Schule auf neuen Wegen," *Die Süddeutsche Zeitung*, 11 October 1945;
    "Tröstliche Jugend," *Die Süddeutsche Zeitung*, 9 November 1945.
48. See, for example: Wacker, "Münchner Kommunalpolitik nach 1945: Nach-
    laßverwaltung oder demokratische Erneuerung?, 39–59, in *Trümmerzeit
    in München;* Fleischer-Schumann, *Das Bildungs- und Erziehungswesen in
    München;* StadtAM, Schulamt 8353; StadtAM, Schulamt 8009; StadtAM,
    Schulamt 8604; StadtAM, Schulamt 8359.
49. See, for instance: Heinz Hürten, ed., *Akten Kardinal Michael von Faul-
    habers: III 1945–1952* (Paderborn, 2002).
50. Tent, *Mission on the Rhine*, 110–63.
51. "Fortschritt im Schulwesen," *Die Neue Zeitung*, 18 October 1945.
52. Referenced in Karl-Heinz Füssl, *Die Umerziehung der Deutschen: Jugend
    und Schule unter den Siegermächten des Zweiten Weltkriegs, 1945–1955*
    (Paderborn, 1994), 100.
53. George F. Zook (President of the American Council on Education) was the
    chairman of the Education Mission to Germany. George F. Zook, *Report of
    the United States Education Mission to Germany* (Washington, DC, 1946),
    33. See also: Tent, *Mission on the Rhine*, 115–18.
54. Josef Hederer, interview by author, tape recording, Munich, 5 August
    2009.
55. Erzbischöfliches Jugendamt München und Freising, ed., *Talente. Aufbruch.
    Leben: Das Erzbischöfliche Jugendamt München und Freising seit 1938* (Mu-
    nich, 2005), 24.

56. United States Army, Europe, ed., *The U.S. Armed Forces German Youth Activities Program 1945–1955* (United States Army, Headquarters Europe, 1956), 6.

57. Andreas Dornheim, *Forever Young? Jugendarbeit im Kreisjugendring München-Stadt von 1945–2000* (Munich, 2004), 99. See also: StadtAM, Schulamt 6628.

58. Armin Ganser, ed., *Zwanzig Jahre Bayerischer Jugendring: Ideengeschichte und Dokumentation; ein Beitrag zur Geschichte der Jugendarbeit nach 1945* (Munich, 1966); StadtAM Kreisjugendring; Arthur Bader, ed., *20 Jahre Kreisjugend München-Stadt 1946–1966* (Munich, 1966); Klaus Dittrich, ed., *I hob a Loch im Balkon! Geschichten vom Kreisjugendring München-Stadt, 1946–1986* (Munich, 1986).

59. United States Army, Europe, ed., *The U.S. Armed Forces German Youth Activities Program*, 4. See also: Institut für Zeitgeschichte Munich (IfZM), OMGUS 5/295–3/2–7; U.S. Military Army Institute, Carlisle, PA, MHI Catalogue, D802.A1 1945–46 G47 1947 (German Youth Activities, Occupation in Europe Series 1945–1946) and D802.A1 1946–47 G47 1948 (German Youth Activities of the U.S. Army 1 July 1946–30 June 1947); United States Army, ed., *German Youth Activities Army Assistance Program Guide* ([Unknown], 1948).

60. See namely the local newspaper publication *The Munich American*.

61. U.S. Military Army Institute, Carlisle, PA, MHI Catalogue, D802.A1 1945–46 G47 1947 (German Youth Activities, Occupation in Europe Series 1945–1946, 3).

62. United States Army, Europe, *The U.S. Armed Forces German Youth Activities Program*, 2.

63. Zahner, *Jugendfürsorge in Bayern*, 77. See also: Kleinschmidt, *Do Not Fraternize*, 206.

64. Kellermann, *The Present Status of German Youth*, 15. See also: ibid., 17.

65. Glaser, *Rubble Years*, 158; Wagner, *Jugendliche Lebenswelten nach 1945*, 58.

66. Josef Hederer, interviews by author, tape recording, Munich, 5 August 2009, 12 August 2009, and 14 July 2010. Josef Hederer (*1927) worked for the GYA in Munich shortly after the war. He experienced ongoing debates first hand. See also: Glaser, *Rubble Years*, 158.

67. "Die Jugend," *Die Süddeutsche Zeitung*, 12 November 1946; "Ausbau der Jugendorganisationen," *Die Neue Zeitung*, 4 January 1946; "Haushaltsjahr für junge Mädchen," *Die Neue Zeitung*, 11 January 1946; U.S. Military Army Institute, Carlisle, PA, MHI Catalogue, D802.A1 1946–47 G47 1948 (German Youth Activities of the U.S. Army 1 July 1946–30 June 1947, 96); Goedde, *GIs and Germans*, 153–56.

68. Alf Lüdtke, Inge Marssolek, and Adelheid von Saldern, eds., *Amerikanisierung: Traum und Alptraum im Deutschland des 20. Jahrhunderts* (Stuttgart, 1996), 11–13; Michael Ermarth, ed., *America and the Shaping of German Society, 1945–1955* (Oxford, 1993); Eberhard Schütz, "Nach dem Entkommen, vor dem Ankommen: Eine Einführung," 1–139, here 119, in *Handbuch Nachkriegskultur*.

69. Landeshauptstadt München, *Ein Neuer Anfang im Wohlfahrts-, Jugend- und Gesundheitswesen*, 53. Karl-Heinz Füssl names three main problems

for the Youth Welfare Office: (1) youth from the Soviet sector; (2) wandering youth; (3) youth over eighteen unwilling to work. Füssl, *Die Umerziehung der Deutschen*, 104. See also: Zahner, *Jugendfürsorge in Bayern*.

70. United States Army, Europe, *The U.S. Armed Forces German Youth Activities Program 1945–1955*, 2.

71. Landeshauptstadt München, *Ein Neuer Anfang im Wohlfahrts-, Jugend- und Gesundheitswesen*, 27.

72. Zahner, *Jugendfürsorge in Bayern*, 97. See also: Kenkmann, *Wilde Jugend*, 353–54.

73. The Bavarian Welfare Office Law (*Bayerische Jugendamtsgesetz*, BayJAG) influenced administrational structures as well but did not play a key role. The Reich Youth Welfare Law (Reichswohlfahrtsgesetz, RJWG) was passed on 14 June 1922, and became law on 1 April 1924. See, for example: Gerhard Potrykus, ed., *Jugendwohlfahrtsgesetz nebst Ausführungsgesetzen und Ausführungsvorschriften der deutschen Länder* (Munich, 1972), 1–3; Benno Hafeneger, *Jugendarbeit als Beruf: Geschichte einer Profession in Deutschland* (Opladen, 1992), 14; Robert Sauter, ed., *75 Jahre Reichswohlfahrtsgesetz. Jugendhilfe zwischen Ordungsrecht und Sozialpädagogik* (Munich, 1999). For the situation in Munich see namely: BayHStAM, Staatskanzlei 13776; Landeshauptstadt München, *Ein Neuer Anfang im Wohlfahrts-, Jugend- und Gesundheitswesen*, 27; Zahner, *Jugendfürsorge in Bayern*, 24–29.

74. Zahner, *Jugendfürsorge in Bayern*, 98–110; Robert Havighurst, *Report on Germany* (New York, 1947), 84.

75. StadtAM, Bürgermeister & Rat 2551. See also: *Bericht des Stadtjugendamtes München über die 'Derzeitige Arbeitslage im Stadtjugendamt,'* quoted in Zahner, *Jugendfürsorge in Bayern*, 84.

76. *Plan über die ergriffenen und zu ergreifenden Maßnahmen zur Behandlung der Jugend zwischen 15 und 22 Jahren*, BayHStA Munich, Staatskanzlei 13776.

77. The content of the ordinances did not change: Ordinance no. 73 (homeless juveniles); Ordinance no. 74 (demoralized girls and women); Ordinance no. 75 (measures against youth up to the age of twenty-five).

78. Selig et al., *Chronik der Stadt München*, 286.

79. BayHStAM, Ministerium des Inneren 92075. The U.S. military government even called for the stricter application of these ordinances: Zahner, *Jugendfürsorge in Bayern*, 63–64.

80. BayHStAM, Ministerium des Inneren 92075.

81. "Salonfähige Mädchen: Pässe für girl-friends," *Der Spiegel*, 15 February 1947.

82. "Junge Vagabunden werden erzogen," *Die Süddeutsche Zeitung*, 8 February 1947.

83. See, for example: "Eine Möglichkeit für junge Menschen," *Münchner Zeitung*, 9 July 1946; "Dörfer für heimatlose Kinder," *Die Süddeutsche Zeitung*, 12 June 1946; "Ohne Schloss und Riegel," *Der Pinguin*, no. 7 (1946).

84. Selig et al, *Chronik der Stadt München*, 286.

85. *Die Süddeutsche Zeitung*, quoted in ibid., 287.

86. Zahner, *Jugendfürsorge in Bayern*, 58–59.

87. Biddiscombe, "Dangerous Liaisons," 626 and 618–20.

88. Zahner, *Jugendfürsorge in Bayern*, 63–64 and 60.

89. OMGUS Public Health and Welfare Branch and Chief of Staff, "Control Fraternization: Memorandum for Record," 29 August 1946, in NA, RG 260 OMGUS 1945–46–15/1,2 of 3.), quoted in Kleinschmidt, *Do Not Fraternize*, 193.

90. "Junge Vagabunden werden erzogen," *Die Süddeutsche Zeitung*, 8 February 1947.

91. Wacker, "Münchner Kommunalpolitik nach 1945: Nachlaßverwaltung oder demokratische Erneuerung?" in Prinz, ed., *Trümmerzeit in München*, 39–59, here 56. Franz Pitzer repeatedly called for stricter reactions. See: StadtAM, Ratsitzungsprotokolle 719/1 Stadtrat-Plenum (26 March 1946), 181; StadtAM, Ratsitzungsprotokolle 702/2, Stadtrat-Plenum (9 September 1947), 1923ff; Franz Kotteder, ed., *Der Krieg ist aus: Erinnern in München nach 1945* (Munich, 2005), 122.

92. "Was ist zu tun?" *Die Süddeutsche Zeitung*, 31 May 1947.

93. "Ordnung und Sicherheit in München: Ein Notschrei des Münchner Polizeipräsidenten," *Der Münchner Stadtanzeiger*, 21 May 1947.

94. BayHStAM, Staatskanzlei 13776.

95. Ibid.

96. Ibid.

97. StadtAM, Ratsitzungsprotokolle 720/2, Stadtrat-Plenum (9 September 1947), 1924f, quoted in Wacker, "Münchner Kommunalpolitik nach 1945: Nachlaßverwaltung oder demokratische Erneuerung?" in Prinz, ed., *Trümmerzeit in München*, 55.

98. The Bavarian state representative questioning the ordinances was liberal-democrat Fritz Linnert (FDP).

99. Paragraph 3 of the Bavarian constitution read: "The youth needs to be protected against exploitation as well as moral, mental, and physical delinquency with the help of state and municipal measures and institutions. Welfare education [*Fürsorgeerziehung*] is only allowed if grounded in a legal foundation." See: *Die Bayerische Verfassung*, December 1946.

100. BayHStAM, Staatskanzlei 113776.

101. Zahner, *Jugendfürsorge in Bayern*, 113.

102. Evans, *Life Among the Ruins*, 173. See also: Mörchen, "'Echte Kriminelle' und 'zeitbedingte Rechtsbrecher.'"

103. "Razzia auf Jugendliche," *Die Süddeutsche Zeitung*, 30 September 1947. See also: Zahner, *Jugendfürsorge in Bayern*, 111.

104. "Der 'gesäuberte' Hauptbahnhof," *Die Süddeutsche Zeitung*, 13 September 1947.

105. "Eine Frau für heute Abend: Mekka der Unterwelt," *Der Spiegel*, 20 September 1947.

106. StadtAM, RA (Polizeiakten) Nr. 77.673 (15 October 1947), quoted in Zahner, *Jugendfürsorge in Bayern*, 114. See also: Selig et al., *Chronik der Stadt München*, 310. Five large-scale raids and thirty-five smaller raids are noted in the police chronicle: Falter, *Chronik des Polizeipräsidiums München*, 105.

107. BayHStAM, Office of the Military Government Bavaria (OMGB) 10/114–2/10 (November 10, 1947), quoted in Zahner, *Jugendfürsorge in Bayern*, 114.

108. "Große Jagd auf kleine Streuner," *Die Süddeutsche Zeitung*, 31 October 1947.
109. Ibid. See also: "Siedlung für heimatlose Jugendliche," *Die Süddeutsche Zeitung*, 10 October 1947.
110. "Gericht," *Der Pinguin*, no. 9. (1947).
111. Landeshauptstadt München, *Ein Neuer Anfang im Wohlfahrts-, Jugend- und Gesundheitswesen*, 27. Youngsters also repeatedly escaped from more rural institutions like the Herzogsmühle in Upper Bavaria. See: Zahner, *Jugendfürsorge in Bayern*, 116.
112. "Große Jagd auf kleine Streuner," *Die Süddeutsche Zeitung*, 31 October 1947.
113. Selig et al., *Chronik der Stadt München*, 301.
114. BayHStAM, Staatskanzlei 13776. 529 individuals came from Upper Bavaria. BayHStAM, Staatskanzlei 13776. See also: BayHStAM, OMGB 10/114–2/10, quoted in Zahner, *Jugendfürsorge in Bayern*, 115. For the age group older than eighteen authorities arrested 180 males and 208 females in Upper Bavaria; for the age group under eighteen years of age they caught fifty-four males and ninety-two females. StAM, RA Nr. 77.673, quoted in ibid., 114. For numbers on Munich see: StaAM, RA Nr. 77.673, quoted in ibid., 117.
115. BayHStAM, OMG 10/114–2/10, quoted in ibid.
116. StaAM, Polizeipräsidium Oberbayern Nr. 63, quoted in ibid.
117. Maximilian Lanzinner, *Zwischen Sternenbanner und Bundesadler: Bayern im Wiederaufbau 1945–1958* (Regensburg, 1996), 179–80.
118. "Ein Deutsches Wunder: Sechzig Jahre Bundesrepublik," *Der Spiegel Geschichte*, no. 2 (2009); "60 Jahre Bundesrepublik: Eine opulente Zeitreise von 1949–2009," *Der Stern Extra*, no. 1 (2009). See also: the popular history shows on German television and in writing, most notably presented by Guido Knopp: Guido Knopp, prod., *Die großen Jahre des 20. Jahrhunderts 1900–1999* (Grünwald, 2000); Guido Knopp, *Unser Jahrhundert: Deutsche Schicksalstage* (Munich, 2000).

PART 2

AMERICANIZATION AND YOUTH CULTURES IN THE MIRACLE YEARS, 1949–1962

CHAPTER 3

Constructing *the Halbstarke* and *the* Teenager

In 1956, the German movie *Die Halbstarken* captured the rise of two new images of youth. Amongst the few movies to look at juvenile delinquency at a time when escapist love stories set in romantic regions dominated the scene, this screenplay built on widespread stereotypes of male and female delinquency embodied by two new images: *the Halbstarke* and *the teenager.* Protagonist Freddy (Horst Buchholz) had all characteristics of this literally semistrong delinquent male youngster: working-class background, interested in motorcycles and cars, aggressive, provocative, and not willing to listen to adults. Freddy's girlfriend Sissy (Karin Baal), on the other hand, embodied a variety of supposed female characteristics found in *the teenager:* sexually promiscuous, materialistic, and disinterested in her role around the house. Towards the end of the movie she encourages Freddy to kill an old man by yelling, "Come on, shoot, Freddy, shoot!"[1] Those seeing the movie thus learned about a new threat to social order while, at the same time, finding comfort in a didactic ending and overall "pedagogical impetus."[2]

Contemporary anxieties regarding the reappearance of delinquent youth again revealed a widespread and highly moralized discourse, and functioned as a way to discuss broader issues. In times of growing prosperity, authorities increasingly feared American mass culture; they were also concerned about an increase in leisure for youth given that young people could spent their time away from adult supervision. At times, such discussions built on earlier debates around *Schmutz und Schund* or smut and filth, two terms capturing widespread fears regarding cheap and dirty literature, magazines, comics, and movies. Such and other conversations epitomized the continuing obsession with juvenile delinquency in the Bavarian capital during the so-called miracle years. According to popular sentiments, the economic miracle and widespread prosperity had led young people of both sexes astray, and away from traditional values, gender mores, and respect for adult authorities. Such behaviors became visual reminders of American influences, a shaky moral order, and changing sexual norms. The reliance on a combination of traditional tools of control and the new power of capitalistic mechanisms within a growing consumer culture eventually helped channel such threats. In the process, authorities once again relied on demonizing, strict policing, and the re-creation of more acceptable and profitable images of youth to ensure stability, moral order, and prosperity.

There was perhaps a youth crisis in the so-called miracle years; yet again, adult authorities consistently manufactured and exaggerated it for self-serving purposes. As before, the construction of juvenile wrongdoing had benefits.[3] Whereas some youngsters did become more demanding given that rites of passage often entailed challenging adult norms, local officials widely exaggerated the extent of deviancy to frame a broader consensus. Moreover, it is clear that the construction of delinquency benefited a variety of traditional and emerging powers trying to influence society. Traditional governmental authorities in particular remained interested in protecting and defending stability, social order, and morality. Bavarian Minister of the Interior August Geislhöringer, for instance, repeatedly pushed for stricter policies against male rowdies.[4] Corporations, on the other hand, hoped to expand their markets by profiting from the growing purchasing power of youth. For them, youth was slowly turning into a lucrative business, and a new, exciting, and at least partially rebellious image of youth could thus be useful. As a result, youth yet again proved to be a powerful rhetorical space and platform for authorities to influence contemporary morals in their attempt to ensure authority and generate revenue.

As discussions about *Halbstarke* and *teenagers* illustrate, local authorities continued to rely on existing mechanisms of social control while also employing new ways to ensure stability. Schooling, youth groups, and the importance of work became ways to keep the young off the streets, and policing urban spaces marked avenues to ensure compliance. To demonize certain misbehaviors further helped create societal pressures. Such campaigns mainly targeted Americanization, a force seen as a powerful threat to German values. To question U.S. influences on culture also became a way for local authorities to emancipate themselves from American rule after 1949. The rise of capitalistic mechanisms interested in a profiting image of youth finally underlines the growth of another rather abstract force interested in constructing and using images of youth.

This second part of *Coming of Age* then focuses on representations of male and female youth in the long 1950s, defined as the miracle years. It sets in with the stabilization and increasing recovery of the West German economy following the currency reform; it ends with the decline of the Adenauer era. To discuss *the Halbstarke* and *the female teenager*[5] throughout these miracle years is again a way to access and capture the construction, normalization, and protection of masculinity, femininity, and authority. No strangers in German history, both images of youth emerged in new and advanced forms during a time when widespread Americanization opened new opportunities for youngsters. Yet similar to the situation in the crisis years, a pervasive adult consensus underlined that contemporary youth is a threat to such postwar prosperity and stability, resulting in a whole array of contemporaries using images of youth to push stricter mechanisms of social control against the young and society overall.

Creating *the Halbstarke*

"The Halbstarke are back!"[6] This worrisome headline appeared on the front page of *Die Süddeutsche Zeitung* in June 1956 and reintroduced a previous image of male delinquency: *the Halbstarke*. That literally semistrong male youngster was supposedly "loitering at restaurants and movie theaters, bothering women of all ages, and rattling around ... with his moped [a slow motorcycle] to show off his vigor;"[7] he also robs kiosks and drives under the influence of alcohol. The paper continued by discussing how this phenomenon emerged all over Western Europe, due to the rise of American youth culture. Fears of rock 'n' roll, uncontrollably dancing young girls or teenagers, and male rowdies comparable to Marlon Brando and James Dean are apparent in this context. The article concluded by noting, "It would be an affirmation of our inabilities if we cannot deal with this disease of Western children."[8] Readers learned about this new threat to social order while, at the same time, hearing about the desire of some to defend a barely established prosperity by taking on the fight against such juvenile delinquents.

The Halbstarke had supposedly reappeared in the miracle years, a time of growing prosperity and return of traditional norms. Following a crisis period and subsequent efforts to rebuild and recover, West

Germany increasingly returned to normality in the 1950s. In Munich, ration cards and most physical signs of war, destruction, and postwar depression had disappeared.[9] As elsewhere, the so-called Marshall Plan had helped rebuild infrastructure and laid the foundation for economic progress.[10] Locals seized the opportunity to consume, enjoy, and relax as an abundance of products returned to stores and filled shelves. In 1955, one customer magazine for a major grocery chain noted, "We are doing better!"[11] The return of several thousand prisoners of war from the Soviet Union plus West German rearmament underlined another step towards normality, while the Cold War offered a binary and conveniently simple world order. Change, on the other hand, was neither welcome on a federal level nor in a state like Bavaria. There, conservative Catholic values and pre-1914 sentiments repeatedly clashed with more liberal urban sentiments. The earlier generally dominated discussions, apparent in repressive gender roles, family structures, and patriarchy. For most, such desire for normalization needed little explanation, as normality became, to follow historian Hanna Schissler, "a powerful tool in the social and ideological reality."[12]

Yet an increasingly prosperous and open West German democracy brought new anxieties and challenges, real and imagined, soon to be embodied by male rowdies or *Halbstarke*. According to contemporary interpretations, generational differences made most youngsters more receptive towards American mass culture, especially compared to adults. Defined by debates around Americanization during the Weimar Republic, anti-American Nazi ideologies, and defeat in war, the older generation deemed the United States in particular as inexperienced, without a culture, and with no societal cohesion. As historians pointed out later on, such adult fears were mostly rooted in historical stereotypes.[13] Yet those favoring traditional class stratifications feared these supposed American characteristics, thinking about U.S. society as faceless and anonymous. According to German historian and philosopher Oswald Sprengler, for instance, the time of the masses would be the downfall of the occident and Western civilization. For him, as for others interested in the revival of traditional norms, Americanization was threatening.[14] Young people, on the other hand, saw the role of the United States in a different light. They grew up in the presence of U.S. soldiers, who had fraternized with them early on. Such experiences exposed many young people to American culture and lifestyle, symbolized by chewing gum, Coca-Cola, and American Forces Network radio.[15] For them, America was the antonym to a devastated postwar Munich and the opposite to the ideals of adults. As one youngster noted, "we were fed up with hearing about the war from the older generation, just fed up—and the alternative for that were the Americans, where everything was different; in our view it was a huge country, rich people, big cars, dominant youngsters."[16]

In the United States, businesses had discovered youth as a potential market relatively early; such influences soon arrived in West Germany as part of Americanization, resulting in widespread concerns. Prior to the arrival of rock 'n' roll music and specific movies like *The Wild One* (1953) and *Rebel Without A Cause* (1955), comic books and other "trash" literature concerned adults. Adults saw the corruptive influences of such products throughout Munich. Aligned with traditional understandings of such Americanization as *Schmutz und Schund,* or smut and filth, contemporaries described these trends as a disease or virus. To them, cheap comic books flooded newsstands to seduce youth, while the sexually provocative content of some publications and "light erotica elicited visceral urges or aroused lurid thoughts about sex and violence, even if they did not graphically depict sexually immoral acts," as one scholar noted.[17] According to conservative authorities, educators, church officials, and other societal groups, the treacherous content of these materials infiltrated and endangered young minds in particular. Oversexualized characters supposedly paint a demeaning picture of love, romance, and marriage while overaggressive and ambiguous protagonists challenged law and order. As a result, youngsters would get increasingly sucked into artificial worlds and avoid reading German literary classics. They would become addicts to comic books while being deprived of "real" cultural opportunities. In 1951, an article in the national news magazine *Der Spiegel* laid out a whole list of dangers. It concluded that comic books are "opium in children's rooms" and hence a threat to the moral composition of the nation.[18] In Munich, numerous newspapers debated such issues at great length, contemplating laws and regulations to protect youth from such filth.[19] Fears of communism within a Cold War climate also played a role as authorities saw the moral composition and cohesion of the state crumbling. West Germany tried to shape its identity, often in contrast to the German Democratic Republic (GDR). While fears of Americanization threatened the moral and societal fabric of the GDR more directly, and made youth a similar battleground for such debates as in the West,[20] local authorities in Munich tried to find a third way, between unfettered American capitalism with its individualized mass culture and a threatening Soviet communism with its austerity. After all, as well-known Catholic priest and public speaker Pater Leppich plainly summarized, "a youth that grows up with brothel-magazines and filthy movies will eventually go to the dogs."[21]

The rise of U.S. popular culture ultimately helped resurrect *the Halbstarke* as the new image for male delinquency in Munich and provided a reference point for contemporaries. Historically, naming male delinquents *Halbstarke* was nothing new. A colloquial term capturing the rebellious characteristics of male youngsters, this image of youth has been around since at least the early twentieth century. Then, as again in the 1950s, contemporaries employed this term to describe delinquent urban youth, supposedly with a working-class background, and thus all the more threatening. In 1905, for example, social commentator Hermann Martin Popert referred to *Halbstarke* as "young fellows, with greasy hats and livid faces;"[22] several years later another description saw *the Halbstarke* as a "young man between fifteen and twenty-two years of age who is part of the degenerate city youth ... [and] has a passionate animosity against order; that is why he hates regularity, as well as everything nice, especially work. ... he tempts others into sin, [and] stimulates their joy for destruction."[23] *Halbstarke* constitute "a mob, a fearsome, threatening power, especially within urban environments."[24] In fact, in Munich a local magazine featured a painting titled "Der Halbstarke" as early as 1918. It showed an indifferent, cigarette-smoking young male, slouching on a window ledge. The caption read, "Oh gosh, now it's over with the magnificent flamboyant life—tomorrow dad comes home from war!"[25] Whereas such references aimed to highlight the need for adult supervision in young people's lives, the image itself also captured a particular working-class or proletarian background. This characterization continued to be prevalent during the National Socialist era, as apparent in references to so-called Wilde Cliques and Edelweiss Pirates in past and present discussions.[26] In Munich, such groups became known by the colloquial term *Blas'n*—literally bubble—in this context,[27] an expression that also reappeared in the 1950s.

By then the media again helped manufacture *the Halbstarke* as a threat to stability. Even though several youngsters did speed around on their mopeds and provoked authorities, none of their behaviors in Munich matched media coverage. The most vivid example for sensationalism and an exaggerated production of male delinquency remains a story by the Munich tabloid *Die Abendzeitung*. In mid-August 1956, this paper reported on an incident involving the "gang of the skulls," a group of young delinquents that had created trouble in West Berlin and elsewhere already.[28] Now such danger had supposedly come to Munich. The main headline read, "Terror by the Gang of the Skulls from the Schwanthalerhöhe suburb—Munich's Police without a Chance." The article described a violent brawl at a local beer garden, triggered because a youngster unintentionally ran into another young man. Then, according to the newspaper, "all hell broke loose." Not shy to employ sensationalist language, *Die Abendzeitung* described the situation as "an attack" and a "major battle" with "loud cries of pain" and 400 guests panicking, eight injured, and two badly injured; the next day someone even found a loaded pistol at the site of this brawl. The paper concluded with the question, "How long should this go on?"[29] This story fit well with other incidents involving *the Halbstarke* and keeping contemporaries on their toes throughout the summer. However, and in some ways similar to the tabloid press and its exaggeration of the events involving mods and rockers in the United Kingdom in spring of 1964,[30] *Die Abendzeitung* completely fabricated this tale. The incident at the beer garden was not simply blown out of proportion, but there was not even a minor confrontation.[31]

Scholars initially believed and relied on such exaggerations. Apparent in the work of mainly conservative commentators, many saw German society in danger. They feared that U.S. popular culture could flood West Germany and undermine existing middle-class norms. Such voices built on pre-1945 fears regarding Americanization and were clearly alarmed about *the Halbstarke*. One scholar described him as "superficial, longing for amusement, indifferent, without taste, and a weird psychopathic inclination towards crime."[32] References to *the Halbstarke* "as wandering around through a well-off German landscape with their clearly diluted sense for life and a frail melancholy"[33] tried to capture his motivations. Well-known pedagogue and sociologist Hans Heinrich Muchow went even further. For him, *the Halbstarke* "de-created" and "de-civilized" society.[34] In a later article Muchow asked, "What is going on with these Halbstarke?" before categorizing him into three different groups: "the primitives," "the educationally frustrated," and "the nihilists."[35] For him, a lack of authority was the root of the problem,[36] and he thereby already provides a glimpse into connections between constructing and controlling youth.

Media coverage and scholarly discussions influenced crime statistics and data, leaving room for questioning the supposed rise of juvenile delinquency. In Bavaria, the Ministry of Justice noted a rise of crime rates among the young by 32 percent between 1954 and 1957; about 10 percent of young adults were convicted every year.[37] At the same time, however, a report by Director of the Munich Youth Welfare Office Kurt Seelmann concluded that such a rise in crime rates would not automatically make the majority of youngsters criminals.[38] Moreover, broad definitions of delinquency again raise serious doubts regarding these numbers. With a maximum of 10 percent of youngsters defined as *Halbstarke* by historians engaging with this topic since the 1950s,[39] male delinquency as constructed by the general public was a minor problem.[40] Only its connection to broader issues and usefulness in defining norms explains why it was blown out of proportion.

Concerns about class traditionally framed *the Halbstarke* and often remained in the center of discussions throughout the 1950s. According to contemporary descriptions, *the Halbstarke* had a working-class background and only a basic education, a claim partially dismissed by some scholars.[41] In Munich, contemporaries noted, those attending secondary schools rarely joined groups of *Halbstarke*.[42] Rooted somewhat in juvenile delinquency statistics, more recent scholarship has questioned and even dismissed broad claims regarding class altogether. Following the notion that "middle-class delinquents hardly end up in statistics,"[43] historians like Thomas Grotum and Sebastian Kurme challenged the empirical basis of this data overall.[44] Such discussions raise questions regarding widespread simplifications in regard to class background and milieu; it also outlines the power of constructs. After all, deeming *the Halbstarke* as a working-class youngster coincided with traditional fears of proletarian youth, even socialism and communism. Doing so was evidently a beneficial and convenient simplification because it dismissed any discussion of middle-class participation, aligned with historic stereotypes, hence increasing fears.

At the same time, to understand *the Halbstarke* as a working-class young male did offer ways to discuss productivity, work habits, and leisure. Aware of the necessity to remain an efficient society, adult contemporaries repeatedly looked at the young when discussing the future. To them, hard work and discipline had brought the nation economic progress; jeopardizing this success now would be devastating. A competitive Cold War context, in which West Germany constantly looked to out-produce its adversary East Germany, could also not tolerate young people wasting time and money by standing on street corners, speeding around with mopeds, or simply doing nothing. Furthermore, and as historian Uta Poiger has convincingly demonstrated when discussing German youth more broadly, West and East Germans wrestled with American cultural imports as a way to define themselves and normality.[45]

Male youth in Munich and elsewhere had supposedly picked up concerning behaviors by going to movies like *The Wild One*, which had opened in Munich on 15 January 1955. Following the story of Johnny Strabler (Marlon Brando) and two rivaling motorcycle gangs, the main character shows little interest in hard work. Young viewers became fascinated with Marlon Brando's style, attitude, and coolness. Soon

male youth in particular hoped to purchase a leather jacket and motorcycle. As outlined by one historian, "Metaphorically, a leather jacket
conveys a talismanic quality of fierceness; the wearer is a different an-
imal, tough, and thick-skinned. He is uncivilized, perhaps brutal, and
so should be respected if not feared."[46] Male youth also imitated hairstyles, wore jeans, and began showing provocative postures. Given a
newly accomplished prosperity and widespread full-time employment,
male youth generally had the resources and time to spend on these new
trends. According to a contemporary study, working male youngsters
had about 116 Deutsche Marks available each week.[47] This income
helped sustain a Brando-like coolness, while a shortened workweek
expanded the time to enjoy it.

A conspicuous style and posture—at times created by youth as a sign
for a specific identity—supposedly went along with certain clothing
and openly defied adult authorities. *The Halbstarke* wore wide shirts
with eye-catching colored fabric, flashy-colored scarves, American
blue jeans, and hats.[48] According to cultural historian Beverly Gordon,
for angry young men, jeans were "the anti-fashion wardrobe that symbolically flaunted the mores of the frightened society at large."[49] Male
youngsters in Munich created their specific style: they either wore their
jeans extremely tight or extremely loose. Both styles ran against contemporary norms because a tight fit was seen as obscenely exposing
the body and folded up jeans that never touched the ground were seen
as a provocative misuse of legwear. Apart from this reading, accentu-
ated contrasts ran against more subtle colors like grey, navy blue, and
brown. A local police report spoke of "well-known clothing (red and
black blousons, blue jeans, and such)."[50] In that sense, bright shirts
worn by male youth visibly and metaphorically disrupted the monot-
ony and conventions of the "stuffy" 1950s. Of course haircuts contributed to such discussions as male youngsters wore long and messy hair,
especially once imitating Elvis Presley's hairstyle became fashionable.
Long sideburns, one curl like rock 'n' roll star Bill Haley, or the so-
called ducktail became stylistic signs and marks of identification for
a now well-endorsed subculture. Yet these haircuts defined resistance
against a variety of norms and traditions, especially when compared
to previous hairstyles within the Nazi youth.[51] Finally, certain postures,
inspired by Marlon Brando and James Dean, added a provocative attitude. According to contemporary scholar and observer Curt Bondy, *the
Halbstarke* "avoids abrupt ruptures in his posture and instead empha-
sizes elastic movement of the whole body."[52] He typically had his hands
in his pockets, chewed gum, or smoked. To lean against something
further sustained such coolness. At that point clothing and outwardly

typical behaviors fulfilled an additional role in literally and metaphorically sustaining the buoyancy of male delinquents. The looks of leather jackets, cowboy boots, and jeans then only increased their relaxed posture and coolness. Such provocative casualness, messy hair, and lanky stance seemed provoking to those favoring discipline and order, resulting in conflicts throughout Munich.

For authorities a newly developing youth motorcycle culture soon became one prominent example of wasting time and money. Many youngsters would have hoped to purchase a motorcycle like Marlon Brando. However, for most a moped was all they could afford. Seen as a cheap substitute, it primarily fulfilled a practical purpose for working youngsters: it brought them to work. As a contemporary academic study about youngsters and motorcycles in Munich suggested, more than one-fifth of all youngsters drove a moped to get to work in the Bavarian capital.[53] Yet in times of demonizing youth such elements received little or no attention in the media. Instead, discussions simply dismissed such practical needs for transportation and focused on how *the Halbstarke* wasted time in garages, back alleys, and entranceways to work on his *Hobel*—literally fad[54] [Figure 3.1]. Some even gave their mopeds female names, like Trixi.[55] One contemporary stated, "The engine ... has become the 'wife of the Halbstarken,' like the rifle the 'wife

Figure 3.1 So-called *Halbstarke* and their mopeds in Munich-Neuhausen, 1959. Courtesy of Geschichtswerkstatt München-Neuhausen e.V.

of the soldier.' At least there is some kind of intimacy between the Halb-starke and engines, which was demanded in the relationship between a soldier and his weapon."[56] Such references underscored a supposed unwillingness of male youth to become fathers, soldiers, and family men, and in that way defying traditional order. Youngsters, on the other hand, enjoyed retooling the exhaust and adding speed—often simply to make sure there was a fabulous echo once they drove be-tween high buildings. On weekends and in evenings, the moped then became a symbol for freedom from strict rules, authoritative adults, and encroaching cityscapes. As one youngster recalled with nostalgia, "Imagine the excitement, when the whole pack was [riding] together."[57] Some traveled on weekends; others simply drove around with friends. Even the study referenced earlier captured this stereotypical *Halb-starke* by noting, "a certain type of male youngster ... uses the tech-nology with coolness and, at the same time, fast pace, all while having comfort without effort ... , just like rock 'n' roll music."[58]

The young did not necessarily need a moped to question popular notions of productivity. In mid-January 1956, *Die Süddeutsche Zeitung* reported, "Semi-grown-ups are standing on street corners." Calling them a topic of concern, the article discussed local anxieties regard-ing *the Halbstarke* and their "so-called 'Blasen.'" According to the pa-per, Blas'n were "loose groups of adolescents that meet daily in certain spots within their quarters of town."[59] All they did was stand around. Eighty such groups supposedly existed in Munich. Some enjoyed the music coming out of jukeboxes, hung out at the movies, or visited fairgrounds; others came to restaurants to play cards and drink. As a seventeen-year-old recalled, "I got a portable record player from my dad. Then we went to [the restaurant] Zur Schanz. We asked the owner if we could play our records. He allowed us to do so in the rear of the restaurant."[60] From then on the youngsters hung out in that restaurant whenever they had a chance. Since they spent money on drinks, the owner was quite happy. Only when he had other guests for lunch he kindly asked them, "Do you mind taking a walk for an hour or so?"[61] Whereas the young enjoyed their own space and newly acquired inde-pendence, authorities worried about the proximity of alcohol and rock 'n' roll music in such environments. The latter was more aggressive and faster than traditional classical music, and for authorities a source of trouble. Aware of rock 'n' roll riots in the United States and later in various cities in West Germany, a local newspaper described the power of rock 'n' roll on youth prior to the opening of *Rock Around the Clock* (1956) in Munich: "They continued to dance ... like lunatics to the rhythms they had heard in the movie theater but had been unable to let off steam right away. They fought with the police.... We hope that Munich's dancing youngsters are able to resist against the rock 'n' roll fever."[62] Another newspaper asked, "Where does the inflammatory character of rock 'n' roll come from?"[63] Most concerning, however, remained the conviction that youth simply wasted their resources and time by standing or sitting around, talking, and playing cards.[64] Adult commentators used such discussions to further strengthen constructs of youth as deviant, especially once compared to the hard work and sacrifice of their parents. As one local journal noted, almost with nostalgia, "Many of us experienced war and after the war what it meant to be hungry. But if you are stuffed [with food] then you forget these times easily."[65]

The young, on the other hand, became increasingly irritated, illustrating a growing divide or gap between actual age groups. As one young voice noted,

> All I hear is leisure ... and by now it has become annoying.... What does the youth do during the weekend? It is almost a given according to some that we have lots of time; adults hover over us watching every step with their microscope to note: Take a look at the youth of today! In our times there was barely any vacation during the year, and no day off on Saturdays. We had to work. But today ...[66]

Many youngsters still lived with their families cramped into small homes or apartments. For them, being out of the house and away from adult supervision seemed only natural. In Munich, many groups had their own meeting point in a certain neighborhood or street. One youngster recalled, "Each quarter of the city had a catwalk, a 'Broadway.' In the suburb of Neuhausen it was the Rotkreuzplatz square, or, as it was referred to in the West of Munich, the Rio."[67] Such spaces "provided various possibilities to let off steam, show off, provoke adults, and present rebellious fashion," another youngster added.[68] For authorities, on the other hand, the street in urban environments had always been the typical scene of crime. In their view, the young were simply loitering and engaging in obnoxious behaviors, provocations, and illegal activities [Figure 3.2]. *Die Süddeutsche Zeitung* noted, "Their imprudence ... terrorizes whole districts."[69] Soon contemporaries feared for their safety passing by certain spots, coming across several youngsters, or walking through specific public spaces. According to a contemporary scholar, these youngsters "act out in groups and ... break societal norms in senseless riots; he [*the Halbstarke*] begins his hooligan-like behavior and 'breaks out'.... He acts ... consciously against adults."[70]

Figure 3.2 Two so-called *Halbstarke* loitering on the streets of Munich, 1959.
Courtesy of Fritz Neuwirth/Süddeutsche Zeitung Photo.

City streets and public spaces also became contested areas for broader discussions about mobility, class, and power. Streets, for example, encapsulated such debates. Even though mopeds were a means to get to work, authorities complained that the young used their bikes to disrupt order and normality. Apart from speeding around with their noisy rides, their mopeds provoked adults also in other ways. Some youths rode on sidewalks while others howled their engines and honked their horns late in the evening. This behavior, said a contemporary commentator, "ran contrary to urban order."[71] *The Halbstarke,* on the other hand, described car owners as "snobby," "spiteful," and "short-tempered" middle-class drivers unwilling to share the road.[72] According to historian Werner Lindner and a subcultural interpretation of these events, the young provoked "bourgeois understandings of order."[73] In this sense, their youthful mopeds challenged adult cars. In one such incident in June 1956, roughly fifty youngsters blocked Munich's Stiglmaierplatz square using their mopeds and bicycles. This showcase of youth's power created a traffic jam and resulted in turmoil. Only the arrival of a riot squad dispersed the youngsters and allowed traffic to flow freely.[74] If traffic order is understood as a sign of social and moral order, then this behavior becomes not simply a traffic violation but also a symbolic act of resistance against "street peace."[75]

Antiauthoritarian behaviors of male youth became apparent in various other contexts as well. Those real and imagined delinquents targeted by adult authorities during the crisis years had already resisted. Unlike *the Halbstarke,* however, previous male youngsters had less support from their peers. Consequences of war in particular left uprooted youngsters of the crisis years with few options. This situation changed due to economic stability in the 1950s. Plus, a group dynamic amongst youth took shape—often only strengthened because of adult demonization. As a result, authorities could not simply rely on their mere presence and authority anymore. Accustomed to stepping in when the younger generation misbehaved, the defiant reaction of youth surprised many adults. A witness cited in *Die Süddeutsche Zeitung* vividly described various incidents, including when a youngster on a moped cut off and "molested" a man and two women who were taking a stroll. After a brief argument, the man—seemingly accustomed to his adult authority—simply slapped the youngster. In response, the latter whistled for his friends. A "horde of partially adolescent boys" attacked the man and beat him unconscious.[76] Similar incidents occurred throughout the summer. According to one contemporary commentator, "responsibility means standardization, order, authority with an intention. But the young in particular are rebelling against this authority with purpose and reason."[77] The most prominent example of disrespect, not only for adult authority but also law enforcement and thereby police order as a whole, took place during the Auer Dult, a yearly fair in Munich. In 1956, the Dult made headlines. "Police Fighting Against a Horde of Youngsters,"[78] read one newspaper. The police eventually moved forward against male youngsters unwilling to leave the fair-grounds at closing. Whereas the police had few problems clearing the area the first night, a day later the situation escalated. According to the municipal court report, roughly 100 youngsters near the bumper cars failed to comply with police orders. Although the police were able to clear the area once again, a horde soon returned. In the end, "the police faced roughly 300 youngsters, were trapped, and had to use baton sticks, while youngsters yelled and threw rocks at police cars."[79]

A growing fear of *the Halbstarke* influenced and framed mindsets, an element that eventually contributed to a tragic climax in late summer of 1956. On 20 August, a seemingly minor incident ended with a tragedy. Early in the morning two brothers with potentially too much to drink, accompanied by a girl, walked home in the Munich suburb of Allach. Around 2:20 A.M., three police officers on their bikes stopped them near the train station. Aware of and most likely concerned about recent incidents involving male youth, the policemen approached the group, suspicious about their behaviors. Once confronted with the two intoxicated brothers, a brief argument took place before both youngsters tried to walk away from the officers. One policeman followed them and soon found himself in a brawl with one of the "suspects." He felt threatened, used his pistol, and shot the youngster. The situation escalated further thereafter and a second police officer now arriving at the scene fired a shot into the air hoping to intimidate the by now outraged second "suspect." Unable to do so, he shot the youngster twice, killing him also. This description is based on police records and broader publications given that exact circumstances are difficult to assess. For the media, however, the situation was clear: the police had acted in self-defense. *Die Abendzeitung* soon arranged this tragedy in line with numerous previous incidents, including occasions when youngsters played simple pranks on pedestrians. These stories painted a threatening picture of *the Halbstarke* and indicated that he clearly questioned accepted norms.[80] That had to put adults into a state of panic.[81]

It did not take long for authorities to fully employ *the Halbstarke* as an argument for more control, thereby again making male delinquents a useful tool. By summer 1956, generalizations regarding male youth already provided a way to control behaviors. At a certain point, every youngster dressing, acting, or behaving "abnormally" was deemed as being a semistrong. As one girl noted, "If I go out with a boy who wears jeans then he is a 'Halbstarker' right away."[82] A male youngster felt similar, stating, "If they [adults] speak about the Halbstarke then they act as if they are discussing leprosy."[83] The ills of society had been defined

and were now embodied by *the Halbstarke,* and, after the tragic incident in Allach, authorities saw the necessity to move forward against
this deviancy. According to *Die Abendzeitung,* "The police hope that
the shots from Allach are a warning sign. Police and riot squads are
ready to break the reign of the Halbstarke."[84] In the regional conservative newspaper *Bayernkurier* State Representative Heinrich Junker
reminded the reader of his previous attempts "to push for more state
authority."[85] Another newspaper quoted Bavarian Minister of the Interior August Geislhöringer on the events. According to him, the police
"must act with full force and if necessary, also brutality.... They need
to hit hard, even against bystanders, so that these issues finally come
to an end."[86] Both individuals had been ready to respond to a largely
constructed and manufactured threat, *the Halbstarke,* for months.

Creating *the Teenager*

Similar to *the Halbstarke,* a representation of female youth as *teenagers*
took shape in the miracle years. Like her male complement, *the teenager* endangered normality during the 1950s: concerned contemporaries blamed her for jeopardizing socially accepted norms, including
economic stability, conservative morals, and gender mores. The latter
referred primarily to traditional family structures rooted in patriarchy
and natalist sentiments. Throughout the miracle years, adult society
deemed marriage sacred and premarital sex immoral—particularly
in conservative Bavaria, where a re-Christianization became evident
throughout this period. This made sexual repression the norm and the
three Ks the center of life for women: *Küche* (kitchen), *Kinder* (children), and *Kirche* (church).[87] In contrast, adults perceived *the teenager,*
who was allegedly spending her time dancing to rock 'n' roll music
and openly displaying her sexuality, as a challenge to morality and in
defiance against existing gender mores. Consequentially, she became a
construct of sexual deviancy marking the abnormal in a society hoping
to hold on to its barely reclaimed normality.[88] As one commentator
noted, in times of "insecurity regarding morals and virtues" within a
bourgeois society, norms need to be in place.[89]

Akin to *the Halbstarke* and in many ways parallel to discussions in
the interwar period,[90] the term *teenager* was not new. Although headlines discussed the production of "a new type"[91] during the 1950s, this
image of youth had a prehistory. Cultural historian Jon Savage traced
it by analyzing numerous literary and scholarly pieces, including *The
Wonderful Wizard of Oz* and *Peter Pan.*[92] He gives psychologist and

educator G. Stanley Hall credit for defining adolescence or youth as "a marvelous new birth" as early as 1904.[93] The *New York Times* referred to "teen-age boys"[94] by 1942 and discussed "teen-age fashion"[95] two years later. In January 1945, the same newspaper even published "A Teen-Age Bill of Rights,"[96] addressing youth between thirteen and nineteen years of age. In that sense, Savage concludes, "the Allies won the war exactly at the moment that America's latest product [*the teenager*] was coming off the production line."[97] In 1948, the West German weekly news magazine *Der Spiegel* already followed the rise of Frank Sinatra in the United States, which was closely tied to the support of "young American girls around sixteen years of age, the 'teen-agers.'"[98] A year later, the same newspaper provided a definition closer to home when referencing the more traditional term *Backfisch*.[99] In the late 1940s, both terms were used interchangeably before a shift towards the American expression became noticeable. In 1958, one publication recalled and explained this transition:

> Back in the days they were Backfische, these young girls between fourteen and nineteen. This word came from the English term "back fish." English fishermen used to throw back small, young fish: those needed to develop, grow. One treats Backfische like young fish: no one took them seriously, they were put back, to grow up. Backfische are teenagers these days.[100]

The term *teenager* was never translated, but simply replaced its predecessor as the primary description of young girls, and, by 1958, had become a new, Americanized social construction of female youth.

Early on in the miracle years, *the teenager* was gendered as female. Although it eventually expanded to include male youngsters by the early 1960s, females clearly dominated this construction of youth throughout the long 1950s. Seen as a young fish similar to the *Backfisch*, these girls were not ready for men and the world. Such aspects distinguished them from young men; it also underlined a specific focus on sexuality and future motherhood. With a female audience in mind, German youth magazines of course framed a majority of their content for girls. Columns included beauty and fashion tips while other female youngsters gave regular advice.[101] This approach included Steffi, the perfect teenager appearing in the youth magazine *Bravo* with issue no. 32, in 1958.[102] Most magazines or newspapers saw *the teenager* also in the context of movie stars like Romy Schneider or Christine Kaufmann, both examples for "cute Teenagers."[103] A popular publication titled *Teenagers* specifically traced the rise of the image in 1958 throughout the West. One piece described an encounter with a female teenager in Greenwich Village, NY; another essay gives a girl from Vienna the chance to tell her story. The overwhelming majority of images featured throughout the publication illustrate female youngsters, while male characters are portrayed as rather effeminate.[104] By the mid-1950s, *the teenager* was clearly a female in her teens.

Appearance defined *the teenager*. Distinctively different from adults and children yet similar to *the Halbstarke,* she invented her own style: tight jeans, all kinds of skirts, different haircuts, in particular pony tails. As one young girl noted, "I wore a pony tail for weeks because one looks nice, I do not need to go to the hairdresser, and it is fashionable;"[105] another youngster stated, "I don't have a pony tail, but short hair. I can look so wonderful disorderly ... [and] I feel more relaxed and more free."[106] This aspect explains why, as noted by social commentator Eric Godal, "If a couple is walking by, it is hard to tell who is she and who is he."[107] *The teenager* also wore bright colors, tight jeans, and worn-out sandals. Her attitude is casual, a little naïve, and openminded. She is driven by curiosity yet walks carefree through her day. Godal added that "sex has little secrets" for her.[108] He also best captured her aura as he was trying to describe her in detail:

> Young people have graceful lines and idiosyncratic movements, like animals. An older woman puts one leg over the other, as conventions taught her. One move, a cliché at this point. Teenagers, on the other hand, move without hesitation and disruptions.... One has to leave them to themselves to try to catch their charming movements. While I paint them, they chew on candy, pickles, and bananas. They drink Coca-Cola, listen to Benny Goodman, and their toes are dancing, while she is looking through magazines. "[The French actress] Bardot got fat," she says, and that's it about Bardot. Or: "[German actor] Horst Buchholz, I could like him, very nice!"[109]

The teenager became an almost mystical female creature as she seemingly questioned prudish, stuffy, and repressive formats simply based on her appearance and aura.

Throughout the 1950s, *the teenager* had more time and space. Due to the economic miracle, the housework at home traditionally completed by wives and daughters became easier and less time consuming. Technological advances had made their way into West German kitchens and washrooms. As one contemporary noted sarcastically, "If a woman today finds a pink mixer or a new vacuum under the Christmas tree then she is usually happy. Imagine grandma's surprise if she would have found a wooden spoon or a mop with a bow on it."[110] Whereas these advances gave *the teenager* more time for leisure, her middle-class status also provided her with more space at home. By the mid-1950s, the economic situation had allowed many middle- and upper-class families to have additional space for their children. Now young girls could hang out with friends in their own rooms and have at least some kind of privacy.[111] Used to constant interference by adults, this marked a major shift for female youth. Once outside the home, movie theatres and ice cream parlors became her prime habitat. Instead of showing off with mopeds or standing on street corners like *the Halbstarke*, they rather enjoyed the rock 'n' roll music often available from jukeboxes in so-called milk bars. One girl recalled:

> We met with friends at certain locations in the city, meaning in milk bars, where we drank milk shakes, coke, or lemonade until 7 P.M.; then we had to go home anyway. Girls could just go to the milk bars, alone or with friends. There was a jukebox, and sometimes, even during the afternoon, dancing was going on. … Many girls dressed up for these events in the afternoon. We wore long, tight pants—jeans were in style—but also tight dresses and skirts with the [so-called] Dior-tuck, which flew open when dancing to rock 'n' roll music.[112]

During the 1950s, *the teenager* also explored new spaces, as she increasingly met with her peers in so-called teenager clubs. Most clubs aligned around similar interests, namely tied to movies, records, and stars [Figure 3.3]. By the late 1950s, an estimated 130,000 teenagers met within such informal settings.[113] In Munich, various clubs had to turn down members because they were beyond capacity. In fact, in 1959 there were at least seventeen different clubs in the Bavarian capital. They included groups like the Jaguar Club, the Midnight Club, or the Presley Club.[114] Some met in restaurants; most, however, mingled in private homes. As a result, *the teenager* had started to claim her own space as these clubs provided a sense of community on the local level and away from constant adult supervision. Girls mingled with others to discuss the latest news and gossip about stars, listened to music, and danced to different tunes. The local radio station *Der Bayerische Rundfunk* even had a teenager party program specifically aimed at *the teenager* and her friends. Many sent in requests regarding their favorite songs, and others wrote to stars asking for autographs and pictures.[115] Some clubs were coeducational. Reminiscent of American attempts to create open youth groups shortly after the war, these clubs provided an alternative framework distinct from traditional youth organizations, and away from adult authorities, regulations, and conventions. Besides, traditional youth organizations had no interest in allowing youngsters to listen to rock 'n' roll music or discuss the newest fashion styles. As one observer described, in teenager clubs "the young can be

Figure 3.3 Young people with a portable record player, living the teenage dream around 1955. Courtesy of Otfried Schmidt/Süddeutsche Zeitung Photo.

like they want to. They want to be among themselves, outside paternalistic structures and without regulations."[116] The reasoning for setting up or joining such clubs thus reached from practicality to privacy: "We did not want to pay a fee to go dancing,"[117] noted one youngster. And there was also no other space for youth in the city: "We did not know where else to go. We know each other for a while, but standing around on street corners, that was nothing [for us]. That's why we founded a club."[118] According to one young girl, "as soon as parents are gone on the weekend, we call each other on the phone to meet up. Everyone brings something to eat and to drink. Sometimes we show up in funny costumes. One day, that was funny, someone came … in a bathrobe."[119] Even though not all teenager clubs were coeducational and casual, their willingness to simply meet up with others was deemed as abnormal in a society that had kept their daughters at home and away from unsupervised mingling with male youth.

Adult authorities labeled teenager clubs as deviant spaces and threats to society, and often feared the worst. Worried about the dissolution of existing structures on a larger level, debates about female youth within teenager clubs became a proxy site for broader discussions. For one, many contemporaries were concerned about the increasing influence of U.S. popular culture and marketing; some even suspected deviant ideological reasons behind these setups. In addition, the coeducational nature of many teenager clubs nourished fears regarding promiscuity. The fact that the Youth Protection Law could not be applied in the private sphere only increased concerns; but it also provided an avenue to critique parents.[120] "This makes it increasingly difficult to introduce the importance of discipline regarding the Youth Protection Law to the young," argued one commentator before asking, how could parents be so trusting?[121] The inability to access teenager parties led some authorities to indulge in more aggressive speculations. According to a rather vicious voice from a contemporary Catholic scholar, "such adapted formats of the teenager party can easily become a 'petting party' (making out); soon the teenager club adopts American formats like 'dating' and 'going steady' … thereby exposing those more mature youngsters to a seemingly unbounded erotic-sexual playfield."[122] In his view, *the teenager* with her unrestrained sexuality was a threat to herself, endangered male youth, and jeopardized moral cohesion of society as a whole. Whereas this commentator used his critique also to put forward anti-American sentiments, a less worried voice referred to such overexaggerated nervousness as a reaction to the lack of a coherent youth movement. In his view, concerned contemporaries, "who then get worried about rare rhythmical excitement [by youngsters], create panic once noticing bad behaviors, and think that having nothing to do or being bored needs to be accompanied with constant nagging."[123] This reference to anxieties adequately described widespread reactions and fears in response to *the teenager* while already proposing—through state-sponsored youth organizations—a solution that would bring the needed supervision.

A growing display of sexuality within popular culture seemingly strengthened adults' worst fears. In 1957, the movie *And God Created Woman* (1956) featuring young French actress Brigitte Bardot and German actor Curd Jürgens opened in Munich. Bardot played Juliette, an eighteen-year-old girl highly aware of her sexuality and natural eroticism. Set in a respectable small-town environment on the French Côte d'Azur, Juliette lives in the moment: she sleeps in, walks around barefoot, lays in the sun naked, and flirts freely. Her natural innocence and beauty as well as her inordinate yearning and appetite for plea-

sure mesmerize millionaire Carradine (Curd Jürgens). Juliette, however, desires the cad Antoine (Christian Marquand). Once he abandons
her, she marries his younger brother. Such impulsiveness and unbri-
dled behavior disturbed order and erupted in an ecstatic scene on the
dance floor: there, she unveils her deceitful character as she plays with
her lovers who are forced to watch her sexually explicit dance to foreign and exotic tunes. For those concerned with sexual repression,
Brigitte Bardot impersonated the untamed and immoral *teenager*: her
hair was wild, her well-proportioned body exposed, and her attitude
feisty though naïve. Such descriptions underlined that her stardom
was mostly based on age, bodily features, and sexuality. Referred to by
the news magazine *Der Spiegel* as a "mixture of infantilism and sex,"[124]
Bardot's behaviors made her, among others, the pin-up teenager exposing a repressive society to sexuality.[125] Not surprisingly, the Catholic
Film Service claimed that her behavior and acting was "animal-like."[126]
Brigitte Bardot, "a symbol of female sensuality in Germany"[127] and beyond, sexualized a sexually repressed 1950s West German society and
provided a new and threatening image of femininity to young girls.

Many girls in Munich and throughout West Germany mimicked Bardot's looks and behaviors, thereby sustaining widespread fears among
adults. Just as *the Halbstarke* aimed to look and behave like Marlon
Brando or James Dean, young girls began imitating the French actress
and stars like her: female youngsters wore tight sweaters, blue jeans,
and a ponytail.[128] 1960s Munich celebrity and sex idol Uschi Obermaier vividly recalled how her room was full of posters of James Dean
and Brigitte Bardot.

> I liked to go to bed early, because there I could dream without being dis-
> turbed. I imagined myself playing in movies, and in my fantasy I always
> looked like Brigitte Bardot. First I wondered what kind of hair I had,
> long straight silver hair, blonde straight hair, or blonde and curly. Then I
> re-enacted the scene in my head—how I approach Jimmy [James Dean]
> as he sits there in front of the house in his car, feet up, wearing a cowboy
> hat. I imagined how I introduced myself, how we kissed, and how he
> pushed his body against mine ...[129]

The youth magazine *Bravo* published a major poster-puzzle of Brigitte
Bardot—the first of its kind—to help teenagers like Obermaier to en-
vision herself as the French actress.[130] These attempts at imitation increased sexual awareness. As noted by historian Dagmar Herzog, for
a "stuffy" and "philistine" West German postwar society, this had to
mark a deviation from traditional norms.[131] In fact, many more conservative newspapers harshly rebuked attempts of the young to mimic

Bardot. One publication claimed, "One can be against girls who get caught up in Bardot and even show that in front of a camera light; one cannot even fall in love with such girls."[132] Sexual openness challenged societal hopes and norms, making attempts to imitate Bardot's looks and behaviors only part of discussions meant to regulate sex "through useful and public discourse,"[133] to follow a Foucauldian framework. Once teenage fashion is seen as a sort of text, then perceptions of abnormal behaviors become even more obvious. Instead of a long and pleated skirt, female youngsters wore jeans or a short skirt. In a time when trousers were still widely seen as defeminizing women, such fashion was a provocation. Since skirts twirled when dancing, female youth showed more skin than socially acceptable in a time when female sexuality was mostly banned from the public sphere.[134]

Rock 'n' roll music most openly challenged, questioned, and endangered sexual repression. Originally rock 'n' roll came to Munich as part of a larger transnational trend. As historian Mark Fenemore rightfully notes when focusing on East Germany, "rock 'n' roll was an international phenomenon that transformed expressions of masculinity and femininity throughout Europe."[135] Opening in West Germany in late 1955, movies like *Blackboard Jungle* (1955) had triggered riots among male youngsters in various cities.[136] Initially more concerned about *the Halbstarke*, anxieties soon shifted to include female sexuality. For historian Uta Poiger, the rise of "Elvis, the Pelvis," by fall 1956 marked a paradigm shift from male aggression to female sexuality altogether.[137] In early December, the youth magazine *Bravo* reported how American "girls scream for Elvis."[138] The same month Elvis decorated the cover of the weekly news magazine *Der Spiegel*. Long articles described various scenes occurring during his concerts in the United States. Set up like a sexual act, young girls are first portrayed as impatiently waiting to see the "god of teenager."[139] Once he appeared on stage, some "sob," some "romantically minded young girls" throw flowers on stage, others their panties.[140] Elvis, on the other hand, is depicted as moving like "a talented striptease dancer."[141] The audience reacts to his "sex-trordiary" behavior.[142] Within a short amount of time, a frenzy spreads through the crowd. Girls became emotionally exhausted after the sexual hysteria reached a climax, like an orgasm. In a time of sexual repression, this behavior encouraged by rock 'n' roll music was simply unacceptable.

To bring sexuality to the forefront became part of discussing traditional gender norms because adult voices often tied such conversations to music and dancing. Traditions had been disrupted during the crisis years as society pressured women to work for recovery. In the

miracle years, women could and certainly should return to their traditional role as angels of the house, obedient wives, and caring mothers.
Patriarchy was again the norm, and self-control for women a necessity.
Seen as the shield guarding against male sexual aggression, it was also
important that young girls did not tempt males to misbehave. Rock 'n'
roll dancing girls literally and metaphorically challenged these understandings and norms.[143] Instead of men leading women, both danced
freely together. This arrangement was contrary to previous dances like
the waltz. Understood as liberating for the young, especially for females, these behaviors disrupted traditions and endangered patriarchy. Not surprisingly, in Munich, only one local dance studio allowed
the jitterbug, and then without any sexual moves.[144] Moreover, with
self-control being a key characteristic of femininity at the time, those
dancing loosely and freely clearly threatened such traditions.[145] After
all, the necessity to control the body applied more to females than
males. They were, according to contemporary stereotypes, morally
weaker and more emotional. Future teenage star and Munich native
Peter Kraus recalled hearing about "girls going wild in America when
listening to the music of Bill Haley."[146] In the movie *And God Created
Woman,* this wildness led almost to a disaster. Exposed to an environment with foreign music, young Juliette is seduced by exotic rhythms.
She dances to the music of four black musicians, swirls around them,
and taps on the table, all in very sexually explicit poses. The scene
gets wild, in particular when her two lovers show up hoping to break
the spell. Juliette refuses, dancing in ecstasy. The situation becomes
hectic, the music faster, until a shot is fired by one of her upset lovers.
Male interference breaks the curse of "jungle music" and underscores
that Juliette had to be protected from such forces, by a man.[147] In a
time of sexual repression and strict gender hierarchies, endangering
patriarchy meant trouble.

Contemporary descriptions of dances all had a note of wildness to
them and became a way to critique Otherness. One girl stated, "Yesterday we put on the hottest new record. That made us dance! One is
completely overcome [by the music]. The guys yelled and went crazy.
Just wonderful."[148] For the scholar quoting her, such behavior was
comparable to some sort of ecstasy and excess; he also worried about
the revolting characteristics embedded within rock 'n' roll tunes. A
contemporary voice in the newspaper *Die Zeit* noted how "mania,"
"excesses," and "orgies" capture young females as she worships her
stars and idols fanatically and dances unworried.[149] The commentator
partially blamed parents and adults, thereby expanding his analysis to
critiquing the moral state of society as a whole. He also questioned the

growing importance of psychoanalysis, the idolization of stars, and
overall greediness within the corporate media culture. The same newspaper referred to another contemporary adult voice who suggested
pouring water on dancers to break this deviant spell.[150] This statement
fell in line with those blaming girls less and instead comparing rock 'n'
roll music and marketing to the fictitious Pied Pieper of Hamelin. He
was a mystical character from a legendary German fairytale seducing
and capturing mice with his pipe to follow him out of the city. Once not
paid for such services, he did the same to local children. Racialized references to the seducing powers of African American or simply "exotic"
music became dominant within various discussions and strengthened
fears of the abnormal and foreign Other.[151]

Similar to previous debates surrounding male youth, discussions
about dancing female youth became a way to create binaries. Youngsters dancing to foreign tunes, going wild on the dance floor, and challenging gender norms and German high culture were seen as deviant;
those keeping social etiquette, respecting patriarchy, and listening to
German—possibly even classical—music, on the other hand, marked
the norm. According to cultural historian Rolf Lindner, this opposition
by contemporaries outlined

> two normative systems: just as ballroom dancing was not only an ex-
> pression of good breeding but also displayed the well-bred person at his
> or her best (tactful, tasteful, and with a sense for boundaries), boogie-
> woogie [broadly defined and incorporating rock 'n' roll] contained a mes-
> sage that went beyond the violation of formal dance rules. The "eccentric
> groove" and "lackadaisical casualness" was a violation of "one doesn't do
> that" conformism, which understood dance rules as a way of disciplining
> the body.[152]

In this sense, female bodies and behaviors in the context of dancing
could weaken societal norms.

For contemporaries, the behavior of young girls in particular also
influenced male youth and their conduct in a negative way. Most voices
described this gender dynamic as one-directional, victimizing men and
solemnly blaming young females. Brigitte Bardot's free mind and im-
pulsive behaviors, for instance, marked a subversive threat to patriarchy. According to an essay by French philosopher and social theorist
Simone de Beauvoir, "She [Bardot] follows her inclinations. She eats
when she is hungry and makes love with the same unceremonious sim-
plicity. Desire and pleasure seem to her more convincing than precepts
and conventions."[153] In *And God Created Woman*, Juliette captures such
sentiments stating, "I live as if I were going to die any moment."[154]

For Beauvoir such behavior "embodies ... the credo that young people of our time are opposed to safe values, vain hopes and irksome constraints."[155] In a society believing in exactly such safe values, this conduct had to be threatening. Bardot did not fit traditional gender mores of an obedient and self-sacrificing wife. To quote conservative West German Family Minister Wuermeling, "it is about self-control, abstinence, and self-denial."[156] For him, "a lack of restraint dissolved society and state,"[157] and endangered male rule. In other words, the misbehaviors of Bardot marked the deviation from traditional gender roles and tempted men. Beyond that, Brigitte Bardot did not restrain her female powers. Instead, she embodied the role of Vladimir Nabokov's *Lolita*, a twelve-year-old sexually premature girl mesmerizing a middle-aged man in the 1955 novel; she also "flatters masculine vanity" and invites "the male to domesticate her."[158] Bardot, like *the teenager*, plays with and challenges masculinity while she herself is portrayed along common stereotypes of femininity. According to Simone de Beauvoir, "The male is an object to her [Bardot], just as she is to him. And that is precisely what wounds masculine pride."[159]

Female misbehaviors also endangered masculinity in more indirect ways. Aware of what impresses girls, male youngsters felt compelled to imitate the behaviors of stars as well. Yet Elvis, among other idols, was in no way following traditional understandings of German masculinity. According to contemporaries, Elvis "steps on stage in a colorful costume, loves to wear purple shirts,"[160] and moves like a woman. That he shook his pelvis was scandalous, particularly in a period when West Germany rearmed and adult authorities looked for disciplined and masculine soldiers for their *Bundeswehr* army. According to historian Uta Poiger, the fact that many saw Elvis as feminized increased fears because any ambiguities regarding his gender threatened masculinity.[161] In the 1950s, males did not shake their pelvises; they also did not wear pink shirts and apply hair products. Yet Elvis did exactly that, and adult contemporaries saw him in a different light compared to more masculine rebels like Marlon Brando and James Dean. Historian Marina-Fischer Kowalski notes, such conduct "was viewed as a violation of masculine standards of behavior."[162] Intrigued by Elvis and others, while also interested in meeting girls, male youngsters did not care about such adult sentiments. Instead, they wore similar haircuts and clothes, some used lots of Brisk or grease to look like Billy Haley, while others grew out their sideburns and wore a ducktail. Girls in particular did so in secret, well aware how their parents and other adults would react.[163] Rarely able to escape adult supervision in general, adults would come down much harder on *the teenager* compared to *the Halbstarke* because due to her age, gender, and sexuality she faced much more scrutiny.

Notes

1. Georg Tressel, prod., *Die Halbstarken* (Berlin, 1956). See also:, "Die Halbstarken und ihr Film," *Die Süddeutsche Zeitung* 2 October 1956; "Ein deutscher Halbstarkenfilm," *Die Frankfurter Allgemeine Zeitung*, 8 October 1956.
2. Manuel Köppen, "Die Halbstarken," 666–69, here 667, in *Handbuch Nachkriegskultur.*
3. Foucault, *Discipline and Punish*, 278.
4. See, for example: "Zuerst der Gummiknüppel," *Der Münchner Merkur*, 22 August 1956.
5. On the most recent acknowledgment of both images see: Wrage, "Neue Jugend: Einleitung," 641–665, in *Handbuch Nachkriegskultur.*
6. "Rückkehr der Halbstarken," *Die Süddeutsche Zeitung*, 21 June 1956.
7. Ibid.
8. Ibid. See also: "Die Halbstarken sind nun wieder da," *Die Welt*, 31 March 1956.
9. Dollinger, *München im 20. Jahrhundert*, 211 and 235. See also: Elisabeth Angermaier, *München. Bewegte Zeiten: Die 50er Jahre* (Munich, 2002), 1; Münchner Aufbaugesellschaft, ed., *Ein halbes Jahrzehnt Schuttbeseitigung und Wiederaufbau in München: Tätigkeitsbericht der Münchner Aufbaugesellschaft m.b.H. für die Zeit von Anfang 1947 bis Ende 1951* (Munich, 1952).
10. Angermaier, *München.*
11. "Die Kluge Hausfrau," *Edeka Kundenmagazin*, no. 39 (1955): 2, quoted in Wildt, "Privater Konsum in Westdeutschland in den 50er Jahren," in *Modernisierung im Wiederaufbau: Die westdeutsche Gesellschaft der 50er Jahre*, ed. Axel Schildt and Arnold Sywottek (Bonn, 1998), 275–89 here 275.
12. Hanna Schissler, "'Normalization' as Project: Some Thoughts on Gender Relations in West Germany During the 1950s," in *Miracle Years*, 359–375, here 360.
13. Lüdtke, Marssolek, and Saldern, *Amerikanisierung*, 9–14.
14. Ibid., 13.
15. Silvia Wickenhäuser, "Amerikanische Reeducation und die deutsche Jugend: Mit besonderer Berücksichtigung von Radio München und AFN München" (M.A. thesis., Ludwig-Maximilians University Munich, 2003).
16. Werner Lindner, *Jugendprotest seit den fünfziger Jahren: Dissens und kultureller Eigensinn* (Opladen, 1996), 47–48. See also: Maase, *Bravo Amerika*, 131; Jarausch, *After Hitler*, 122–23.
17. Luke Springman, "Poisoned Hearts, Diseased Minds, and American Pimps: The Language of Censorship in the Schund und Schmutz Debates," *German Quarterly* 68, no. 4 (1995): 408–29, here 413. See also: Dolle-Weinkauff, *Comics* (Weinheim/Basel, 1990), here 96–172.

18. "Opium der Kinderstube," *Der Spiegel,* 21 March 1951.

19. BayHStAM, Staatskanzlei 13776; BayHStAM, Ministerium des Inneren 92079–92084; "Ein bayerisches Gesetz gegen Schmutz und Schund," *Die Abendzeitung,* 31 October 1949; "Gesetz gegen 'Schmutz und Schund,'" *Die Süddeutsche Zeitung,* 31 October 1949; "Sittenromane—'haarsträubend,'" *Der Münchner Merkur,* 6 December 1949; "Wohnungen und Arbeit wieder wichtiger als Schmutz- und Schundgesetz," *Die Süddeutsche Zeitung,* 4 January 1950; "Zu diesem Schund und Schmutz," *Die Neue Zeitung,* 3 February 1950.

20. Poiger, *Jazz, Rock, and Rebels;* Fenemore, *Sex, Thugs and Rock 'N' Roll;* Janssen, *Halbstarke in der DDR.* See also: Alan McDougall, *Youth Politics in East Germany: The Free German Youth Movement, 1946–1968* (Oxford, 2004).

21. Günther Mees and Günter Graf, eds., *Pater Leppich Spricht: Journalisten hören den 'roten' Pater* (Düsseldorf, 1952), 45.

22. Hermann Martin Popert, *Helmut Harringa: Eine Geschichte aus unserer Zeit* (Dresden, 1905).

23. Clemens Schultz, *Die Halbstarken* (Leipzig, 1912), 7–8.

24. Ibid., 33/34.

25. *Jugend, Münchner Illustrierte Wochenschrift für Kunst und Leben* 48 (1918): 959. Accessible at Universitätsbibliothek Heidelberg, Heidelberger historische Bestände, http://diglit. ub.uni-heidelberg.de/diglit/jugend, [last accessed 6 January 2015].

26. Günther Dehn, *Großstadtjugend: Beobachtungen und Erfahrungen aus der Welt der großstädtischen Arbeiterjugend* (Berlin, 1919); Peukert, "Die Halbstarken," 534; Hans Heinrich Muchow, "Zur Psychologie und Pädagogik der 'Halbstarken' (I)," *Unsere Jugend* 8 (1956): 388–94, here 388. See also: Curt Bondy, *Jugendliche stören die Ordnung: Bericht und Stellungnahme zu den Halbstarkenkrawallen* (Munich, 1957), 13–16; Günther Kaiser, *Randalierende Jugend: Eine soziologische und kriminologische Studie über die sogenannten 'Halbstarken'* (Heidelberg, 1959), 13–21; Thomas Grotum, *Die Halbstarken: Zur Geschichte einer Jugendkultur der 50er Jahre* (Frankfurt am Main, 1994), 20–43; Sebastian Kurme, *Halbstarke: Jugendprotest in den 1950er Jahren in Deutschland und den USA* (Frankfurt am Main, 2006), 178–85; Arno Klönne, "Jugendprotest und Jugendopposition: Von der HJ-Erziehung zum Cliquenwesen der Kriegszeit," in *Bayern in der NS-Zeit,* ed. Martin Broszat, Elke Fröhlich, and Falk Wiesemann (Munich, 1983), 527–620, here 594.

27. *Münchner Stadtzeitung,* 9 March 1956, quoted in Geschichtswerkstatt Neuhausen e.V., ed., *Vom Rio zum Kolobri—Halbstark in Neuhausen: Jugendkultur in einem Münchner Stadtteil 1948–1962* (Munich, 2001), 17–18 and 87–88.

28. References to the Gang of the Skulls (*Totenkopfbande*) were in the news after the screening of the film *The Wild One,* in 1953. Katja Scherl, "'Det is doch wie Kino,'" in *Medienkultur und soziales Handeln,* ed. Tanja Thomas (Wiesbaden, 2008), 119–41, here 127.

29. "Terror der Totenkopfbande von der Schwanthalerhöhe," *Die Abendzeitung,* 14–15 August 1956. See also: StadtAM, Schulamt 8271.

30. Cohen, *Folk Devils and Moral Panics.* See also: Gilbert, *A Cycle of Outrage.*

31. BayHStAM, Ministerium des Inneren 81082; MonM, 4° Mon 3831: Seelmann, "Das Halbstarken-Problem in München," (1957), 10; "Wir sind keine 'Halbstarken'!," *8-Uhr Blatt,* 7 September 1956; Geschichtswerkstatt Neuhausen, ed., *Vom Rio zum Kolobri,* 11; Kurme, *Halbstarke,* 29.

32. Friedl Schröder, "Gefahr und Not der Halbstarken," *Allgemeine Deutsche Lehrerzeitung* 8, no. 17 (1956): 326–28, here 326.

33. William S. Schlamm, *Die Grenzen des Wunders: Ein Bericht über Deutschland* (Zurich, 1959), 137.

34. Muchow, "Zur Psycholgie und Pädagogik der Halbstarken, (I)," 393. See also: Axel Schildt, *Moderne Zeiten: Freizeit, Massenmedien und 'Zeitgeist' in der Bundesrepublik der 50er Jahre* (Hamburg, 1995), 176.

35. Muchow, "Zur Psychologie und Pädagogik der Halbstarken, (II)," 446.

36. Hans Heinrich Muchow, *Sexualreife und Sozialstruktur der Jugend* (Reinbek bei Hamburg, 1959), 136. See also: Walter Sagitz, "Das Problem der 'Halbstarken' in psychologischer Sicht," *Neue juristische Wochenschrift* 12 (1959): 806–807; Schildt, *Moderne Zeiten,* 153

37. ABL, StBBd, II, no. 45, 455, quoted in Zahner, *Jugendfürsorge in Bayern,* 191. In 1950, 12.5 percent of young adults (nineteen to twenty-two years of age) were convicted; in 1955, 7.9 percent, and 9.1 percent in 1956. See: ABL, StBBd, I, no. 9, 214, quoted in ibid.

38. MonM, 4° Mon 3831: Seelmann, "Das Halbstarken-Problem in München," (1957), 4–5.

39. Günther Kaiser speaks of 5 percent. Kaiser, *Randalierende Jugend,* 54. See also: Scherl, "'Det is doch wie Kino'," 119. Jürgen Zinnecker sees a maximum of 10 percent involved in this kind of behavior. Jürgen Zinnecker, "'Halbstarke,' die andere Seite der 68er-Generation," in *Protestierende Jugend,* ed. Ulrich Hermann (Weinheim, 2002), 461–85, here 468. Werner Lindner talks about 3 to 5 percent. Lindner, *Jugendproteste seit den fünfziger Jahren,* 27. See also: Kurme, *Halbstarke,* 350.

40. Geschichtswerkstatt Neuhausen, *Vom Rio zum Kolobri,* 15; Lindner, *Jugendprotest seit den fünfziger Jahren,* 31–32.

41. Bondy, *Jugendliche stören die Ordnung,* 55.

42. Geschichtswerkstatt Neuhausen, *Vom Rio zum Kolobri,* 34.

43. Goodman, quoted in Kurme, *Halbstarke,* 309.

44. Ibid. Grotum, *Die Halbstarken,* 208.

45. Poiger, *Jazz, Rock and Rebels.*

46. Lily Phillips, "Blue Jeans, Black Leather Jackets, and a Sneer: The Iconography of the 1950s Biker and its Translation Abroad," *International Journal of Motorcycle Studies* 1, no. 1 (2005), [no page numbers]. See also: Mick Farren, *The Black Leather Jacket* (New York, 1985), 66; Alison Lurie, *The Language of Clothes* (New York, 1981), 232.

47. Ruth Münster, *Geld in Nietenhosen* (Stuttgart, 1961), 47.

48. Kaspar Maase, "Entblößte Brust und schwingende Hüfte: Momentaufnahme von der Jugend der fünziger Jahre," in *Männergeschichte—Geschlechtergeschichte: Männlichkeit im Wandel der Moderne,* ed. Thomas Kühne (Frankfurt am Main/New York, 1996), 193–217.

49. Beverly Gordon, "American Denim: Blue Jeans and Their Multiple Layers of Meaning," in *Dress and Popular Culture*, ed. Patricia A. Cunningham and Susan Voso Lab (Bowling Green, 1991), 31–45, here 33. See also: MonM, 4° Mon 3831: Seelmann, "Das Halbstarken-Problem in München," (1957), 14; Geschichtswerkstatt Neuhausen, *Vom Rio zum Kolobri*, 35, 46, and 76; Phillips, "Blue Jeans, Black Leather Jackets, and a Sneer."

50. StadtAM, Polizeidirektion München 922.

51. Peter Kraus, "Entenschwanz & Ponyfransen," in *Bravo 1956–2006*, ed. Teddy Hoesch (Munich, 2006), 100–113; Maase, *Bravo Amerika*, 120; Arne Andersen, *Der Traum vom guten Leben: Alltags- und Konsumgeschichte vom Wirtschaftswunder bis heute* (Frankfurt am Main, 1999), 212–13.

52. Bondy, *Jugendliche stören die Ordnung*, 25. See also: Kurme, *Halbstarke*, 192–95.

53. Heinz Schimetschke, "Der jugendliche Motorradfahrer" (Ph.D. diss., University of Munich, 1958), 37. See also: Statistische Jahrbücher für die Bundesrepublik Deutschland, quoted in Martin Limpf, *Das Motorrad: Seine technische und geschichtliche Entwicklung, dargestellt anhand der einschlägigen Fachliteratur* (Munich, 1983), 78.

54. Geschichtswerkstatt Neuhausen, *Vom Rio zum Kolobri*, 109.

55. Schimetschke, "Der jugendliche Motorradfahrer," 61.

56. Klaus Hartmann, quoted in Jürgen Zinnecker, *Jugendkultur 1940–1985* (Opladen, 1987), 147. See also: Bodo Mrozek. "Halbstark! Aus der Urgeschichte der Popkultur," *Merkur* (2008): 630–35, here 633.

57. Grotum, *Die Halbstarken*, 204.

58. Schimetschke, "Der jugendliche Motorradfahrer," 45. See also: Schildt, *Moderne Zeiten*, 162; Dietmar Fack, "Jugend, Motorrad und Stadterfahrung: Die Kontinuität subkultureller motorsportlicher Milieus in der modernen Industriegesellschaft," in *Jahrbuch Jugendforschung 5*, ed. Jürgen Zinnecker and Hans Merkens (Wiesbaden, 2005), 95–120.

59. "An der Ecke stehen die Halbwüchsigen," *Die Süddeutsche Zeitung*, 14–15 January 1956.

60. Geschichtswerkstatt Neuhausen, *Vom Rio zum Kolobri*, 98. See also: "Rückkehr der Halbstarken," *Die Süddeutsche Zeitung*, 21 June 1956.

61. Geschichtswerkstatt Neuhausen, *Vom Rio zum Kolobri*, 98.

62. *Die Abendzeitung*, 29–30 September 1956, quoted in Geschichtswerkstatt Neuhausen, *Vom Rio zum Kolobri*, 66.

63. "Außer Rand und Band: Woher kommt die aufreizende Wirkung von Rock 'n' Roll?" *Die Zeit*, 4 October 1956. See also: "Neu in Deutschland: Außer Rand und Band (USA)," *Der Spiegel*, 3 October 1956; "Rock and Roll: Der Rhythmus der Gelangweilten," *Die Süddeutsche Zeitung*, 9 August 1956.

64. Wolfgang Hopker, "Mehr Freizeit—aber wozu? Vierzig-Stunden-Woche und die neue deutsche Gesellschaft," *Die politische Meinung* 2, no. 12 (1957): 46; Michael Gallmeier, "Freizeit: Ein Problem der Gegenwart in Sicht der Erzieher," *Welt der Schule* 11, no. 7 (1958): 289–29; Wolfgang Neubelt, "Der Streit um die Freizeit," *Unsere Jugend* 11 (1959): 121–24; Walther Becker, "Automatisierte Freizeit," *Unsere Jugend* 11 (1959): 407–11; Hanns Ott, "Freizeitgestaltung oder Freizeitbildung," *Deutsche Jugend*

5, no. 3 (1957): 107–13; Franz Metzger, "Die Musikbox als aktuelles Freizeitangebot der Jugendpflege?" *Deutsche Jugend* 8 (1960): 124–28.

65. *Caritas* 56, no. 2/3 (1955): 65, quoted in Zahner, *Jugendfürsorge in Bayern,* 173.

66. Sarah Sonntag, "Am Samstag fängt die Woche an ...," *Deutsche Jugend* 8 (1960): 226–30, here 229.

67. Geschichtswerkstatt Neuhausen, *Vom Rio zum Kolobri,* 93.

68. Ibid., 85. Other such spaces included: the parking space at the corner Juta-/ Leonrodstraße street, or the area of the former Max-II-barracks. Ibid., 85–86.

69. "An der Ecke stehen die Halbwüchsigen," *Die Süddeutsche Zeitung,* 14–15 January 1956. See also: Günther Kaiser, "Die Kriminalität der sogenannten Halbstarken," *Unsere Jugend* 9, no. 7 (1957): 301–9.

70. Kaiser, *Randalierende Jugendliche,* 44.

71. Heinz Kluth, "Die Halbstarken': Legende oder Wirklichkeit," *Deutsche Jugend, Zeitschrift für Jugendfragen und Jugendarbeit* 4 (1956): 495–503, here 497.

72. Schimetschke, "Der jugendliche Motorradfahrer," 57.

73. Lindner, *Jugendproteste seit den fünfziger Jahren,* 63.

74. Geschichtswerkstatt Neuhausen, ed., *Vom Rio zum Kolobri,* 14; MonM, 4° Mon 3831: Seelmann, "Das Halbstarken-Problem in München," (1957), 11–12.

75. Gerhard Fürmetz, "'Kampf um den Straßenfrieden': Polizei und Verkehrsdiziplin in Bayern zwischen Kriegsende und beginnender Motorisierung," in *Nachkriegspolizei: Sicherheit und Ordnung in Ost- und Westdeutschland 1945–1969,* ed. Gerhard Fürmetz, Herbert Reinke, and Klaus Weinhauer (Hamburg, 2001), 199–228.

76. "An der Ecke stehen die Halbwüchsigen," *Die Süddeutsche Zeitung,* 14–15 January 1956. See also: "Weil er getadelt wurde, schlug er zu," *Der Münchner Merkur,* 15 May 1956; "Ein Halbstarker, Halbschwacher und der Watschenbaum," *Der Münchner Merkur,* 13 July 1956; StadtAM, Polizeipräsidium München; StadtAM, Schulamt 8271; Günter Raschen, "Die Krawalle der 'Halbstarken' als Probleme der Erwachsenen," *Unsere Jugend* 9, no. 1 (1957): 10–15.

77. Gallmeier, "Freizeit," 290. See also: Hopker, "Mehr Freizeit—aber wozu?," 46.

78. "Dreimal Tumult auf Dult," *Die Süddeutsche Zeitung,* 7 August 1956. See also: "Dultstraße geräumt," *Der Münchner Merkur,* 7 August 1956; "Das hat die Auer Dult noch nie gesehen: Polizei im Kampf gegen Horde von Jugendlichen," *Die Abendzeitung,* 6 August 1956; "In der Maxburg werden Rowdies klein," *Der Münchner Merkur,* 24 January 1957; MonM, 4° Mon 3831: Seelmann, "Das Halbstarken-Problem in München," (1957), 9–10.

79. Geschichtswerkstatt Neuhausen, *Vom Rio zum Kolobri,* 14. See also: StadtAM, Polizeidirektion München 922; StadtAM, Schulamt 8271; StadtAM, Stadtchronik (1956); *Die Süddeutsche Zeitung,* "Sie machten auf der Au Radau," January 24, 1957; Mrozek, prod., *Bürger, Antibürger, Intellektuelle (2). Die motorisierte Rebellion,* radio program Bayerischer Rundfunk, aired 10 March 2009 (8:30 P.M.–), 24.

80. "Halbwüchsige gefährden die Straßen der Stadt," *Die Abendzeitung*, 22 August 1956. See also: Falter, *Chronik des Polizeiäsidiums München*, 126; StadtAM, Stadtchronik (1956).

81. "Zuerst der Gummiknüppel," *Der Münchner Merkur*, 22 August 1956; "Bei 'Halbstarken' hilft Erziehung mit Stärke," *Bayernkurier*, 1 September 1956; "Die tödlichen Schüsse von Allach waren Notwehr," *Der Münchner Merkur*, 13 September 1956. Two other incidents occurred in Munich that claimed lives of youngsters. See: Geschichtswerkstatt Neuhausen, *Vom Rio zum Kolobri*, 165.

82. Edith Göbel, *Mädchen zwischen 14 und 18: Ihre Probleme und Interessen, ihre Vorbilder, Leitbilder und Ideale und ihr Verhältnis zu den Erwachsenen* (Hannover, 1964), 315.

83. Ibid. See also: Zinnecker, *Jugendkultur 1940–1985*, 22; Jürgen Zinnecker, "'Halbstarke,' die andere Seite der 68er-Generation," in *Protestierende Jugend: Jugendoppostion und politischer Protest in der deutschen Nachkriegsgeschichte*, ed. Ulrich Hermann (Weinheim, 2002), 461–85, here 461.

84. "Halbwüchsige gefährden die Straßen der Stadt," *Die Abendzeitung*, 22 August 1956.

85. "Bei 'Halbstarken' hilft Erziehung mit Stärke," *Bayernkurier*, 1 September 1956.

86. "Zuerst der Gummiknüppel," *Der Münchner Merkur*, 22 August 1956.

87. Ralph Willett, *The Americanization of Germany, 1934–1949* (New York, 1989), 125; Claudia Ingenhoven and Magdalena Kemper, "Nur Kinder, Küche, Kirche? Der Frauenfunk in den fünfziger Jahren," 134–37, in *Perlonzeit*. See also: Merith Niehuss, "Kontinuität und Wandel der Familie in den 50er Jahren," 316–34, in *Modernisierung im Wiederaufbau: Die westdeutsche Gesellschaft der 50er Jahre*, eds. Axel Schildt and Arnold Sywottek (Bonn, 1993); Robert Moeller, "Reconstructing the Family in Reconstruction Germany: Women and Social Policy in the Federal Republic 1949–1955," *Feminist Studies* 15, no. 1 (1989): 137–69; Erica Carter, *How German Is She? Postwar West German Reconstruction and the Consuming Woman* (Ann Arbor, 1997); Sara Lennox, "Constructing Femininity in the Early Cold War Era," in *German Pop Culture: How 'American' Is It?* ed. Agnes C. Mueller (Ann Arbor, 2004), 66–80; Schütz, "Nach dem Entkommen, vor dem Ankommen," 134, in *Handbuch Nachkriegskultur*.

88. Uta Poiger, "Rock 'n' Roll, Female Sexuality, and the Cold War Battle over German Identities," *Journal of Modern History* 68, no. 3 (1996): 577–616, here 578.

89. Theodor Dolezol, "Die Spontanen und ihre Organisatoren," *Deutsche Jugend* 8 (1960): 470–75, here 471.

90. Peukert, *Jugend Zwischen Krieg und Krise.*

91. Hans Heigert, "Ein neuer Typ wird produziert: der Teenager," *Deutsche Jugend* 7 (1959): 117–21, here 117.

92. Jon Savage, *Teenage: The Creation of Youth Culture* (New York, 2007), xv and 453.

93. G. Stanley Hall, *Adolescence: Its Psychology and its Relations to Physiology, Anthropology, Sociology, Sex, Crime, Religion, and Education*, Vol. 1 (New York/ London, 1922), xv.

94. "A 'Teen-ager cited: Pharmacist's Mate, 19, Saved Life of Marine in Solomons," *New York Times*, 1 November 1942.
95. "Teen-Age Fashions," *New York Times*, 1 October 1944.
96. "A Teen-Age Bill of Rights," *New York Times Magazine*, 7 January 1945.
97. Savage, *Teenage*, 465.
98. "Gleiche Chance für Frankie," *Der Spiegel*, 24 April 1948.
99. "Miss Dynamit," *Der Spiegel*, 11 June 1952. See also: Catherine Dollard, "The *alte Jungfer* as New Deviant: Representation, Sex, and the Single Woman in Imperial Germany," *German Studies Review* 29, no. 1 (Feb. 2006): 107–26, here 109; David Ehrenpreis, "The Figure of the Backfisch: Representing Puberty in Wilhelmine Germany," *Zeitschrift für Kunstgeschichte* 67, no. 4 (2004): 479–508; Christine Bartmann and Heinz-Hermann Krüger, "Vom Backfisch zum Teenager: Mädchensozialisation in den 50er Jahren," in *'Die Elvis-Tolle die hatte ich mir unauffällig wachsen lassen': Lebensgeschichte und jugendliche Alltagskultur in den fünfziger Jahren*, ed. Heinz-Hermann Krüger (Opladen, 1985), 84–101, here 99.
100. Eric Godal and Rolf Italiaander, eds., *Teenagers: Mit Beiträgen von 26 Autoren* (Hamburg, 1958), 7. See also: Willett, *The Americanization of Germany 1945–1949*, 126; Erica Carter, "Alice in the Consumer Wonderland: West German Case Studies in Gender and Consumer Culture," 185–214, here 199, in *Gender and Generations*, ed. Angela McRobbie and Mica Nava (Houndmills, 1984); Carter, *How German Is She?*
101. "Bravo Schönheitsstips," *Bravo*, no. 17 (1956), no. 2 (1957), and no. 4 (1958); "Bravo Modetips," *Bravo*, no. 37 (1957), no. 39 (1957), no. 4 (1958). See also: "Modehaus Bravo," 432–39, in *Bravo 1956–2006;* Isabella Belting, "Als Mutter jung war…," 14–20, in *Nylon & Caprisonne: Das fünfziger Jahre Gefühl*, ed. Isabella Belting (Wolfratshausen, 2001). According to one study, *Bravo* had roughly 1.66 million readers in 1962 (West Germany and West Berlin), two-thirds of them female. Helmut Ehrmann, ed., *Bravo-Leser stellen sich vor* (Munich, 1961) 15. See also: Maase, *Bravo Amerika*, 104 and 262.
102. "Steffi," *Bravo*, no. 32 (1958). Steffi ended her career in 1959. Maase, *Bravo Amerika*, 143–44; Martin Hussong, "Jugendzeitschriften von 1945–1960: Phasen, Typen, Tendenzen," in *Zwischen Trümmern und Wohlstand: Literatur der Jugend 1945–1960*, ed. Klaus Doderer (Weinheim/Basel, 1988), 521–85, here 568–80.
103. Wiebke Nieland, "Frauenbilder in Bravo," 82–83, in *Bravo 1956–2006*.
104. Adriaan van der Veen, "Das Mädchen von Greenwich Village," 23–31, in *Teenagers*. See also: Fritz Habeck, "Ein Wiener Mädchen erzählt," 54–56, in ibid.
105. Rolf Italiaander, "Die Antworten der Teenagers," 124–60, here 129, in ibid.
106. Ibid. See also: Angela Delille and Andrea Grohn, "Backfische, Teenager, Frühreife," 42–55, here 50–51, in *Perlonzeit*.
107. Eric Godal, "Ich zeichne junge Menschen," 11–15, here 12–14, in *Teenagers*.
108. Ibid.
109. Ibid. See also: Ingeborg Weber-Kellermann, "Mit Pferdeschwanz und Petticoat: Kindheit in den fünfziger Jahren," 13–22, in *Perlonzeit*.

110. Janet Wolff, *Kaufen Frauen mit Verstand?* (Düsseldorf, 1959), 183. See also: Angela Delille and Andrea Grohn, "Komfort im Reich der Frau," 126–33, in *Perlonzeit;* Andersen, *Der Traum vom guten Leben,* 91.

111. Silke Kurth and Petra Mallwitz, "Vom Privileg zur Grundausstattung: Der lange Weg zum Modellkinderzimmer," in *Vom Trümmerkind zum Teenager: Kindheit und Jugend in der Nachkriegszeit,* ed. Doris Foitzik (Bremen, 1992), 82–89; Katrin Pallowski, "Wohnen im halben Zimmer: Jugendzimmer," 23–29, in *Perlonzeit.*

112. Delille and Grohn, eds, *Perlonzeit,* 37. See also: Andersen, *Der Traum vom guten Leben,* 222.

113. Heigert, "Ein neuer Typ wird produziert," 117. See also: Bartmann and Krüger, "Vom Backfisch zum Teenager," here 99.

114. Paula Linhart, "Von der Teenager-Mode zur Teenager-Bewegung," *Unsere Jugend* 11 (1959): 313–16, here 313.

115. Bayerischer Rundfunk, Historisches Archiv Munich (BRHistAM), Tanzmusik 01.01.1953–31.12.1963; (BRHistAM), Bayerischer Rundfunk (Sommerprogramm 1959). See also: Wanderer and Silbereisen, "Teenager-Party und Jugendschutz," *Unsere Jugend* 11 (1959): 380–81; "Jugendclubs und ihre Statuten," *Die Zeit,* 4 February 1954.

116. Dolezol, "Die Spontanen und ihre Organisatoren," 472.

117. Ibid.

118. Ibid.

119. Linhart, "Von der Teenager-Mode zur Teenager-Bewegung," 314.

120. See, for example: "Weniger von 'Halbstarken,' mehr von ihren Eltern reden," *Die Welt,* 7 July 1956.

121. Linhart, "Von der Teenager-Mode zur Teenager-Bewegung," 314.

122. Heinz Loduchowski, *Teenager und Koedukation? Jugend der freien Welt in Gefahr* (Freiburg, 1960), 12–13.

123. Hans Tietgens, "Zwischen 15 und 25: Die Heranwachsenden," *Deutsche Jugend* 7 (1959): 362–67.

124. "Brigitte Bardot," *Der Spiegel,* 30 September 1959. See also: "Gier nach Liebe," *Der Spiegel,* 8 August 1956.

125. "Pariser Luft," *Der Spiegel,* 6 June 1956; "Brigitte Bardot," *Der Spiegel,* 4 November 1959. See also: Geschichtswerkstatt Neuhausen, *Vom Rio zum Kolobri,* 52.

126. Brigitte Tast and Hans-Jürgen Tast, eds, *Brigitte Bardot: Filme 1953–1961: Anfänge des Mythos B.B.* (Hildesheim, 1982), [no page number].

127. Poiger, *Jazz, Rock, and Rebels,* 171.

128. Rainer Eisfeld, *Als Teenager träumten: Die magischen 50er Jahre* (Baden-Baden, 1999), 75.

129. Uschi Obermaier and Olaf Kraemer, *High Times: Mein wildes Leben* (Munich, 2007), 16–17. For other examples see: Gabriele Dietz, "Sozius-Miezen: Halbstarke Mädchen," 32–41, here 38–39, in *Perlonzeit.*

130. Hoesch, ed., *Bravo 1956–2006,* 265–73. For covers of *Bravo* see: ibid., 56.

131. Herzog, *Sex after Fascism,* 106.

132. "Entblösste halbjüngerchen a la Brigitte Bardot," *Der Spiegel,* 10 July 1957.

133. Foucault, *History of Sexuality,* 25.

134. Poiger, *Jazz, Rock, and Rebels,* 103; Wilfried Breyvogel, "Provokation und Aufbruch der westdeutschen Jugend in den 50er und 60er Jahren," 445–59, here 453, in *Protestierende Jugend;* Belting, "Als Mutter jung war …," 14–20.

135. Fenemore, *Sex, Thugs and Rock 'N' Roll,* 132. See also: Kaiser, *Randalierende Jugend,* 20.

136. "Neu in Deutschland," *Der Spiegel,* 9 November 1955; "Neu in Deutschland: Außer Rand und Band (USA)," *Der Spiegel,* 3 October 1956. Such riots occurred primarily in the Ruhr area in West Germany.

137. Poiger, *Jazz, Rock, and Rebels,* 171.

138. "Mädchen schreien für Elvis," *Bravo,* no. 16 (1956). See also: "Schwarm von Millionen," *Bravo,* no. 15 (1956).

139. "Der Über-Rhythmus," *Der Spiegel,* 26 September 1956.

140. "Elvis, the Pelvis," *Der Spiegel,* 12 December 1956. In his biography, author Jerry Hopkins speaks of "hysteria." Jerry Hopkins, *Elvis: A Biography by Jerry Hopkins* (New York, 1971), 119.

141. "Elvis, the Pelvis," *Der Spiegel,* 12 December 1956. *Der Spiegel* frequently referred to Elvis as the "hip-shaking champion" (*Hüftwackel-Champion*). See: "Elvis Presley," *Der Spiegel,* 4 December 1957; "Elvis Presley," *Der Spiegel,* 4 June 1958.

142. "Elvis, the Pelvis," *Der Spiegel,* 12 December 1956: See also: "Meldungen von der Rock-'n'-Roll-Front," *Der Spiegel,* 26 September 1956.

143. Bartam and Krüger, "Vom Backfisch zum Teenager," 84–101, here 94.

144. *Die Süddeutsche Zeitung,* 15 January 1955, quoted in Geschichtswerkstatt Neuhausen, *Vom Rio zum Kolobri,* 66.

145. Eisfeld, *Als Teenager träumten,* 45.

146. Peter Kraus, *I Love Rock 'n' Roll: Keine Zeit zum alt werden* (Heidelberg, 2006), 80. See also: "Außer Rand und Band: Woher kommt die aufreizende Wirkung von Rock 'n' Roll?" *Die Zeit,* 4 October 1956; Poiger, "Rock 'n' Roll, Female Sexuality, and the Cold War Battle over German Identities," 583.

147. Eisfeld, *Als Teenager träumten,* 43–52, passim; Poiger, "Rock 'n' Roll, Female Sexuality, and the Cold War Battle over German Identities," 582; Maase, *Bravo Amerika,* 94.

148. Walter Becker, "Rock'n-Roll: Symbol der Auflehnung," *Ruf ins Volk* (1958): 27–28, here 27.

149. "Das große Schütteln über die Jugend," *Die Zeit,* 27 September 1956.

150. *Die Zeit,* 31 October 1958, quoted in Andersen, *Der Traum vom guten Leben,* 219.

151. Becker, "Rock-'n-Roll: Symbol der Auflehnung," 27; Walter Becker, "Der 'Siegeszug' des Rock'n Roll," *Ruf ins Volk* (1958): 90–91, here 90; Schildt, *Moderne Zeiten,* 177.

152. Rolf Lindner, "Jugendkultur: Stilisierte Widerstände," in *Immer diese Jugend! Zeitgeschichtliches Mosaik 1945 bis heute,* ed. Deutsches Jugendinstitut (Munich, 1985), 14–24, here 14. Translation from: Sabine von Dirke, *'All Power to the Imagination!' The West German Counterculture from the Student Movement to the Greens* (Lincoln, 1997), 26.

153. Simone de Beauvoir, *Brigitte Bardot and the Lolita Syndrome* (New York, 1972), 16.
154. Ibid., 16–17.
155. Ibid., 18.
156. Dietrich Haensch, *Repressive Familienpolitik* (Reinbek bei Hamburg, 1969), 51. See also: Peter Kuhnert and Ute Ackermann, "Jenseits von Lust und Liebe?" 45, in *'Die Elvis-Tolle die hatte ich mir unauffällig wachsen lassen.'*
157. Ibid., 102.
158. Beauvoir, *Brigitte Bardot and the Lolita Syndrome*, 14–15.
159. Ibid., 20–21. See also: Jean Améry, *Teenager-Stars: Idole unserer Zeit* (Rüschlikon-Zurich, 1960), 79–84; Bernard d'Eckardt, *Brigitte Bardot: Ihre Filme, ihr Leben* (Munich, 1982).
160. "Elvis, the Pelvis," *Der Spiegel*, 12 December 1956. See also: Geschichtswerkstatt Neuhausen, *Vom Rio zum Kolobri*, 68.
161. Poiger, "Rock 'n' Roll, Female Sexuality, and the Cold War Battle over German Identities," 579.
162. Marina Fischer-Kowalski, *1958-Hooligans and 1968-Students: One Generation and Two Rebellions* (Vienna, 1982), 36.
163. Krüger, *'Die Elvis-Tolle, die hatte ich mir heimlich wachsen lassen'*; Kraus, "Entenschwanz & Ponyfransen," 100–113.

CHAPTER 4

Controlling Youth and Society in the Miracle Years

In 1958, social commentators noted that dancing, rock 'n' roll music, comic books, and several other namely American products endangered the young and society as a whole. It is not surprising "that our culture is moving backwards [and] becoming more primitive,"[1] one voice noted. Psychologist Wolfgang Brudny made a similar argument. He surveyed the reaction of children at numerous movie theaters in Munich throughout the 1950s.[2] By then, of course, *the Halbstarke* and *the teenager* fully embodied contemporary fears, as both images symbolized threats to stability: he endangered productivity and moral order; she primarily jeopardized gender mores. As a result, and similar to discussions regarding *the delinquent boy* and *the sexually deviant girl* in the crisis years, both images of youth eventually provided authorities with the leeway to expand mechanisms of social control.

To step in against youth, however, was a complicated issue. Since May 1949 West Germany had been a democracy, grounded in the *Grundgesetz* common law that protected civil liberties and restricted random government interference in many areas. This framework meant that although local authorities might fear growing Americanization and had fought against it in numerous ways,[3] they had limited possibilities to censor such influences. Moreover, the young had more means, freedoms, and confidence compared to the crisis years. Young males in particular often worked full time and contributed to recovery, productivity, and overall stability. For them, it became their right to do what they wanted after work, especially if they were over the age of eighteen. Finally, corporations had discovered youth as consumers, giving them even more say and power. As a result, adult authorities had a harder time single handedly restricting the doings of young people in these miracle years.

Soon traditional local authorities and a growing commercial sector
nonetheless took on this challenge. In Munich, two conservative politicians in particular demanded stricter measures against primarily male
youth. Member of the State Parliament Heinrich Junker introduced
an urgency measure. It outlined the threat posed by *the Halbstarke* and
provided support for additional policing, stricter laws, and more supervision; Member of the conservative Bavarian Party (BP) and Minister
of the Interior August Geislhöringer repeatedly called for a stringent,
possibly even brutal, police response in light of *the Halbstarke*.[4] In a
way, traditional conservative voices partially stuck in old mindsets
spearheaded responses in Munich. The public's reactions against the
rhetoric of Geislhöringer, at least, plus limitations based on shared
governance, ultimately averted the implementation of most proposals.
Apart from facing similar policies, *the teenager* also dealt with more
indirect pressures. In particular, conservative West German Family
Minister Franz-Josef Wuermeling and religious officials on the local
level repeatedly enforced pious sentiments specifically targeting young
women.[5] In that sense, discussions of shame and guilt combined with
strict rules against female youth became powerful ways to restrict teenage bodies and behaviors, as females once again faced a stigmatization
based on age, gender, and sexuality.[6] The growing influence of the commercial sector finally became a new and powerful force controlling
youth as business interests quickly discovered the growing purchasing power of the young.[7] Since rebellious *Halbstarke* and overly sexual
teenagers were not lucrative in a repressive overall environment, a major rebranding effort created a more tolerable and profitable construct
of youth. By the early 1960s, this corporate model of male and female
youth embodied a new stage in life, between childhood and adulthood,
now grounded, of course, in the need to purchase this teenage lifestyle.

Controlling *the Halbstarke*

Direct attempts to control *the Halbstarke* became increasingly noticeable by the mid-1950s. Following broader discussions about rebels and
rowdies elsewhere, local authorities had long anticipated the arrival
of this threat. Earlier campaigns against smut and filth had already
targeted subversive foreign influences, and provided some leeway to
expand overall surveillance.[8] Plus police officers had by now begun
monitoring public spaces as a way to disperse and prevent any gath-
erings of male youth in the first place. As a police report from March
1956 noted, "Most recently, the semigrown are trying to gain ground

on different corners at Münchner Freiheit square. As observed, they were sitting around on handrails ..., wearing well-known clothing (red and black bomber jackets, blue jeans, and such), or standing on street corners, teasing each other, molesting pedestrians, or calling someone names."[9] The report confined, "they are under close observation within such spaces and directed to move along and disperse, something they do most of the time without protest.... So far we could not catch them in the act [of committing a crime], so that there is no basis for prosecution."[10]

In light of a perceived increase in incidents, local officials soon coordinated their efforts. Influenced by looming fears, August Geislhöringer and the Ministry of the Interior outlined "measures against the wildness of the young" by May 1956.[11] After referencing various newspaper articles and thereby building on constructs of male youth as *Halbstarke* to justify their approach, the actual blueprint called for specific actions against the young. It outlined how "constant supervision of youngsters by the police is only partially feasible."[12] Instead, the blueprint proposed a more comprehensive approach. Authorities should focus on "educating, supporting, and assisting the young in order to prevent criminal acts altogether."[13] These youth-saving measures in combination with police observations could partially prevent brawls and riots. The initial blueprint resulted in a far-reaching directive for the police. The measure noted, "In light of several incidents it has become obvious that wild and delinquent youngsters seriously endanger law and order. It is therefore necessary that the police during its patrols and other duties specifically focus on these individuals, and aim to prevent and prosecute criminal acts."[14]

Such initial attempts and sentiments provided the basis for a comprehensive five-point plan, passed on to law enforcement in June 1956. According to the directive, local policemen should observe public spaces frequented by gangs of adolescents on a regular basis. "Acts of mischief are sufficient ... and evident if youngsters bother others."[15] This broad definition of misbehaviors provided an avenue for preemptive measures. A second point stated, "If youngsters are seen within the proximity of locations that constitute a moral danger," then they need to be dispersed right away.[16] Such immoral spaces included street fairs, certain squares, and train stations. Restaurants regularly visited by youngsters also had to be monitored very carefully. One of those places was the Weisse Kreuz restaurant in the quarter Neuhausen. Here, local youngsters met to play games, drink, and hang out.[17] Other places invited youngsters to dance. Concerned about the rebellious potential of rock 'n' roll, the directive mirrored such fears. According to point three, all youngsters "participating in dance events" after a certain time or within an immoral environment had to be "removed" immediately. The next point noted that youngsters driving motorcycles and mopeds "were a particular threat." Given that not all youngsters broke existing traffic laws, authorities noted, "a punitive disruption ... can occur if the act of driving is not meant for reaching a destination but merely for entertainment, for instance, driving around city blocks. ... Driving back and forth with a rattling moped is furthermore a disorderly breach of peace. As a result, such trips have to be prevented."[18] Reminiscent of attempts to limit and control movements of supposed vagrants during the crisis years, police officers now had proper cause and the opportunity to stop youngsters on their mopeds. Finally, the directive outlined measures addressing possible resistance. Well aware of an increasing willingness of male youngsters to question authorities, it underscored the state's desire to show little mercy, stating, "Resistance against governmental authority has to be broken."[19] In early summer, local authorities became proactive regarding a supposedly looming threat of youth.

This directive increased tensions on the streets. Constantly aware of potential delinquents, the police began profiling, criminalizing, and harassing young males based on their clothing, posture, or location. For example, those standing on street corners became targets of repeated controls. Police patrols checked for identification before dispersing them altogether. According to a contemporary journal, authorities acted "randomly against shabby, delinquent, and criminal youngsters and adolescents."[20] In fact, the biker magazine *Das Motorrad* had to protest against such stereotyping, stating that not everyone wearing a leather jacket was automatically a criminal.[21] Since many felt wrongfully accused and profiled, resistance against the police increased. That then became a sign for the rise in juvenile delinquency for authorities. The cycle arguably created a tense environment and panic, which fostered overreactions, sustained simplistic understandings of youth, and at least partially explains the uncompromising behaviors of some youngsters in the summer of 1956.

Instead of reconsidering their measures, however, events on the streets of Munich merely encouraged those determined to defend the state and public order. Initially facing only limited opposition amongst more liberal officials on the state level, two conservatives took up the task to fight *the Halbstarke* in Munich: Member of Parliament Heinrich Junker (CSU) and Minister of the Interior August Geislhöringer (BP). The latter saw "law and order jeopardized by the behavior of youngsters."[22] Such rhetoric indicated inherent fears regarding public safety and social order, and followed widespread constructions of youth as deviant. Newspapers like *Der Münchner Merkur* had also called for "drastic measures against Halbstarke"[23] by early June, consequently indicating to Junker and Geislhöringer that their stricter approach had at least some public support.

Initial attempts by State Representative Junker to push for more rigorous laws did not succeed. In the last meeting of the Cultural Committee within the state government before the summer break, he put forward an urgency measure, titled "Measures for the Protection of Youth." It proposed:

1. Steady observation of movie theatres, restaurants and parks and intervention without restraint by the police regarding disturbances of public order and safety.
2. Observation of young drivers, especially those with mopeds whose undisciplined behavior not only endangers other drivers but also pedestrians.
3. Strict opposition against any formation of gangs.
4. Breaking any resistance against state authority by the Halbstarke within legal boundaries.
5. Directives for prosecutors to request prosecution regarding the misdeeds of the Halbstarke.[24]

Fellow party member Otto Schedl asked for further retributions, noting, "state institutions need to be instructed to check if guardians have breached their duty of supervision or failed in other ways. If necessary, authorities need to utilize and apply punitive measures."[25] Although Junker had conservative support, the proposal needed the approval of other coalition members. After a heated discussion, "social democrats (SPD) and liberals (FDP) favored a pedagogical approach."[26] According to the official transcripts, mainly the social democratic caucus did not feel comfortable with the proposed restrictions. State Representative and social democrat Rudolf Schlichtinger in particular "underlined that the buzzword Halbstarke seems unsuitable.... Generally speaking today's youth is not worse than the youth overall; it is just different and that is not surprising, if one recalls that these youngsters were born at the beginning of World War II."[27] Fellow party member Fritz Grässler agreed, arguing, "The state of the youth is dramatized.... I want to warn against popularizing the buzzword 'Halbstarke' making it into a term that already smells like crime."[28] Whereas no other representative seemed as concerned about this issue as these two voices, the SPD and the FDP as parties generally favored a more liberal approach:

they both hoped for more discussions and a thorough investigation first—instead of quick and strict restrictions imposed on youth shortly before the upcoming summer break. In the end, the committee merely agreed with the initial request to investigate the problem at hand in more detail, hence limiting initial conservative yearnings for a more direct response.[29]

With parliament and city council in recess during the summer months, discussions about expanding policing against *the Halbstarke* gained momentum. Minister of the Interior August Geislhöringer in particular used this temporary vacuum of governing and his authority to push for harsher measures. Fed up with the inabilities of other institutions to maintain public order, Geislhöringer opposed what he called "sloppy humanist sentiments" regarding the young.[30] He did not want to give "the impression that the state is powerless!"[31] As a result, Geislhöringer demanded measures against all delinquent behaviors and specifically noted that harsh brutality, if necessary, has to be considered. In this sense he followed previous conversations around corporal punishment, an issue that had played an important role in the crisis years regarding the reorganization of schooling. He specifically proposed the expansion of police forces and wanted the police throughout the state of Bavaria to have access to baton sticks: "They should beat without mercy and should even obstruct those watching, so that such troubles finally end."[32] Influenced by growing anxieties and media outrage, Geislhöringer had substantial support. *Der Münchner Merkur* at least stated that Geislhöringer "is right. It is about time that Munich is cleansed from the Halbstarke."[33] The local evening newspaper and tabloid *8-Uhr Blatt* underlined that a meeting initiated by Geislhöringer would finally bring "relief."[34] Letters to the editor agreed with such sentiments. A concerned citizen wrote to *Die Süddeutsche Zeitung* in favor of stricter laws and deterrence. Using *the Halbstarke* as a way to sustain arguments for the reestablishment of a West German army, the author noted, "there is no better argument for quick remilitarization than how things developed so far." The panicked submission was without a name because "by now one has to be careful about sharing one's identity if hoping to avoid retributions and revenge aimed against oneself and one's family from such juvenile gangsters and youngsters who are not even afraid to brawl with armed policemen."[35] Geislhöringer himself also received numerous supportive letters. Such backing poured into his Munich office from all over West Germany. One such submission described "juvenile criminals as the foremost enemy of the state;" it also thanked the minister "in the

name of roughly a hundred thousand old, weak, war victims" for taking on this issue.[36]

However, local authorities in the city of Munich did still not agree
with Geislhöringer. Governed by a social democratic majority, they
saw the problem in less dramatic terms, and were thus less inclined
to move forward against *the Halbstarke*. For them, it was—if at all—an
exaggerated problem that would eventually fade away. The virtual denial of the existence of *the Halbstarke* problem also had more selfish
reasons: it limited the state's influence onto the local level. Munich had
its own city police until 1975—described by the newspaper *Die Süddeutsche Zeitung* as the mayor's little army at one point.[37] As a result,
authorities were extremely careful to mention issues of concern. It was
consequently not surprising that a meeting initiated by Geislhöringer
and city officials on 17 August did not bring the outcome the former
had hoped for.[38] Instead, several city officials questioned and eventually stopped the minister and his more stringent approach.[39] Deputy
Mayor Adolf Hieber and the Criminal Director Andreas Grasmüller at
this point even spoke about "exaggerated reports," claiming that the
fuss about *the Halbstarke* was "constructed."[40] In their view, existing
measures were more than adequate to deal with the problem.[41]

Yet an enduring support of some media outlets plus the events in
Munich-Allach more explicitly encouraged conservative voices to continue their efforts against the threat of *the Halbstarke*. In response to
SPD and FDP resistance, *Die Abendzeitung* published a long list of incidents of juvenile delinquency happening in the last months. This in-
ventory included the riots at the Auer Dult but also minor incidents,
like youngsters splashing pedestrians with water.[42] The shooting in
Allach also gave conservatives led by Geislhöringer and Junker a vantage point to push their agenda. Soon Junker reminded the readers of
regional newspapers about his earlier attempts to expand mechanisms
of control. And whereas Geislhöringer admitted that "shooting right
away" was not the answer, he still stood by his proposals in favor of
baton sticks and the surveillance of immoral and delinquent spaces,
now sharing such views on a national level.[43] Outspoken support for
such comments from all over West Germany again strengthened his
position. One such letter to Geislhöringer stated, "the more vehement
and forceful you clamp down, the more thankful people will be!" Another submission in the same context underlined that—compared to
the United States—"it was not too late" to act against *the Halbstarke*.[44]
At the same time, however, the shooting in Allach also raised concerns
regarding police brutality and Geislhöringer's rhetoric. The national

newspaper *Die Frankfurter Allgemeine Zeitung,* for instance, wondered "if not all of us [should] react a little more coolly towards the 'buzz-word' describing youthful delinquents, unlike—as recently demanded in Bavaria—rushing the police in with baton sticks?"[45] A political cartoon in a regional Bavarian paper portrayed Geislhöringer as a "fully strong" cowboy in a wild-west stand off against the "semistrong."[46] Such debates increasingly polarized society along political beliefs, regional contexts, and also age.

Discussions eventually resumed in the city council after the summer. At the first meeting on 11 September, conservative council member Franz Fackler put forward "urgency measure no. 47." It stated, "various well-known incidents and their reception within the public put the problem of the so-called 'Halbstarken' in Munich on the agenda; this problem has to be taken seriously not only in the interest of the young but also to protect the reputation of Munich." The proposal hoped for an open discussion and an in-depth analysis of the problem. Similar to Junker's earlier attempt, Fackler also wanted to strengthen the role of the police. To avoid comparisons to his unsuccessful predecessors, however, Fackler toned down his rhetoric. He specifically underlined that "in contrast to the opinion of others we do not believe that this problem can be solved by employing brute force; instead we push for consistent assistance for the young." Fackler also proposed additional resources for youth work. The council agreed with Fackler's general sentiments and assessments, but after a brief discussion deemed the term *Halbstarke* insufficient. Several council members even reminded their colleagues that youth had been delinquent before. The meeting ultimately adjourned after all members voiced their support for a general inquiry to study the problem.[47] Although Fackler had hoped for more, the council—like the state legislature—at least decided to investigate the problem.

Scrutinizing to Control

In October 1956, the state government put forward its report on juvenile delinquency in Munich not only to frame subsequent proposals and debates but also as a way to use *the Halbstarke* as a means to increase the state's influence overall. The Ministry of Culture and Education had taken a leading role during the creation of this blueprint. After numerous meetings, revisions, and constant discussions, a thirty-two-page "Memorandum Regarding the Problem of Semi-Grown-Ups" was submitted to state parliament. The report began with a by now standard dismissal of the term *Halbstarke* before outlining "typical characteristics of current juvenile delinquency." According to several statistics, juvenile crime was on the rise. This increase, according to the report, underlined "flawed trends" within society. The memorandum also briefly mentioned that girls are less likely to be criminals due to their "female mentality." While this understanding excluded female delinquency from rowdy behaviors, female sexual deviancy was still a concern. A precise breakdown of offenses then outlined that there were bigger problems at hand, including postwar destitution, a lack of adult supervision, and declining morals. In addition, the report named "inner reasons" for such troubles, namely a lack of support from adults and an increasing exposure to smut and filth in the media. Such language set the stage for several subsequent proposals. Moving directly from constructed meanings to precise mechanisms of social control, the Ministry of Culture and Education asked for more funds for schools and youth groups; it also called for better coordination between schools, teachers, and parents. Another proposal put the Ministry of the Interior in charge of creating stricter guidelines against "alluring entertainment." The level of enforcement of existing laws by the police had to be left up to the cities. According to the state proposal, however, more needed to be done. In this context, the report specifically pointed to Munich as a space with high crime. The memorandum also called on the Ministry of Justice to streamline the judicial process to ensure a coordinated application of the law. More funds, more law enforcement, and more coordination were needed to deal with these elements, the state memorandum concluded.[48] In this sense, this directive clearly illustrates that delinquent youth also provided a potential avenue for state authorities to gain more influence in the Bavarian capital.

The city of Munich acknowledged this proposal, but continued to follow its own approach. Coordinated by City Schools Inspector Anton Fingerle, its approach relied on the coordination of a variety of institutions. Numerous letters and reports from local schools and actual youth groups influenced the proposal. In this sense, the Bavarian capital included the voices of the young early on, possibly as a way to weaken the state's attempts to gain more say. In fact, the local city youth ring outlined the lack of funding for traditional youth organizations as one reason for *the Halbstarke;* it also proposed to build a racetrack where the young could drive around with their mopeds. Of course, most institutions consulted by authorities hoped for additional resources: local schools noted that too many students in one class limited their ability to teach and educate the young.[49] In a way, investigating *the Halbstarke* problem became a convenient avenue for local institutions to ask for more money and support.

The inclusion of the actual young still marked a dramatic shift in discussions. Shortly after the original meeting of the city council in September 1956, Council Member August Mühlbauer had invited the young to a "Young Citizens and Youth Forum" in Munich's Hofbräu-hauskeller restaurant.[50] The title of the event was, "Do Halbstarke Exist?"[51] During the meeting, social democratic State Representative Rudolf Schlichtinger briefly introduced the topic of concern, at times directed at the supposed male delinquents present at the event. The latter, above all, critiqued the term *Halbstarke*. One youngster insisted, "We are not 'Halbstarke'!"[52] Others agreed: "We are not Halbstarke, but we are provoked. If in the evening we stand around at some corner, talking, if someone sees us on our mopeds, or if we play our music at a restaurant, then it is always the same: 'Look, here they are, the Halb-starke, they miss the army.'"[53] Several undercover policemen attending the meeting heard similar statements from these supposed "anticiti-zens;"[54] they also learned that the young simply looked for a place to mingle and to let off steam—to be young.

The lack of such city spaces for youth in Munich should not have been surprising. During the crisis years Munich tried to accommodate a seemingly endless amount of refugees, making the reconstruction of housing a main priority. Spaces for youth, on the other hand, had been a secondary concern, especially once traditional institutions for youth reappeared. As a result, lower- and working-class youngsters in particular felt not only a lack of adequate housing but also the need for more open spaces: they rarely had their own rooms and could also sel-dom afford to escape the city and enjoy the beauty of its surroundings. Besides, once the U.S. Military Government began playing a less active role, open youth groups in the city like the GYA, which were accessible to all and less controlled, closed their doors, or traditional adult-super-vised setups absorbed them. There, authorities monitored youngsters closely, making sure the young did what they were told. American mu-sic was certainly not welcome or allowed in such environments. Ac-cording to one youngster, even in more open settings "there is always a youth worker that wants you to do 'something meaningful.'"[55] As a re-sult, youth hung out at movie theaters or in ice cream parlors instead. For those without the needed financial means, street corners in work-ing-class neighborhoods became their space. Here, they had hoped, they could enjoy themselves without constant supervision. When the young shared such information at the meeting with authorities, it be-came apparent that both sides had never spoken to each other about such problems. Authorities had feared *the Halbstarke* throughout the last weeks and months without ever making the attempt to approach the actual young. Once this initial step had taken place, then solutions became quite obvious: more spaces for the young within Munich's urban landscape.

Aware of the potential of such meetings, organizers continued conversations and tried to capitalize from their success. In October 1956, politicians and authorities discussed the current situation with youngsters at a local trade school. Again, supposed *Halbstarke* voiced their opinions. One stated, "We are condemned to be the Halbstarke and thereby act like them."[56] Another youngster reiterated the common view that there was no space for youth in the city by asking, "Where can we go in the city without raising suspicion?"[57] These and many other statements indicated that the young had closely and critically followed debates. According to one young participant, "The Halbstarke is a topic of concern only in an effort to sustain the importance of the military";[58] another one noted that this image merely provided sensationalist headlines for the media. Rudolf Schlichtinger reported on the triumph of such meetings in January 1957;[59] he was also amongst those not shy to self-righteously promote his own ability to potentially solve *the Halbstarke* problem.

Such meetings eventually helped shift media reporting. With national media outlets like the newspaper *Westdeutsche Allgemeine Zeitung* reporting on attempts to invite gang leaders in the Bavarian capital early on,[60] local papers soon followed. *Die Süddeutsche Zeitung* wondered, "Off the streets, but where to?"[61] Even the sensationalist tabloid *Die Abendzeitung* ultimately revised its approach. Originally responsible for the fake headlines about the gang of skulls, it had warned authorities of *the Halbstarke* until late August; it then changed its tone after the public forum at the Hofbräuhauskeller restaurant, not without one more final story: only a week after the initial meeting, *Die Abendzeitung* invited the young to its agency, underlining the newspaper's attempt to profit from these shifts. The paper extensively covered every step of how *the Halbstarke* showed up at its office in Munich. In a climactic description it then debunked the storyline noting that these male youngsters were not any different from other boys.[62] Indeed, *Die Abendzeitung* from thereon forward actively helped defuse the situation. For example, it forwarded a report to the police including the youngsters' "complaints about the behaviors of the police. The debate was factual and serious, and it became obvious that an open conversation between these youngsters and the police was crucial in order to deal with tensions."[63] The tabloid initially condemning and actively constructing *the Halbstarke* now tried to mediate on behalf of the young, and in that way still spoke for them. Still married to the idea of publishing on *the Halbstarke* in some way—and possibly realizing the potential within youth as future readers—*Die Abendzeitung* also proposed to set up a rock 'n' roll concert in Munich. This concert took place at the Deutsche Museum and marked a striking success. As the "first major youth party" in Munich,[64] it included local stars like "the German Bill Haley" Paul Würges, and Max Greger.[65] In addition, it was among the first appearace of rising new teenage idol Peter Kraus. He described the situation, noting, "I see excited faces, girls and boys pounding along with the rhythm. Unbelievable!"[66] A contemporary commentator followed up on this statement, writing,

> The hall with 2,500 [available] seats was packed. The young people did not show up—as expected—in their "Halbstarken clothes," but in their "Sunday dress".... There was one uncomfortable situation, when they could have released their energy by destroying the seating. The jazz orchestra leader, however, calmed down the excited crowd with a couple of humorous and fine statements, and the event continued without any problems.[67]

Die Abendzeitung proudly noted the applause for the concert and the success of such rock 'n' roll events. But at the same time, subsequent conversations about the need for spaces for youth also outlined underlying adult strategies: to get the young off the streets. Authorities interested in the well-being of the young and those hoping to have such delinquents in sight understood the power of music as a way to lure youngsters into a controlled space. The concert at the Deutsche Museum did exactly that. According to one adult contemporary, promoting the construction of additional open youth facilities can provide "order and morals needed so desperately."[68]

Overall, efforts to involve *the Halbstarke* and bring them off the streets continued beyond these events. Kurt Seelmann became the driving force behind this new method. Director of the Youth Welfare Office since 1955, he approached the topic in a more practical manner. Seelmann regularly invited local youngsters for discussions into his office and tried to build lasting relationships with young people throughout his tenure. Seelmann also made a specific attempt to rebuild the relationship between the police and the young. Those youngsters interested in a local event sponsored by the city of Munich had to go to the local police station to get tickets. This setup helped decrease animosities between both groups and further defused a tense environment. Soon described by the media as "the father of the Halbstarke,"[69] Seelmann set up various programs for the young, thus taking discussions about "bored rioters" seriously.[70] Additional funding made such initiatives possible. In this sense, the city listened to youth and offered what they hoped for; but it also meant that youth again found itself within organized formats and under official adult supervision.[71]

Controlling *the Teenager*

The tolerance for *teenage* misbehaviors was lower compared to that for *the Halbstarke,* thus falling in line with previous discussions of youth in the crisis years. Whereas male youngsters faced retribution for their rebellious behaviors aimed directly at authorities, female youngsters feared stringent measures due to age, gender, and sexuality. In addition, a growing infiltration and invasion of female spaces by American products increasingly worried authorities.[72] Besides, adults perceived those out dancing as challenging morality within a sexually repressive 1950s society, describing such misbehaviors as provocations "against the norms of female grace and male chivalry."[73] As a result, they often replied with harsh retributions in response to seemingly minor incidents.

Parents, neighbors, and even strangers helped control female youth. The role of parents as a first line of defense became even more important than before given American influences. Historically less visible in a repressive society, adult authorities generally confined female youth to the domestic sphere. Especially after puberty parents rarely allowed their daughters to leave the house for leisurely activities. The possibility of meeting male youngsters was a risk far too high for many. Sexual repression, pushed by a nervous and partially paranoid society, influenced these sentiments and limited the possibilities of *the teenager* to even get into trouble. Young girls faced strict rules because middle-class families in particular were concerned about religious morality embedded within conservative values and would not jeopardize their social and moral status. At times, such struggles took place over seemingly benign objects. As one young female recalled, "My dad hated make-up. First I put on slightly colored lipstick and some black eyeliner. He went wild. He also did not like when I had bangs [hair]. The forehead had to be visible."[74] Furthermore, the so-called "pimping paragraph" was still in place, punishing everyone who encouraged or merely provided an apartment for unmarried relationships. Actually, in May 1953 local law enforcement shut down a space within a building in Munich deemed deviant; the owner was sent to prison based on the accusation that she

encouraged relations between unmarried couples.[75] This public scrutiny of sexuality combined with historic stereotypes exposed *the teenager* in particular to the public gaze and repression.

Some recent scholarship provides additional insights into such dynamics, notably the work of historian Peter Wensierski. He notes regarding female deviancy:

> Sexual danger lurked everywhere, especially in music from the United
> States. In her room Gisela drew a small image of Elvis on the wall. Her
> mother had forbidden her to hang up photos or posters from movies.
> Once her mother saw the painting she yelled, "of all, it has to be that
> Elvis! With his … pelvis shaking!" There was a major fight and Gisela
> had to remove Elvis. If her idol Elvis was actually on the radio for once,
> she turned it on louder and enjoyed his music at the window. She had to
> pay for this brief moment of joy. "The neighbors called the local Youth
> Welfare Office, because they felt that the music was too loud. The next
> day a welfare worker came."[76]

The local official was a frequent and unannounced guest because a single mother raised Gisela. Statements like "That does not suit a girl!"[77]
became the standard warning voiced by the official. However,

> most dangerous remained the neighbors because they seemed to spend
> their whole day watching the street from behind the curtains. The girl
> [Gisela] thus met up with friends outside the neighborhood. She liked
> the bold youngsters on their mopeds. If she ever rode with one of them
> she made sure to get off a couple blocks down the street and walked
> home, passing by the spies behind their curtains.[78]

Females dancing to rock 'n' roll music were also a prime concern
of adult contemporaries. Whereas Youth Protection Laws and discussions regarding *the Halbstarke* provided some leverage to keep *the
teenager* away from dance floors, authorities could not restrict jukeboxes available in countless milk bars or cafés. By 1957, there were
already 12,000 jukeboxes throughout West Germany; three years later
there were 50,000.[79] Youngsters could now meet at ice cream parlors
or restaurants during the day to listen and dance to rock 'n' roll music.
As one youngster remembered, "We met whenever we could at ice-
cream parlors…. There, we drank milkshakes and danced."[80] Authorities soon wondered about these immoral spaces, asking "How about
youth protection regarding these jukeboxes?"[81] Yet in most instances
it was well-placed guilt and shame that was supposed to keep *the
teenager* away from these deviant spaces. The youngster cited above
followed her statement by saying, "This was not acceptable, this was
not right."[82] Female sexuality also played a key role as contemporaries

hoped to strengthen traditional values. If seen within certain environments, then *the teenager* risked besmirching her good reputation and
purity, and potentially that of her family. Broad definitions of what that
meant became tools to control young girls. For example, female purity
was juxtaposed with being a prostitute, and simply spending time in
an ice-cream parlor while rock 'n' roll music was playing could be constructed as being immoral. Even if young girls cared little about such
pressures, their parents wanted to avoid public shame. Teenage pregnancy was the worst-case scenario, and demonizing sexual relations
instead of discussing possible dangers remained the norm.

Those young females who defied societal pressures generally faced
institutionalization. Scholar Annette Lützke wrote about female deviants in the Rhineland and noted,

> contrary to male youth, criminal behaviors did not play a major role
> regarding young girls. Seemingly normal behaviors like "running away,"
> "staying out late at night," and "bad manners," on the other hand, be-
> came deemed as "sexual deviancy." Until well into the early 1970s "roam-
> ing around," going to dance clubs, smoking and putting on make-up
> were seen as "sexual deficits" and "dangerous passions."[83]

Lützke also argues that authorities institutionalized girls based on
their cultural interests. Adult officials deemed listening to rock 'n' roll
music, idolizing Elvis, and mimicking certain behaviors as abnormal, and reason enough for juvenile detention;[84] other scholars agree
with such interpretations.[85] As outlined by Wensierski, "those [female
youngsters] ending up in a foster home rarely arrived there because
they were foster children or criminals."[86] Instead, throughout the 1950s
girls ended up in disciplinary institutions based on minor incidents
and bagatelles. In fact, the girl Gisela introduced earlier used cacao
and water to fabricate her own make-up. While in front of the mirror
she was trying to mimic the pout and other facial expressions of Brigitte Bardot. For her mother, neighbors, and the local youth welfare
officer such behaviors were a sign of sexual and moral deviancy. This
construal brought Gisela into a religious institution for young girls.[87]
Of course, authorities could not take children away without parental
consent. However, legal guardians like Gisela's mother regularly saw a
stay in a disciplinary institution as a way to straighten out their children. In a time when Family Minister Wuermeling, among others,
preached purity, restraint, and self-denial, rigid reactions in response
to even the most minor misbehaviors seemed more than justifiable.

Once committed to such institutions, life for young females was
hard. In the state of Bavaria, church officials generally supervised and

ran such youth detention. Youngsters had to follow strict regulations, which meant a life of abstinence similar to a monastery. As outlined by Wensierski when discussing these issues more broadly, beatings or cold water became regular tools to bring *the teenager* back from the abyss towards deviance.[88] To be locked away, to constantly feel guilty, and to endure a variety of other harsh treatments affected those experiencing such retributions for the rest of their lives. The limited scholarship on girls sent to such institutions paints a dismal picture. According to a recent study, in 1952, authorities institutionalized 79.2 percent of those girls in such facilities due to their supposed "sexual deviancy"; in 1959, roaming around was the main reason for being admitted to an institution.[89] Most girls had a lower-class background, although a slight shift is apparent by the mid-1950s.[90] Throughout their time in these institutions, young women learned how to take their role within society: they were trained how to cook, iron, and wash, and they also learned how to be obedient. As one scholar points out, "preparation for marriage" was the prime objective.[91] Patriarchy called for self-sacrificing wives and mothers, characteristics *the teenager* lacked. As a result, young women became aligned with their role in society, while young men if sent to similar homes had to work in the fields.[92] Historian Maria Fischer-Kowalski is thus right when hinting at continuities and concluding, "there probably never was any other young generations—before or after them—that had so large a proportion ending up in penitentiaries and jails (despite the considerable changes in judicial policies)."[93]

Conforming, Commercializing, and Re-Creating Youth

Apart from such direct retributions, adult contemporaries also found ways to deal with teenager clubs. Authorities employed similar tactics as these put forward against *the Halbstarke* and his street-corner societies. In Munich, local officials had made specific attempts to get *the teenager* into supervised spaces early on. To bring her to concerts like the one at the German Museum was one way to approach this problem. But more measures seemed necessary to prevent unmonitored activities among female youngsters within teenager clubs more specifically. Since direct control was impossible within the private sphere, the Youth Welfare Office in Munich pursued a different route. Rooted in the intention to help, authorities created public forums and spaces for *the teenager* to mingle with others. Whereas such offers gave local clubs potentially more opportunities for various activities, it also lured *the teenager* out of unsupervised private spaces. In Munich, for instance, the Youth Welfare Office not only sponsored a teenager newspaper but also provided access to facilities in local youth centers and schools. Soon youth workers had access and could monitor club activities given that they were the ones providing funding and facilities.[94] Moreover, increased direct funding allowed traditional and largely supervised youth organizations like the City Youth Ring to expand its programs. Clubs like the Karo-Rot-Club, on the other hand, received much less support. With such setups authorities increasingly pulled *the teenager* out of a less-controlled private sphere and back into traditionally supervised formats.[95] In little time clubs had been either fully absorbed or at least partially conformed. As one adult commentator noted in this context, it was quite "pleasant" how quiet it had become regarding free youth clubs.[96]

Apart from local institutions, numerous marketing organizations equally began trying to influence teenager clubs. Increasingly aware of the purchasing power of youth, various businesses saw teenager clubs and their parties as useful access points into a growing youth culture and potential markets. Soon, the teenager club in the Munich suburb of Harlaching had some product placement in an article about "Blue Jeans—The Blue Miracle" in its first newsletter.[97] This article discussed the history of Levi Jeans while showing a conveniently placed Levi Jeans commercial on its back cover.[98] Similar examples of such early advertisement appeared elsewhere, including an article about the Teenager Club 17 and its "visit of the teenager-café Nestlé."[99] Nestlé became the corporate sponsor of Munich's Teenager Club 17, and even opened up a little café for teenagers. The reaction to such growing influence was mixed. One young contributor to a teenage magazine noted, "It would be nice if businesses would give their 'surplus funds' to youth clubs, youth organizations, and other institutions;"[100] other youngsters felt mocked. Wondering when "commercial success became equal with quality,"[101] they questioned increasingly conformist narratives. Some even wondered why everyone, and all of a sudden, claimed to speak for them. One young voice nicely summarized such sentiments in a letter to a Munich teenager magazine *Harlach-Pinguin* in 1959. Titled "Teenager—Fair Game for Business Men,"[102] the author described how a whole industry literally attacks the young:

> But neither the word Halbstarke nor the word Teenager is from them. Picked-up, mocked, and used! Something has to be done for the young, they argued with an alarmed voice…. Yet there was no help to be expected from adults. That is why I call on the young: keep your eyes and ears open, check everything offered to you! Don't let those use you who

only care about your money, and nothing else. Resist against such attempts and respond by showing off your own powers.[103]

The gradual commercialization of youth marked a much larger paradigm shift, especially with the rise of a "newly developing teenager-
consumption industry."[104] According to historian Jürgen Zinnecker, up
until the mid-1950s the "young were organized, activated, and steered
... by state, political, and pedagogical institutions."[105] Though granting
youth limited agency with this analysis, Zinnecker is right when he
notices that after that time another force came into play: the commercial sector. This power became very visible given the availability
of products like movies and music specifically created for the young;
yet the commercial sector also increasingly played an important role
as "secret co-educators"[106] of youth because it helped frame, construct,
and eventually control youth and society.

That the commercial sector specifically targeted *the teenager* and *the
Halbstarke* was not surprising. According to a study by the Society for
Market Research in 1959, West German youngsters had an average
of forty Deutsche Marks available each month, adding up to a total
spending capacity of roughly 2.6 billion Deutsche Marks a year in West
Germany.[107] Whereas such numbers underlined the growing purchasing power of the young, success stories regarding this new market
from the United States painted a promising picture for corporations.[108]
After all, as some noticed quickly, "the teenager ... was not only an actual and potential consumer ... but also the consumer of the future. In
addition, youngsters greatly influenced the consumer choices of their
parents."[109] Soon different groups sought out ways to target the youth,
and tap into "the money in blue jeans,"[110] resulting in savvy marketing
approaches in place by the late 1950s.

In order to make male and female youth profitable, however, it had
to be reinvented. Although *the Halbstarke* and *the teenager* were purchasing certain products, additional commercialization seemed difficult: rebellious youngsters from a working-class background were a
limited market too closely associated with juvenile delinquency and
trouble; overly sexual females could not be promoted in a sexually repressive society. These limitations resulted in a major rebranding effort. The youth magazine *Bravo* was on its forefront. Soon to become
a "guide to normality,"[111] it was among the first to see the real potential
of marketing youth. It had followed the less successful magazine *Die
Rasselbande* to become the supposed mouthpiece of youth by the end
of the decade.[112] For fifty pennies, this *Magazin für Film und Fernsehen*
discussed the life of TV and movie stars as well as popular music and

culture. It ran stories on Marilyn Monroe, rowdies, and James Dean. Brigitte Bardot was on the cover of *Bravo* nine times and stories about James Dean dominated early editions.[113] As a perfect platform to utilize, frame, and eventually conform images of youth, *Bravo* openly dismissed the rebellious behaviors of *the Halbstarke*. It employed various approaches and questioned the existence of *the Halbstarke* altogether. In September 1956 an article read, "*Bravo* Demands: An End with This! There is not a Halbstarken generation and no Halbstarke danger! There are a couple of rowdies, those have always been around."[114] It proposed a more open-minded solution similar to the one in Munich. In this case, the city of West Berlin had approached *the Halbstarke,* and *Bravo* happily reported on it: "The mayor provided a space for the young and paid for an excellent jazz-band. A happy end because a mayor for once used his brain and not the baton stick!"[115] At the same time, however, *Bravo* actively used the term *Halbstarke* to distinguish its own concept of youth: a newly defined teenager. The magazine followed gangsters and juvenile delinquents in various publications and frequently referenced the term *Halbstarke*. These were, according to the magazine, not the majority of youngsters; the magazine also used the term *Halbstarke* to describe the rough life of new teenage star and actor Horst Buchholz, who, of course, had overcome his difficult past to become the new teenager.[116]

The popularity of Elvis provided another excellent platform and stage to reframe juvenile deviancy, embodied by *the Halbstarke* and *the teenager.* The rise of Elvis had created an outrage. He was, after all, moving around his pelvis and seducing German youth to challenge sexual repression; his music made the young go wild while his haircut was just shocking. *Bravo* had closely followed his rise, always ready to show the appropriate outrage. Yet again and again, *Bravo* also defused rumors by clearing up simple misunderstandings, primarily about Elvis. In one *Bravo* story the magazine explained the "scandal" around the second bed in Elvis's bedroom: it was meant for his parents, to tell him a goodnight story, and keep him company so he could fall asleep.[117] Anecdotes like this one made him a more acceptable star. By 1958, Elvis was then drafted into the U.S. Army, an event that provided an even better platform to reframe this rebellious star. *Bravo* followed his introduction into the military as part of a transition from overly sexual rebel to clean-cut gentleman stationed in West Germany. First, the U.S. Army cut his hair, and he lost his sideburns. *Bravo* skillfully used this change in appearance to outline that the well-known ducktail, displayed by many youngsters, was not fashionable anymore. Moreover, Elvis now wore a uniform. Whereas *Bravo* generally remained rather critical towards West German militarization, the look of a uniform—as seen on the cover of *Bravo* in fall 1958—visibly underscored that Elvis had conformed to societal norms[118] [Figure 4.1]. John Lennon noted in this context later on that Elvis died when he joined the army,[119] thus more directly describing what one scholar has portrayed as being nor-

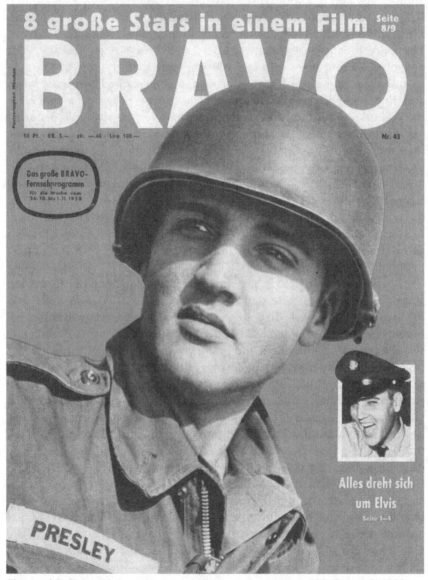

Figure 4.1 Elvis and the army: cover of the youth magazine *BRAVO*, no. 43, 1958. Courtesy of *BRAVO*.

malized through military service.[120] Once Elvis sang the German folk song "Muss i denn zum Städtele hinaus" (Wooden Heart) with a puppet in 1960,[121] he had silenced widespread concerns amongst adults, paved the way for remaining delinquents to normalize, and helped stabilize traditional norms.[122]

While there now was an avenue for leaving delinquency behind, *Bravo* also provided the perfect alternative idol for the new male-teenager: Munich native Peter Kraus. Ever since one of his first major shows at the concert in the Deutsche Museum in the Bavarian capital *Bravo* had vigorously promoted him. The magazine put Kraus on numerous covers and made him the first male "puzzle of stars." A series titled "When Teenagers Dream—The Peter Kraus Story" had also provided the adequate narrative for the rise of Kraus.[123] According to one educator, this should be "tolerated.... Better to have Peter Kraus as an idol than none at all. He merely tries to seduce youngsters to yodel, not to become criminals."[124] Kraus was thus a produced-teenage star without any rebellious characteristics; he was also an excellent marketing product. Soon the new male teenager could buy numerous records and, of course, the official Peter Kraus pullover.[125] Again, not all youngsters liked this transition. Those interested in harsher tunes saw him as a fluffy rip-off. In fact, during the event Record Hop in Munich's Löwenbräukeller restaurant in February 1960 local youngsters showed their distaste. When the disk jockey tried to play Peter Kraus's song "Tiger," he found himself against an angry crowd.[126] Savvy marketing strategists reacted to such incidents, hoping to profit from these dissatisfied groups as well. As a result, they created the more rebellious Ted Herold, the star of "tough guys."[127] His success remained limited, as he could never enthuse real rock 'n' roll fans. But his appearance did outline how advanced business models meant to target youth had developed in a short amount of time.

Bravo also pushed female stars, most notably Cornelia "Conny" Froboess.[128] She had been a star since she sang about bringing bathing trunks to the beach as a child. With her short haircut and bubbly attitude she was nowhere near a sexually deviant female youngster. According to social commentator Jean Améry, she was harmless and would certainly not seduce anyone: "With her the youth is in good hands, like in a monastery. No smell of whisky, no smoke of cigarettes, no new crap: best prewar goods in sterile plastic postwar wrapping. The conformism of conny-formism is everything worried parents and educators ever dreamed of."[129] Youth was indeed in safe hands, and by the early 1960s, Conny and Peter—the "teenage-couple made in heaven"[130]—dominated popular youth culture and made youth profitable [Figure 4.2]. They played in movies like *Wenn die Conny mit dem Peter* (1958) or *Conny und Peter machen Musik* (1960). These romantic comedies followed traditional slapstick formats, often with a didactic ending. As a fusion of youth culture and escapist *Heimatfilm,* main

Figure 4.2 Teenage stars Conny and Peter: cover of the youth magazine *BRAVO,* no. 52, 1958. Courtesy of *BRAVO.*

characters questioned authority in a controlled manner. Soon this version of youth became a platform for sharing a simplistic and conservative morality. Love, friendship, family, and other traditional values were in the center of the plot. The movie *Wenn die Conny mit dem Peter,* for instance, evolved around life at school, love, and music. Instead of oversexualized dancing and deadly dares, Conny and Peter worked together to make money for an upcoming music festival. That they snuck out school to fulfill this fantasy was their worst crime. According Améry, "these movies were not teenager films but fairy tales for children."[131] Commercialization had helped tame and calm the rebellious nature of *the teenager* and *the Halbstarke,* and made them into a fun, conformist, and apolitical marketing product for male and female youth between thirteen and nineteen.

Soon an appropriate and fitting teenage idol seemed available for everyone, especially for young females. Initially constructed as a sexually deviant girl endangering gender roles, reproduction, and the family, *the teenager* increasingly shed all of these characteristics. *Bravo* again provided the requisite narrative. As outlined by journalist Wiebke Nieland, *Bravo* featured certain types or images of femininity. First, there was "the successful businesswoman,"[132] embodied by triumphant stars like Caterina Valente. In this context *Bravo* underscored the hard work it took to make it in a male-dominated world. Caterina was emancipated. After all, she could get a cab in New York City by herself. Nonetheless, she still relied on a caring husband. According to *Bravo,* "The hungry Caterina loves to be fed by Eric," her husband and provider.[133] The second image featured in *Bravo* was "the sex symbol."[134] Most notably embodied by Brigitte Bardot, the youth magazine made sure to demonize her scandalous behaviors more and more. *Bravo* described her as "a girl like Satan,"[135] and frequently illustrated how "she is playing a brutal game: today she kisses him, tomorrow she is pushing him away."[136] The third image was the cute teenager. This was Romy Schneider, the "ideal teenager."[137] Working closely with her mother, Romy was nowhere near erotica, sex, or other deviancies. Instead, she always had a smile on her face and was truly innocent. In 1960, social commentator Jean Améry noted, "Romy and blue jeans, Romy and rock 'n' roll, Romy and 'Bonjour Tristesse,' Romy and 'necking' in the car—no, that does not go together, that does not make sense, that does not work."[138] According to Nieland, "These three types of women are juxtaposed with the image of a caring mother. In the life of a young woman this societal model marked the prime purpose and objective of her path through life."[139] *Bravo* illustrated this setup in numerous publications. Apart from aligning stars like Caterina Valente with the role of the obedient wife and mother, *Bravo* also openly dismissed questionable behaviors. In fact, the youth magazine publically shamed Hungarian actress Eva Bartok because five different men could supposedly be the father of her child. At the same time, *Bravo* promoted the image of actress Ruth Leuwerik as "the mother of the nation."[140] It was thus not surprising that Ruth Leuwerik as well as Romy Schneider remained among the top three for the fan prize OTTO in the late 1950s. By then, being a teenager was an accepted pre-stage towards adulthood and part of the road towards becoming a caring mother and obedient wife within a patriarchal and still rather conservative society.

Apart from utilizing the rich and famous to reframe *the teenager*, *Bravo* also created its own image of female youth: Steffi. In August 1958, she first appeared in *Bravo*.[141] In numerous editions thereafter, she defended the young against adults. In the first episode of her weekly diary-like column, Steffi wrote that all adults "think youngsters are stupid."[142] She noted, "Of course we Teenagers (and twenty-year-olds) are upset about the lack of understanding from 'adults.' It is especially distressing to hear how upset they are about us.... Even discussions about the 'Halbstarke' are upsetting—especially since no one can tell me, what a 'Halbstarke' even is."[143] That she stood up for youth made her a more credible figure and a supposed representative of the young. Yet the fictional persona Steffi was only slightly reminiscent of *the teenager*. Not rebellious or overly sexual, she defined what it meant to be normal. In fact, her persona was a productive fiction. Instead of a young girl writing her column, it had been a retired male schoolteacher all along.[144] Thus domesticated, normalized, and commercialized by a dominant male structure interested in profit, Steffi became the proto-type of a new marketing product. *Bravo* knew that overly rebellious characteristics could hinder profit. Hence, in her column, Steffi walked a fine line between conservative values and some challenges to rigid societal structures. Steffi proudly wore blue jeans and would not mind being called deviant for doing so; she also enjoyed the music of Peter Kraus. Being young was, after all, fun.[145] But Steffi also respected her parents, especially her father.[146] Steffi as the new teenager was modern when it came to youth culture but still traditional regarding her moral values, ideals, and lifestyle choices. She stated, for example, that it is something "wonderful to be a girl because one does not have to initiate conversation."[147] In a patriarchic society, men carried conversations. Steffi also did not shy away from more difficult topics. She dealt with teenage pregnancy when one of her friends got pregnant. Whereas she did not judge her friend directly, she still raised concerns when wondering if that girl could be happy now that she was missing school and getting married.[148] Thus siding with traditional norms, Steffi helped sustain conservative sexual morals, making sure to demonize early sexual relations along the way. She also reasserted the idea that politics remained a male domain. Indeed, she admitted, "I do not understand anything about politics,"[149] illustrating that *Bravo* was not neutral but quite conservative when it came to societal norms and gender roles. If she ever made a political comment, she was sure to frame it kindly to avoid offending anyone. To speak out against racial discrimination in the United States in one of her diary entries, for instance, was safe.[150] Too much political discussion, however, namely around more divisive issues, could harm business, and *Bravo* thus avoided it altogether—a trend most notable in the 1960s. In this sense, Steffi was herself a true marketing product, and she hence fit in with "the international standardization of a youth generation."[151]

In order to further sustain this new image of youth, the division between adults and youngsters was crucial. Arguably, *Bravo* came up with various ways to construct and strengthen generational differences. Apart from Steffi's frequent references to adults, it was the series "Wir & Ihr," or "Us & You,"[152] that most clearly exemplifies such attempts. Two teenagers and two adults discussed a topic of concern, like, "Should a young girl be allowed to go to London?"[153] Of course, discussions also touched on natalist ideas, noting, for instance, that having a child is a blessing for any relationship. Whereas opinions were not always divided based on age, the discussion format as such sustained categories of us vs. them, with the Other being an adult. As a result, this forum became a way to construct, highlight, and sustain generational differences in the context of what youngsters should and should not do; it also created a community of youth as conceived by *Bravo*.

Overall, such approaches helped align teenagers with the newspaper and made sure that *Bravo* kept its preferable and profitable audience; it also sustained the arrival of youth as an interlude before becoming domesticated within the traditional family.[154] Throughout this process, *Bravo* never hid its attempts to frame and thereby partially control images of youth. According to the magazine, "We steer, but you [the young] decide where the journey will take us."[155] Whereas it would not steer the magazine into troubling and thus unprofitable waters, the magazine gave the young a voice. Youth was not simply a vessel to be filled, exploited, and used. Instead, *Bravo* remained connected to its readers and broader audience on numerous levels. Such aspects allowed it to pick up trends early and ensured its success as a trendsetter. As a result, commercialization was not equal to victimization. Instead, some of the young actively participated in creating this new image of youth. When discussions about sexuality became more open and profitable, then *Bravo* was on the forefront regarding these issues and at that point made sure, as one scholar put it, to help in "stabilizing the heterosexual matrix in West Germany's youth culture."[156] Surveys were thus important. Yet the most imperative feedback remained circulation numbers,[157] as profit was rarely equated with quality. It was thus not surprising that *Bravo* did not take any risks regarding political discussions, and even neglected engaging with or even acknowledging the student movement of the 1960s. After all, protesting youngsters and politics were potentially dangerous for profit.

In 1958, West Germany experienced so-called rock 'n' roll riots. In West Berlin, Hamburg, Essen, and Stuttgart numerous youngsters went wild during concerts of Bill Haley, and destroyed the interior of various venues. Local authorities in Munich followed Haley's tour and news stories with great alarm. One official sent a concerned letter to the Minister of the Interior underlining how "these Halbstarke and their hysterical female entourage" go wild at such concerts.[158] *Die Süddeutsche Zeitung* illustrated that a simple spark could make the young go crazy.[159] The more conservative newspaper *Die Bayerische Staatszeitung* later summarized the events by describing Haley's performance as "loud noise (this is in no way singing)" that provided the background for rioting.[160] For that newspaper such discussions set the stage for outlining the need to clamp down on popular youth culture right away. As news from rock 'n' roll riots poured into Munich, the paper attracted support. Local educators, social commentators, and numerous groups argued and petitioned for the termination of a scheduled Haley concert in Munich. According to one petition, attempts to let the American rock 'n' roll star play in the Bavarian capital "would exacerbate primitive instincts within the young" and "mock all previous attempts to deal with the problems of youth."[161] However, neither city nor state officials had the authority to prevent the event. Trouble seemed to return to Munich.

Haley's gig in Munich did not end in a riot. The renter of the concert venue and several others involved in the production made sure to impose a high insurance rate as a way to protect themselves. Financial liabilities were thus employed to target any potential provocations by the band that could spark riots. But this was not the only reason youth did not go wild. After all, youngsters knew little about higher liabilities for stars. Still, no aggressive *Halbstarke* or sexually open *teenager* started a riot. Munich, compared to other cities, seemed to have its youngsters under control. With juvenile delinquency never the problem it was made out to be in the first place, the dialogue between city officials and the young had also helped defuse some situations. In addition, *the Halbstarke* and *the teenager* had been conformed since their original arrival or reappearance in the early 1950s. Deemed less rebellious and provocative, youngsters in their teens were now teenagers. Once some youngsters went wild at Bill Haley concerts elsewhere then the new teenager was ready to dismiss this deviation from the teenage norm.[162] In fact, Steffi, Conny Froboess, and Peter Kraus publicly shunned and slandered rioters, and *Bravo* provided the forum for such comments.[163] Hence, the new teenager internalized mechanisms of control and took the role of officials and authorities. This development was a sign for the growing power of youth within society; but it was also an indication that stringent mechanisms of control remained in place.

At the same time the appearance of *the teenager* and *the Halbstarke* had changed the role of youth. Female youth now had more options when growing up. Whereas various limitations remained in place, the rhetoric regarding *the teenager* had created certain niches. By the end of the decade, for example, it was socially accepted to listen to partially normalized rock 'n' roll tunes, as long as the future role as a mother remained untouched. Americanized youth culture and British pop music thus continued to dominate Munich's history in subsequent periods as artists like The Beatles, The Rolling Stones, or Jimi Hendrix increasingly defined a whole generation. Moreover, male youngsters had employed the image of *the Halbstarke* to demand changes regarding youth policies. Although this social group remained under surveillance at the Auer Dult and other events in the upcoming years,[164] actual youngsters now had a say regarding facilities for youth. According to city officials Anton Fingerle and Kurt Seelmann in a newspaper interview in March 1959, the young had numerous open youth groups, parties, and other events to go to; they were also engaged in a dialogue with the police. Besides, Seelmann was in contact with ten *Blas'n*. Although this newspaper article pointed out that there were still not enough open youth facilities, authorities quoted in the article highlighted that riots had ended.[165] One commentator even spoke to the benefits of the panic, stating, "The public had become aware of the problems certain age groups face through its panicked reaction to the misdeeds of so-called 'Halbstarke.'"[166] In this sense, a perceived threat creating a public outrage had led to promising debates and at least some positive changes for the young.

Attempts to consolidate and protect normality throughout the miracle years are easily traceable when discussing youth. As illustrated in this section, embodiments of delinquency became ways to recapture supposed threats to productivity, stability, and moral order; controlling and—at times—reframing these images meant also controlling society, and ensured continuity of traditional values and beliefs. According to adults, youth should be working hard all week and use their leisure in a productive way; it also meant settling down and having a family, especially for young girls. Even though 1950s Munich remained a very traditional place,[167] change was visible. As some youngsters increasingly left their assigned role in the shadow of social constructs, they felt that youth was a force in history. Supported by commercial interests, they saw how authorities, as one scholar put it, feared the new "power of the teenagers."[168] Soon they found allies willing to support them, either because they truly wanted to help or because they hoped to make a profit or advance their careers. Hence, the agency of youth began to increase as the grip of adult authorities within an increasingly democratic structure slowly shrank. This reading captures underlining tensions and illustrates that the miracle years were only static on the surface, and that continuities *and* changes are visible as Munich slowly came of age.

Notes

1. Becker, "Rock'n Roll: Symbol der Auflehnung," 27.
2. "Die Reiz-Überflutung," *Der Spiegel,* 11 July 1956. See also: Jürgen Kniep, *"Keine Jugendfreigabe!" Filmzensur in Westdeutschland 1949–1990* (Göttingen, 2010), 360–61.
3. Discussions focusing on smut and filth (*Schmutz und Schund*) in the post–World War II period illustrate a rich history of trying to censor Americanization and foreign influences, often by employing youth as the underlining reasoning. See: Kniep, *"Keine Jugendfreigabe!"* For the situation in Munich in particular see, for instance: BayHStAM, Ministerium des Inneren 92084; BayHStAM, Ministerium des Inneren 92083.
4. Heinrich Junker (CSU) was a member of the Bavarian parliament (1950–1970). He eventually became Bavarian Minister of the Interior in 1962. See: Kock, ed., *Der Bayerische Landtag,* 437. August Geislhöringer was member of the Bavarian parliament (1950–1958) and Minister of the Interior between 1954 and 1957. See: ibid., 421. Debates circling around how to respond to *the Halbstarke* emerged throughout West Germany. See: Kurme, *Halbstarke,* 244.
5. Franz-Josef Wuermeling, *Ehe und Familie Heute;* Wuermeling, *Familie: Gabe und Aufgabe* (Cologne, 1958). See also: Schenda, "Die Familie als Bollwerk gegen den Kommunismus," 90–98, in *Vom Trümmerkind zum Teenager;* Herzog, *Sex after Fascism,* 73, 98, and 119.
6. Cox, "Girls in Trouble," 192–205, in *Secret Gardens, Satanic Mills.* See also: Angela Delille and Andrea Grohn, "Fräulein Grünschnabel: Backfische, Teenager, Frühreife," 42–55, in *Perlonzeit.*

7. Münster, *Geld in Nietenhosen,* 39. See also: Helmut Lamprecht, *Teenager und Manager* (Munich, 1965); Schildt, *Moderne Zeiten,* 161–62; Siegfried, *Time Is on My Side.*
8. See endnote 3.
9. StadtAM, Polizeidirektion München 922. See also: Kurme, *Halbstarke,* 196.
10. StadtAM, Polizeidirektion München 922.
11. BayHStAM, Ministerium des Inneren 92087.
12. Ibid.
13. Ibid.
14. BayHStAM, Ministerium des Inneren 81082. See also: "Mit voller Kraft gegen Halbstarke," *Die Süddeutsche Zeitung,* 4 June 1956.
15. BayHStAM, Ministerium des Inneren 81082.
16. Ibid.
17. Geschichtswerkstatt Neuhausen, *Vom Rio zum Kolobri.*
18. BayHStAM, Ministerium des Inneren 81082.
19. BayHStAM, Ministerium des Inneren 92087.
20. *Zentralblatt für Jugendrecht und Jugendwohlfahrt* 46, no. 6/7 (1956), here 151, quoted in Zahner, *Jugendfürsorge in Bayern,* 183.
21. *Das Motorrad,* no. 24 (1958), quoted in, Mrozek, prod., *Bürger, Antibürger, Intellektuelle (2),* 5. See also: Mrozek. "Halbstark!" 630.
22. *Allgemeine Deutsche Lehrerzeitung* 8, no. 17 (1956), here 329, quoted in Kurme, *Halbstarke,* 186.
23. "Scharfes Durchgreifen gegen Halbstarke," *Der Münchner Merkur,* 2–3 June 1956. See also: BayHStAM, Ministerium des Inneren 81082.
24. Geschichtswerkstatt Neuhausen, *Vom Rio zum Kolobri,* 19.
25. Ibid.
26. Kock, *Der Bayerische Landtag,* 117.
27. Mrozek, prod., *Bürger, Antibürger, Intellektuelle (2).* See also: Geschichtswerkstatt Neuhausen, *Vom Rio zum Kolobri,* 19–20; Kock, *Der Bayerische Landtag,* 116.
28. Mrozek, prod., *Bürger, Antibürger, Intellektuelle (2).*
29. Zahner, *Jugendfürsorge in Bayern,* 177–78.
30. "Geislhöringer wurde gestoppt," *Die Welt,* 17 August 1956.
31. Ibid.
32. "Zuerst der Gummiknüppel," *Der Münchner Merkur,* 22 August 1956. See also: *Mittelbayerische Zeitung,* 17 August 1956, quoted in BayHStAM, Ministerium des Inneren 81082.
33. "'Halbstarke' werden immer stärker," *Der Münchner Merkur,* 17 August 1956.
34. "Staatsaktion gegen die Halbstarken," *8-Uhr Blatt,* 17 August 1956.
35. "An Redaktion SZ," *Die Süddeutsche Zeitung,* 17 August 1956.
36. BayHStAM, Ministerium des Inneren 81082. See also: "Zuerst der Gummiknüppel," *Der Münchner Merkur,* 22 August 1956; "Unter der Lupe," *8 Uhr-Blatt,* 25 August 1956; "Die Autorität der Polizei muss unter allen Umständen gewahrt bleiben," *Mittelbayerische Zeitung,* August 1956.
37. *Die Süddeutsche Zeitung,* 22 January 1954, quoted in Gerhard Fürmetz, "Polizei, Massenprotest und öffentliche Ordnung: Großeinsätze der Münchner Polizei in den frühen fünfziger Jahren," in *Öffentliche Ordnung in der*

Nachkriegszeit, ed. Christian Groh (Ubstadt-Weiher, 2002), 78–106, here 86. See also: Michael Sturm, "Zwischen Schwabing und Fürstenfeldbruck: Die Stadtpolizei München in der Reformzeit der Bundesrepublik," in *Die Geschichte des Erfolgsmodells BRD im internationalen Vergleich,* ed. Jörg Calließ (Rehburg-Loccum, 2006), 147–72.

38. StadtAM, Stadtchronik (1956).
39. "Geiselhöriger wurde gestoppt," *Die Welt,* 17 August 1956.
40. "Keine Banden in München sagt Hieber," *Die Abendzeitung,* 18–19 August 1956
41. "Halbwüchsige gefährden die Straßen der Stadt," *Die Abendzeitung,* 22 August 1956.
42. Ibid.
43. "Drastische Maßnahmen gegen Halbstarke," *Die Welt,* 19 September 1956.
44. BayHStAM, Ministerium des Inneren 81082.
45. "Die Erfindung der Halbstarken," *Die Frankfurter Allgemeine Zeitung,* 7 September 1956.
46. "Wildwest in München: Halbstarker und Ganzstarker," *Main-Echo,* 31 August 1956.
47. StadtAM, Ratsitzungsprotokolle, Sitzungsprotokoll 729/1–4 (1956).
48. BayHStAM, Ministerium des Inneren 92087 (Denkschrift zur Problematik der Halbswüchsigen). The state report appeared on 2 October 1956. Juvenile crime rose by 35% between 1947 and 1955. See also: BayHStAM, Ministerium des Inneren 92089; "Zwischen Lausbubenstreich und Gewalttat," *Die Süddeutsche Zeitung,* 30 November 1956.
49. StadtAM, Kreisjugendring no. 10. See also: StadtAM, Schulamt 8271; BayHStAM Ministerium des Inneren 92087.
50. StaAM, Plakatsammlung 1848–2008, 1073 (1956); "Die 'Blasen' nehmen kein Blatt vor den Mund: Diskussion vor dem Jugendforum," *Der Münchner Merkur,* 17 September 1956; Geschichtswerkstatt Neuhausen, *Vom Rio zum Kolobri,* 164.
51. "Die 'Blasen' nehmen kein Blatt vor den Mund: Diskussion vor dem Jugendforum," *Der Münchner Merkur,* 17 September 1956.
52. "Wir sind keine 'Halbstarken,'" *8-Uhr Blatt,* 7 September 1956
53. "Jugendliche setzen sich gegen 'Halbstarke' zur Wehr," *Die Süddeutsche Zeitung,* 8 September 1956. See also: Bondy, *Jugendliche stören die Ordnung,* 23–24.
54. Mrozek, prod., *Bürger, Antibürger, Intellektuelle (2).*
55. Rainer Dorner, "Halbstark, Rock'n Roll Existenzialismus," in *Bikini: Die Fünfziger Jahre: Kalter Krieg und Capri-Sonne: Fotos, Texte, Comics, Analysen,* ed. Eckhard Siepmann (Reinbek bei Hamburg, 1983), 164–69, here 166.
56. StadtAM, Schulamt 8271.
57. Ibid.
58. Ibid.
59. "Die Raben von Rio sagen uns ihre Meinung," *Quick,* 29 September 1956.
60. "Die Bandenführer bitte melden: München lädt jugendliche 'Blasen' zum offenen Gespräch ein," *Westdeutsche Allgemeine Zeitung,* 17 September 1956. See also: BayHStAM, Ministerium des Inneren 81082.

61. "Weg von der Straße, aber wohin?" *Die Süddeutsche Zeitung,* 17 September 1956; "Jugendliche setzen sich gegen 'Halbstarke' zur Wehr," *Die Süddeutsche Zeitung,* 8 September 1956. See also: *Mittelbayerische Zeitung,* 24 October 1956, quoted in Zahner, *Jugendfürsorge in Bayern,* 183.

62. "Halbwüchsige gefährden die Straßen der Stadt," *Die Abendzeitung,* 22 August 1956.

63. StAM, Polizeidirektion München Nr. 11011, quoted in Zahner *Jugendfürsorge in Bayern,* 181. See also: *Die Süddeutsche Zeitung,* 20 September 1956, quoted in ibid., 184.

64. Geschichtswerkstatt Neuhausen, *Vom Rio zum Kolobri,* 69.

65. Florian Fricke, *München rockt: Die wilde Zeit an der Isar* (Munich, 2007), 8.

66. Peter Kraus, *Wop-baba-lu-ba: Mein ver-rocktes Leben* (Wien, 1990), quoted in Geschichtswerkstatt Neuhausen, *Vom Rio zum Kolobri,* 69.

67. Bondy, *Jugendliche stören die Ordnung,* 109–10. See also: "Beifallstürme bei Jazzkonzert für Münchner Jugend," *Die Abendzeitung,* 20 November 1956; Geschichtswerkstatt Neuhausen, *Vom Rio zum Kolobri,* 40.

68. Hans Heigert and Werner Wirsing, *Stätten der Jugend* (Munich, 1958), 11. See also: MonM, 4° Mon 3831: Seelmann, "Das Halbstarken-Problem in München" (1957), 28–46, passim.

69. Gerhard Fürmetz, "Anwalt der Jugend," in *'Schwabinger Krawalle:' Protest, Polizei und Öffentlichkeit zu Beginn der 60er Jahre,* ed. Gerhard Fürmetz (Essen, 2006), 141–50, here 141.

70. "Aufstand gegen die Langeweile," *Bild am Sonntag,* 27 January 1957. See also: "Über die Behandlung von Blasen: Der neue Leiter des Jugendamtes stellt sich vor," *Die Süddeutsche Zeitung,* 20 September 1956.

71. Munich's city report surfaced piece by piece. StadtAM, Schulamt 6244; StadtAM, Schulamt 8271. See also: "Modewort 'Halbstarke' ist irreführend," *Der Münchner Merkur,* 27 November 1956; "Fingerle hält seine Hand über die Jugend: 'Sofortprogramm' des Stadtschulrats," *Die Süddeutsche Zeitung,* 30 October 1956; "Zuschuss für Jugendheim," *Die Abendzeitung,* 13 December 1956.

72. See, for example: Waltraut Küppers, *Mädchentagebücher der Nachkriegszeit: Ein kritischer Beitrag zum sogenannten Wandel der Jugend* (Stuttgart, 1963); Kuhnert and Ackermann, "Jenseits von Lust und Liebe?" 43–83, here 75/76, in *'Die Elvis-Tolle, die hatte ich mir unauffällig wachsen lassen';* Bartam and Krüger, "Vom Backfisch zum Teenager," 84–102, in ibid. Heide Funk, "Mädchenalltag: Freiraum nach geleisteter Pflicht," 37–46, in *Immer diese Jugend;* Erika Dichtl, "'Nylon's, Tanzen, Märchenprinz:' Ein Neuhauser Teenager in der Halbstarkenzeit," 78–81, in *Vom Rio zum Kolobri.*

73. Krüger, "Vom Punk zum Emo,' 16, in *inter-cool 3.0.*

74. Jutta Scheerbarth (*1943), quoted in Rüdiger Bloemke, *Roll Over Beethoven: Wie der Rock 'n' Roll nach Deutschland kam* (St. Andrä-Wörden, 1996), 119.

75. *Der Münchner Merkur,* 5 May 1953, quoted in Geschichtswerkstatt Neuhausen, *Vom Rio zum Kolobri,* 44–45.

76. Peter Wensierski, *Schläge im Namen des Herren: Die verdrängte Geschichte der Heimkinder in der Bundesrepublik* (Munich, 2006), 17.

77. Ibid.
78. Ibid., 19. See also: Lieselotte Pongratz and Hans Odo Hübner, *Lebensbewährung nach öffentlicher Erziehung* (Neuwied/Darmstadt, 1959); Annette Lützke, "Öffentliche Erziehung und Heimerziehung für Mädchen 1954 bis 1975: Bilder 'sittlich verwahrloster' Mädchen und junger Frauen" (Ph.D. diss., University-Gesamthochschule Essen, 2002).
79. Maase, *Bravo Amerika*, 78. See also: Lindner, *Jugendprotest seit den fünfziger Jahren*, 42.
80. Susanne Ostermann (*1943), quoted in Bloemke, *Roll Over Beethoven*, 120.
81. B., "Musik dröhnt aus Automaten," *Ruf ins Volk* (1957): 76, here 76. See also: Franz Metzger, "Die Musikbox als aktuelles Freizeitangebot der Jugendpflege?" *Deutsche Jugend* 8 (1960): 124 –28.
82. Ostermann, quoted in Bloemke, *Roll Over Beethoven*, 120.
83. Lützke, "Öffentliche Erziehung und Heimerziehung für Mädchen 1945 bis 1975," 281.
84. Ibid., 246 and 282.
85. Sabine Pankofer, *Freiheit hinter Mauern: Mädchen in geschlossenen Heimen* (Weinheim, 1997); 241–50; Sabine Hering, "Verwahrloste Mädchen' als Zielgruppe öffentlicher Erziehung: Ein Rückblick auf die Jahre 1945–1965," in *Sozialpädagogik: Vom Therapeutikum zur Weltgesellschaft. Systematischen und historische Beiträge*, ed. Diana Franke (Baltmannsweihler, 2005), 135–50; Eva Gehltomholt and Sabine Hering, *Das verwahrloste Mädchen: Diagnostik und Fürsorge in der Jugendhilfe zwischen Kriegsende und Reform (1945–1965)* (Opladen, 2006).
86. Wensierski, *Schläge im Namen des Herren*, 9.
87. Ibid., 19.
88. Ibid., 51.
89. Gehltomholt and Hering, *Das verwahrloste Mädchen*, 76.
90. Ibid., 86–87.
91. Ibid., 91.
92. Wensierski, *Schläge im Namen des Herren*, 49 and 64. See also: Pankofer, *Freiheit hinter Mauern;* Hering, "Verwahrloste Mädchen' als Zielgruppe öffentlicher Erziehung."
93. Fischer-Kowalski, *1958-Hooligans, 1968-Students*, 6. See also: Gehltomholt and Hering, *Das verwahrloste Mädchen*, 85–86.
94. StadtAM, Kreisjugendring no. 11; Fingerle, *München*, 132–36; Landeshauptstadt München, *Zur Geschichte der Erziehung in München;* Josef Hederer, interview by author, tape recordings, Munich, summer 2009 and summer 2010.
95. Zahner, *Jugendfürsorge in Bayern*, 181; Geschichtswerkstatt Neuhausen, *Vom Rio zum Kolobri*, 153. See also: Heigert and Wirsing, *Stätten der Jugend;* Lothar Böhnisch, "Historische Skizzen zur offenen Jugendarbeit," (I), (II), *Deutsche Jugend* 32 (1984): 460–70 and 514–20; Lindner, *Jugendprotest seit den fünfziger Jahren*, 75–78; Bondy, *Jugendliche stören die Ordnung*, 114.
96. Dolezol, "Die Spontanen und ihre Organisatoren," 474.
97. BayStaBiM, *Teenager. Zeitschrift für die Jugend* (Harlaching-Pinguin), no. 1 (1958).

98. BayStaBiM, *Teenager. Zeitschrift für die Jugend*, no. 7 (1959).
99. BayStaBiM, *Teenager. Zeitschrift für die Jugend*, Sonderheft (1959).
100. Ibid. See also: StadtAM, Kreisjugendring no. 11.
101. Maase, *Bravo Amerika*, 148.
102. StadtAM, Schulamt 8271, "Unsere Leser schreiben!" *Harlaching-Pinguin*, no. 7 (1959).
103. Ibid.
104. Krüger, "Vom Punk zum Emo," 16, in *inter-cool 3.0*.
105. Zinnecker, "'Halbstarke': Die andere Seite der 68er-Generation," in *Protestierende Jugend*, 461–85, here 475–76.
106. Ulrich Beer, *Geheime Miterzieher der Jugend: Macht und Wirkung der Massenmedien* (Düsseldorf, 1961). See also: Grotum, *Die Halbstarken*, 219.
107. Münster, *Geld in Nietenhosen*, 47. See also: Lindner, *Jugendproteste seit den fünfziger Jahren*, 44. Siegfried, *Time Is On My Side*.
108. Münster, *Geld in Nietenhosen*, 7.
109. Ibid.
110. Ibid.
111. Winfried Krüger, "Jugendzeitschrift 'Bravo': Anleitung zur Normalität," in Deutsches Jugendinstitut, ed., *Immer diese Jugend!*, 363–74. See also: Eisfeld, *Als Teenager träumten*, 51 and 70.
112. Schildt, *Moderne Zeiten*, 169; Nina Lammers, "*Bravo* und die Mediennutzung von Jugendlichen," 265–271, here 271, in *50 Jahre Bravo*, ed. Archiv der Jugendkulturen e.V. (Berlin, 2006). *Bravo* started with roughly 64,000 (63,981) issues. Deutsches Jugendinstitut, ed., *Immer diese Jugend!*, 364; Klaus Farin, "50 Jahre Bravo: Ein Projekt des Archiv der Jugendkulturen e.V.," 9–23, here 9, in *50 Jahre Bravo*. See also: Manfred Berger, "Bravo: 50 Jahre Pubertätserotik und Teenie-Pop," *Unsere Jugend* 58 (2006): 341–44, here 341; Martin Hussong, "Jugendzeitschriften von 1945–1960: Phasen, Typen, Tendenzen," in Doderer, ed., *Zwischen Trümmern und Wohlstand*, 521–85.
113. "Ich war Jimmys Freund," *Bravo*, no. 9 (1957). See also: "James Dean rettete ein Mädchen," no. 9 (1957); "Sensationelle Bilder: James Dean wie ihn keiner kennt," *Bravo*, no. 3 (1957).
114. "Halbstarke und Polizisten Herhören," *Bravo*, no. 4 (1956). See also: "Angeklagt: Die POLIZEI!" *Bravo*, no. 9 (1957).
115. "Halbstarke und Polizisten Herhören," *Bravo*, no. 4 (1956).
116. "Weil Mutter Hunger hatte," *Bravo*, no. 19 (1956); "Halbstarker! König! Hochstapler!" *Bravo*, no. 30 (1957); "Halbstarker! König! Hochstapler!" no. 36 (1957).
117. "Die Elvis-Presley-Story," *Bravo*, no. 15 (1957). See also: "Die Elvis-Presley-Story," *Bravo*, no. 8 (1957); "Die Elvis-Presley-Story," *Bravo*, no. 9 (1957); "Die Elvis-Presley-Story," *Bravo*, no. 14 (1957); "Elvis nach Deutschland," *Bravo*, no. 28 (1958).
118. "Alles dreht sich um Elvis," *Bravo*, no. 43 (1958).
119. Sheila Whiteley, *Too Much Too Young: Popular Music Age and Gender* (New York, 2003), 170.
120. Katja Scherl, "'Zeig Deine Orden, Elvis!' Banal Militarism als Normalisierungsstrategie," in *Banal Militarism: Zur Veralltäglichung des Militäri-*

schen im Zivilen, ed. Tanja Thomas and Fabian Virchow (Bielefeld, 2006), 307–32.

121. Bloemke, *Roll Over Beethoven*, 100.

122. Maase, *BRAVO Amerika*, 126.

123. "Neuer Name: Peter Kraus," *Bravo*, no. 5 (1957). See also: Bloemke, *Roll Over Beethoven*, 126; Kraus, "Entenschwanz & Ponyfransen," 100–13. The series "When Teenagers Dream: The Peter Kraus Story" was first announced in November 1958. See, for instance: *"Wenn Teenager träumen— Die Peter-Kraus Story,"* *Bravo*, no. 47 (1958), no. 48 (1958), no. 49 (1958). See also: Geschichtswerkstatt Neuhausen, *Vom Rio zum Kolobri*, 69.

124. Améry, *Teenager-Stars*, 97. See also: Kraus, *40 Jahre Rock 'n' Roll;* Kraus, *I Love Rock 'n' Roll.*

125. Hoesch, ed. *Bravo 1956–2006*, 452–57, here 454. Freddy Quinn and Roy Black played similar roles.

126. Geschichtswerkstatt Neuhausen, *Vom Rio zum Kolobri*, 70.

127. Ibid.

128. *Der Spiegel*, "Cornelia (Conny) Froboess," August 26, 1959.

129. Améry, *Teenager-Stars*, 97/98. See also: Veronika Ratzenböck, "'Steig ein in das Traumboot der Liebe:' Deutsche Schlager der 50er Jahre," 177–181, in *Perlonzeit*; Poiger, *"Rock'n'Roll, Female Sexuality, and the Cold War Battle over German Identities,"* 610.

130. Geschichtswerkstatt Neuhausen, ed., *Vom Rio zum Kolobri*, 70. See also: "Conny & Peter," *Der Spiegel*, November 12, 1958; *Bravo*, [cover], no. 44 (1958); Wrage, "Neue Jugend: Einleitung," 650, in *Handbuch Nachkriegskultur.*

131. Améry, *Teenager-Stars*, 115. A variety of movies fit into this framework, including those with Roy Black and Uschi Glas.

132. Nieland, "Frauenbilder in *Bravo*," in *Bravo 1956–2006*, 80–99, here 82.

133. Ibid., 82.

134. Ibid.

135. Ibid., 92.

136. Ibid.

137. Ibid., 88. See also: Baumann and Krüger, "Vom Backfisch zum Teenager," 88, in *'Die Elvis-Tolle, die hatte ich mir heimlich wachsen lassen,'* 88.

138. Améry, *Teenager-Stars*, 55.

139. Nieland, "Frauenbilder in *Bravo*," in *Bravo 1956–2006*, 82.

140. Ibid., 98

141. "Steffi," *Bravo*, no. 32 (1958).

142. Ibid.

143. "Steffi," *Bravo*, no. 41 (1958).

144. See, for instance: Kaspar Maase, "Auf dem Weg zum zivilen Habitus: Rock 'n' Roll, Teenager, BRAVO und die US- Populärkultur in der zweiten Hälfte der 50er Jahre," 7-38, here 8, in *Amerikanisierung der Alltagskultur? Zur Rezeption US-amerikanischer Populärkultur in der Bundesrepublik Deutschland und in den Niederlanden*, eds. Kaspar Maase, Gerd Hallenberger, and Mel van Elteren (Hamburg, 1999).

145. "Steffi," *Bravo*, no. 39 (1958); "Steffi," *Bravo*, no. 41 (1958); "Steffi," *Bravo*, no. 33 (1958); "Steffi," *Bravo*, no. 34 (1958).

146. "Steffi," *Bravo*, no. 32 (1958); "Steffi," *Bravo*, no. 45 (1958); "Steffi," *Bravo*, no. 50 (1958).

147. "Steffi," *Bravo*, no. 35 (1958).

148. "Steffi," *Bravo*, no. 41 (1958).

149. "Steffi," *Bravo*, no. 33 (1958).

150. "Steffi," *Bravo*, no. 44 (1958).

151. Ingrid Volkmer, "Teenager: Ausgangspunkt medialer und ästhetischer Kommerzialisierung der Jugendphase," 142–152, here 151, in *Jugend 1900–1970: Zwischen Selbstverfügung und Deutung*, ed. Dieter Baacke, Heinrich Lienker, Ralf Schmölders, and Ingrid Volkmer (Opladen, 1991).

152. The series "Us & Them" (*Wir & Ihr*) began in January 1962. "Wir & Ihr," *Bravo*, no 1. (1962).

153. "Wir & Ihr," *Bravo*, no. 9 (1962).

154. "Wir & Ihr," *Bravo*, no. 30 (1962); "Wir & Ihr," *Bravo*, no. 32 (1960); "Plötzlich war alles anders! Mit dem Kind kam die große Wende," *Bravo*, no. 34 (1962); "Durch Opfer rettete ich meine Ehe," *Bravo*, no. 36 (1962).

155. *Bravo* no. 45 (1957), quoted in Maase, *Bravo Amerika*, 109.

156. Lutz Sauerteig, "Die Herstellung des sexuellen und erotischen Körpers in der westdeutschen Jugendzeitschrift BRAVO in den 1960er und 1970er Jahren," *Medizinhistorisches Journal* 42 (2007): 142–79, here 142.

157. Run of 30,000 at start, 200,000 within the first twelve months, and 523,000 by mid-1959. By spring 1960 a survey spoke of 1.66 million readers of *Bravo* (FRG/ West Berlin). Maase, *BRAVO Amerika*, 104.

158. BayHStAM, Ministerium des Inneren 92090.

159. "Streiflicht," *Die Süddeutsche Zeitung*, 30 October 1958.

160. "Verdienen an einer skeptischen Generation: Die Bilanz der Bill-Haley-Gastspiele," *Bayerische Staatszeitung*, 21 November 1958.

161. BayHStAM, Ministerium des Inneren 92090. See also: "Saat der Gewalt," *Der Spiegel*, 5 November 1958.

162. "Streiflicht," *Die Süddeutsche Zeitung*, 10 October 1958; "Billy Haley heizt in Stuttgart ein," *Die Süddeutsche Zeitung*, 1–2 November 1958; "Saat der Gewalt," *Der Spiegel*, 5 November 1958; "Verdienen an einer skeptischen Generation: Die Bilanz der Bill-Haley-Gastspiele," *Bayerische Staatszeitung*, 21 November 1958; Dollinger, ed., *München im 20. Jahrhundert*, 247.

163. See, for instance: "Steffi," *Bravo*, 14 November 1958; "Wenn Teenager träumen," *Bravo*, 21 November 1958.

164. StadtAM, Polizeidirektion München 11083.

165. "Was wurde aus dem Programm für Münchner Halbwüchsige," *Die Süddeutsche Zeitung*, 31 March 1959.

166. *Die Innere Mission* 46, no. 11 (1956): 339, quoted in Zahner, *Jugendfürsorge in Bayern*, 184.

167. Scholars refer to a "revival" of old norms, at least when referencing teenagers. See: Bartam and Krüger, "Vom Backfisch zum Teenager," in *'Die Elvis-Tolle, die hatte ich mir unauffällig wachsen lassen,'* 101.

168. Grace Hechinger and Fred M. Hechinger, *Die Herrschaft der Teenager* (Gütersloh, 1965). See also: Schildt, *Moderne Zeiten*, 177.

PART 3

POLITICAL ACTIVISM IN THE
PROTEST YEARS, 1962–1973

CHAPTER 5

Constructing *the Student* and *the Gammler*

"Hell is loose in Schwabing!"[1] This headline appeared in the newspaper *Der Münchner Merkur* on 25 June 1962. On several warm summer nights, the Schwabing quarter, close to downtown Munich, became the setting for major youth riots and protests. The article noted,

> Whereas the first turmoil on Thursday ... happened due to some kind of impulse, the riots on Friday and Saturday ... were initiated by rowdies. At the second and third turmoil, ... hundreds of youngsters (on average twenty years of age) banded together, destroyed cars, threw fireworks, bottles, and rocks, until the police went forward brutally with batons.[2]

Unable to identify the nature and reasoning for such sudden riots, authorities and the media initially worried about the return of *the Halbstarke*. Former mayor Thomas Wimmer even feared that the events in Schwabing could be a starting point for "some nasty surprises ... in the future."[3] Yet partially sparked by the police, unrests turned into political protests, pushing *the student* as the new construct of youth into the epicenter of discussions.

Throughout the 1960s, repeated riots and demonstrations reflected a larger struggle over the form and nature of West German democracy. Arguably initiated by the events in Schwabing, and repeatedly tied to the takeover of city spaces, debates about youth politicized society at large. For many, *the student*—and to an extent *Gammler* buns—as an emerging image of youth embodied a new generation and discourse. Born after World War II, these youngsters questioned adult authority and political frameworks, the latter leading to intense debates about higher education, the Cold War, and emergency laws. In 1966, the two major parties within the Federal Republic created a grand coalition with a supermajority, further encouraging protests and the organization of youth. These developments were new within West Germany's democracy,[4] and raised historic fears about political instability as experienced during the years of the Weimar Republic. In fact, at the height of protests in spring 1968 one state representative noted, "If Bonn is not to become Weimar, then the Bavarian capital cannot have the image of 1918 and become a fertile ground for extreme disruptions and an opportune arena for violent struggles."[5] As elsewhere, *the student* thus embodied disorder and fear, making this image of youth a discursive space or microcosm for broader conversations.

Again, the construction of *the student* and *the Gammler* as disruptive, violent, and possibly antidemocratic forces had its benefits.[6] Situated within the so-called protest years (1962–1973), the rise of both images emerged as frozen political structures embodied by aging chancellor Konrad Adenauer slowly dissolved. After a brief interlude government headed by Ludwig Erhard, a grand coalition between the two major parties—the conservatives (CDU/CSU) and the social democrats (SPD)—formed a government from 1966 until 1969. Their supermajority brought people to the streets and helped create the Extraparliamentary Opposition (APO), a movement that authorities interested in traditional democratic structures belittled as angry young men. While there was perhaps a real crisis around youth, it was again consistently defined only as that and exaggerated overall for self-serving purposes. As a result, youth once more proved a powerful rhetorical space for larger discussions and provided the leverage for expanding mechanisms of social control.

Although constructions of youth as *students* and *Gammlers* followed similar trends as during previous decades, a growing ability and broader willingness of the actual young to help frame its own image became increasingly apparent. With more power and influence, namely once comparing such dynamics to the situation during the crisis years, young people played a more active role. Even though authorities and primarily the media continually described them as violent and antidemocratic, the young pushed a counternarrative and tried to tell their own stories. This struggle over what youth means during the protest years illustrates the growing diversity of a young democratic structure, as well as the increasing power and interest of young people to construct an image of youth.

The third and final part of *Coming of Age* thus highlights the rise of *the student* and *the Gammler* during the protest years. In 1962, the politicization of youth took shape on the streets in Schwabing, marking an awakening of a new generation. From that point forward, young people increasingly asked inconvenient questions, challenged authorities, protested, and organized. Continuing tensions plus the inability of adult authorities to defuse the situation led to a climax in 1968 and the death of two individuals on the streets of Munich. As a result—and beginning in the wake of the riots in Schwabing—to control *the student* and *the Gammler,* and with that certain city spaces, became important. Local authorities re-evaluated outdated police tactics, relied on surveillance and spatial planning, and tried to streamline judicial processes. The young, on the other hand, began organizing and fighting back, resulting in continuing riots on the streets of Munich, dynamics that ultimately helped the Bavarian capital grow up.

Creating *the Student*

Not surprisingly, protests initiating a shift in discourse and introducing *the student* began in Schwabing, the young and vibrant quarter of Munich. Located just north of the city center, its main boulevard Leopoldstraße runs all the way from the Siegestor Arch of the Victor to Münchner Freiheit square. The Ludwig-Maximilians University—the largest university in West Germany at the time—was located in Schwabing; the Academy for the Arts and the Technical College was nearby. In the early 1960s, these three institutions brought roughly 20,000 students to the city.[7] As the bohemian part of town, Schwabing was also the home of countless artists and musicians. Studios, sidewalk stands, restaurants, cafés, movie theaters, and a busy nightlife attracted mainly students and youngsters. Actually, the Director of the Youth Welfare Office, Kurt Seelmann, described this Schwabing "state of mind"[8] in the early 1960s with a reference to new trends among young males, noting, "the environment was almost exclusively inhabited by extremely nice young people (even though some of them might have had a full beard)."[9] On warm and beautiful days thousands pushed along the main boulevard to enjoy its atmosphere, as many sat outside to have coffee or ice cream. In the evening, restaurants and bars filled up quickly as music, cabarets, and theaters intrigued visitors and locals alike. Those over eighteen had few problems enjoying themselves on rock 'n' roll dance floors and in jazz clubs, while underage individuals could take pleasure in musicians on street corners. For authorities and residents, such noise and constant activity became concerning and irritating, and the latter repeatedly called upon the police to deal with breaches of peace. Law enforcement then broke up street musicians and pavement artists, leaving many to wonder how such behavior aligned with the city's new slogan, "Munich, an embracing metropolis."[10]

An increase in disruptions became apparent by 1962, and ultimately triggered the riots in June. Earlier that month, a university riot developed when the police tried to clear a crowd of about two thousand individuals after a jazz concert near the university.[11] On 20 June the police responded to a similar call, as youngsters supposedly "made disrupting noises by playing music, clapping, even dancing and yelling."[12] When arriving at the Wedekindplatz square in Schwabing, the police noticed a group of street musicians, and roughly 150 listeners. As the patrol rolled up to the scene, onlookers welcomed them with whistles and boos, while some even threw bottles and started yelling, "Nazi state."[13] The police eventually began clearing the area, against the opposition of many onlookers. A day later, the police again dealt with three youngsters making music at the Monopteros monument before a similar situation escalated later the same day. That time, the police tried to disperse a crowd of several hundred people who were listening to five musicians in Schwabing. The musicians disrupted the peace, while onlookers blocked parts of the main road. As a result, the police tried to escort the musicians away from the scene, only to face an upset audience believing the officials had arrested the young performers. Some bystanders surrounded the police car; others released air from its tires. The police officers, on the other hand, called for reinforcement, and the riots of Schwabing began.[14]

For the next five days, Schwabing saw an unprecedented disruption of public peace. Sparked by a seemingly minor incident, hundreds of people began blocking the streets. In the following days, between 10,000 and 20,000 protestors participated in similar events.[15] Emerging riots played out along almost the same script each night: a crowd assembled on the Leopoldstraße boulevard throughout the day; in the evening, some began blocking the street. Reminiscent of incidents when *the Halbstarke* obstructed traffic at the Stiglmaierplatz square several years earlier, protestors stepped onto the street, carrying tables and chairs, sat down on tram tracks, and refused to move. Several couples danced on the street, which gave the protests a playful and provocative character [Figure 5.1]. As one participant recalled, "Initially, it was quite amusing, [and] the people enjoyed making fun of the police."[16] The police, on the other hand, conceptualized them as "disruptive to traffic."[17] Leopoldstraße boulevard in particular was a main access route to downtown Munich at the time. Once initial orders to disperse remained mostly unanswered, police units began dispersing the gathering with force. In groups, the police tried to push people

Figure 5.1 Dancing on the streets during the so-called riots in Schwabing, 1962. Courtesy of Otfried Schmidt/Süddeutsche Zeitung Photo.

off the streets. Unable to distinguish between onlookers and participants, officers used their batons indiscriminately; some even rode their horses into street cafés. The crowd, on the other hand, started throwing beer bottles and other objects. Chaos ensued as the police began detaining protestors at the same time as others tried to flee. Eventually, the police were able to clear the streets again, at least until disruptions resumed the next evening.

The events in Schwabing caught public authorities and adult contemporaries by surprise. Munich had seen relative stability and order since the end of panics surrounding *the Halbstarke*. Those conflicts took place in working-class neighborhoods, and not in the middle-class bohemian area of Schwabing. Moreover, whereas politicians feared communism, they rarely connected such concerns to youth. If anything, then fears surrounding the vibrant and, at times, chaotic buzz of Schwabing worried authorities. As a result, Mayor Hans-Jochen Vogel came to Schwabing wondering about the nature of these disruptions. He hoped to defuse the situation, and approached a group of protestors. As he recalled later,

> After a longer discussion, I was able to convince a group about the uselessness of additional blockades and brawls with the police. My plea to consider Munich's prestige made an initial impression, [and] this group dispersed. Encouraged by this success, I approached a second group. ... This time, however, I was ... pushed into an entrance way as people threw stink bombs, yelled at me ... , and demanded the release of all those arrested.[18]

For such protestors, the situation had been incited by police brutality, indiscriminate arrests, and unnecessary violence. Unable or unwilling to abide by the requests of demonstrators, the mayor retreated as the police continued to move forward with batons. Director of the Youth Welfare Office Kurt Seelmann was also caught by surprise. On his way to get ice cream, he found himself in the middle of the unrest. Seelmann tried to get in contact with authorities, hoping to soothe the situation. At some point, a police officer told him to keep moving. Seelmann noted later, "in order to make me speed up, he hit me with a baton on the back."[19] Seelman had established a dialogue between the young and the police for years, but that night he wondered if "all such efforts had been in vain."[20]

Although covering the events extensively, the media and the general public also had a hard time framing what happened in Schwabing. An editorial in *Der Münchner Merkur* aimed to distinguish between bystanders caught by surprise, a minority of "rowdies" who threw rocks, and "mainly students";[21] it also asked its readers "What do you make of these riots?"[22] The tabloid *8-Uhr Blatt* reported on the criminal character of the "rioting masses";[23] it also—similar to other publications—simply resurrected earlier images of *the Halbstarke*[24] by stating, for example, "That shabby looks and character do not make an artist and attendance in lectures do not make a student is common knowledge. But that hundreds of pseudo-artists and quasi-academics have worked with loitering Halbstarke in order to beat the last sense out of Schwabing is depressing."[25] Rumors about a group of "three-hundred Halbstarke, as 'reinforcement,' on their way from Frankfurt and Düsseldorf" to Schwabing, appeared as well.[26] Letters to the editors

painted a similar picture: some commentators saw *the Halbstarke* involved in the riots while others had detected "rioting students" and
"academics."[27] Many also categorized participants as local students
and outside agitators. According to Mayor Hans-Jochen Vogel, on
Saturday night it was "mainly the scum of various quarters," which
showed up in Schwabing.[28] Only Director of the Youth Welfare Office
Kurt Seelmann questioned these sentiments and descriptions openly,
given that he had experienced police brutality first hand and person-
ally knew many of supposed *Halbstarke.*[29]

The media and officials eventually began framing the events in
Schwabing as student protests, tied to clandestine communist activities and thus in line with broader 1960s political discussions. Throughout the riots, the police had arrested 248 individuals; 106 of them were
students, a fact not surprising given general profiling of youth. For
authorities, this finding was sufficient evidence that students were the
most dominant group within the riots. That those captured were mainly
between eighteen and twenty-nine years old sustained such claims.
Moreover, with only thirteen women arrested, female youth seemed
to play only a secondary role.[30] This conclusion made male students
the prime targets even though data suggests that students in general
and male students in particular were not the only groups protesting.[31]
Apart from framing the riots as a new kind of protest,[32] recent events—
namely new Cold War tensions due to the construction of the wall in
Berlin in August 1961—also influenced the creation of this threat. The
police chief saw "political implications" at hand in Schwabing, and
blamed secret communist support and subversive forces.[33] After all,
the five musicians triggering the riots had supposedly played Roma-
nian folk songs.[34] One of the musicians later recalled that his interest
in the Russian author Fyodor Dostoyevsky became sufficient evidence
to further sustain these accusations.[35] Besides, authorities had arrested
several youngsters with connections to East Germany: they arrested
Peter Schmitt as a supposed leader, only because he had visited East
Germany in 1958/59 and sustained friendships into the GDR.[36] The
most important evidence of communist involvement was a flyer by the
illegal Communist Party (KPD) that surfaced during the riots. The media discussed this flyer at great length, speculated about a communist
conspiracy, and even feared an invasion.[37] Such constructions of students as communist tools contradicted the experiences of protestors,
who saw the events unfold as "something completely coincidental and
spontaneous, without any political objectives."[38] Even an internal report from the Office for the Protection of the Constitution saw no connection between the leaflet and the KPD.[39] For many authorities such

findings mattered little given their understandings and interpretation of events, plus an increasing state of hysteria.

While the media and local authorities increasingly stereotyped and demonized young participants and bystanders alike, the events in Schwabing politicized individual participants over time. As one voice recalled years later, the riots "did affect me, as one can imagine. The authoritarian state showed its vigor, which I thought we had overcome, and I consequently believed that the majority of the police had to be fascists. I was thus politicized in a heartbeat, and lost all trust into politics."[40] Others saw their initial experiences in 1962 in the context of their subsequent involvement in protests. One individual later noted that in 1962 defying authorities was "highly political."[41] The events even affected those who did not participate. Subversive activist and cofounder of the alternative community Kommune I Dieter Kunzelmann "did not leave his house [in Munich] during the riots."[42] He still noted, "I experienced for the first time that hundreds of people showed solidarity with guitar-playing bums and that it took such a minimal cause for law and order to turn into chaos. This experience impressed me much, so that in the following years I used every situation to experience it in another form."[43] Then nineteen-year-old Andreas Baader was also arrested in Schwabing. Police officers overheard him stating, "I saw them [the police] beating innocent people yesterday. One man was beaten brutally and then kicked. A woman was beaten to the ground; they [the police] need a beating; something like this ought to be in the news, with photos."[44] For authorities this statement was sufficient to prove his active role in the riots, and they arrested Baader. Although released after twelve hours, Baader's mother later recalled how he came home that night and said, "There is something foul in a state where the police moves forward against singing youngsters."[45] These experiences in no way fully explain Baader's later role within the leftist-terrorist Red Army Faction (RAF) but the events in Schwabing marked a watershed moment for him and many other contemporaries, and only proved originally misleading understandings of the riots as political a reality.

In response to police brutality, many participants began organizing.[46] In July, a group of fourteen local residents established the Community Initiative for the Protection of Civil Liberties. It hoped to prevent "a police state,"[47] and tried to raise awareness by setting up meetings, printing leaflets, holding press conferences, and writing letters to editors. In the first leaflet from 16 July it called for witnesses in an attempt to find evidence to prosecute police officers.[48] In a resolution, it outlined, "Until now, there has been no proof regarding obstruction of police order (which is interesting, when recalling the broad use of batons!)."[49] A year after the riots, second chairmen of the initiative outlined the rights of citizens in the student magazine *profil*.[50] The initiative was eventually dissolved due to financial problems and internal animosities, leaving student organizations like the General Student's Committee (AStA) in charge. That organization in particular had hoped to defuse and de-escalate the situation early on. On the fourth day of the riots, it had called on students "to not support such consciously provoked turmoil, which have nothing to do with student and 'Schwabing freedom.'"[51] Shortly after the riots, AStA had then condemned the criminal behavior of participants but also criticized police brutality. While claiming that these had "not been student riots,"[52] AStA also organized a forum to discuss the events. More than three hundred people showed up. In a lively discussion, participants focused on the role of the police during the riots. Two speakers aiming to defend the role of the police were booed; another speaker noted, "The respect I had for the police is gone. There were lots of rowdies, yes, but most of them wore a uniform."[53] Such sentiments received lots of applause, as many had lost respect for authorities and now looked to politicize existing organizational formats like AStA "to protest against such [state] arbitrariness!"[54]

The Rise of *the Student*

As a watershed moment, the riots and protests of Schwabing marked the appearance, construction, and awakening of *the student*. With virtually no memories of the war and National Socialism, this new image of youth came of age during the late 1950s, when artificial divisions along generations became all the more evident. As the years passed, a wider public debate helped create such generational cohorts. In 1957, sociologist Helmut Schelsky already defined a "skeptical generation";[55] six years later, the weekly news magazine *Der Spiegel* deemed this age cohort as the "exaggerated generation."[56] The magazine embedded it within international trends, noting that this generation is "cool, confident, [and] condescending."[57] They are the "kids of Marx and Coca-Cola,"[58] who consume as never before, follow Beat music, love The Beatles, wear miniskirts, and question authorities. U.S. popular culture, among other foreign influences, had made the young more international. Furthermore, argued *Der Spiegel*, "Their use of sex is even more irritating for adults, [and] a source of youth-bashing and youth-idolization."[59] Popular culture, a degree of internationalism, and their disruptive politics made *the student* a force for change and a threat to traditional order.

Similar to previous images of youth, constructions of *the student*— defined as a young, politically active, male, middle-class urbanite—had a history. Historically, the German term *Student* primarily refers to those attending universities and colleges. It is distinguished from the term *Schüler* for elementary and secondary school students and consequently refers to an older age cohort. In the Federal Republic, *Schüler* generally left school in their late teens, becoming college students in their early twenties. *Student* also infers male youth, given that female youngsters could not attend German universities until the late nineteenth century. By the 1960s, the situation had changed, of course, although males still dominated higher education. Moreover, according to historian Harald Lönnecker, German universities have been understood as hotbeds of liberalism, dissent, and delinquency.[60] Student riots in 1848 come to mind when thinking about the political activism of this construct, as do *Burschenschaften* fraternities. Again, such events remain tied to a male population. Social class restricted and limited access to higher education for most young people, an aspect that changed after World War II. Beginning in the 1950s, an expansion in higher education grounded in postwar prosperity became noticeable, opening up this career path for more individuals. In many ways, however, students remained tied to the middle class. Spatially, the home of students was the university. Located within the center of major cities, student quarters emerged around such places of higher education. Schwabing was one of these university spaces, where *the student* could spend time in coffee shops, restaurants, or bars like the Big Apple and the PN. Numerous bands played in these clubs, including future stars like Jimi Hendrix.[61] At the same time, *Gammler*—young bums traveling through Europe—hung around on street corners, sold various items along the Leopoldstraße boulevard, and prepared a spot for the night in this center of "the German sleeping-bag movement."[62] In other words, contemporaries built on historical understandings that saw *the student* as an urbanite who engaged in excessive drinking, disorder, and immorality,[63] making this image of youth a threat to stability.

Age and class also defined *the student* and helped misrepresent larger dynamics. Youngsters went to college in their late teens and early twenties. The average age of all those arrested in 1962 was twenty-five, with most students being a little younger.[64] In short, *the student* was older than eighteen and would not get in conflict with the Law for the Protection of Youth. Whereas this made *the student* more threatening than previous social constructions of youth, the middle-class background brought anxieties of youth away from working-class *Halbstarke* and into the sphere of *the teenager*. Such emphasis, regardless of a broad range of participants, demonstrates the strength of *the student* as a social construct. However, as historian Kristin Ross noted in the context of protests in France, "May '68 had very little to do with the social group—students or 'youth'—who were its instigators. It had much more to do with the flight from social determinations, with displacements that took place outside of their location in society, with a disjunction, that is, between political subjectivity and the social group."[65] She ultimately argues that the events were reduced to a student and generational revolt. Similar trends were visible in Munich, where authorities constructed *the student* as the prime force behind the protests. This neglect of other participants allowed contemporaries to frame potential opposition around university environments along delinquency and generation, especially after the events in Schwabing.

The revival of *the student* as a male youngster was tied to his appearance, an interpretation that simply neglected the role and power of young females or deemed them as irrelevant. Early descriptions noted that *the student* had a full beard. Kurt Seelmann described this type of youngster when recalling his visits to Schwabing,[66] and the police at the riots had only taken photos of suspects with beards—even if witnesses described some participants as "tall, blond, and neat."[67] The police arrested a French student as a ringleader simply because he had a full beard.[68] Similar arrests took place at protests in the GDR, indicating parallels between both German states when it comes to constructions of male youth in the 1960s.[69] Moreover, emerging stereotypes assigned young women a narrow role within the student movement. After all, the police only arrested thirteen women during the riots in Schwabing.[70] Most student organizations also had male leaders, an element again visible in other countries. At least until the mid-1960s authorities and adult onlookers saw and understood young women simply as accessories for male protestors. Newspapers wrote about "twen" girls—those in their twenties—standing by and watching male rioters in Schwabing, or female "'vagabonding-bees following [male] bums."[71] According to one contemporary, "females had to be beautiful, fashionable, sexy, intellectual, and ready to serve."[72] Such female passivity was supposedly grounded in their curiosity and sexual promiscuity and explains why authorities might have been blind towards early female participation. According to historian Kristina Schulz, "participation of women was simply overlooked,"[73] as the media focused more on their looks. Indeed, in Munich, local newspapers wrote about "the necks of Schwabinger art brides" and "open blouse wearing" women protestors,[74] thus putting female bodies, not their actual protests, values, and concerns, into the center of discussions. As the wife of student leader Rudi Dutschke, Gretchen Dutschke-Klotz, later recalled, women "were disposed of at will" if they did not fit this ideal.[75] Such stereotypes continued later on. According to the news magazine *Der Spiegel,*

> It was the highest form of female participation if a girl ... yelled "Shut up!" during a meeting of the Student Social Union (SDS). Tired gals of the revolution put their stylistic haircuts in the way of the water cannon representing the executive power of the state; they join their comrades at teach-ins, sit-ins, and demonstrations; and they also help them in matters of love. But they remain silent once it comes to ... underlying male determination for strict German order present with organizational structures.... Now they feel frustrated.[76]

As one historian noted in a similar context, "That politically conscious males did not behave in any way different towards women, but were sometimes even more brutal and exploitive, all the while situating themselves within a narrative of emancipation," was upsetting.[77] As a result, and although the women's movement did not gain steam until the late 1960s,[78] the early role of female participants rarely concerned male protestors, authorities, or even historians.

At the same time, appearance also became a way to protest. Similar to *the Halbstarke* and *the teenager,* actual students used different styles to resist contemporary norms. Male youngsters made long hair, beards, and casual clothing part of a purposeful shabbiness, and turned such style into a statement against middle-class values. So-called *Gammler* bums—youngsters living on the streets and traveling through Europe—openly defied norms. As one young female contemporary recalls, "'dressing up' meant refusal against revolutionary consciousness," turning rags into a revolutionary statement.[79] Clothing again became political, apparent at a ceremony for the opening of a new student apartment complex in Munich in 1967. Although an official occasion, AStA Chairman Rolf Pohle wore corduroys and a turtleneck. After Pohle made a brief political statement regarding the lack of democratic frameworks, the representative from the Ministry of Culture and Education felt provoked and snapped, stating, "Wear a proper suit before talking about democracy!"[80] Apparently a ragged style and appearance played an important role when constructing, detecting, and identifying *the student;* yet it also visibly distinguished those unwilling to conform to a traditional and orderly view of democracy.

This political nature of *the student* was in line with a long history, yet unusual compared to previous images of youth, which was stereotyped as delinquent during the crisis years and had little agency and power. The situation had improved in the miracle years, due to the rise of youth culture and new opportunities. *The student*, on the other hand, had a long history of being political, visible in the promotion of national and liberal ideals throughout the nineteenth century, as at the Hambach Fest in 1832.[81] In the 1960s, such interest in politics was present due to debates about Germany's Nazi past, partially triggered by the Adolf Eichmann trial. In fact, after the riots in Schwabing one member of the Community Initiative specifically referred to this trial in a press conference to defend the initiative's claims for justice.[82] In 1963, the Frankfurt-Auschwitz trials brought discussions about the Holocaust even more into the limelight, giving youngsters the opportunity to confront adults with uncomfortable and, at times, unreasonable questions and accusations. Parents and adult authorities as such lost credibility, even more through apparent continuities between the former Nazi state and West Germany. On the federal level, former member of the Nazi Party Kurt Georg Kiesinger became the third chancellor of West Germany in 1963. In Munich, Bavarian Minister of Culture and Education Theodor Maunz in particular sparked debates. He had been professor of jurisprudence providing commentaries on National Socialist laws throughout the Nazi period. According to historian Dieter Deiseroth, such individuals at least indicated "a limited break with the fascist past."[83]

Unwilling to accept such realities, the new generation found ways to respond: "It started harmlessly," activist Alois Aschenbrenner recalled. "For instance, wearing police uniforms ... to the university to then stand in front of the podium of two professors—[Prof. Reinhart] Maurach too, because he was an old fascist, a criminal law commentator, back in Hitler's times. We wanted to raise awareness regarding such unwillingness to deal with the past."[84] At the riots in Schwabing, some individuals had provoked the police yelling "Nazi state," "Gestapo," and "Nazi police."[85] Later, students would interrupt the commemoration for the resister Scholl siblings because they saw such an event as hypocrisy. According to an official report, students "disturbed the ceremony by dropping leaflets, uncoiling a banner with slogans like 'Nazis out,' 'Murderers celebrate their victims.' There were supposedly brawls. The demonstration ... was primarily aimed against speaker Prof. Buszmann and other professors ... because of their supposed National Socialist past."[86]

Apart from discussing the Nazi past, student protests circled around numerous other issues. As historian Konrad Jarausch summarized in a broader context, student protests in general incorporated three dimensions: debates regarding student subculture, the improvement of educational opportunities, and political activism.[87] In the postwar period, opposition often arose within the context of West German rearmament, soon coordinated within annual Ostermärsche Easter marches.[88] In March 1964, for example, the Kampagne für Demokratie und Abrüstung (Campaign for Democracy and Disarmament) had organized a demonstration in Munich, titled "From Cologne to Warsaw: Nuclear-Weapon Free!"[89] Annual events grew dramatically by 1968[90] because of the need for education reform. In 1964, pedagogue George Picht had described this "misery of education" in great detail: a lack of facilities, teachers, and basic funding.[91] Soon students began demanding more funding for institutions of higher education, direct input into university governance, and broader structural reforms. Also, as one young contemporary from Munich put it, "The indifference of the administration and senseless traditions"[92] needed to go. Conservative contemporaries and authorities, on the other hand, feared leftist student groups undermining the university.[93] Hence, they tried to limit democratization throughout the university, pushing young protestors on the streets. In July 1965, "the largest demonstration in the postwar period"[94] took place in Munich when around 10,000 protestors demonstrated in favor of education reform.[95]

International issues, most notably the War in Vietnam, fueled student opposition as well, especially once the conflict in Southeast Asia intensified. Two-thirds of the young were willing to take their protest to the streets,[96] namely in front of the U.S. consulate and the Amerikahaus in Munich.[97] Protestors repeatedly carried an effigy of U.S. President Lyndon B. Johnson to highlight their opposition, participated in sit-ins in the middle of the street, or disrupted celebrations of German-American friendship.[98] At times, protests turned violent, as demonstrators threw rocks at U.S. institutions, or used a small rocket to drop leaflets over the McGraw barracks in Munich to encourage desertion among U.S. soldiers.[99] Aware of the American role as the guarantor of West German freedom within the Cold War, political authorities became worried. *The student's* anti-imperialist agenda became also visible during the brief visit of the Iranian shah in Munich in 1967. Protestors welcomed the shah with boos once he arrived at the central train station, and demonstrations and disruptions followed him to the National Theatre, the Old Art Gallery, and City Hall. The police tried to keep order in an attempt to prevent brawls between *the student* and an accompanying group of shah supporters,[100] fearing further radicalization of *the student* and general disorder.

Soon embodying a complex mixture of antiestablishment characteristics, *the student* also became the symbol of anti–emergency law protests. According to the Germany Treaty from 1952, the United States, France, and Great Britain held the right to interfere in internal relations in case of an emergency. These rights would remain in place until the West German parliament passed adequate emergency laws.[101] Since the late 1950s, the conservatives (CDU/CSU) led by Chancellor Konrad Adenauer and later Ludwig Erhard had tried at various times to pass such laws. However, they needed the support of the social democrats (SPD) to get the two-thirds majority necessary to change the constitution. In the early 1960s, the SPD opposed various proposals, claiming such plans would restrict democratic processes and civil liberties. Soon discussions about the emergency laws faced a stalemate. In 1966, the CDU/CSU and the SPD then formed a Grand Coalition. As the first coalition between conservatives and social democrats in the Federal Republic, the Grand Coalition had a supermajority of 450 to 49 votes in parliament.[102] Theoretically, this alliance was more than enough to get a two-thirds majority needed to change the constitution. As more serious conversations regarding emergency laws took shape, questions around a lack of oversight given the limits of parliamentary opposition and concerns around far-reaching emergency laws took shape, mostly outside traditional frameworks.

The leftist Socialist German Student Union (SDS) and the Campaign for Disarmament had increasingly coordinated such efforts, eventually formed the board Emergency of Democracy, and later aligned itself partially with the Außerparlamentarischen Opposition (Extraparliamentary Opposition, APO).[103] Initially, such organizations had been part of a student council, as each group was broadly aligned with a political party. There had been the Social Democratic University Group as well as a more conservative Munich Student Union.[104] Soon, however, various individuals formed alternative organizations, especially in Schwabing. The undogmatic and artistic group Subversive Action, for instance, met in a cellar. Here, they read and discussed Theodor Adorno, Herbert Marcuse, Karl Marx, and others; their objective was to "expose societal repression."[105] Regular participant Dieter Kunzelmann later became a founding member of the Kommune I in West Berlin, a politically motivated commune set up to provide an alternative to traditional middle-class family structures. Elsewhere, people simply discussed political issues in restaurants and bars. Many visited different groups each night, participated in debates, and networked. According to one contemporary, during the 1960s "a left subculture sprouted on every corner in Schwabing,"[106] outside traditional, hierarchical, and adult-approved organizations. Throughout West Germany, such groups often aligned themselves with the APO.[107] Sustained mainly by the Socialist Student Union (SDS), this Extraparliamentary Opposition has commonly been described as synonymous with the student movement.[108] Rather diverse throughout the years, the APO played a key role in Munich and gained broad support beyond students, mainly after the formation of the Grand Coalition in 1966 and the push for emergency laws. According to scholar Rolf Seeliger, an alienation from traditional parties was a major reason for the rise of the APO.[109] Soon local student groups like the SDS and the Humanist Union worked together, apparent in attempts to democratize the university. Events like "Democratic Action January 1968"[110] and subsequent protests brought much attention, and some local politicians even joined calls for more democracy. Most political authorities, however, feared this extraparliamentary format. Bringing to mind attempts to push *the delinquent boy* into structured political setups during the crisis years, local politicians noted that protestors should join a traditional party. Such voices clearly favored structured political arrangements, perceived APO as an antiparliamentary force, and feared politically organized young people overall.

The Arrival of *the Gammler*

Adult authorities also worried about those youngsters simply dropping out of society altogether. A phenomenon soon embodied by *Gammler* bums, this image of youth disrupted class strata and traditional morals in the most visible form. Most came from middle-class backgrounds[111] yet chose to simply travel around Europe, bumming around Leopoldstraße boulevard in Schwabing, begging for money, sometimes playing protest songs, or painting on sidewalks[112] [Figure 5.2]. According to one contemporary description, *Gammler*

> have messy hair and beards, [and] wear ragged and audacious clothes. The Gammler takes it easy, while leaning against walls or sitting on stairs. The Gammler is not walking but rambling, slouching, looking lost, worn out, disinterested. At night the Gammler is sleeping outside, in parks, in grit boxes, run-down cars, and unfinished buildings.... The Gammler is not interested in money or ownership, could be compared to the Greek philosopher Diogenes, just sitting in the sun, thinking and discussing with other Gammlers. They live for the moment.[113]

Figure 5.2 A group of so-called *Gammler* at the Monopteros monument in the English Garden park in Munich, 1968. Courtesy of Hans Enzwieser/Süddeutsche Zeitung Photo.

Similar behaviors had sparked the riots in 1962, thus making local authorities worried right away. In addition, officials feared Americanization, especially once hearing about similar situations in the United States. In June 1966, one Munich police official spent six weeks touring the United States, stopping in no less than seventeen cities. He concluded, "for the liberalization of our laws we have to pay a price. ... We need to put even more emphasis on preemptive measures, [and] ... attempts to influence the young have to be expanded. Additional means of control are necessary for Beatclubs, Gammler, and pseudo-artists."[114] Moreover, in a society valuing hard work, order, and discipline, the attitude and appearance of *the Gammler* marked "a crawling revolution,"[115] and a threat to social order. References to National Socialism surfaced right away, as adults commented, "During Hitler's times this would not have been possible"; another curious bystander called for forced labor,[116] substantiating a survey conducted by the polling group Allensbach in 1968, in which more than 50 percent of those asked about *Gammler* wanted them sent to compulsory work camps.[117] Comments about gassing these bums could be heard on the streets of Munich and elsewhere then and later on,[118] and outline the presence of the Nazi past on street corners; such references also illustrate how youth yet again became a platform for talking about moral values, social norms, postwar order, and the past.

Again, the media and local authorities hyped the arrival of the protesting *student* and the noncompliant *Gammler* in Munich. Although a minority movement,[119] vagrant and vagabonding youth soon dominated front pages. *Der Spiegel* as well as local newspapers widely discussed *the Gammler.*[120] In addition, authorities sustained such constructs. One member of the local city council stated that "445 out of 608 Gammler are under twenty-one years of age. These numbers indicate that such behavior was a problem of the young and not so much a societal problem."[121] Some local authorities saw such deviancy rooted in a feeling of adventure; others detected an unwillingness to conform, criminal energy, and even increased drug use.[122] In fact, by 1965 an internal survey within the police revealed a growing criminalization of and discrimination against young people overall. Thirty-one percent of police officers saw *the student* as their enemies.[123] Historian Werner Linder described such profiling as an "unscrupulous *marginalization* and *criminalization* of these individuals."[124] Speculations about alcohol, crime, sexual orgies, and venereal diseases, at times, accompanied these narratives. Some even wondered if *Gammlertum* or bumming around could lead to socialism, an interesting dynamic given that authorities in East Germany feared it could lead to capitalism. Described by one historian as "a provocation par excellence,"[125] connections to students became increasingly fluid. At the same time, fears regarding *the student* remained high, especially due to sensation-alist reports. A caption in *Die Deutsche Nationalzeitung,* for instance, read "Stop [student leader] Dutschke now! Or there will be a civil war. Hunt Nazis—but flatter communists?" Below the headline, five images showed the student leader.[126] Rooted in fears regarding instability and communism, it was the Springer press in particular that became a sup-porter of conservative policies. Springer was the most powerful press conglomerate in West Germany, publishing newspapers like *Die Welt* and *Die Bildzeitung.* For *the student,* noted one historian, "the Springer press symbolized everything that was wrong with society: inadequate engagement with the Nazi past, the authoritarianism and lack of de-mocracy, and the pervasive influence of anticommunism."[127]

Again, a binary emerged, pitting two groups against each other along age or generation. On one side, there were adult authorities, more con-servative in their values, and in favor of social order, traditional moral-ity, and structured political processes. On the other side, there was *the student* and *the Gammler:* mainly young, middle-class males, and their female companions, disruptive to political order. As one contemporary summarized, when adults talked to the *Gammler* in Munich, then "two opposites meet: the bourgeoisie owners against those without owner-ship, the clean against the unclean, the working against those dismiss-ing work."[128] This atmosphere left little space for complexities or even conversation between both groups, and put Munich arguably on a path towards its most violent postwar protests yet.

1968 in Munich

The visit of the shah in Munich marked the beginning of further es-calation, triggered by events in West Berlin. After a brief visit in the Bavarian capital, the shah and his wife faced demonstrators at West Berlin's city hall on 2 June. In contrast to Munich, the local police did not separate supporters of the Iranian leader and protestors. Instead, it stood by as followers of Shah Pahlavi used sticks to beat demonstra-tors and bystanders alike. Chaos ensued, and the situation escalated as undercover policeman Karl-Heinz Kurras shot twenty-six-year-old Benno Ohnesorg.[129] News of Ohnesorg's death spread quickly, reaching Munich in an instant. Three days later, about seven thousand demon-strators marched silently through the city, some with signs reading "Benno Ohnesorg, Political Murder"; protestors lay down a wreath at a memorial at the square in Remembrance of the Victims of Fascism,[130] illustrating their interpretation of events. In the following months, the death of Ohnesorg created a tense and volatile situation within the Bavarian capital. Closely linked with the situation in West Berlin, many followed the trial against Kurras. He was acquitted several months later, raising fears amongst Munich's authorities in regard to retaliation from *the student*. Demonstrations continued, while inciting remarks by local Munich authorities that students were "stupid and primitive"[131] hardly served to soothe tensions.

Several months later, tensions in West Berlin again triggered protests in the Bavarian capital. In spring 1968, Josef Bachmann tried to kill student leader Rudi Dutschke. On 11 April, Bachmann approached Dutschke outside a pharmacy. Once the student leader confirmed his identity, Bachmann shot him three times.[132] Again, news spread quickly to Munich and elsewhere.[133] Whereas Dutschke survived the attack, many blamed a larger media campaign against *the student* for the assassination attempt. Publicist Axel Springer in particular became the target of protestors, together with conservative and reactionary voices.[134] As then student Hanfried Brenner recalled later, "Of course we became active right away, ... and mobilized Schwabing."[135] The official reaction by Chancellor Kiesinger and others did little to abate such anger.[136] Indeed, conservative Bavarian politician Franz-Josef Strauß stated, "with these scoundrels there is nothing to talk about; every word is wasted on them."[137] For him, Munich and the Federal Republic tumbled towards another unstable Weimar Republic.

The fears of authorities materialized soon thereafter, as protests took place throughout Munich. Already at the night of the assassination attempt, roughly 200 to 300 "mostly younger people"[138] marched from the university to the office building of Springer Publishing, the Buchgewerbehaus building. As participating protestors remembered, the police were not prepared for such demonstrations.[139] Soon some protestors climbed on the roof, destroyed windows, and tagged walls. One slogan read "Murder, Springer"; another banner recalled the names of the victims, "Ohnesorg, Dutschke."[140] Groups of protestors yelled, "Today Dutschke, Tomorrow Us!" and "Springer, Murder!"[141] Around 1:00 A.M., some demonstrators entered the building and engaged workers in discussions in an attempt to convince them to join protests. As one protestor noted, "it was no problem getting into the building."[142]

Once able to clear the situation and disperse the crowd, local law enforcement made sure it would not be caught by surprise again. As a result, authorities began closely monitoring *the student* around Schwabing throughout the next days. Officials hence noticed the distribution of leaflets calling for "the seizure of the Buchgewerbehaus building in Munich";[143] protestors also "planned to prevent the delivery of the daily tabloid *Die Bildzeitung*," a Springer publication.[144] Increasingly losing the advantage of surprise, roughly three hundred protestors showed up at the Buchgewerbehaus building the next evening. Again, according to official records, "Some demonstrators tried to get into the building. [This time] police officers positioned within the area prevented such [efforts]."[145] Around 8 P.M. that evening, the police called on protestors to clear the access road. Eventually, law enforcement moved forward, using water cannons. A group of six protestors, seemingly directing the riots from their white Chevrolet car nearby, were soon soaked by those water cannons.[146] Demonstrators responded by throwing rocks. A chaotic scene developed: many protestors resisted, while others merely continued to discuss current political issues with police officers. The police followed their newly developed police tactic and tried to avoid direct involvement. By midnight the majority of the demonstrators had dispersed and authorities began clearing the road to allow the free flow of traffic and with that the delivery of Springer newspapers.

After days of protests throughout the Easter weekend, the situation at last escalated on 15 April. Following a longstanding tradition, a diverse group of protestors joined the Easter march taking place that day. Inspired by the events in West Berlin, the march brought more people together than ever before. Throughout West Germany, roughly 300,000 people protested. Some carried signs; others simply came along in an attempt to demonstrate against the emergency laws, war, or the Springer press. In 1968, many also showed their sympathy for Rudi Dutschke.[147] After an initial gathering and various speeches, roughly 1,500 protestors marched to the Buchgewerbehaus building.[148] Again, some began blocking the entrance with various objects, hoping to prevent the delivery of newspapers; some also sat in the middle of the street. This time the police moved forward with less restraint, especially when protestors threw rocks. At least sixteen people were injured;[149] two individuals—young journalist Klaus Frings and student Rüdiger Schreck—were hit by an object and died in the hospital.[150] The protests in Munich had reached a sad climax.

In the months following the death of Frings and Schreck, the situation calmed down as local authorities and protestors began evaluating the overall events.[151] An official report surfacing in early September blamed various student organizations and *the student* more directly; it also gave a profile of offenders based on gender, family status, age, and profession. According to this, 219 protestors had been originally indicted, only twenty-one of them female. More than 75 percent of all were between eighteen and twenty-nine years of age; a majority were unmarried male youngsters. Only 33 percent of arrested protestors were enrolled at the university, and thus actual students.[152] That aspect, however, seemingly bothered no one given the power of *the student* as the contemporary construct of youth during the protest years. Protestors took a step back as well, rethinking what had happened. On 17 April, AStA organized an event, in which a group of demonstrators marched to the Königsplatz square in downtown Munich, rallying around the slogan, "Against political murder, terror, violence, and anarchy." Many carried signs reading "Terror neither from the right nor from the left!," "One death is enough," and "Rocks are no political arguments."[153] Subsequent discussions among participants and bystanders about the question who was at fault for the two deaths continued long into the night. Although between thirty and eighty individuals walked over to the Buchgewerbehaus building, that day the police did not have to intervene. A similar demonstration took place six days later. Following the motto "Is there a new beginning?"[154] roughly six thousand participated. Again, politicians from all major parties as well as student leaders from several organizations spoke at the Königsplatz square.[155] The situation seemingly calmed down, and conversations between various sides became a possibility.

The eventual return of harsh rhetoric indicated the continuing power of *the student* as a discourse. Voices in the media and responses of protestors, at times, continued to paint a grim picture. In fact, a reporter for *Der Bayerische Rundfunk* radio compared student leaders to monks during the inquisition;[156] the ultraconservative newspaper *Christ und die Welt* even saw *the student* on the way towards becoming asocial, and warned of "a dangerous path from opposition to isolation to antisociality."[157] Student organizations like the SDS, on the other hand, did not fully dismiss violence as a legitimate means of politics. For them, the events in West Berlin had only sustained fears of a totalitarian state. As one participant noted, "We do not act according to Gandhi, but according to Marx, Engels, Lenin, and Mao."[158] Nonetheless, protests against the emergency laws in May 1968 remained mostly nonviolent [Figure 5.3]. On 20 May, for example, roughly 2,500 marched to the main office of local labor unions, hoping to convince workers to join their movement.[159] Yet the Easter riots had deterred many, limiting the appeal of the protests. Several days later, protestors tried to politicize the public by disrupting a theater performance with "emergency-go-ins."[160] They had little success. Other demonstra-

Figure 5.3 Students protest against the Emergency Laws at Stachus square in Munich, 1968. Courtesy of Marlies Schnetzer/Süddeutsche Zeitung Photo.

tions and actions followed, and, according to Police Chief Manfred Schreiber, "demonstrations continued without major disruptions."[161]

Whereas the overall appeal of the protest movement appeared to decline in the coming weeks, minor skirmishes continued. In May 1968, the emergency laws passed in the German Bundestag; a year later, higher education reform also moved through the legislature. At that point, it became more difficult for protestors to rally behind various issues. Yet even beforehand many individuals had withdrawn their support, especially once they saw the violence in April and the unwillingness of some leaders to condemn it altogether. Soon former protest leaders left certain organizations, or radicalized even more. AStA leader Rolf Pohle joined the newly forming left-wing terrorist group, the Red Army Faction (RAF).[162] Actions continued beyond 1969, however.[163] In February protestors occupied Munich's Academy for the Arts to protest against conservative elites, the old establishment, and the proposed university reform.[164] Some occupiers wrote slogans on walls reading, "SS-University" or "Nazi-Kiesinger"[165] to illustrate their protests; others set up a motorbike race within the building as a way to provoke the state legislature.[166] Of course, that race in particular, combined with some other behaviors, made it much easier for authorities to frame this occupation as vandalism. Minister for Culture and Education Ludwig Huber had consequently little difficulty convincing a majority in parliament to end the rule of the mob.

It took a couple more years until *the student* left the limelight altogether. This had to do particularly with the fact that some local authorities tried to hold on to this image of youth as long as possible. In a memorandum regarding "the interference of teaching and research ... by disturbances of students,"[167] one professor tried to resurrect fears. Whereas he acknowledged that the situation in 1969 did not compare to that of 1968, the memorandum outlined a lack of publicity regarding ongoing disturbances. Away from the public sphere, students now used what he described as "guerrilla war" tactics: "The university is helpless ... within this grueling war of nerves."[168] Yet the lack of major issues of contestation and the end of the Grand Coalition left less room for such voices to be heard. In June 1970, *Die Süddeutsche Zeitung* could thus report on the "disarmament of the Easter marchers"[169] already even if authorities continued to reference and employ *the student* until 1973.

Notes

1. "In Schwabing ist der Teufel los," *Der Münchner Merkur,* 25 June 1962.
2. Ibid.
3. "Was halten Sie von den Krawallen?" *Der Münchner Merkur,* 26 June 1962.
4. According to Hanna Schissler, these protests "fundamentally questioned West German 'normality.'" Schissler, "'Normalization' as Project," 361, in *Miracle Years.*
5. Kock, *Der Bayerische Landtag 1946–1986,* 182. See also: Fritz Allemann, *Bonn ist nicht Weimar* (Cologne, 1956); "Wird Bonn doch Weimar?" *Der Spiegel,* 13 March 1967.
6. Foucault, *Discipline and Punish,* 278.
7. In the winter semester 1962/63, Munich registered 20,032 students. Bay-HStAM, Staatskanzlei 13619. See also: Ludwig-Maximilians-Universität München, ed., *Ludwig-Maximilians-Universität München* (Neukeferloh/ Munich, 2001). The numbers increased dramatically in the following years, reaching more than 30,000 by 1968. See: Manfred Schreiber, "Das Jahr 1968 in München," in *1968: 30 Jahre danach,* ed. Venanz Schubert (St. Ottilien, 1999), 35–54, here 41.
8. Ernst Hofenrichter, "Unsterbliches Schwabing," in *Lebendiges Schwabing,* ed. Rolf Flügel (Munich, 1958), 218–30, here 218; Franziska Bilek, *Mir gefällts in München: Ein Geständnis in Bildern und Worten* (Munich, 1958); Fricke, *München rockt.*

9. Stefan Hemler, "Aufbegehren einer Jugendszene: Protestbeteiligte, Verlauf und Aktionsmuster bei den 'Schwabinger Krawallen," in *'Schwabinger Krawalle'*, 25–57, here 27. See also: StAM, Polizeidirektion München 11129.

10. Michael Sturm, "'Wildgewordene Obrigkeit'? Die Rolle der Münchner Polizei während der 'Schwabinger Krawalle,' in *'Schwabinger Krawalle'*, 59–105, here 60. See also: Anton Fingerle, *München: Heimat und Weltstadt* (Munich, 1963).

11. StAM, Polizeidirektion München 11131; StAM, Polizeidirektion München 11129. See also: *Information des AStA der Universität München*, "Studentenkrawalle: Jazz in der Uni," 18 June 1961; Sturm, "Wildgewordene Obrigkeit," in *'Schwabinger Krawalle'*, 62.

12. StAM, Polizeidirektion München 11129. See also: StAM, Polizeidirektion München 11131.

13. StAM, Polizeidirektion München 11129.

14. Bernd Drost, prod., *Gestern und Heute: 'Schwabinger Krawalle'* (Munich, 1990); Oktavia Depta, prod., *Wolfram Kunkel und die Schwabinger Krawalle* (Munich, 2009).

15. StAM, Polizeidirektion München 11131.

16. Gerhard Fürmetz," Fünf Protestmnächte mit weitreichenden Folgen: Die 'Schwabinger Krawalle' vom Juni 1962," in *Auf den Barrikaden*, 71–79, here 71.

17. Ibid. See also: BayHStAM, MJu 24032, quoted in Hemler, "Aufbegehren einer Jugendszene," in *'Schwabinger Krawalle'*, 47–48; Max Thomas Mehr, ed., *Drachen mit tausend Köpfen: Spaziergänge durch linkes und alternatives Milieu* (Neuwied/Darmstadt, 1982), 53–58; Fritz Fenzl, *Münchner Stadtgeschichte* (Munich, 1994), 238–41; Geschichtswerkstatt Neuhausen, *Vom Rio zum Kolobri*, 155–56; Michael Farin, ed., *Polizeireport München 1799–1999* (Munich, 1999), 392; Fricke, *München rockt*, 12–14.

18. Hans-Jochen Vogel, *Die Amtskette: Meine 12 Münchner Jahre* (Munich, 1972), 45–46. See also: StAM, Polizeidirektion München 11129.

19. Fürmetz, "Anwalt der Jugend," 146, in *'Schwabinger Krawalle'*.

20. Ibid., 147.

21. "Gaudi und Rowdy," *Der Münchner Merkur*, 23–24 June 1962. See also: "Das ist kein Spaß mehr!" *Der Münchner Merkur*, 25 June 1962; "Nächtlicher Krawall in der Leopoldstraße," *Der Münchner Merkur*, 23–24 June 1962. *Die Süddeutsche Zeitung* described the events in a similar fashion: "Treibjagd auf die Rowdys," *Die Süddeutsche Zeitung*, 27 June 1962; "Aufstand der Massen in Schwabing," *Die Süddeutsche Zeitung*, 23–24 June 1962.

22. "Was halten sie von den Krawallen?" *Der Münchner Merkur*, 26 June 1962.

23. *8-Uhr Blatt*, 23 June 1962, quoted in Andreas Voith, "'Tanz der Gummiknüppel' und andere Sensationen: Zur Presseberichterstattung über die 'Schwabinger Krawalle,'" in *'Schwabinger Krawalle'*, 107–123, here 111.

24. Ibid. See also: "Riesenkrawall in Schwabing," *Abendzeitung-Nachtausgabe*, 22 June 1962;

25. "Schwabinger Ungeist 62," *8-Uhr Blatt*, 24 June 1962.

26. "In München ging ein unrühmliches Kapitel zu Ende," *8-Uhr Blatt*, 30 June 1962.
27. "Für uns war es jedesmal eine Erlösung," *Die Süddeutsche Zeitung*, 7–8 July 1962.
28. "Nacht für Nacht: Tumulte in Schwabing," *Die Süddeutsche Zeitung*, 25 June 1962.
29. Seelmann-Bericht, quoted in Fürmetz, "Anwalt der Jugend," in *'Schwabinger Krawalle'*, 141–50. See also: "Krawalle im Meinungsstreit," *Der Münchner Merkur*, 29 June 1962.
30. StAM, Polizeidirektion München 11129.
31. BayHStAM, Ministerium des Inneren 97954.
32. StAM, Polizeidirektion München 11129.
33. BayHStAM, Ministerium des Inneren 97954.
34. Karsten Peters, ed., *'1200 Jahre Schwabing:' Geschichte und Geschichten eines berühmten Stadtviertels* (Munich-Gräfelfing, 1982), 126. See also: Diethart Krebs, "Zur Geschichte und Gestalt der deutschen Jungenschaft," *Neue Sammlung* 6 (1966): 146–70, here 152–62.
35. Depta, prod., *Wolfram Kunkel und die Schwabinger Krawalle*.
36. BayHStAM, 97954.
37. See, for instance: "Im Rathaus: Ruhe nach dem Sturm," *Der Münchner Merkur*, 28 June 1962; "Die erste Nacht ohne Krawall," *Der Münchner Merkur*, 28 June 1962.
38. Fürmetz, "Fünf Protestnächte mit weitreichenden Folgen: Die 'Schwabinger Krawalle' vom Juni 1962," in *Auf den Barrikaden*, 71–79, here 71.
39. The fact that East German reporters discussed the events in Schwabing and even sent journalists to Munich increased fears. "So blässt man ungewollt in Ulbrichts Horn," *Der Bayernspiegel*, 3 July 1962.
40. Julius Schittenhelm, in *München rockt*, 13. See also: BayHStAM, Staatskanzlei 13612; StAM, RA 101155.
41. Sturm, "Wildgewordene Obrigkeit?" in *'Schwabinger Krawalle'*, 76.
42. Dieter Kunzelmann, *Leisten sie keinen Widerstand! Bilder aus meinem Leben* (Berlin, 1998), 36. See also: Stefan Hemler, "'Nicht aus dem Haus gegangen:' Die 'Subversiven' und die 'Schwabinger Krawalle,' in *'Schwabinger Krawalle'*, 173–74.
43. Kunzelmann, *Leisten sie keinen Widerstand*, 37.
44. Bundesarchiv Koblenz (BundAK), Stammheim-Akten, Band 6, quoted in Klaus Stern and Jörg Herrmann, *Andreas Baader: Das Leben eines Staatsfeindes* (Munich, 2007), 44.
45. Ibid., 49. According to this biography, Baader's "career as a protestor began at that date [26 June 1962, in Schwabing]." Ibid., 43.
46. A group called Provisional Committee in Defense of Democratic Rights in Schwabing planned a meeting on 26 June 1962 at the Monopteros monument at the English Garden Park. 250 people showed up. Participants discussed the events before dispersing. BayHStAM, Ministerium des Inneren 97954; "Die fünfte Krawallnacht," *Der Münchner Merkur*, 27 June 1962.
47. StadtAM, Ratsitzungsprotokolle, Sitzungsprotokoll 735/16 (1962). See also: StAM, Polizeidirektion München 11132; Esther Arens, "Lektion in Demokratie: Die 'Schwabinger Krawalle' und die Münchner 'Interessen-

gemeinschaft zur Wahrung der Bürgerrechte,' in *'Schwabinger Krawalle'*, 125–40, here 127.

48. StAM, Polizeidirektion München 9049 (Flugblatt zur Untersuchung der Polizei).
49. StAM, Polizeidirektion München 11132.
50. "Im Waffenlärm," *profil*, no. 3 (May 1963). See also: Arens, "Lektion in Demokratie," in *'Schwabinger Krawalle'*, 137.
51. "AStA distanziert sich," *Der Münchner Merkur*, 26 June 1962.
52. "Es waren keine Studentenunruhen," *Die Süddeutsche Zeitung*, 3 September 1962.
53. "Studentenschaft und die Schwabinger Krawalle," *Die Süddeutsche Zeitung*, 5 July 1962.
54. "Gegen diese Willkür mußt du demonstrieren!" *Welt am Sonntag*, 1 July 1962.
55. Helmut Schelsky, *Die skeptische Generation: Eine Soziologie der deutschen Jugend* (Düsseldorf, 1957).
56. "Übertriebene Generation," *Der Spiegel*, 2 October 1967.
57. Ibid. Henning Wrage writes about the commercialization, referencing the lemonade *Bluna*. Wrage, "Neue Jugend: Einleitung," in *Handbuch Nachkriegskultur*, 650. See also: Axel Schildt and Detlef Siegfried, eds, *Between Marx and Coca-Cola: Youth Cultures in Changing European Societies, 1960–1980* (New York, 2006). The concept of generations remains methodologically "slippery" but useful when tracing new constructs. Stephen Lovell, "Introduction," in *Generations in Twentieth-Century Europe*, ed. Stephen Lovell (New York, 2007), 9; Jarausch, *After Hitler*, 164.
58. "Übertrieben Generation," *Der Spiegel*, 2 October 1967.
59. Ibid.
60. Harald Lönnecker, "Studenten und Gesellschaft, Studenten in der Gesellschaft: Versuch eines Überblicks seit Beginn des 19. Jahrhunderts," in *Universität im öffentlichen Raum*, ed. Rainer Christoph Schwinges (Basel, 2008), 387–438. See also: Lindner, *Jugendproteste seit den fünfziger Jahren*, 106–16.
61. Frick, *Münchne rockt*, 39–41.
62. "Schalom aleichem," *Der Spiegel*, 19 September 1966.
63. Lönnecker, "Studenten und Gesellschaft: Studenten in der Gesellschaft," 387–390.
64. Hemler, "Aufbegehren einer Jugendszene," in *'Schwabinger Krawalle'*, 29.
65. Kristin Ross, *May '68 and Its Afterlives* (Chicago, 2002), 2–3. George Lipitz notes in a similar context, "youth activists did play an important role in the political struggles of the decade, but they represented specific interest groups and constituencies among youth, not youth as a whole." Georg Lipitz, "Who'll Stop the Rain? Youth Culture, Rock 'n' Roll, and Social Crisis," in *The Sixties: From Memory to History*, ed. David R. Farber (Chapel Hill, 1994), 206–34, here 206.
66. Hemler, "Aufbegehren einer Jugendszene," in *'Schwabinger Krawalle'*, 27.
67. "'Alles Material übergeben,'" *Der Münchner Merkur*, 29 April 1968.
68. Sturm, "Wildgewordene Obrigkeit," in *'Schwabinger Krawalle'*, 79. See also: Karl Stankiewitz, *München '68: Traumstadt in Bewegung* (Munich, 2008). 24.

69. McDougall, *Youth Politics in East Germany*, 191.
70. BayHStAM, Staatskanzlei 11129. See also: Hemler, "Aufbegehren einer Jugendszene," in Fürmetz, ed., '*Schwabinger Krawalle*', 29.
71. "Schalom aleichem," *Der Spiegel*, 19 September 1966. See also: Ute Frevert, "Umbruch der Geschlechterverhältnisse? Die 60er Jahre als geschlechtspolitischer Experimentierraum," 642–60, in *Dynamische Zeiten: Die 60er Jahre in den beiden deutschen Gesellschaften*, ed. Axel Schildt and Detlef Siegfried (Hamburg, 2000).
72. Inga Buhmann, *Ich habe mir eine Geschichte geschrieben* (Munich, 1977), 164.
73. Kristina Schulz, *Der lange Atem der Provokation: Die Frauenbewegung in der Bundesrepublik und in Frankreich 1968–1976* (Frankfurt am Main, 2002), 78.
74. "In München ging ein unrühmliches Kapitel zu Ende," *8-Uhr Blatt*, 30 June 1962.
75. Gretchen Dutschke-Klotz, *Wir hatten ein barbarisch schönes Leben. Rudi Dutschke: Eine Biographie* (Cologne, 1996), 81. See also: Marita Krauss, "1968 und die Frauenbewegung," in *1968: 30 Jahre danach*, 133–62, here 146.
76. "Die rosa Zeiten sind vorbei," *Der Spiegel*, 25 November 1968.
77. Buhmann, *Ich habe mir eine Geschichte geschrieben*, 164.
78. See namely: Krauss, "1968 und die Frauenbewegung," in *1968: 30 Jahre danach*.
79. Gerl-Falkovitz, "Milde Verklärung? Erlebnisse als Studentin '68," in *1968: 30 Jahre danach*, 60. See also: Marion Grob, *Das Kleidungsverhalten jugendlicher Protestgruppen im 20. Jahrhundert am Beispiel des Wandervogels und der Studentenbewegung* (Münster, 1985), 224–309; Sabine Weißler, "Unklare Verhältnisse: 1968 und die Mode," in *1968: Handbuch zur Kultur- und Mediengeschichte der Studentenbewegung*, ed. Martin Klimke and Joachim Scharloth (Stuttgart, 2007), 305–10.
80. Studentenwerk München, ed., '*Wo geht's hier zum Studentenhaus?*' 75 Jahre *Studentenwerk München* (Munich, 1995), 44. See also: Hanna-Barbara Gerl-Falkovitz, "Milde Verklärung? Erlebnisse als Studentin '68," in *1968: 30 Jahre danach*, 55–69, here 59; Günter Gerstenberg, *Hiebe, Liebe und Proteste: München 1968* (Munich, 1991), 9.
81. Konrad Jarausch, *Deutsche Studenten 1800–1970* (Frankfurt am Main, 1984).
82. "OB Dr. Vogel beging 'Landfriedensbruch,'" *8-Uhr Blatt*, 28 July 1962.
83. Dieter Deiseroth, "Kontinuitätsprobleme der deutschen Staatsrechtslehre(r): Das Beispiel Theodor Maunz," in *Ordnungsmacht? Über das Verhältnis von Legalität, Konsens und Herrschaft*, ed. Dieter Deiseroth, Friedhelm Hase, and Karl-Heinz Ladeur (Frankfurt am Main, 1981), 85–111, here 103. See also: "Aufgeblickt, himmlische Herrscharen," *Der Spiegel*, 4 December 1967; "Diese Herren," *Der Spiegel*, 19 February 1968.
84. Alois Aschenbrenner, quoted in Bayerischer Rundfunk, Die 68er–40 Jahre danach, accessible at http://archive.is/005H6, [last accessed 11 March 2014].

85. StAM, Polizeidirektion München 11131; StAM, Polizeidirektion München 11129. See also: "Das ist kein Spass mehr!" *Der Münchner Merkur,* 25 June 1962.

86. StAM, RA 101154. See also: "Zwischenfälle bei Gedenkstunde für die Weiße Rose," *Die Süddeutsche Zeitung,* 24–25 February 1968; "Die Leitbilder der Geschwister Scholl," *Die Süddeutsche Zeitung,* 2–3 March 1968.

87. Jarausch, *Deutsche Studenten,* 9. As Jarausch underlines, the term *student* often carries a negative connotation.

88. Karl Otto, *Vom Ostermarsch zur APO: Geschichte der außerparlamentarischen Opposition in der Bundesrepublik 1960–1970* (Frankfurt am Main, 1977); Hans Konrad Tempel and Helga Tempel, "Ostermärsche gegen den Atomtod," 11–14, in *30 Jahre Ostermarsch: Ein Beitrag zur politischen Kultur der Bundesrepublik Deutschland und ein Stück Bremer Stadtgeschichte,* ed. Christoph Butterwegge (Bremen, 1990).

89. StadtAM, Zeitgeschichtliche Sammlung 190/5 quoted in Protest Chronicle Munich (1964), accessible at http://protest-muenchen.sub-bavaria.de, [last accessed 11 March 2014]. See also: "Studenten-Protest gegen Atomrüstung," *Die Süddeutsche Zeitung,* 21 May 1958; "Drei Tage nächtlicher Protest der Studenten," *8-Uhr Blatt,* 23 June 1958; "Schweigemarsch der Studenten," *Die Süddeutsche Zeitung,* 19 May 1958; "Schwache Teilnahme an den Ostermärschen," *Der Münchner Merkur,* 4 April 1961; "Sie kämpfen gegen die Atombombe," *Die Süddeutsche Zeitung,* 24 April 1962.

90. "Ostermaschierer rufen zu Aktionen auf," *Die Süddeutsche Zeitung,* 16 April 1968; StadtAM, Zeitungsarchiv 178.

91. George Picht, *Die deutsche Bildungskatastrophe: Analyse und Dokumentation* (Olten, 1964). See also: Jürgen Habermas, *Protestbewegung und Hochschulreform* (Frankfurt am Main, 1969); Ernst Nolte, *Sinn und Widersinn der Demokratisierung der Universität* (Freiburg, 1968).

92. Fricke, *München rockt,* 67.

93. Hans Julius Schoeps and Christoph Dannenmann, eds., *Die rebellischen Studenten: Elite der Demokratie oder Vorhut eines linken Faschismus?* (Munich/Esslingen am Neckar, 1968).

94. "Studenten demonstrieren für bessere Bildungschancen," *Die Süddeutsche Zeitung,* 2 July 1965. See also: "Studentendemonstration," *Der Münchner Merkur,* 24 June 1965; "Konvent der Uni München kritisiert den Bundeskanzler," *Die Abendzeitung,* 9 July 1965; "Studenten gehen auf die Barrikaden," *Der Münchner Merkur,* 25 June 1965; "'Priorität für Bildungspolitik,'" *Der Münchner Merkur,* 1–2 July 1967; "Bildungspolitik mit Provinz-Niveau," *Die Süddeutsche Zeitung,* 3 July 1967; Dollinger, *München im 20. Jahrhundert,* 275.

95. "10,000 Studenten demonstrierten gestern in München," *Der Münchner Merkur,* 2 July 1965.

96. "Zwei Drittel zum Protest bereit," *Der Spiegel,* 19 February 1968. See also: "Diesen Krieg kann niemand gewinnen," *Der Spiegel,* 4 March 1968; "Bereit, auf die Straße zu gehen," *Der Spiegel,* 12 February 1968; Eckhard Siepmann, "Vietnam: Der große Katalysator," in *CheSchahShit: Die Sechziger Jahre zwischen Cocktail und Molotow,* ed. Eckhard Siepmann (Berlin, 1984), 125–27.

97. "Antiamerikanische Demonstration von Polizei in München aufgelöst," *Die Süddeutsche Zeitung*, 28 May 1965; "Zwei Demonstranten mit Transparenten verhaftet," *Die Süddeutsche Zeitung*, 27 July 1965; "Verwarnung wegen Auflauf," *Der Münchner Merkur*, 10 November 1965; "Demonstranten gegen den Vietnam-Krieg," *Die Süddeutsche Zeitung*, 25 February 1966.

98. dpa-Foto, Fotomuseum, quoted in Protest Chronicle Munich (1965), accessible at http://protest-muenchen.sub-bavaria.de, [last accessed 11 March 2015]. See also: StadAM, Stadtchronik (1968); StAM, RA 101154.

99. StadtAM, Stadtchronik (1968); BayHStAM, Staatskanzlei 13619. See also: Protest Chronicle Munich (1968), accessible at http://protest-muenchen .sub-bavaria.de, [last accessed 11 March 2015]; "Aufruf zur Desertation war vergeblich," *Die Abendzeitung*, 9 May 1968; "Vietkong-Fahne vor US-Kaserne," *Der Münchner Merkur*, 9 May 1968; "Parolen gegen den Vietnam-Krieg," *Die Süddeutsche Zeitung*, 9 May 1968.

100. BayHStAM, Staatskanzlei 13617; Protest Chronicle Munich (1967), accessible at http://protest-muenchen.sub-bavaria.de, [last accessed 11 March 2015]; *Der Münchner Merkur*, quoted in "Sanfte Polizei Welle," *Der Spiegel*, 19 June 1967. See also: Dollinger, *München im 20. Jahrhundert*, 284.

101. The Germany Treaty (*Deutschlandvertrag*) was signed on 26 May 1952. Several changes make the version from 23 October 1954 the basis for further discussions. Accessible at http://www.documentarchiv.de/brd/dtlvertrag.html, [last accessed 11 March 2014].

102. Joachim Eichhorn, *Durch alle Klippen hindurch zum Erfolg: Die Regierungspraxis der ersten Großen Koalition (1966–1969)* (Munich, 2009).

103. The Socialist German Student Union (Sozialistischer Studentenbund, SDS) was initially the student organization of the social democrats (SPD). By 1961, it split with the party. See, for instance: Tilman Fichter and Siegward Lönnendonker, *Macht und Ohnmacht der Studenten: Kleine Geschichte des SDS* (Hamburg, 1998), 45–91; Willy Albrecht, *Der Sozialistische Deutsche Studentenbund (SDS): Vom parteikonformen Studentenverband zum Repräsentanten der neuen Linken* (Bonn, 1994).

104. Other main groups included: GAST (Gewerkschaftlicher Arbeitskreis der Studenten) and the LSD (Liberale Studenten Deutschlands). See mainly: Stefan Hemler, "Wie die 68er-Revolte eines ihrer liberalen Kinder fraß: Eine kurze Geschichte der Humanistischen Studenten-Union, erzählt am Beispiel Münchens," *Vorgänge. Zeitschrift für Bürgerrechte und Gesellschaftspolitik* 40, no. 155 (2001): 49–61.

105. Alexander Holmig, "Die aktionistischen Wurzeln der Studentenbewegung: Subversive Aktion, Kommunie I und die Neudefinition des Politischen," in *1968: Handbuch zur Kultur- und Mediengeschichte der Studentenbewegung*, 107–88, here 107. See also: Kunzelmann, *Leisten Sie keinen Widerstand!;* Wolfgang Dressen, Dieter Kunzelmann, and Eckhard Siepmann, *Nilpferd des höllischen Urwalds: Spuren in eine unbekannte Stadt: Situationisten, Gruppe SPUR, Kommune 1* (Giessen, 1991); Aribert Reimann, *Dieter Kunzelmann: Avantgardist, Protestler, Radikaler* (Göttingen, 2009), 43–122.

106. Fricke, *München rockt*, 76.

107. Hemler, "Von Kurt Faltlhauser zu Rolf Pohle," in Schubert, ed., *1968: 30 Jahre danach*, 209–42; Hemler, "Wie die 68er-Revolte eines ihrer liberalen Kinder fraß."

108. Pavel Richter, "Die Außerparlamentarische Opposition in der Bundesrepublik Deutschland 1966 bis 1968," 35–55, here 37, in *1968: Vom Ereignis zum Gegenstand der Geschichtswissenschaft*, ed. Ingrid Glicher-Holtey (Göttingen, 1998); Gerhard Bauß, *Die Studentenbewegung der sechziger Jahre in der Bundesrepublik und West Berlin* (Cologne, 1977); Rob Burns and Wilfried van der Will, *Protest and Democracy in West Germany: Extra-Parliamentary Opposition and the Democratic Agenda* (London, 1988); Hans Dollinger, ed., *Revolution gegen der Staat? Die außerparlamentarische Opposition: Die neue Linke* (Bern, 1968); Karl Otto, ed., *APO: Außerparlamentarische Opposition in Quellen und Dokumenten (1960–1970)* (Cologne, 1989).

109. Rolf Seeliger, *Die außerparlamentarische Oppostion* (Munich, 1968). See also: Stankiewitz, *München '68*, 21–22.

110. StadtAM, Stadtchronik (1968); Stankiewitz, *München '68*, 21. See also: Protest Chronicle Munich (1968), accessible at http://protest-muenchen.sub-bavaria.de, [last accessed 10 March 2015].

111. StAM, Polizeidirektion München 15622. See also: "Schalom aleichem," *Der Spiegel*, 19 September 1966.

112. Else Pelke, *Protestformen der Jugend: Über Beatniks, Gammler, Provos und Hippies* (Donauwörth, 1969); Klaus Weinhauer, "Eliten, Generationen, Jugenddelinquenz und innere Sicherheit: Die 1960er Jahre und frühen 1970er Jahre in der Bundesrepublik," in *Recht und Justiz im gesellschaftlichen Aufbruch (1960–1975): Bundesrepublik Deutschland, Italien und Frankreich im Vergleich*, ed. Jörg Requate (Baden-Baden, 2003), 33–58, here 49. See also: Herbert Reinke, "'Leute mit Namen': Wohlstandskriminelle, Gammler und Andere," 539–553, here 550, in *Repräsentationen von Kriminalität und öffentlicher Sicherheit: Bilder, Vorstellungen und Diskurse vom 16. bis zum 20. Jahrhundert*, ed. Karl Härter, Gerhard Sälter, and Eva Wiebel (Frankfurt am Main, 2010). *The Gammler* also had a prehistory, an aspect noted by various scholars. See, for example: Walter Hollstein, "Gammler und Provos," *Frankfurter Hefte* 22 (1967): 409–10.

113. Pelke, *Protestformen der Jugend*, 8.

114. Manfred Schreiber, quoted in Falter, *Chronik des Polizeipräsidiums München*, 169.

115. Hollstein, "Gammler und Provos," 414; Margaret Kosel, *Gammler, Beatniks, Provos: Die schleichende Revolution* (Frankfurt am Main, 1967). See also: Walter Hollstein, "Hippies im Wandel," *Frankfurter Hefte* 23 (1968): 637–46.

116. Peter Fleischmann, prod., *Herbst der Gammler* (Munich, 1967). See also: M. F., "Keine Toleranz für Gammler?" *Deutsche Jugend* 16 (1968): 93–94.

117. Weinhauer, "Eliten, Generation, Jugenddelinquenz und innere Sicherheit," 49.

118. Fleischmann, prod., *Herbst der Gammler*. For similar discussions around punks elsewhere see, for example: Mike Dennis and Norman LaPorte, *State and Minorities in Communist East Germany* (New York, 2011), 165.

119. Kosel, *Gammler, Beatniks, Provos*, 10.
120. "Schalom Aleichem," *Der Spiegel*, 19 September 1966.
121. StadtAM, Ratsitzungsprotokolle, Sitzungsprotokoll 741/13 (1968). See also: StAM, Polizeidirektion München 15622.
122. Walter Becker, *Jugend in der Rauschgiftwelle* (Hamm, 1968); Hans Böttcher, *Sind Gammler Ganoven? Einige Auffälligkeiten und Anfälligkeiten der heutigen Jugend* (Gladbeck/Westfalen, 1968); Hollstein, "Hippies im Wandel," 641; Bernd Werse, *Cannabis in Jugendkulturen. Kulturhistorische Betrachtungen zum Symbolcharakter eines Rauschmittels* (Berlin, 2007), 190–200. See also: Robert Stephens, *Germans on Drugs: The Complications of Modernization in Hamburg* (Ann Arbor, 2007), 20–21. For discussions in Munich see: Hanna-Barbara Gerl-Falkovitz, "Milde Verklärung?" in *1968: 30 Jahre danach;* BayHStAM, Staatskanzlei 13617; Schreiber, "Das Jahre 1968 in München," in *1968: 30 Jahre danach*; Vogel, *Die Amtskette*, 179–80; Stankiewitz, *München '68.*
123. Sturm, "'Wildgewordene Obrigkeit'?" in *'Schwabinger Krawalle'*, 104.
124. Lindner, *Jugendprotest seit den fünfziger Jahren*, 87.
125. Reinke, "'Leute mit Namen,'" 550. See also: "Schwabinger Tragikkomödie," *Bayerische Staatszeitung*, 29 June 1962; BayHStAM, Ministerium des Inneren 97954.
126. "Stoppt Dutschke jetzt!" *Die Deutsche Nationalzeitung*, 22 March 1968.
127. Carole Fink, Philipp Gassert, and Detlef Junker, "Introduction," in *1968: The World Transformed* (Cambridge, 1993), 1–27, here 12.
128. Kosel, *Gammler, Beatniks, Provos*, 10.
129. "Schah-Reise," *Der Spiegel*, 31 July 1967; "Tod vor der Oper," *Der Spiegel*, 5 June 1967; "Knüppel frei," *Der Spiegel*, 12 June 1967; "Haß in der Mitte," *Der Spiegel*, 19 June 1967; Knut Nevermann, ed., *Der 2. Juni 1967: Studenten zwischen Notstand und Demokratie* (Cologne, 1967); Jürgen Henschel, "Der 2. Juni: Das Ohnesorg-Foto," in *CheSchahShit*, 114–15.
130. "Schweigemarsch für Ohnesorg," *Der Münchner Merkur*, 6 June 1967. See also: Protest Chronicle Munich (1967), accessible at http://protest-muenchen.sub-bavaria.de, [last accessed 9 March 2015].
131. "AZ Umfrage zu Studentenunruhen: Durch Provokation zur Diskussion?" *Die Abendzeitung*, 28 November 1967.
132. Ulrich Chaussy, "Das Attentat auf Rudi Dutschke," in *CheSchaShit*, 132–37; Nevermann, *Der 2. Juni 1967;* Nick Thomas, *Protest Movements in 1960s West Germany: A Social History of Dissent and Democracy* (Oxford/New York, 2003), 165–81.
133. For coverage of the attack on Rudi Dutschke within Munich see, for instance: "Ostermaschierer rufen zur Aktionen auf," *Die Süddeutsche Zeitung*, 16 April 1968;" "Straßenschlacht in Schwabing: Nach dem Attentat auf Dutschke," *Die Süddeutsche Zeitung*, 13–14 April 1968; "Lieber ein roter als ein toter Dutschke," *Die Abendzeitung*, Ostern 1968. See also: Media Archive Springer at: http://www.axelspringer.de/artikel/Online-Datenbank-Medienarchiv68_1086007.html, [last accessed 11 March 2015]; Andreas Renz, *Die Studentenproteste von 1967/68 im Spiegel der Münchner Presse* (Munich, 1992).

134. "Stoppt Dutschke jetzt!" *Die Deutsche Nationalzeitung,* 22 March 1968. See also: Bauß, *Die Studentenbewegung der sechziger Jahre in der Bundesrepublik und West Berlin,* 71–111; Hans Dieter Müller, *Press Power: A Study of Axel Springer* (London, 1969); Florian Kain, *Das Privatfernsehen, der Axel Springer Verlag und die deutsche Presse: Die medienpolitische Debatte in den sechziger Jahren* (Münster, 2003).

135. Quoted in Ulrich Chaussy, "Tod in München—Frings und Schreck: Die Eskalation bei den 'Osterunruhen' 1968 in München," in *Auf den Barrikaden,* 89–100, here 90.

136. Kurt Georg Kiesinger, quoted in Thomas, *Protest Movements in 1960s West Germany,* 177; Kurt Georg Kiesinger, *Die große Koalition 1966–1969: Reden und Erklärungen des Bundeskanzlers,* ed. Dieter Oberndörfer (Stuttgart, 1979), 186–87, here 186.

137. Arnulf Baring, *Machtwechsel: Die Ära Brandt-Scheel* (Stuttgart, 1982), 77. See also: Uwe Wesel, *Die verspielte Revolution: 1968 und die Folgen* (Munich, 2002), 35.

138. StAM, RA 101154.

139. StAM, Polizeidirektion München 11134. See also: Chaussy, "Tod in München—Frings und Schreck," 90, in *Auf den Barrikaden.*

140. StAM, RA 101154. See also: StadtAM, Polizeipräsidium München, Filmsammlung 16mm, Nr. 13; StadtAM, Polizeidirektion München 9570/3; Gerhard Fürmetz, *Protest oder 'Störung'? Studenten und Staatsmacht in München um 1968* (Munich, 1999), 47–48 and 53–55; Vogel, *Die Amtskette,* 181–83; Mehr, ed., *Drachen mit tausend Köpfen,* 59–60; Gerstenberg, *Hiebe, Liebe und Proteste München 1968,* 30–33; Protest Chronicle Munich (1968), accessible at http://protest-muenchen.sub-bavaria.de, [last accessed 11 March 2014].

141. StAM, RA 101154.

142. Reinhard Wetter, quoted in Chaussy, "Tod in München," in *Auf den Barrikaden,* 92.

143. StAM, RA 101154.

144. Ibid.

145. Ibid.

146. Chaussy, "Tod in München," in *Auf den Barrikaden,* 96–97.

147. "Ostermaschierer rufen zur Aktionen auf," *Die Süddeutsche Zeitung,* 16 April 1968. See also: StadtAM, Polizeipräsidium München, Filmsammlung 16mm, Nr. 12; StAM, RA 101154.

148. Ibid.

149. Dollinger, *München im 20. Jahrhundert,* 289.

150. StAM, RA 101154. See also: Chaussy, "Tod in München," in *Auf den Barrikaden,* 98–100; Stankiewitz, *München '68,* 37–41.

151. "154 Strafverfahren gegen Demonstranten," *Die Süddeutsche Zeitung,* 17 April 1968; "'Anschlag auf rechtstaatliche Ordnung,'" *Die Süddeutsche Zeitung,* 25 April 1968; "Verlorenes Wochenende," *Der Spiegel,* 22 April 1968.

152. StAM, RA 101154. According to this official report, 77.2 percent were between eighteen and twenty-nine years of age; 33.8 percent were students.

153. Ibid.

154. Ibid. See also: Dollinger, *München im 20. Jahrhundert*, 289; StadtAM, Stadtchronik (1968).

155. BayHStAM, Staatskanzlei 13617; BayHStAM, Staatskanzlei 900050; "Nach der Straßenschlacht die Redeschlacht," *Der Münchner Merkur*, 25 April 1968; "Ich bitte ums Wort," *Die Abendzeitung*, 10 May 1968. Various newspapers also discussed student groups in more detail. See, for example: "Die politische Hochschulgruppen—was denken und was wollen sie?" *Die Welt*, 27, 29, 30 April 1968; Fürmetz, *Protest oder 'Störung'?* 48; Volkhard Brandes, *Wie der Stein ins Rollen kam: Vom Aufbruch in die Revolte der sechziger Jahre* (Frankfurt am Main, 1988), 165; Stankiewitz, *München '68*, 52–55; Protest Chronicle Munich (1968), accessible at http://protest-muenchen.sub-bavaria.de, [last accessed 11 March 2014].

156. BayHStAM, Staatskanzlei 13617. See also: Antje Eichler, *Protest im Radio. Die Berichterstattung des Bayerischen Rundfunks über die Studentenbewegung 1967/1968* (Frankfurt am Main, 2005).

157. "Studenten, Mikrokosmos des fünften Standes: Der gefährliche Weg," *Christ und die Welt*, 3 May 1968.

158. *Die Süddeutsche Zeitung*, 18 April 1968, quoted in Gerstenberger, *Hiebe, Liebe und Proteste München 1968*, 34. See also: BayHStAM, Staatskanzlei 13617; "Wir hauen auf den Putz," *Der Spiegel*, 13 May 1968; "Ohne uns ware es viel schlimmer gekommen," *Der Spiegel*, 22 April 1968.

159. Gerstenberger, *Hiebe, Liebe und Protests München 1968*, 44.

160. Peter Schult, "Panoptikum der Exoten?" in *Drachen mit tausend Köpfen*, 52–64, here 49.

161. Schreiber, "Das Jahre 1968 in München," in *1968: 30 Jahre danach*, 50. See also: BayHStAM, Plakatsammlung 26476; IfZM, Plakatsammlung (May 1968); Protest Chronicle Munich, accessible at http://protest-muenchen.sub-bavaria.de, [last accessed 11 March 2014]; H. Jürgen Gießler, *APO-Rebellion Mai 1968: Die letzten Tage vor Verabscheidung der Notstandsgesetz: Dokumentation und Presseanalyse dieser Tage vor dem 30. Mai 1968* (Munich, 1968), 39–54.

162. Stankiewitz, *München '68*, 25. For internal discussions within various student organizations see, for example: StAM, RA 101146; Stefan Hemler, "Von Kurt Faltlhauser zu Rolf Pohle: Die Entwicklung der studentischen Unruhe an der Ludwig-Maximilians-Universität München in der zweiten Hälfte der sechziger Jahre," 209–242, in *1968: 30 Jahre danach*. See also: Michael Sturm, "Tupamaros München: 'Bewaffneter Kampf,' Subkultur und Polize, 1969–1971," in *Terrorismus in der Bundesrepublik: Medien, Staat und Subkulturen in the 1970er Jahren* (Frankfurt am Main, 2006). 99–133.

163. BayHStAM, Staatskanzlei 113612; StAM, Polizeidirektion München 15971; StAM, RA 101149; "Anzeige gegen Rektorats-Besatzer," *Der Münchner Merkur*, 7 February 1969; "Rektorats-Stürmern droht Strafanzeige," *Die Abendzeitung*, 7 February 1969; Fürmetz, *Protest oder 'Störung'?* 34.

164. StAM, RA 101147; StAM, Polizeidirektion München 15975; StAM, Polizeidirektion München 16006; "Kultusministerium schließt Akademie," *Die*

Süddeutsche Zeitung, 21 July 1969; "Klage gegen Akademie-Schließung," *Der Münchner Merkur,* 22 July 1969; "Radikale Studenten stürmten die Akademie der Künste," *TZ,* 20 February 1969; "Studenten besetzen die Kunstakademie," *Der Münchner Merkur,* 21 February 1969; "Kultusministerium schloß gestern die Münchner Akademie der Bildenden Künste," *Die Abendzeitung,* 21 February 1969; "Münchner Hochschule von Studenten besudelt und demoliert," *Bild,* 21 February 1969; "Studenten siegten," *Die Abendzeitung,* 26 February 1969; "Akademie wieder eröffnet," *Der Münchner Merkur,* 26 February 1969. See also: Thomas Zacharias, "Zwischen Ende der Nachkriegszeit und Anfang der Altbausanierung: Die Akademie von 1968 bis 1989," in *200 Jahre Akademie der bildenden Künste München,* ed. Nikolaus Gerhart, Walter Grasskamp, and Florian Matzner (Munich, 2008), 112–21, here 116; Cornelia Gockel, "Revolution war gestern: Kunst und Protest an der Akademie der Bildenden Künste in München," in *Auf den Barrikaden,* 223–40.

165. StAM, RA 101147.
166. *Bayerische Rundfunk* Archiv, "Motorrad-Rennen in der Kunstakademie," 5 February 2015, accessible at, http://www.br.de/radio/bayern2/wissen/kalenderblatt/0502-motorradrennen-kunstakademie-muenchen-100.html [last accessed 28 February 2015].
167. StAM, RA 101151. See also: StAM, RA 101146; Hemler, "Wie die 68er-Revolte eines ihrer liberalen Kinder fraß."
168. StAM, RA 101151.
169. "Die Ostermaschierer rüsten ab," *Die Süddeutsche Zeitung,* 21 June 1970.

CHAPTER 6

Controlling Protestors in the Protest Years

When asked about the 1960s in Munich for a recent publication, Mayor Hans-Jochen Vogel briefly referred to shifting policies. "We had two deaths and endured vicious quarrels; this gave the conflict between students and authorities a certain intensity. We had to deal with that, but quite differently than we did during the riots of Schwabing 1962."[1] Vogel illustrated how Munich had had the chance to learn from earlier events. Initially caught by surprise during the riots and protests in Schwabing in 1962, the former mayor hints at a learning curve. But how did local officials defend its understanding of democracy in the light of protestors? How did the city contain *the student* and *the Gammler*?

As for many onlookers and protestors, the events in Schwabing too marked a turning point for local authorities. Initially surprised and overall unable to cope with the new threat, the police faced criticism by the general public. This backlash resulted in a new approach regarding the control of protesting youngsters. Known as *die Münchner Linie* or the Munich Line, the police moved from active intervention towards preemptive and more targeted measures. More precisely and in response to the riots in Schwabing, law enforcement put the young in Schwabing under constant surveillance. Promoted as de-escalation and restraint, this new approach targeted youth more secretively. In this sense, *the student* and *the Gammler* had become valuables tool to justify the installation of a police state in Schwabing.

Again, a diverse set of adult protagonists framed and controlled both images. Since 1960, Hans-Jochen Vogel from the Social Democrats Party (SPD) was mayor of Munich. As the youngest mayor in West Germany at the time, the riots of Schwabing were among his first challenges in office. Additionally, newly installed Police Chief Manfred Schreiber modernized the police by moving away from pre-1933 tactics; he also presented Munich as a tolerant and open-minded city. At the same time, state authorities got involved as well, especially given that *the student* disrupted university settings. Conservative voices dominated politics there and even had an absolute majority in the Bavarian parliament by 1962. Apart from the president of Bavaria, Hans Ehard, and his successor Alfons Goppel, it was in the roams of the Ministry of the Interior, the Ministry of Culture and Education, and the Ministry of Justice to take action. In addition, conservative party leader and future Bavarian president Franz-Josef Strauß was also anxious to get involved and make his mark as a politician. He demanded more rigorous restrictions against *the student* and *the Gammler*, only to be superseded by the right-wing Nationalist Party (NPD).[2] Together with the media and various other social commentators, these authorities in particular set out to control a threatening minority in an attempt to defend their conception of West German democracy while ultimately hoping to prevent the instabilities of the Weimar Republic.

Unlike previously, however, the actual young were increasingly organized and actively participating in debates, especially after the riots in Schwabing. More and more aware of their voices and power, many joined community initiatives and other organizations. Some student groups like AStA shifted between politically moderate in 1962 to more radical positions throughout the later period. This radicalization became also visible in organizations like the socialist group SDS. Student leaders and organizers included Rolf Pohle and Reinhard Wetter, while Dieter Kunzelmann and Fritz Teufel often helped represent *the student*. Soon such groups relied on their own publications: they printed leaflets and newspapers, or made their voices heard in interviews within the mainstream media. These comments contested, disrupted, and—at times—altered discussions, and challenged the monopoly of authorities to frame images of youth. Young people's abilities to organize and resist had an impact on state responses and mechanisms of control, arguably resulting in more subtle attempts to regulate society.

Police Brutality in Schwabing

In the early 1960s, harsh restrictions aimed against the young were still in place. Fears, panics, and larger circumstances tied to the rise of *the Halbstarke* and *the teenager* had criminalized both groups and resulted in various means of control. The police patrolled the streets looking for loitering *Halbstarke,* and they monitored traffic, wondering about the young cruising through the city on their mopeds. Authorities also observed certain clubs playing rock 'n' roll music. These concerns brought police patrols to Schwabing early on. Seen as the young, vibrant, and bohemian part of town, Schwabing offered a variety of entertainment. Youngsters could hang out with friends at ice cream parlors, movie theaters, or on street corners; they could also listen to their favorite tunes on jukeboxes located in bars and various restaurants. In addition, Schwabing was close to the university, a location that brought countless students to Leopoldstraße boulevard. Whereas the Youth Protection Law prohibited youngsters to frequent bars or clubs in the evening,[3] *the student* could move around more freely. As a space for the young, Schwabing meant potential trouble for those concerned about juvenile delinquency.[4]

Police patrols on duty in Schwabing focused on several issues. Expected to keep law and order, their most imminent task was to limit disruptions of peace and public order. Especially on warm summer nights, numerous noise complaints reached police headquarters. After receiving such calls, a unit of two officers would generally arrive at the scene to disperse the source of trouble. Those disquieting the peace usually followed orders without problems. Sentiments gradually changed in the early 1960s, however. Then, more and more youngsters felt harassed by overly zealous police measures. As a new generation, many of the young also rejected orders of their predecessors almost instinctively. On 21 June 1962, one such minor incident proved the last straw, as constant control and harassment of youngsters had led to the Schwabing riots, surprising local authorities. In this sense, in 1962, a diverse group of youngsters not only dismissed calls to end their music but also fought back. With little prior experiences regarding large crowds, overwhelmed police officers followed chaotic orders and the pre-1933 tactic—"mount, march out, dismount, clear, mount, retreat, [and] eat."[5] Mayor Vogel and subsequent court decisions were consequently correct overall when noting that the police "was acting according to the wording of the law."[6]

The use of such police strategies was not a coincidence. Apart from being rooted in outdated tactics, the response was embedded within larger postwar attitudes. To control the young and those disturbing the peace by force was acceptable at the time. It was a reflection of current political and societal values. To clear streets employing batons as a way to ensure the free flow of traffic was seen as an appropriate measure by most of Munich's citizens in the early 1960s. Munich had experienced an enormous rise in traffic—not least due to the lack of a subway system—making main routes like Leopoldstraße boulevard essential.[7] Furthermore, the street was a potential space for social conflicts, plus the police were supposed to protect the state against internal threats in the first place. Public order was important as many contemporary authorities and officials vividly recalled the chaotic situation during the Weimar years. Hence, authorities saw a robust democracy that fought back as essential in their attempts to prevent similar events in Munich. At the same time, many had experienced National Socialism. As outlined by historian Nick Thomas,

> Hans-Jochen Vogel, the SPD Mayor of Munich, declared that "in the Munich City Council sit many men and women who were hunted down and robbed of their freedom between 1933 and 1945. The police president was also a political victim. They are all, as I am myself, certainly no friends of rubber truncheons," but he justified the police tactics, saying "the police cannot allow the destruction of the peace and the law-breaking on the streets of a democratic state in homage to a mistaken concept of freedom."[8]

This understanding of democracy as static, state-supported, and constantly under attack partially explains the behavior of authorities; it also indicates the use of the past to justify present actions. The fact that stringent retributions seemed to work and people eventually cleared the streets at some point strengthened these ideals [Figure 6.1].

After the riots in Schwabing and brutal police reaction, city authorities supported the police without hesitation. Mayor Hans-Jochen Vogel, the city council, and the honorary Council of the Elders stood by the police, not least because the city council and the mayor as elected bodies were in charge of the police. It was thus not surprising when authorities avoided blaming each other. At the first meeting of the city council shortly after the events,[9] the recent riots had been added to the agenda at the last minute. Actual discussions were cut short. Instead, council members listened to a report by Police Chief Anton Heigl before, according to *Die Süddeutsche Zeitung,* "praising the police."[10] Council Member Georg Fischer from the social democrats (SPD) noted, the police did not "clear the area until *after* traffic was disrupted, property damaged, and even lives of citizens endangered."[11] The SPD Caucus led by Mayor Vogel published a proclamation after the meeting, concluding, "The Social Democratic Caucus of the city council regrets any kind of actions that call for police intervention; yet it cannot dismiss such police assignments because they are in the interest of security for our citizens."[12] The SPD Caucus also promised, "If violations [by the police] occurred then there will be a proper inves-

Figure 6.1 Police arrest a youngster during the "Schwabing Riots," 1962. Courtesy of Otfried Schmidt/Süddeutsche Zeitung Photo.

tigation. The Caucus will discuss its results and draw its conclusions. We pass on our sympathy to those guiltless caught in the middle of the events."[13] This brief acknowledgment of potential missteps seemed superficial given the magnitude of recent events in Schwabing.

Punishing *the Student*

Authorities equally applied the full force of the law after the riots, regardless of evidence. They wanted to convict all those arrested during the events. However, initial hearings of early cases outlined problems with evidence. In the trial against twenty-year-old Karl Kristan, for instance, the police had not even sufficient evidence to indicate why it had kept him in custody for sixty-seven days. A police officer initially claiming he knew the accused only to partially retract his original testimony later on. According to *Der Münchner Merkur*, the trial became "a farce."[14] For authorities, however, even such lack of evidence did not automatically result in the dismissal of a case, an aspect that captures desires to blame and persecute *the student* at all costs. One of the musicians, initially at the scene in Schwabing, experienced this after his arrest. Without much evidence against him, the police searched his room hoping to unearth links to communism; he was also interrogated at his work. This questioning took place in front of his boss, making it all the more uncomfortable and intimidating. In the end, he faced a 150 Deutsche Mark fine for "improper use of the sidewalk."[15]

Subsequent trials continued to illustrate the exaggerated response of the judicial system. In late September 1962, a male youngster was accused of participating in the riots. He noted, "I wanted to see how someone is arrested for once," and thus decided to come to Schwabing.[16] There, according to various witnesses, he was "particularly active":[17] he walked slowly across the street to disrupt traffic, encouraged others to sit on the road, and failed to follow police orders. That the attorney detected "anarchic"[18] characteristics in the accused did not help his defense. He was eventually sentenced to eleven months in a juvenile prison. Other youngsters experienced similar verdicts. A twenty-three-year-old French journalist had to go to jail for mocking the police and "banding together" with others.[19] In one case the statement by a youngster that his friend was more active than him brought that friend to jail and to court. Sentences ranged from pedagogical measures or community service to much stricter verdicts, and the judicial review seemed to care surprisingly little about broad generalizations and limited evidence. In fact, twenty-one-year-old student of medicine Elmar was sentenced to six months in juvenile prison because he supposedly kicked a journalist. According to the verdict, "more self-restraint and reason should be expected from a student coming from a good family."[20] Even Director of the Youth Welfare Office Kurt Seelmann was initially indicted based on his mere presence at the event,[21] an aspect that underlines the stark judicial response of local courts.

Accused participants, bystanders, and victims had little leverage. Often without the means or support to push for convictions of police officers, those individuals deciding to put forward a complaint could only rely on an inadequate judicial review. Police officers rarely recalled when they were involved in what brawl. If they did, then they kept it to themselves. A strong and largely institutionalized bias within the judicial system towards law enforcement plus the chaotic scenes during the riots did not help. That victims had no way of identifying police officers, who had no visual identifications, made prosecution virtually impossible. As a result, courts dismissed many accusations based on a lack of evidence,[22] and the first actual trial against a police officer did not occur until February 1963. Then, a policeman accused of heavy assault against a student faced charges.[23] The officer had twice pushed student Klaus Staudt onto the side of the road. Staudt severely injured his knee. In this case, the accused faced six weeks in prison and a fine of 200 Deutsche Marks. Yet over the course of the trials, only fourteen out of 248 police officers were convicted.[24] In May 1963, an editorial in *Die Süddeutsche Zeitung* summarized the judicial review of Schwabing, stating that 25 percent of all civilians initially arrested were convicted while only 1 percent of police officers. "This is," the editorial concluded, "simply shocking."[25]

The role of Kurt Seelman finally gave some credibility to those pushing back already. Caught up in the riots plus a victim of police brutality, Seelman spoke out against the police. His credibility grounded in his role within the city administration and adult age made him a powerful voice. According to mayor Hans-Jochen Vogel, "it was the case of Kurt Seelmann in particular" that inspired others to speak up against the police.[26] At least then the mayor met with victims, showed his sympathy, and promised that "violations by police officers will not be covered up."[27] At the end, however, only a couple of police officers faced charges, making it all look like a cover-up and embarrassment for the city of Munich, now promoting itself as a cosmopolitan metropolis and tourist destination.

The Birth of the Munich Line

While the judicial process took shape and complaints continued to pour in, local decision makers began revisiting police tactics. In the first meeting of the city council after summer break, authorities focused on possible changes to general strategies as well as identification numbers for police officers, the latter being quickly dismissed because of privacy issues and fears of discrimination.[28] Discussions about tactics, on the other hand, continued, increasingly shaped by a public debate and new insights. City Council Member Georg Fischer (SPD) addressed Police Chief Anton Heigl during the council meeting in October directly, noting, "It should not happen again that the police walk around without clear guidance, like chickens."[29] When Anton Heigl did not react to this criticism, conservative Council Member Peter Schmidhuber (CSU) got short, stating, "If you are not going to respond, then I wonder why we even discuss this issue."[30] This incident, amongst others, underlined Heigl's inability or unwillingness to communicate with authorities and the press. His attempts to emphasize that Munich's police were "not barbarians"[31] in the newspaper *Welt am Sonntag* was not enough to rebuild a by then damaged reputation. Soon Heigl became a prime target of the media, and a symbol for static, outdated, and traditional administrational structures.

His illness and sudden death in a tragic accident eventually allowed the city of Munich to replace Anton Heigl with a younger, more communicative, and less predisposed police chief. According to Mayor Vogel, Manfred Schreiber perfectly fit this description and also followed more current police tactics.[32] Another official referenced continuities within the mindset of the city police when discussing Heigl's replacement and noted, "It had been quite difficult to impose new guidelines for training and fill the structure of the police with more democratic formats. The understandings of some participants in the war [World War II] and now members of the police was simply overshadowed by militaristic ideologies."[33] Local leadership hoped that thirty-seven-year-old Manfred Schreiber could more easily address these issues. He had been the public face of the police in Munich even before Heigl's death. As Schreiber acknowledged himself, "To better the relationship between police and public" became his main objective following the riots.[34]

Although technically legal given outdated police standards, the police had certainly not played a positive role in the riots. Changes seemed necessary, especially once public pressure increased. After initial debates on various levels, a broad proposal outlined more detailed possibilities. First, officials thought about hiring a psychologist to better prepare police officers for stressful situations. Second, authorities debated whether to purchase an additional water cannon. State officials had underlined the necessity for this in the past, and most agreed that the use of a water cannon during the riots in Schwabing would have defused the situation. Only Anton Heigl—among a few others—had stated that a water cannon would be empty too quickly, forcing the police to withdraw while protestors regrouped. In addition, the police discussed the need for new procedures. During the riots, a lack of coordination had become apparent: time and again supervisors left police officers behind or with little to no guidance. A clear structural framework seemed necessary, as were concisely worded demands to be read to rioters. Discussions surrounding the purchase of a video and audio vehicle finally addressed the need to gather evidence.[35]

After extensive debates, the city of Munich endorsed this so-called Munich Line, a police reform grounded in post-riot lessons. One of the reports summarized its content in thirteen points. These included better schooling of the police, more coordination, more flexibility in response to rioters, the need for more street and undercover patrols, and the necessity to employ a psychologist.[36] In an interview with the news magazine *Der Spiegel*, Manfred Schreiber, who in many ways personified the Munich Line, specifically commented on the need for a psychologist. In a surprisingly blunt statement he noted, "the police ... do not have access to the best and the brightest; that is why one could only weed out those not useful for the police; to school the rest by employing psychological techniques is necessary to get as close as possible to the ideal police officer."[37] Psychologist Rolf Umbach and eight others took on this role, and soon trained police officers for different scenarios.[38] Such psychological training included ways to remain calm when provoked by a rebellious crowd. Apart from a psychological division, the police also established a film and audio crew to gather evidence.[39] An emphasis on better cooperation with the press and an increased attention to public relations in general indicated that the police wished to avoid bad publicity in the future.[40] In the evaluation of police historian Josef Falter, the Munich Line meant the "internal and external modernization of the city police,"[41] arguably—one could add—to primarily better public perceptions.

The Munich Line became the pride of the city police. Proudly promoted and applied in the following years, authorities saw it as a step towards de-escalation and cooperation. Compared to other cities still relying on pre-1933 tactics, the Bavarian capital did indeed lead the way towards more tolerance. According to Police Chief Schreiber, "not beating or hitting, but convincing ... and guiding are in the foreground today. The police tactic is based on the tactic of demonstrators, knowledge based on the psychology of the masses, and the general environment."[42] The new Munich Line also incorporated the press, and aimed to limit provocations, all in an effort to mainly avoid bad publicity. Streamlining police tactics and procedures was meant to create stricter hierarchies and limit mistakes. In order to avoid a lack of evidence after a riot, the police would now carefully document any misbehavior of protestors with cameras; that the use of recording devices helped dismiss calls for police identification was all the more reason to implement such setups.[43]

Overall then, the implementation of the Munich Line did not indicate a change of heart. Even though the police became more open and less brutal, previous attempts to move forward against rioting youngsters were not dismissed. Instead, the Munich Line merely acknowledged that brutal behaviors would bring negative publicity to the police and could escalate a situation. One official report had stated without hesitation, "events [in Schwabing in 1962] were without precedence after the war, and have been dealt with in the best manner possible given the situation."[44] Police Chief Manfred Schreiber agreed with such sentiments.[45] Actually, the Munich Line was not a soft approach, but more a way to appear more modern, gather more evidence, and act preemptively. In a way, this framework marked a shift towards more nuanced and subtle tactics of social control, still to be used to target youth, but now much more in line with Munich's self-image as an international, cosmopolitan, and open metropolis. The role of police officer Rudolf Mayer during a demonstration in November 1969 underlines this most clearly: Mayer linked his arms with protestors and joined them in their demonstration through Munich. From then on informally known as Unterhak-Mayer arm-linking Mayer, his behavior symbolized the positive and de-escalating role of the Munich Line for years to come[46]—without acknowledging that even his mere presence at the head of demonstrations underlined that mechanisms of control had gained access to previously protected spaces within protest movements.

Monitoring Schwabing

With the official approval of the Munich Line, authorities imposed an intricate system of social control. Instead of running the risk of bad publicity and collective resistance, the police took a more indirect and preventive approach. This included much more clandestine work. Most notably, shortly after the riots in Schwabing, undercover police patrols on foot increased dramatically, especially during summer months. A direct order outlined that "younger officers in particular"[47] need to patrol in Schwabing: this would limit detection among a primarily young crowd. The directive also specifically stated that these undercover patrols should not provoke or spark disruptions. Instead, they needed to observe as events unfold, only to step in once a situation has calmed down or disruptive individuals were isolated. Precise reports indicating disruptions and concerning behaviors were recurred at 8 P.M. every night. From spring until fall every year, officials put forward a similar directive. If the weather was nice and *the student* and *the Gammler* was out, then undercover agents were on duty walking and observing Schwabing.

The daily reports produced by such patrols give detailed insights into how authorities perceived youth. Still wary of a repeat of the June 1962 riots, patrols documented any potential threat. On 10 June 1964, for instance, a patrol noted "two twenty-two-year-old American students ... because they played guitar on a bench" at the Leopoldstraße boulevard.[48] Such behaviors could spark a riot again, they warned. A week later, the police followed up on a call complaining about "a crowd of students storming the cinema box office."[49] When they arrived the supposed threat had disappeared. On a Saturday in July the police noted "two students sitting on a doorstep.... Whereas one was singing foreign songs, the other one played along with the guitar."[50] This conduct was threatening, and the police on duty made sure to write down as much information about these musicians as possible. Two days later, a patrol reported how "students and those, who claim to be students," were selling paintings.[51] For those on duty even that was a potential threat. The next day, a patrol responded to another breach of peace regarding the music of young street musicians. In this instance "the students reduced the volume of their music without problems" once notified.[52] Yet the threat such individuals posed to society was highlighted in the evening report. To keep an eye on *the student* and *the Gammler,* note any misbehavior, and preemptively write down everything about certain youngsters was seen as vital in attempts to prevent future riots and gather evidence for later.

Not all disruptions led to a citation. Whereas some patrols pressed charges once they had isolated the violator and felt safe from collective resistance, others took the relaxed climate of Schwabing into account. According to one report, "the daily situation at the Leopoldstraße boulevard might violate laws in various ways, yet this is well-known in higher ranks and seen virtually as a normal state for Schwabing. It is officially tolerated."[53] Aware of such lenient tendencies amongst some officers, Police Chief Manfred Schreiber soon clarified the official standpoint of the police. As Schreiber stated in official orders, "Painting on the sidewalk or making music is prohibited. Such individuals need special attention because their behaviors inherently carry additional potential for disruptions of law and order."[54]

The creation of a massive data system including information about supposedly disruptive individuals soon supported surveillance efforts and prosecution. Rooted in a directive from June 1964, "all incidents connected to the situation at the Leopoldstraße boulevard and its surroundings have to be centrally collected, indexed, and stored at the police station."[55] A complex system based on various color codes organized the data. For example, the letter L scribbled on a card with a green pencil underlined the urgency of a specific note. Such setups allowed the police to determine disruptive individuals without problems; it also provided valuable evidence once a youngster faced criminal charges.

Police presence increasingly deterred disruptions. In June 1965, Manfred Schreiber noted, "Mainly students have become more careful as they hope to avoid citations"[56] and conflicts with the law. That everyone could read about the presence of undercover police officers in newspapers significantly helped deter disruptive forces. For local authorities, these measures turned out to be an excellent preemptive tool as they successfully intimidated and controlled *the student* and *the Gammler* in Schwabing[57]—even if constant surveillance and the collection of data could not prevent all disruptions. Many youngsters became simply more cautious as they spent time in public spaces, talked loudly, and sometimes used a moment of solitude to play music.

Nonetheless, in late fall of 1965, the city council of Munich decided to tighten restrictions, using urban design as a tool of control. In a nonpublic meeting on 14 November, a report backed by the police and the city park service outlined the problem while providing an adequate solution. According to the official record of the meeting, "during the summer dangers regarding disruptions of order remain high. ... Based on years of supervision and numerous experiences by the police, it has become obvious that Wedekindplatz square [in Schwabing] in particular remains an attraction for so-called Gammler and a starting point for disruptions of all kinds."[58] Such unruly forces included local youngsters and travelers from all over. "They occupy the benches and the area of Wedekindplatz square from early in the morning until late at night."[59] In order to deal with such disruptive individuals the report proposed a new spatial concept for this area: "Only the cultivation of plants at Wedekindplatz square can bring relief. The new spatial concept would limit the behaviors described above. ... Legally the police would also have leverage to tighten control in this area, because the space left after spatial restructuring needs to be clear for pedestrians; trespassing onto [then planted] city park property is a misdemeanor."[60] The report even outlined that some plants are better than others and suggested the "use of thorny groves so as to avoid trespassing. ... Planting roses would further increase the threshold within the population to damage this public space."[61] The city council agreed with the proposal, and city planners went to work. Over the winter months, authorities remodeled the public area around Wedekindplatz square; city services narrowed the sidewalk and planted thorny bushes.

The use of spatial planning fulfilled its immediate objective, yet the overall setup ultimately failed. When the next surveillance season started in April 1966, a report noted, "The proposed remodeling and plantation of Wedekindplatz square has been completed, so that additional opportunities regarding police action are more likely possible."[62] As additional reports indicate, the police had no problem bringing this disruptive space formerly used by potentially unruly youngsters under control. Few stepped into the bushes, aware that their thorns are un-

comfortable. Those who simply blocked the sidewalk could be cited
for disrupting the flow of traffic. Although spatial planning had helped
remold an urban environment to fit the needs of local law enforcement
without exposing the authorities to public scrutiny, the larger plan
to expel clusters of disruptive youth from city spaces failed. Instead
of showing up in supervised youth organizations, as authorities had
hoped, the young found new spaces to hang out. In the 1960s, many
moved into the area around the University and the Academy of the
Arts; those loitering in the summer also hung out in local parks. To
remodel all parks was impossible given its disposition as an area for
public leisure and recreation. In this sense, the success of Wedekindplatz square in Schwabing did not solve the problem, and it would take
decades until authorities considered including the young into urban
planning processes and providing spaces for them within Munich as a
way to deal with the situation.

Constant surveillance of Schwabing also brought *the Gammler* more
specifically into the limelight. Since at least 1964, this homeless young
bum had been spotted mainly in Schwabing. *The Gammler* came from
a middle-class background and should have attended college or gotten
a job. Instead, such youngsters decided to live on the streets, supposedly sold drugs, and tainted the image of the city, all behaviors that
raised fears. These anxieties had already influenced the redesign of
Wedekindplatz square, a favorite spot of *the Gammler* in Schwabing.
By the mid-1960s numerous authorities and social commentators had
voiced additional concerns. According to some, *Gammlers* literally and
metaphorically besmirched the clean city of Munich, and many feared
their lifestyle choices.[63] By 1966, even national newspapers picked up
the story. With numerous *Gammlers* on the cover, *Der Spiegel* introduced, among others, Helga Reiners, age twenty, who hung out in Munich begging for "pennies, a sip of your beer, and a smoke from your
cigarette."[64] For one commentator of the conservative Springer press,
Gammlers were "the ugliest the twentieth century has seen."[65] Whereas
such aspects unmistakably aligned *the Gammler* with delinquents and
criminals, these references once more also provided an avenue to act
against youth within Schwabing.

After closely observing *the Gammler* in the aftermath of the riots,
conservative authorities eventually had had enough. In 1966, one city
council member of the Conservative Socialist Union (CSU) demanded
the police to "reduce Gammlerism ... to an appropriate amount"[66]—
whatever that entailed. The Nationalist Party (NPD) hoped for even
stricter measures. In a party leaflet it called for "measures ... to deal
with the whole problem ... in a radical way and along public senti-

ments."[67] These voices had support from high up. In a directive to state ministries of the interior, conservative Chancellor Ludwig Erhard asked for precise information regarding *the Gammler*. Erhard wanted to know, "in what manner do Gammler threaten law and order; are Gammler similar to vagabonds; do Gammler riot and vandalize; and are there foreigners among the Gammlers."[68] Together with local authorities he was "ready to fight against Gammler and delinquents."[69]

To take on *the Gammler* was not that simple, yet existing mechanisms of control following the Schwabing riots helped authorities. Forced to work with laws in place at the time, Police Chief Manfred Schreiber outlined, "Dirt in itself is not a crime."[70] But since the *Gammler* problem was most evident in Schwabing, the police simply employed existing measures. Schreiber even added more police officers believing that such "reinforcement was necessary because the entertainment quarter [Schwabing] had become increasingly popular."[71] Now the police paid attention "specifically ... to the Gammler,"[72] collected, filed, and indexed all information about such bums; they also wrote weekly reports for Police Chief Schreiber and a monthly Gammler report for local newspapers. The creation of such data helped authorities in their attempts to spot and interrupt disruptive forces early on; it also raised awareness and deterred *the Gammler*.[73] As one contemporary voice noted, "the cops patrol and control [certain areas] four, five times each and every day."[74] Once spotted on daily patrols, the police could charge *the Gammler* according to a variety of laws. When they were seen bumming around in the park, they could face five days in jail due to a violation of landscape and park orders or trespassing; if *the Gammler* was sitting on the sidewalk, he or she either had to pay a fine of forty-five Deutsche Marks, or spend three days in jail for disruption of traffic. Constant control for identification gave authorities the most helpful avenue to harass *the Gammler*. A newspaper described in 1966,

> For the first time in the history of Schwabing seven long-haired "Gammler" were called off the trees in the English Garden. They had spent the night there and were now welcomed by the Munich police. The wake-up call was "ID check." Initially, these jobless young gentleman with their mop tops [hair] spent their short nights ... in the English Garden park. There they faced trespassing charges. On the grass ... they got too cold. "The first snow will deal with this problem," noted a local and optimistic police officer.[75]

The news magazine *Der Spiegel* reported on one instance in which one youngster was jailed for blasphemy. He had carried a sign stating, "Jesus was also a Gammler."[76] In addition, large-scale raids through-

out the late 1960s underlined authorities' willingness to crack down
on this social group as they had against *the delinquent boy* and *the
sexually deviant girl* during the crisis years. The southern part of the
English Garden city park was systematically searched various times.
By early 1968, local law enforcement had detained 600 male and 135
female youngsters for a variety of reasons.[77] Twenty-year-old Helmuth
Waitschies, for instance, was caught spending the night in a shabby
hut with three girls and was sent to prison for four weeks;[78] others
went to prison because they had been unable to provide evidence of
residency or appropriate means to sustain themselves. Countless youngsters experienced a similar fate, encouraging the newspaper *Der Münchner Merkur* to name 1967 a record year regarding arrests.[79] In that
sense, existing mechanisms seemed to be an excellent tool against different and hence abnormal behaviors detected among the young, *students* and *Gammlers* alike.

Over the course of several summers, authorities seemed to bring
the Schwabing problem under control. According to an official report
released in February 1968, the numbers of wandering youth bumming
around in Schwabing slowly decreased, and Schwabing became cleaner;
yet the same report remained unsure how international trends like the
hippie movement or the rise of a drug culture would influence the situation in the future. It thus advised authorities to stay alert, and continue to watch out for *the student* and *the Gammler.*[80]

Coping with *the Student* in 1968

Apart from minor disruptions, the visit of the shah in 1967 marked the
first real test of the Munich Line. Partly applied at a Rolling Stones
concert in 1965,[81] this new tactic had been useful when trying to defuse
hostile situations during that particular visit. Whereas numerous individuals protested, blocked streets, and disturbed public order, the police were able to separate opposing groups. In addition, it did not allow
protestors to provoke police officers. The approach of standing back
instead of stepping in initially sparked criticism: many wondered if the
soft line of the police was appropriate for authorities aiming to keep
law and order. News regarding the escalation of a similar situation in
West Berlin changed such attitudes. There, the police were unwilling
to separate pro-shah protestors from demonstrators but stepped in vi-
olently later on. The situation soon escalated, leading to the death of
Benno Ohnesorg. Once hearing about this tragedy, local officials and
the media in Munich became quite satisfied with the Munich Line.

Then, in the following months, the university became the center of protests. There, student organizations met to organize demonstrations before marching from the university through the city. To control this environment was thus important. Apart from regular patrols within the university area and Schwabing as a whole, the police soon looked for a way to monitor newly forming student organizations. To infiltrate such groups undercover became a prime objective. This intrusion could give authorities insights into the structure and composition of certain organizations and groups; it would also allow the police "to detect possible threats prior to the actual event."[82] *Die Süddeutsche Zeitung* described such attempts as "Mao's tactics";[83] the Minister of the Interior Bruno Merk vehemently supported the approach. In his view, "subversive behaviors of disruptors could only be controlled by 'quasi subversive' measures of authorities."[84] The local police had the blessing to move forward, and in the following months it sent undercover officers to various student meetings, especially those of more radical groups like the SDS. They hoped to find out more about future protests and disruptions. In order to avoid detection, young officers generally took on such tasks. On their secret missions, such undercover police officers collected data on leaders and other participants. Based on those reports, officials created individual files on various protestors, student groups, and leading figures. These included photos, newspaper clips, and police reports.[85] Whereas such data was useful for potential future investigations and convictions, a mere presence also gave authorities enough information about plans to prevent surprises. Coordination between different agencies was key in that process, and had worked well ever since undercover agents patrolled the streets of Schwabing. In fact, local authorities connected to the Immigration Office to access information about Iranian émigrés living in Munich before the shah visited the city. According to *Der Spiegel* at least, those in opposition to the shah, or merely with a questionable attitude, faced a curfew while the shah was in the city.[86] A potential visit by student leader Rudi Dutschke sparked similar conversations amongst local authorities. One such discussion circled around preemptively detaining Dutschke, if he should approach the Bavarian capital,[87] and is a striking example for mechanisms of social control authorities deemed acceptable in this fight against *the student*.

In general, local authorities did little to hide their attempts to infiltrate student life, and many therefore knew about surveillance. Police Chief Schreiber and Minister of the Interior Merk spoke freely about their desire and ability to spy on student organizations; both even gave an interview to the more conservative student paper *Konturen* in

May 1968 regarding their actions.[88] This openness, they hoped, would deter *the student* from attending certain meetings while underlining the constant presence of law enforcement. For potential protestors, on the other hand, such infiltration only sustained their views of an increasingly restrictive state. Actually, at one teach-in in December 1967 demonstrators detected an undercover police officer.[89] Though these instances were uncommon, detected police agents played into the hands of those believing that the state employed fascist and totalitarian surveillance methods, infiltrated universities, and subverted freedom of academia, speech, and assembly. In this sense, exposure and detection merely heightened anxieties, and contributed to an ever-growing polarization by early 1968.

As division increased, various authorities began presenting themselves as protectors of society and proposed ways to further strengthen and expand mechanisms of social control. Originally less strict in his outlook,[90] Minister of the Interior Bruno Merk at this point employed fierce rhetoric to directly attack *the student* and the SDS. He noted in the newspaper *Die Süddeutsche Zeitung,* "Whoever thinks doing damage to property and assault in order to push one's own agenda against a majority is not far away from those who try the same by using bombs."[91] For him, amongst others, newly imposed measures including infiltration seemed insufficient. Of course, such voices also repeatedly used these discussions to strengthen their own political profile. Merk, at least, felt that the police were unable to deal with this situation, thus favoring a more stringent reaction than Police Chief Schreiber.[92] Munich's police initially brushed off such accusations. Yet divisions emerged even within the state government, especially once the leader of the conservative party (CSU), Franz-Josef Strauß, voiced his views. Minister for Culture and Education Ludwig Huber felt pressured by Strauß and others to do more. Indeed, in February 1968, Strauß sent Huber an angry telegram encouraging him to move forward more fiercely against "such leftist terror."[93] In his view, a left, radical, and threatening minority of students staged protests in Munich and elsewhere, and that needed to stop. At the same time, *Der Münchner Merkur* questioned Munich's "soft approach" against protestors altogether. Are "gloves instead of batons"[94] the solution? Huber was irritated, and responded with an annoyed letter to Strauß. He voiced his antipathy regarding "the form and the publication [in the media] of this [private] correspondence." Huber made clear that the state government "is fully aware of its constitutional obligation and political duty to the state of Bavaria."[95]

Others were upset about the supposed lax application of available measures. In February 1968, Minister of Justice Philipp Held advised local judges to "fight against such criminal behaviors quickly and effectively."[96] Police and various administrational authorities likewise pushed for more efficiency. Police Chief Manfred Schreiber agreed, stating, "a liberalization of the law" would worsen the situation.[97] He had been upset several years earlier when the federal government consisting of conservatives and liberals had passed a new criminal proceedings law. Since it forced the police, among other measures, to notify those arrested about various procedures, some saw it as "a criminal protection law."[98] Now, such measures limited the ability of authorities to move forward swiftly. Authorities also became increasingly frustrated with demonstrations. With little means to restrict the Right of Assembly granted in the Constitution, attempts to impose requirements when registering a protest gave authorities some leverage. City officials could demand registration for certain events, and in that process they pushed for compliance with certain codes of conduct and rules. Those taking responsibility for scheduled demonstrations had little issues with such restrictions, and simply completed the necessary paperwork. Once protests took place, however, such previous agreements were often broken. To then catch those breaking the rules was almost impossible. Cameras helped, but many soon figured out how to sneak around these documentation devices; participants at demonstrations also employed passive resistance like sit-ins or teach-ins. These provocations further limited the ability of the police to avoid direct engagement and escalation.

At this time, *the student* was not only a recipient of retribution. Reasonably educated and aware of civil liberties within a democracy, most protestors took advantage of their rights. For those less versed regarding judicial processes, student organizations set up assistance groups, one actually led by well-known student leader Rolf Pohle himself.[99] These organizations outlined the necessity to remain silent, once arrested, and handed out contact information for judicial assistance at demonstrations. A group set up by the Extraparliamentary Opposition shared its contact information during the Easter march in 1968,[100] for example, thus preparing demonstrators for various eventualities. Most groups also remained active beyond certain riots. For instance, after the Easter riots the Judicial Assistance Group of the Extraparliamentary Opposition ran a small ad in the local newspaper, looking for eyewitnesses to the riots.[101] The need for evidence became vital when it came to trials and also challenged the monopoly of state authorities' views of the events. Soon court rooms became spaces for the continuation of discussions and struggles as protests continued within such environments. Student leaders like Rolf Pohle "feared a cover-up" by local authorities;[102] Mayor Hans-Jochen Vogel and other officials, on the other hand, questioned the role of student groups and called on the Extraparliamentary Judicial Assistance to actually put forward their supposed evidence.[103] Such endless debates outlined how student organizations constructed authorities as a threat in response to their own demonization. The result was a stalemate, as both sides relied on vague evidence to accuse each other, making it almost impossible to move forward against actual criminals. That neither the circumstances surrounding the death of Klaus Frings nor Rüdiger Schreck were ever fully uncovered was thus not surprising [Figure 6.2].

Reacting to the Easter Riots

Preemptive measures could not avert the riots at the Buchgewerbe-haus building. Whereas local authorities had previously considered arresting Dutschke to prevent his possible visit to Munich, they could not

Figure 6.2 Conclusion of a student protest in honor of Klaus Frings and against "Political Murder, Terror and Violence as an Instrument of Politics." One banner reads, "Rocks are no arguments." Munich, 1968. Courtesy of Fritz Neuwirth/ Süddeutsche Zeitung Photo.

stop information regarding the attempted assassination of the student leader from reaching the Bavarian capital. Unlike other cities, however, Munich had experienced a similar situation in 1962. During the riots in spring 1968, the police followed its Munich Line, smothered protestors, and avoided provocations.[104] Demonstrators, on the other hand, aimed to disrupt such attempts by resisting passively, and by trying to specifically provoke authorities. Their prime objective during the riots was to expose the police as part of a fascist system. Over the course of the Easter weekend, the situation climaxed with the death of two individuals, a reporter and a student. The Munich Line had paradoxically claimed two victims. Neither demonstrators nor authorities were prepared for that tragedy.

Throughout the protests, Chancellor Kurt Georg Kiesinger felt the need to take a stand. Without any executive power within the states, he asked several ministers of the interior if they felt up to the task.[105] Of course, no state asked for help. Getting federal assistance meant transferring some state power to the federal level. More specifically, this option was not feasible for a state with antifederalist tendencies, like Bavaria. Even the news about the death of Klaus Frings and later Rüdiger Schreck did not change such sentiments, and local officials felt they had everything under control even thereafter.

Once the riots ended, city officials still drew a positive conclusion. Apart from keeping law and order most of the time, the police and other authorities had worked together efficiently. In a city council meeting on 22 April, members congratulated themselves. Although shocked by the death of Klaus Frings and Rüdiger Schreck, one member noted, "The police completed the assignment in a satisfying manner" and did "excellent" work; another member outlined, "The psychological schooling of the police had brought wonderful results." Police Chief Manfred Schreiber agreed, of course, and proudly asserted, "The Munich Line had stood the test." In his view, authorities had reacted well. The water cannon, though welcomed by some protestors as a cooling system, had repeatedly dispersed the crowd. In addition, most police officers did not fall for provocations. Instead, many of them carried on political discussions with protestors, thus creating outlets for them and helping to humanize law enforcement officers.[106] The slogan was, "Where discussions happen there is no brawl."[107] Within the self-congratulatory environment of the council meeting, the deaths of two individuals seemed of little importance. Instead, participants applauded themselves and worried little about the underlying motives of protestors, and how such should be approached in the future. In effect, everyone agreed as the meeting adjourned: a tight system of social control and the Munich Line had protected social order. Only Mayor Hans-Jochen Vogel seemed a little uneasy about the possibility of someone leaking the content of the meeting to the press, as the council's position and lack of empathy might be misunderstood by the general public.[108]

Numbers seemingly sustained positive evaluations. By 17 April, authorities indicted 180 individuals;[109] fifty-three additional cases were added later on, based on witnesses and photos.[110] According to one statistic from 16 April, 110 individuals were taken into custody after the Easter march on Monday. Surprisingly, only thirty-three of them were university-attending students.[111] The rest were a mixture of high school students and adults alike, with diverse backgrounds and motivations. This diversity did not seem to matter in a time when *the student* was seen as the dominant threat to society.

State officials were also pleased with the way local authorities had dealt with the riots. On 24 April, the Bavarian parliament discussed the events. After commemorating the deaths of Frings and Schreck, fears of "Bonn becoming another Weimar" became visible.[112] This comparison loomed throughout debates as authorities feared for democratic structures. Anxieties seemed all the more prominent in Munich given the city's own experiences following World War I. In November 1918, a socialist revolution led by Kurt Eisner had helped oust the Bavarian monarchy, and later on events like the Beer Hall putsch had threatened existing structures. As a result, for many officials the true test for any democratic state arose when it had to defend itself but still could maintain law and order. After several comments along these lines, Minister of the Interior Bruno Merk shared his interpretation of the events taking place over Easter. He explained difficulties facing the police, namely in regard to withstanding provocations and finding sufficient evidence to persecute demonstrators. Throughout his explanations, he emphasized that officials should abstain from "generalizations" and "too many emotions" regarding *the student* or the young generation.[113] To stay calm seemed important. At the same time, Merk did exactly what he noted should not be done: That is, to raise fears. During his speech, he insisted that the state did not simply face an extraparliamentary opposition but was fighting against an antiparliamentary resistance in the form of a Maoist revolution: "I am amazed at the fact that some democrats still refuse to take that into account."[114] The general assembly cheered in response to such remarks. When he assured the audience that the police needed to use batons and weapons in self-defense, fellow conservatives applauded. Social democrats interrupted him during his speech once he talked about the events on Friday because some of them felt that the situation was not handled properly. For others, the arrest of forty-one individuals that day was simply not enough. Towards the end, Minister of Culture and Education Ludwig Huber underlined the possibility of passing stricter disciplinary measures; Minister of Justice Philipp Held called for "a quick and efficient prosecution."[115] Bavarian President Alfons Goppel eventually closed the session by ensuring his audience, "the state is safe."[116]

Overall, state authorities could be satisfied. The Ministry of Culture and Education had cooperated efficiently with the Ministry of the Interior. In mid-April, the latter had forwarded a list of 134 students who had come into conflict with the law during the protests. The Ministry of Culture and Education passed this information to universities, directing them to take appropriate actions. These consisted of disciplinary sanctions including the removal of students from the university.[117] In addition, Minister of the Interior Merk had called for a quick judicial review throughout the riots. According to him, "It is good that justice is done quickly. It is necessary and right that the crimes committed in the riots are prosecuted."[118] Those convicted of a crime faced severe punishments.[119] Most were accused of creating a brawl or a mass resistance against governmental authorities and breach of public peace. The first sentence was announced only a couple of days after the riots: student Gerhard Rothmann had to go to prison for seven months.[120] Other participants, like Heinz Koderer and Alois Aschenbrenner, were sent to prison for nine and four months;[121] student leader Rolf Pohle faced charges of leadership during the Easter riots. As a student of jurisprudence, a conviction and three months in prison destroyed his chances of becoming a judge in the future.[122] Although these sentences were partially repealed later on, at the time authorities moved forward efficiently. According to Bavarian Minister of the Interior Bruno Merk, "the police had everything under control,"[123] the state was not in jeopardy of experiencing another Weimar, and officials did not need to employ additional measures of social control.

Within a short time, however, it became obvious that the prosecution of *the student* did not move forward so smoothly. Although the police had made an effort to precisely document criminal behavior during the Easter riots and beyond, such proof was not always useful evidence in court. Also, during the riots, the police had to rely on images taken by journalists from *Die Bildzeitung* because "the camera vehicle [of the police] was too expensive to use."[124] The press photos could only provide limited references because they were not taken for prosecutorial purposes. Moreover, the continuing resistance of some protestors disrupted the judicial process. Well aware of their rights, many of those arrested refused to cooperate with authorities and remained silent—consequently slowing down the judicial process significantly. It soon dawned on authorities that various judicial assistance groups had adequately prepared them, and they would continue to do so as long as protests and antagonisms persisted. The Extraparliamentary Judicial Assistance Group even presented its own report on the Easter riots in June 1968.[125] Eighty-two pages long, it was based on numerous statements from witnesses. Although it was rooted in attempts to demonize authorities, such evidence had to be taken seriously, especially because other groups, including the German Association for Journalists, also questioned the judicial process. Even the newspaper *Der Münchner Merkur* and the broadcasting cooperation *Der Bayerische Rundfunk* eventually joined such calls.[126] Such pressure put additional limitations on the police and only led to further delays.

Such setbacks soon raised concerns and complaints amongst authorities. State officials hoped for more preemptive interference and a stricter application of the law by the police. But to set up preventative measures was difficult as the German Constitution guaranteed a Right of Assembly. Police Chief Manfred Schreiber also did not want to move away from his beloved Munich Line.[127] In his view, it was the fault of the judges. According to Schreiber, they should just consider "the partially subversive nature" of certain crimes, and not let protestors get away so easily.[128] Bavarian Minister of Justice Philipp Held, on the other hand, pushed back and blamed other factors.[129] Yet data supported Schreiber's general claims. Until 1 May 1969, the Higher Regional Court in Munich had investigated 478 cases; only ninety-seven of them resulted in convictions.[130] The 233 individuals arrested throughout the Easter riots took a long time to make their way through the judicial system.[131] Such low numbers and frequent delays indicate that initial efforts to reach suspended sentences as a way to "educate" *the student* was ultimately declined.[132]

Judicial and University Reform

Local authorities saw an upcoming judicial reform as an excellent opportunity to approach a variety of issues regarding the control of youth. West Germany's penal code was indeed in dire need of revision. Still partly based on laws from 1871, attempts to revise outdated measures had been on the agenda of the federal government since 1949. According to *Der Spiegel,* in the 1960s "verdicts remain tied to the ideological standpoint of the judge,"[133] a problematic dynamic for any democracy. Local Bavarian authorities and officials, on the other hand, hoped that reform would help streamline the judicial process, and make the persecution of *the student* much easier. For them, the situation was out of control, and the government needed much more power.

The most prominent voice in that context remains conservative leader and Bavarian politician Franz-Josef Strauß. In several meetings of subcommittees in the West German parliament he specifically opposed "a soft approach."[134] Whereas, as he noted, he "did not favor a police state or terror of justice," he believed that "each citizen has the right for protection from criminal elements and authorities the duty to protect the state from revolutionary upheavals."[135] Strauß referred to recent developments within the state of Bavaria; he also more particularly referenced *the student* to sustain his claims. In fall 1968 protestor Reinhard Wetter was indicted for various crimes in the context of his opposition.[136] Sentenced to eight months of juvenile detention, he served his term in Ebrach near Bamberg in Northern Bavaria. Throughout June and July 1969 some protestors from all over West Germany came to the Bamberg area to show their support for Wetter. They set up a camp and hoped to spark protests within the region. However, only a couple of minor brawls broke out because the local population did not show much sympathy for them.[137] Nonetheless, Franz-Josef Strauß understood the events in Ebrach as another attack on the state. Apart from sending a letter to Bavarian President Goppel asking him to move forward against such individuals, Strauß also noted that those protesting in Bamberg "behave like animals, which makes it impossible for current laws to apply."[138] According to Strauß's continuing demonization, "APO revolutionaries urinated and defecated in public."[139] In December 1969 he pointed out that they supposedly trashed a county office, urinated on documents, and stole religious ornaments from the local cemetery. "One female student fornicated with two men in public and in front of three- to six-year old children."[140] None of his accusations could be proven or sustained, and the statement as such led to criticism from various sides. Even the German Judges Association condemned his use of "Nazi vocabulary."[141] Strauß, on the other hand, did not concede easily, and called members of the Extraparliamentary Opposition "mentally ill,"[142] thus continually trying to benefit from his own construct of juvenile delinquency.

Yet a shift on the federal level made it increasingly difficult for those in favor of more stringent measures against *the student*. In October 1969, Willy Brandt became the first social democratic chancellor and the head of a new coalition. Brandt and the social democrats (SPD) had not won the elections. Instead, Kurt Georg Kiesinger and the conservative party received the most votes. In this sense, a majority of the

people in West Germany seemed at least content with the way conservatives dealt with current problems. However, the liberals shifted
coalitions. This possibility had become available ever since social
democrats (SPD) and liberals (FDP) supported the same presidential
candidate. A variety of internal frictions between conservatives and
liberals then lead to the first SPD-FDP coalition, marking a major shift
in West German politics;[143] it also influenced debates regarding *the
student*. Willy Brandt's credo of "daring more democracy"[144] emerged
partially in response to calls by the young as some members of this
coalition hoped to bring *the student* back into society. Ongoing discussions about judicial reform provided an avenue for reaching out to
those under investigation, especially once numerous well-known intel-
lectuals favored such an amnesty.[145]

Conservatives throughout West Germany and particularly in the
state of Bavaria pushed back. As the media reported, they had "res-
ervations"[146] and certainly opposed an amnesty.[147] Such concerns of
"the law and order faction" even within Brandt's coalition government
resulted in an initial delay.[148] As conversations resumed in early 1970,
so did fears. In spring 1970 Bavarian Justice Secretary Josef Bauer
sent a letter to Federal Minister of Justice Gustav Heinemann outlining his distress regarding a possible amnesty more specifically. In his
view, such a measure would encourage delinquent behavior in the future and jeopardize stability.[149] His letter did not result in the desired
outcome. In March the social democrats and liberals passed judicial reform, including an amnesty for protestors. Demonstrators like
Fritz Teufel saw it as too weak; conservatives understood it as a post-
legalization of unlawful protests.[150] Either way, and similar to the situation in other countries, the protests seemed over and SPD and FDP
could at least hope that *the student* would cast votes for them in the
future.

Yet in Munich discussions continued, now tied to the attempt of the
Bavarian government to pass university reform as a way to control *the
student*. Such conversations had gained momentum since late 1968,
especially once protestors had shifted their focus away from emergency laws[151] and towards disrupting academic life.[152] As a result, local
authorities had concentrated on getting police access to institutions
of higher education to dissolve meetings of student organizations and
prevent further disruptions—a tricky attempt given current law.[153] In
a meeting on 10 January 1969 representatives of the police, the Ministry of the Interior, and university officials had already looked into this
issue and possible responses, including the possibility of checking stu-

dent identification cards. This approach, they had hoped, would prevent disruptors from infiltrating higher education, inciting university students, and disturbing lectures. Most officials had deemed such an approach as impractical and "unfeasible"[154] although, as one official had noted then, "factual jurisdiction of the police also includes universities."[155] Conversations briefly shifted in early February 1969 when the Ministry of the Interior considered an accelerated judicial process if existing disciplinary measures and convictions based on compensation for damage turned out to be insufficient.[156] On 13 February 1969, several members of the conservative CSU, led by Professor Friedrich August von der Heydte, also proposed more stringent penalties to protect what he saw as the freedom of academic affairs. This proposal included cuts to certain scholarships,[157] an approach many conservatives believed could "end the spook" of left-radicalism within various student organizations.[158] One member of Parliament went even further when stating,

> Let's end the uproar of so-called students.... We fight against the use of our tax money if such is given to these elements that do not have any real work on their minds but only pranks.... Expel students, or we will not pay taxes anymore. Give them a snow shovel and send them to work camps so that they learn how to work.[159]

By the summer of 1969, Bavarian authorities also pushed more directly for a comprehensive disciplinary law.[160] Whereas many believed such a reform would break "the dictatorship of learners against teachers,"[161] Minister of Culture and Education Huber did not want to wait for its passage on the federal level. Instead, he—among other mainly conservative state ministers—followed the lead of the state government of North Rhine-Westphalia and signed on to a broader agreement. This document also touched on "the standardization of disciplinary measures at universities."[162] In addition, Ludwig Huber proposed a provision regarding "behaviors of order within the university."[163] Conservative Bavarian authorities consequently continued to employ *the student* as a way to push for additional measures of social control although protests had decreased significantly and broader federal dynamics had favored a more cooperative approach.

Not surprisingly, demonstrations in opposition to such proposals surged within Munich, aimed primarily against Huber. Protestors now more specifically tied to university environments relied on the power of student bodies and various organizations to dismiss governmental attempts to interfere in academic life and within university spaces.

Early on, various protestors had simply blocked the decision-making process within disciplinary committees. Authorities had become frustrated with such efforts, apparent in a report by university professor Paul Bockelmann.[164] To expand state rule within academia by limiting student governance and overall participation in various forums soon ranked high on the agenda of authorities given such early pushbacks in such spaces. Soon opposition against Huber's university reform became much more organized and coherent. Supported mostly by left-leaning organizations, student groups began defining the proposed reform as another emergency law. Moreover, different groups organized. In February 1969, ten student organizations had already signed a resolution against the Bavarian emergency law[165] while some had occupied Munich's Academy for the Arts;[166] the student newspaper *unireport* had proclaimed its decisive "No! Regarding the CSU-Emergency Law!" by 1969.[167] In the following weeks and months, Huber became enemy number one for demonstrators because he was pushing for "more state power within lecture halls."[168] Unable to prevent him from signing the law, protestors continued to demonize the minister by demonstrating against the possibility of a new and more restrictive university reform.

Attempts to control and student responses in the form of protests reached a final climax in 1973. Then, more than 20,000 students joined the opposition against Huber's successor in Munich,[169] the new Minister of Culture and Education Hans Maier. The latter also pushed for more stringent mechanisms of control; he even called for "a separate university police."[170] According to his proposal, the state had to hold domestic power over the university. In Munich, Maier asked for "more state authority [and] less autonomy"[171] overall and continued to push for the states' ability to "exercise domestic authority;"[172] he also hoped the state would be able to expel rebellious students. Compared to other state legislatures, this approach seemed radical. While Bavarian state officials simply continued to demonize *the student* as left-radicals in their attempts to shape university reform,[173] states led by a social democratic government had allowed more student participation and governance within the university as a whole. In that sense, Maier and others tried to avoid more democratization and broader shifts within the university setup—and they took advantage of *the student* as an initially constructed threat as long and as much as possible.

Actual students fought back. During a visit at a Bavarian university Maier experienced the nature of protests as masked protestors interfered with several meetings. "A brawl developed," *Der Spiegel* wrote in 1973, and after "extreme chaos the students left the assembly hall again."[174] Protestors had organized and used their power to directly challenge what they saw as undemocratic and illegal state interference; some of them had also more fully endorsed *the student* as their identity given issues at hand.

In the end, Hans Maier and other conservative Bavarian officials seemingly succeeded. The Act of Higher Education for Bavaria passed in December 1973, before the federal Framework Law for Higher Education. Similar to the situation in other conservative states,[175] this law "beefed up the disciplinary powers of the university authorities;"[176] the reform also limited student participation within the university. The strongly politicized student group AStA, for instance, was dissolved. Such new restrictions and authoritative measures ended remaining concerns of authorities for now.[177]

The protest years in Munich might have ended in 1973; images of youth, however, continued to haunt discourses thereafter. In fact, by the mid-1970s images of youth shifted along broader discussions tied to the end of economic progress and environmental issues. The oil crisis outlined economic instability and the "Limits of Growth" debate increased fears regarding environmental degradation. Constructs of youth followed such narratives, now seen as environmentally conscious, in support of direct democratic processes, and more likely to vote for the German Green Party. Previous stereotypes tied to *the Gammler* remained in place particularly around connections between youth and drugs. In the 1980s, discussions around armament brought the peace movement back into the public limelight as thousands protested against the return to harsh Cold War rhetoric that endangered planet and future. Again, youth mattered.[178] In the 1990s, references to inner city youth became a way to discuss immigration at a time when a united Germany wondered about its national and potentially nationalistic identity. Such conversations continue as Turkish male youngsters in particular have become the new threat. In February 2011, for example, an article in the news magazine *Der Spiegel* referred to male youth as Halbstarke. In this context the article tries to capture complex relationships and dynamics regarding young male Halbstarke with an immigrant background within Berlin-Neukölln's urban topography.[179] In other words, although some normalization is apparent and broad hysteria and panic much less common, youth remains a discursive space, at this point tied to immigration, housing, crime, and education.

Notes

1. Hans-Jochen Vogel (*Aus heutiger Sicht*), quoted in Stankiewitz, *München '68*, 55.
2. Christian conservative (CSU) and former state representative Heinrich Junker was minister of the interior until 1966. His successor was Bruno Merk (1966–1977). Throughout the timeframe discussed, Bavaria had three different ministers of culture and education. Theodor Maunz (CSU) was in power until 1964, followed by Ludwig Huber (CSU) (1964–1970) and Hans Maier (1970–1986).
3. Youngsters under the age of sixteen had to be home by 8 P.M., those under the age of eighteen by 10 P.M.
4. For the situation in Schwabing prior to 1962 see, for instance: Ernst Hoferichter, "Unsterbliches Schwabing," 218–30, in *Lebendiges Schwabing;* Fritz Lutz, *Über den Dächern von München* (Munich, 1966).
5. Schreiber, "Das Jahr 1968 in München," in *1968: 30 Jahre danach*, 38. See also: Sturm, "Wildgewordene Obrigkeit," in *'Schwabinger Krawalle'*, 67.
6. Vogel, *Die Amtskette*, 45.
7. Gerhard Fürmetz, "Polizei und Verkehrsdiziplin in Bayern," in *Nachkriegspolizei*, 199–228, here 203–4; Peter Borscheid, "Auto und Massenmobilität," in *Die Einflüsse der Motorisierung auf das Verkehrswesen von 1886 bis 1986*, ed. Hans Pohl (Stuttgart, 1988), 117–41, here 123; Klaus Zimniok, *Eine Stadt geht in den Untergrund: Die Geschichte der Münchner U- und S-Bahn im Spiegel der Zeit* (Munich, 1981).
8. Thomas, *Protest Movements in 1960s West Germany*, 42.
9. StadtAM, Ratssitzungsprotokolle, Sitzungsprotokoll 735/85 (1962).
10. "Der Stadtrat lobt die Polizei," *Die Süddeutsche Zeitung*, 23 June 1962.
11. "Der Krawall bleibt auf der Tagesordnung: Heigl vor dem Polizeiausschuss: Bedauern für die unschuldig Betroffenen," *Die Süddeutsche Zeitung*, 6 July 1962. See also: "Krawalle doch noch auf der Tagesordnung: Stadtrat diskutiert den 'Fall Schwabing,'" *Der Münchner Merkur*, 5 July 1962.
12. Ibid.
13. Ibid.
14. "Erste Krawall-Verhandlung," *Der Münchner Merkur*, 31 August 1962. See also: "In Schwabing festgenommen," *Die Süddeutsche Zeitung*, 21 September 1962.
15. Oktavia Depta, prod., *Wolfram Kunkel und die Schwabinger Krawalle*.
16. "Elf Monate für jugendlichen Randalierer," *Die Süddeutsche Zeitung*, 27 September 1962.
17. Ibid.
18. Ibid.
19. "Krawall-Prozesse," *Die Süddeutsche Zeitung*, 28 September 1962. See also: "Krawall + Diebstahl = 1 Jahr 4 Monate," *Die Süddeutsche Zeitung*, 5 October 1962; "Es war ein Rädelsführer, sagt der Richter," *Die Süddeutsche Zeitung*, 19 October 1962.
20. "Medizinstudent als Aufwiegler," *Der Münchner Merkur*, 5 April 1963.
21. "Keine Ermittlungen gegen Seelmann," *Die Süddeutsche Zeitung*, 18 December 1962; "Verfahren gegen Seelmann eingestellt," *Die Abendzeitung*,

18 December 1962. See also: Fürmetz, "Anwalt der Jugend," in *'Schwabinger Krawalle'*, 141–50.

22. StadtAM, Ratssitzungsprotokolle, Sitzungsprotokoll 735/85; StadtAM, Ratssiztungsprotokolle, Sitzungsprotokoll 735/14 (1962); StadtAM, Stadtchronik (1962). See also: "In Schwabing festgenommen," *Die Süddeutsche Zeitung*, 21 September 1962.

23. "Am Aschermittwoch: Krawallprozess," *8-Uhr Blatt*, 25 February 1963; "Erster Polizisten-Prozeß in Sachen Schwabing," *Die Süddeutsche Zeitung*, 28 February 1963. For the verdict see: "'Ein Polizeibeamter muss ruhig Blut bewahren,'" *Die Abenzeitung*, 1 March 1963. For a previous trial against a prison guard see: "'Ich bin doch immer gut zu den Gefangenen,'" *Der Münchner Merkur*, 29 November 1962.

24. Michael Sturm, "'Unruhestifter' und Polizisten vor Gericht: Das juristische Nachspiel der 'Schwabinger Krawalle,'" in *'Schwabinger Krawalle'*, 175–203, here 176.

25. "Als ob nichts gewesen wäre," *Die Süddeutsche Zeitung*, 27 May 1963.

26. Vogel, *Die Amtskette*, 47. See also: BayHStAM, Ministerium des Inneren 97954.

27. "Vogel: Bedauern und Mitleid," *Der Münchner Merkur*, 7 April 1963. See also: "Oberbürgermeister will einrenken, Beschwerdeführer bei Dr. Vogel: Sachliches Gespräch über Krawalle," *Der Münchner Merkur*, 7 April 1963.

28. StadtAM, Ratssitzungsprotokoll, Sitzungsprotokoll 735 (1962).

29. Ibid.

30. Ibid. See also: "Mit Heigl unzufrieden," *Die Süddeutsche Zeitung*, 11 October 1962.

31. "Wir sind keine Barbaren!," *Welt am Sonntag*, 1 July 1962.

32. Vogel, *Die Amtskette*, 48.

33. "Der Gummiknüppel steht erst an sechster Stelle: Die Schwabinger Krawalle aus Sicht der Polizei-Strategen," *Die Süddeutsche Zeitung*, 3 July 1962. See also: Schreiber, "Das Jahre 1968 in München," in *1968: 30 Jahre danach;* Drost, prod., *Gestern und Heute*.

34. Manfred Schreiber, quoted in Falter, *Chronik des Polizeipräsidiums München*, 150.

35. StAM, Polizeipräsidium München 11051.

36. StAM, Polizeidirektion München. See also: Vogel, *Die Amtskette*, 49; Manfred Schreiber, "Münchens Polizei: Kein Staat in der Stadt," in *München und seine Polizei*, ed. Manfred Schreiber and Ernst Krack (Wiesbaden, 1964), n.p.; Schreiber, "Das Jahr 1968 in München," in *1968: 30 Jahre danach*, 39; Sturm, "'Wildgewordene Obrigkeit'?," in *'Schwabinger Krawalle'*, 100–105.

37. "Psycho," *Der Spiegel*, 26 February 1964. Schreiber later partially revised his comments. See: "Mitteilungen des Personalrats" Nr 90/64, quoted in Falter, *Chronik des Polizeipräsidiums München*, 155–56.

38. Peters, ed., *'1200 Jahre Schwabing'*, 126–28; Rolf Umbach, "Konfliktzentrum Straße," in *München und seine Polizei*, 18–19; StAM, Polizeidirektion München 11055.

39. Cameras and audio vehicles were available by November 1964.

40. StAM, Polizeidirektion München 11055.

41. Falter, *Chronik des Polizeipräsidiums München*, 155.
42. Manfred Schreiber (*Jahresbericht 1967*), quoted in ibid., 176.
43. StAM, Polizeidirektion München 11129. See also: Manfred Schreiber, "Die 'Schwabinger Krawalle,'" *Die Polizei* 56 (1965): 33–37, here 35. Discussions regarding the identification of policemen made its last appearance after the protests in 1968. See: StadtAM, Ratssitzungsprotokolle, Sitzungsprotokoll 741/13 (1968).
44. Falter, *Chronik des Polizeipräsidiums München*, 144.
45. Manfred Schreiber, "Die'Schwabinger Krawalle.' Versuch einer Zwischenbilanz," *Die Polizei* 55 (1964): 37–40. On the Munich Line not being a soft approach see, for instance: Falter, *Chronik des Polizeipräsidiums München*, 176.
46. Schreiber, "Das Jahr 1968 in München," in *1968: 30 Jahre danach*, 40. See also: "Zollstock angelegt," *Der Spiegel*, 18 July 1977; "Der 'Unterhak-Mayer' ist tot," *Merkur-Online*, 22 October 2010.
47. StAM, Polizeidirektion München 11130. Controls began on 29 May 1964, 14 May 1965, and 27 April 1966. See also: "Polizeipatrouillen in Schwabing," *Der Münchner Merkur*, 29 June 1962; "Schwabing ist ein unruhiges Pflaster," *Der Münchner Merkur*, 27–28 June 1964.
48. StAM, Polizeidirektion München 11130.
49. Ibid.
50. Ibid.
51. Ibid.
52. Ibid.
53. Ibid.
54. Ibid.
55. Ibid. See also: Sturm, "'Wildgewordene Obrigkeit'?" in *'Schwabinger Krawalle'*, 102.
56. StAM, Polizeidirektion München 11130.
57. Ibid. See also: "Schwabing ist ein unruhiges Pflaster," *Der Münchner Merkur*, 27–28 June 1964.
58. StAM, Polizeidirektion München 11130.
59. Ibid.
60. Ibid.
61. Ibid.
62. Ibid.
63. StAM, Polizedirektion München 15622.
64. "Schalom aleichem," *Der Spiegel*, 19 September 1966.
65. Ibid.
66. "Wiar a Kropf," *Der Spiegel*, 23 October 1967. See also: StAM, Polizeidirektion München 15622.
67. "Schalom aleichem," *Der Spiegel*, 19 September 1966.
68. Ibid.
69. Ibid.
70. "Wiar a Kropf," *Der Spiegel*, 23 October 1967.
71. StadtAM, Ratssitzungsprotokolle, Sitzungsprotokoll 741/13 (1968).
72. StAM, Polizeidirektion München 15622.
73. Ibid. See also: StadtAM, Pressesammlung no. 134.

74. Kosel, *Gammler, Beatniks, Provos*, 96. Margaret Kosel notes that the police in Munich had some kind of gentlemen's agreement with *the Gammler:* they could sleep in certain areas but had to disappear during the day. However, most sources question this understanding, and her interpretation might be based on only a couple of instances.

75. *Die Presse* (1966), quoted in Fricke, *München rockt*, 62.

76. "Wiar a Kropf," *Der Spiegel*, 23 October 1967.

77. StAM, Polizeidirektion München 15622. *Der Spiegel* spoke of 637 *Gammlers* for the year 1967. "Wiar a Kropf," *Der Spiegel*, 23 October 1967.

78. Ibid.

79. Ibid.

80. On deterrence and official reports regarding *the Gammler* throughout this time see, for example: StAM, Polizeidirektion München 15622. As rightfully outlined by Georg Lipitz, *the Gammler* was also incorporated by the commercialization and development of an underground "'youth' culture economy." See: Lipitz, "Who'll Stop the Rain?" 213. See also: Weinhauer, "Eliten, Generation, Jugendelinquenz und innere Sicherheit," 43.

81. Schreiber, "Das Jahr 1968 in München," in *1968: 30 Jahre danach*, 39; Fricke, *München rockt*, 33–34.

82. StAM, Polizeidirektion München 17432.

83. *Die Süddeutsche Zeitung*, 15 March 1968, quoted in Fürmetz, *Protest oder Störung?* 46.

84. StAM, RA 101154. See also: Stankiewitz, *München '68*, 24.

85. StAM, Polizeidirektion München 8888; StAM, Polizeidirektion München 8922; StAM, Polizeidirektion München 8999. See also: Fürmetz, *Protest oder Störung?* 47 and 52.

86. "Tod vor der Oper," *Der Spiegel*, 5 June 1967.

87. StAM, Polizeidirektion München 16580; Fürmetz, *Protest oder Störung?* 47.

88. BayHStAM, Studentische Gruppen an der LMU München 6, quoted in Fürmetz, *Protest oder Störung?* 37.

89. StAM, RA 101154.

90. "Innenminister Bruno Merk zeigt Verständnis für Studentenunruhen," *Die Abendzeitung*, 14 February 1968.

91. "Merk greift den SDS an," *Die Süddeutsche Zeitung*, 12 March 1968.

92. Wolfgang Zorn, *Bayerns Geschichte seit 1960*, ed. Rolf Kießling (Regensburg, 2007), 28. See also: "Wachsam nach rechts und links," *Die Süddeutsche Zeitung*, 14 February 1968.

93. BayHStAM, MK Reg. VI/133, quoted in Fürmetz, *Protest oder Störung*, 31 and 38.

94. "Samthandschuhe statt Knüppel," *Der Münchner Merkur*, 10 February 1968.

95. BayHStAM, Staatskanzlei 13617.

96. BayHStAM, Ministerium des Inneren 90051, quoted in Fürmetz, *Protest oder Störung?* 61. See also: StAM, RA 101190.

97. Schreiber, "Das Jahr 1968 in München," in *1968: 30 Jahre danach*, 40.

98. Ibid. See also: Weinhauer, "Eliten, Generationen, Jugenddelinquenz und innere Sicherheit," 45. This minor revision passed on 19 December 1964 (implemented 1 April 1965). See: BGBl. 1964, 1067, quoted in Falter, *Chronik des Polizeipräsidiums München*, 162.

99. "Nach der Straßenschlacht die Redeschlacht," *Der Münchner Merkur,* 25 April 1968.

100. StAM, RA 101122.

101. *Die Abendzeitung,* without title, 22 April 1968.

102. "'Alles Material übergeben,'" *Der Münchner Merkur,* 29 April 1968. See also: "Kripo beschuldigt Rechtshilfestelle," *Der Münchner Merkur,* 26 April 26, 1968; "Kontroversen Studenten: Polizei," *Der Münchner Merkur,* 23 April 1968.

103. StAM, RA 101154. See also: "'Alles Material übergeben,'" *Der Münchner Merkur,* 29 April 1968.

104. BayHStAM, Ministerium des Inneren 90050; BayHStAM, Staatskanzlei 13620. See also: Fürmetz, *Protest oder Störung?* 33; Schult, "Panoptikum der Exoten?" in *Drachen mit tausend Köpfen,* 52–64, here 54,

105. "Einer wird gewinnen," *Der Spiegel,* 22 April 1968.

106. StadtAM, Ratssitzungsprotokolle, Sitzungsprotokoll 741/13 (1968).

107. Fricke, *München rockt,* 67.

108. StadtAM, Ratssitzungsprotokolle, Sitzungsprotokoll 741/13 (1968).

109. StAM, Polizeidirektion München 9570/ 10.

110. BayHStAM, Ministerium des Inneren 90051.

111. StAM, RA 101154. See also: "Verlorenes Wochenende," *Der Spiegel,* 22 April 1968.

112. BayHStAM, Staatskanzlei 13617.

113. Ibid.

114. Ibid. See also: "'Anschlag auf rechtstaatliche Ordnung," *Die Süddeutsche Zeitung,* 24 April 1968.

115. BayHStAM, Staatskanzlei 13617. See also: StAM, RA 101154.

116. BayHStAM, Staatskanzlei 13617.

117. BayHStAM, MK Reg. VI/133, quoted in Fürmetz *Protest oder Störung?* 31.

118. "Endlich! Schnellgerichte gegen die Rädelsführer!" *Bild (Berlin),* 17 April 1968.

119. StAM, RA 101154.

120. "Erster Demonstrant verurteilt: 7 Monate," *Telegraf,* 17 April 1968.

121. StAM, Polizeidirektion München 16393; Landgericht München I, 9 July 1968, quoted in Fürmetz, *Protest oder Störung?* 62 and 71.

122. StAM, Polizeidirektion München 15994, quoted in Fürmetz, *Protest oder Störung?* 62. Pohle received amnesty in 1970 but flunked the second exam. See: StAM, RA 101112, quoted in Fürmetz, *Protest oder Störung?* 62. Most documents regarding prosecution are not accessible due to privacy restrictions. For some insights see: Fürmetz, *Protest oder Störung?* 66–86.

123. BayHStAM, Staatskanzlei 13612.

124. StadtAM, Ratssitzungsprotokolle, Sitzungsprotokoll 741/13 (1968). See also: StAM, Polizeidirektion München 9570/3.

125. StAM, Polizeidirektion München 9570/9.

126. "Neugierig genügt," *Der Spiegel,* 15 July 1968. Later on, students also protested at trials. Whereas this would sometimes delay procedures, it did not affect the actual outcomes of trials. See: StAM, Polizeidirektion München 15982; StAM, Polizeidirektion München 16394; StAM, Polizei-

direktion München 9566. See also: Fürmetz, *Protest oder Störung?* 69–72; Gerstenberg, *Hiebe, Liebe und Proteste München 1968,* 59–63, passim.

127. BayHStAM, Staatskanzlei 13621; BayHStAM, Ministerium des Inneren 90051; StAM, Polizeidirektion München 15970.

128. Fürmetz, *Protest oder Störung?* 63.

129. BayHStAM, Staatskanzlei 13620. See also: StAM, RA 101192.

130. BayHStAM, Staatskanzlei 13620.

131. StAM, RA 101154. See also: BayHStAM, Staatskanzlei 13621 quoted in Fürmetz, *Protest oder Störung?* 61 and 66.

132. StAM, Polizeidirektion München 17432, quoted in Fürmetz, *Protest oder Störung?* 68.

133. "Die Richter sind in einer schwierigen Lagen," *Der Spiegel,* 3 November 1969. See also: "Datum: 1. Dezember. Betr.: Amnestie," *Der Spiegel,* 1 December 1969; "Jede unfriedliche Demonstration ist ein Graus," *Der Spiegel,* 15 December 1969. On amnesty see: "Schlechtes Theater," *Der Spiegel,* 1 December 1969; "Datum: 1. Dezember. Betr.: Amnestie," *Der Spiegel,* 1 December 1969.

134. BayHStAM, Staatskanzlei 13622.

135. Ibid.

136. Fürmetz, *Protest oder Störung?* 61. Together with others, Reinhard Wetter wrote an in-depth analysis of the German prison system. In more than 200 pages, he outlines methods, objectives, and other aspects of imprisonment. Reinhard Wetter and Frank Böckelmann, *Knast Report* (Frankfurt am Main, 1972). See also: IfZM, ED 328/9, quoted in Fürmetz, *Protest oder Störung?* 61.

137. BayHStAM, Ministerium des Inneren 89991. See also: "Schlägerei in Bamberg," *Die Süddeutsche Zeitung,* 21 July 1969.

138. BayHStAM, Staatskanzlei 13622; "Strauß verunglimpft Studenten in Ebrach," *Der Spiegel,* 22 December 1969.

139. "Nichts zu finden," *Der Spiegel,* 22 December 1969.

140. Ibid.

141. Ibid. See also: BayHStAM, Staatskanzlei 13622.

142. Wolfram Bickerich, *Franz-Josef Strauß* (Düsseldorf, 1996), 226.

143. Baring, *Machtwechsel.*

144. Willy Brandt and Wolther von Kieseritzky, *Mehr Demokratie wagen: Innen- und Gesellschaftspolitik 1966–1974* (Bonn, 2001).

145. BayHStAM, Staatskanzlei 13622 (25 November 1969): An Mitglieder und stellvertr. Mitglieder des Bundesrates der BRD: Amnestie für Demonstranten; "Datum: 1. December 1969. Betr.: Amnestie," *Der Spiegel,* 1 December 1969. This article was signed by: Arnold Arndt, Ernst Bloch, Heinrich Böll, Alexander Mitscherlich, Kurt Scharf, and Thomas and Heinrich Mann.

146. "CDU-Vorbehalte gegen Novelle zu den Demonstrationsdelikten," *Die Welt,* 5 December 1969.

147. "Keine Amnestie für Demonstranten," *Die Süddeutsche Zeitung,* 5 December 1969. See also: "Hearing zum Demonstrationsgesetz: Strafrechtler, Studenten und Polizeibeamte sollen zu Reform aussagen," *Der Münchner Merkur,* 5 December 1969.

148. "Amnestie," *Der Spiegel,* 29 December 1969.

149. BayHStAM, Staatskanzlei 13620.
150. "Ein Schlußstrich," *Die Zeit*, 27 March 1970. See also: "Einer für alle," *Der Spiegel*, 18 January 1971. The law (Straffreiheitsgesetz bei Demonstrationsvergehen) was passed on 20 May 1970. See also: Fürmetz, *Protest oder Störung?* 62–63.
151. "Der unbequeme Staatsbürger Schmid," *Der Münchner Merkur*, 16 December 1968; "Beim Demonstrieren etwas zu weit gegangen," *Die Süddeutsche Zeitung*, 8 December 1968; "Jetzt muss er für den Sitzstreik sitzen," *Die Süddeutsche Zeitung*, 16 December 1968.
152. BayHStAM, MK Reg. VI/134, quoted in Fürmetz, *Protest oder Störung?* 40. Protests continued. Students, for instance, occupied the Institute for Journalism located in the *Amerikahaus* on 12 February 1969. See: Fürmetz, *Protest oder Störung?* 41. See also Sub-Bavaria (1969), accessible at http://protest-muenchen.sub-bavaria.de, [last accessed 11 March 2015].
153. BayHStAM, Staatskanzlei 13617. Professor of Law Peter Lerche's report was passed on to the Bavarian State Government in January 1968. See also: Fürmetz, *Protest oder Störung?* 36.
154. BayHStAM, Ministerium des Inneren 90050.
155. Ibid. A representative from the Ludwig-Maximilians University, the Technical University, and the Academy for the Arts were present at this meeting, as was Police Chief Manfred Schreiber. See also: Fürmetz, *Protest oder Störung?* 30.
156. BayHStAM, Ministerium des Inneren 92243, quoted in Fürmetz, *Protest oder Störung?* 39.
157. BayHStAM, Staatskanzlei 13620, quoted in Fürmetz, *Protest oder Störung?* 31–32.
158. BayHStAM, MK Reg. VI/453, quoted in Fürmetz, *Protest oder Störung?* 41.
159. *Die Süddeutsche Zeitung*, 15 February 1968, quoted in Gerstenberg, *Hiebe, Liebe und Proteste München 1968*, 16.
160. BayHStAM, NK Reg. VI/188 and 189, quoted in Fürmetz, *Protest oder Störung?* 32; BayHStAM, Staatskanzlei 13620; Andreas Reich, ed., *Bayerisches Hochschulgesetz. Kommentar* (Bad Honnef, 1977); "Mit dem Latein am Ende," *Der Spiegel*, 14 July 1969 until 13 October 1969 [weekly series]; "Für große Reformen ist eine Utopie nötig," *Der Spiegel*, 17 November 1969.
161. *Bayernkurier*, quoted in "Das Mißtrauen ist nahezuh absolut," *Der Spiegel*, 19 February 1973.
162. Staatsvertrag über die Grundsätze zur Reform der wissenschaftlichen Hochschulen und über die Vereinheitlichung des Ordnungsrechts an den Hochschulen, 27 March 1969, BayHStAM, MK Reg. VI/188, quoted in Fürmetz, *Protest oder Störung?* 32.
163. BayHStAM, Studentenschaft des Freistaats Bayern 7 (April 1969), quoted in Fürmetz, *Protest oder Störung?* 32–33.
164. Paul Bockelmann, "Professorenstreik?" *Deutsche Richterzeitung* (July 1969): 219, quoted in BayHStAM, Staatskanzlei 13622.

165. StAM, Polizeidirektion München 9216, quoted in Fürmetz, *Protest oder Störung?* 32 and 58.

166. StAM, RA 101147; StAM, Polizeidirektion München 15975; StAM, Polizeidirektion München 16006.

167. *unireport* 2, no. 9 (1969), in Universitätsarchiv Munich, Flugblätter und Zeitungen 1967–1971, quoted in Fürmetz, *Protest oder Störung?* 38; StAM, Polizeidirektion München 9216, quoted in Fürmetz, *Protest oder Störung?* 58. See also: IfZM, Dn 358 (Zeitschrift apo press, Nr. 7/II), quoted in Fürmetz, *Protest oder Störung?*.

168. "Mehr Staat im Hörsaal?" *Der Spiegel,* 19 February 1973.

169. "Das Mißtrauen ist nahezu absolut," *Der Spiegel,* 19 February 1973. See also: IfZM, ED 328/37, quoted in Fürmetz, *Protest oder Störung?* 32; StAM, RA 101150.

170. "Ungeheurer Umbruch," *Der Spiegel,* 29 January 29, 1973.

171. "Das Mißtrauen ist nahezu absolut," *Der Spiegel,* 19 February 1973. See also: "Ungeheurer Umbruch," *Der Spiegel,* 29 January 1973.

172. "Das Mißtrauen ist nahezu absolut," *Der Spiegel,* 19 February 1973.

173. "Ruf aus Bayern," *Der Spiegel,* 6 November 1972.

174. "Das Mißtrauen ist nahezu absolut," *Der Spiegel,* 19 February 1973. See also: Fürmetz, *Protest oder Störung?* 59: BayHStAM, Plakatesammlung 27464; StAM, Polizeidirektion München 15996 (June 1969).

175. At the time social democrats governed the states of Bremen, Hamburg, (West) Berlin, Hessen, and North-Rhine Westphalia. Baden-Württemberg, Rhineland-Palatine, and the Saarland had a conservative leadership. See: "Das Mißtrauen ist nahezu absolut," *Der Spiegel,* 19 February 1973.

176. Thomas, *Protest Movements in 1960s West Germany,* 142. See also: Zorn, *Bayerns Geschichte seit 1960,* 56–57.

177. For the Act of Higher Education for Bavaria (Bayerisches Hochschulgesetz, BayHSchG), especially regarding disciplinary measures, see article 76 (Ordnungsverstöße und Ordnungsmaßnahmen) and article 77 (Verfahren). See: Reich, ed., *Bayerisches Hochschulgesetz.* See also: Fürmetz, *Protest oder Störung?* 34; "Herzog Doppelzunge," *Der Spiegel,* 19 May 1969. For later developments see namely: Peter Dallinger, Christian Bode, and Fritz Dellian, *Hochschulrahmengesetz: Kommentar* (Tübingen, 1978).

178. See, for instance: Schildt and Siegfried, *Between Marx and Coca-Cola;* Roger Karapin, *Protest Politics in Germany: Movements on the Left and Right since the 1960s* (University Park, 2007).

179. "Endstation Vorstadt," *Der Spiegel,* 28 February 2011.

Conclusion

Coming of Age discusses six dominant images or constructions of youth. Arising out of the ashes of World War II, *the delinquent boy* marked threats to recovery. Instead of helping to rebuild society, he roamed around, spent time engaged in the black market, and had supposedly no interest in political participation or leadership. *The sexually deviant girl* fraternized and endangered society by spreading venereal diseases; she also challenged gender roles and racial categories. Adult contemporaries mobilized both images to express perceived threats for recovery. In the miracle years, youth once again became a space for discussing and criticizing Americanization. Influenced by a growth in youth culture, two images stepped into the limelight: *the Halbstarke* as a working-class male youngster who wasted time on street corners and rebelled against social norms; and *the teenager* with her middle-class background, desire to dance to rock 'n' roll music, and claim to leave home and kitchen. Both constructs of youth challenged the return of traditional conceptions of normality. Initiated by protests in Schwabing in 1962, *the student* and *the Gammler* threatened the political cohesion and overall order. Mostly seen as male images of older youngsters with female companions, *the student* in particular began organizing outside accepted political structures and formats. His economic background and education, in combination with open dissent, challenged the future of the nation; he also unearthed fears of Munich becoming another Weimar.

Gendered roles and binaries are apparent when analyzing these images of youth. Contemporaries constructed males as delinquent if they abstained from work, failed to prepare for future leadership positions, and challenged broader traditional norms; female deviancy, on the other hand, was tied to sexuality. Gender, sexuality, and age mattered and played a key role when defining and constructing female misbehaviors all through this time period. These surprisingly consistent patterns mark continuities throughout modern history; they also capture a lack of scholarly debate surrounding female youth more specifically because juvenile delinquency remains a male concept. As scholars we need to understand interactions between male and female youth if we want to get a better sense of everyday dynamics, interactions, and relationships—as apparent in *Coming of Age* for the context of Munich.

Space mattered as well because certain locations helped define and characterize juvenile delinquency. The Bavarian capital has been a social democratic island, surrounded by a conservative rural environment, for decades. As a result, traditional stereotypes regarding the dangers of cityscapes, loose law enforcement, and a lack of social order are all the more apparent in Munich. Street corners, dark alley ways, or train stations became collaborators in constructing youth as delinquent: time and again adult authorities construed young people seen within these environments as deviant by default. Not surprisingly, young people became increasingly active in evading such deviant spaces and adult supervision overall. As demonstrated in *Coming of Age,* they began challenging spatial frameworks in their attempt to create spaces for youth. Conflicts surrounding juvenile delinquency thus played out within certain city spaces: black markets and the areas surrounding American barracks in the crisis years; street corners and milk bars in the 1950s; or parts of Schwabing, the university or even courtrooms during the protest years. Some scholarship has addressed such connections to space[1] but specific historical studies focusing on juvenile delinquency seldom keep these important frameworks in mind.

The actual young had agency throughout this transitional period in modern German history, and it clearly increased as Munich came of age. Throughout the crisis years, young people had comparable little input or power concerning the construction of youth. Many protested once picked up and detained to supposed educational facilities; most tried to evade raids the best they could. Yet overall U.S. officials and local authorities had an easy time to create and manufacture threatening images of male and female delinquency to then pick up delinquents on the streets of Munich. The rise of youth cultures and a widespread commercialization of West German society throughout the 1950s then showed a slight shift. Youth had become profitable and the young gained a little more agency. Soon young people organized themselves in groups and clubs, and began contributing to the constructions of youth. This trend continued in the following years, triggered by the political awakening of young people in the Schwabing riots in 1962. Young males and females increasingly organized in community initiatives and student organizations, and they found ways to spread their own views and constructs of youth. Alternative media outlets, or the simple willingness to speak up and provoke, thus complicated broad narratives and simplistic constructs around juvenile delinquency in Munich. Such growth of agency ultimately diversified society, a process that captures an overall democratization.[2] Historian Dieter Rink argues that youth cultures have provoked German society over the years, and such exposure to difference has made West Germany more tolerant. Society has, according to Rink, "abstained from criminalizing, excluding, and destructing" various youth cultures since the 1970s.[3] *Coming of Age* agrees with this interpretation although it is important to note that authorities often became simply more subtle in their responses.

The analyzed images of youth were social constructs and created representations. Homelessness, black-marketeering, and fraternization among the young did exist. But in the postwar period in Munich, these were much more complex phenomena. At best 10 percent of the young population overall could be broadly described as *the Halbstarke*. The supposed widespread nature of *the teenager* is more difficult to assess. However, sources suggest that she was also a limited phenomenon, if she existed at all. In the mid-1950s, most girls could rarely leave the house and if they did could not simply go into a nightclub to dance. Milk bars or maybe their own rooms remained their prime space, always near authorities. *The student* and *the Gammler* were not the only carriers of protests, and the latter in particular was a small yet visible group. At times, carefree or careless youngsters found themselves demonized as Gammlers throughout the 1960s, a dynamic speaking to the power of this construct in Munich as elsewhere.[4] Similarly, at the riots and protests in Schwabing, not even half of those arrested were students; at the protests at the Buchgewerbehaus building six years later, students played a key role in organizing but did not carry out the protests themselves. Instead, it was a broader movement of protestors aimed against emergency laws, the War in Vietnam, and various other issues. Over time, this changed, and by the early 1970s actual university students more fully endorsed *the student* as their identity. In general, however, authorities exaggerated juvenile deviancy throughout this period in Munich because it was beneficial.

Not surprisingly, most of these representations of young people are still evident in current historiography and a broader collective memory. *The delinquent boy* and *the sexually deviant girl* haunt discussions regarding the immediate postwar period. Both images have been reproduced by a variety of scholars to underline the devastation after the war. In that sense, juvenile delinquency became a symbol for the state of postwar Munich. *The Halbstarke* has elicited numerous publications to this day. Most of them do not go beyond a brief acknowledgment regarding the limited visibility of this image; some even reproduce questionable characteristics, making sporadic references to the possibility of a moral panic insufficient. *The teenager* has seen less scrutiny overall—apart from broad and general references to the rise of American youth culture. Some recent conversations have added some complexities, namely in the context of discussing the youth magazine *Bravo*. Finally, *the student*—more so than *the Gammler*—has become an almost mystical image, and has taken on a life of its own. Some see the democratization of society rooted in the arrival of *the student;* others nervously recall the end of traditional values, established morals, and social order. In fact, a high-ranking Munich police officer noted in 2009, "I am eighty-two years old and have managed to block out the events [occurring in the Bavarian capital in 1968]. I do not want to be reminded of them and do not want to get upset."[5] Protestor Reinhard Wetter, on the other hand, noted in a similar context that he does not want to participate in attempts to revisit the events of 1968 in Munich. He believes that too many simplifications and generalizations are apparent.[6] Personal recollections of those that came of age at that time sustain these dynamics as individuals align their memory along age, political leanings, and broader historical context. This then explains the widespread popularity of music, movies, or other cultural elements coming out of this timeframe, and the perhaps larger impact of the 1950s and 1960s on Germany's collective memory overall.

The existence of images of delinquency also hints at the constructed nature of intergenerational conflicts. Adults define and defend existing societal norms. This setup makes conflicts between different age groups—defined, at times, as generation gaps—seemingly inevitable. The young are generally more vulnerable and thus exposed to discrimination. Although most societies rely on these hierarchies, *Coming of Age* exposes the fact that intergenerational differences are largely constructed and not inescapable. Rooted in a continuing emphasis on juvenile delinquency and supposed misbehaviors, the media, various authorities, and a diverse mixture of other societal groups continually nourished distrust towards the young—and do so to this day. After all, the existence of delinquency is beneficial, making efforts to cultivate and, at times, promote, intergenerational conflicts a surprisingly widespread, lucrative, and persistent phenomena: institutions rely on generational differences to gain legitimacy, and marketing strategists hoping to make money off the young continually sustain generational divides. The actual young also define their identity based on exaggerated and partly imagined differences from adults. Actually, throughout the 1960s "'generation' served protesters ... as a political argument,"[7] as noted by one scholar. Pierre Bourdieu said it best, stating that "both youth and old age are socially constructed in the conflict (*lutte*) between the young and the old."[8]

Connections between constructing and controlling remain central to this volume. Interested in the benefits of constructing youth as deviant, *Coming of Age* demonstrates how social constructions can become powerful tools of social control. As indicated throughout this study, once adults framed youth as deviant, then each image of youth became a way to control the actual young, and society as a whole. By 1946, the existence of *the delinquent boy* allowed authorities to justify large-scale raids in less orderly areas of town; at the same time, the appearance of *the sexually deviant girl* justified broad and invasive health regulations; it also helped demonize fraternization. Later, the construction of *the Halbstarke* helped impose stricter traffic laws and brought more funds to traditional youth groups. Besides, police had a justification to increase surveillance of certain parts of town, namely working-class neighborhoods. Female youngsters demonized as *the teenager* faced stringent measures as well. Simply listening to rock 'n' roll music and idolizing Elvis was reason enough to be sent to juvenile detention, a frightening dynamic that speaks to the power of such discourses. Commercialization eventually provided another way to conform and domesticate youth: the promotion of an apolitical and consuming youngster, the new teenager, opened a profitable space in a fearful society. The events in Schwabing in 1962, combined with a politicization during the 1960s overall, allowed authorities to create the Schwabing police state: undercover police officers patrolled the streets and collected data, law enforcement infiltrated student groups, and city officials utilized urban planning to reclaim spaces mostly frequented by the young. The latter indicates again how space mattered, not only when constructing youth as deviant but also when trying to control the young.

The mere existence of certain constructions of youth became perhaps the most powerful tool of social control. As this microhistory demonstrates, defining and marking someone as an "abnormal Other" was a way to control their behaviors. Moreover, constituting norms and standards for all became a way to normalize society. Both trends affected Munich's formative years. Girls shortly after the war did not want to be called *Veronika Dankeschön*. They thus made sure to stay away from supposed deviant city spaces and avoided conversations with U.S. American soldiers, if at all possible. Similarly, many male youngsters worked hard and aligned with the demands of authorities; only then, they hoped, could they avoid being seen as delinquents. Shortly after the war, that was extremely difficult because scarcities pushed the young—like many others—to the black market or to the U.S. Military Government for resources and work. In the 1950s, lines became a little more blurred. Some male youngsters used certain elements of U.S. popular culture to create their own identities and subcultures. Their active participation in the construction of *the Halbstarke* makes an analysis of who constructed these images more complicated. The fact that authorities even perceived youngsters simply driving their mopeds to work as deviant and threatening nonetheless outlines the power of this construct. This means, in some cases, it was a stigma to be called a *Halbstarke*, and any behavior along these lines had to be prevented; other youngsters enjoyed the attention and used this image to provoke, to test boundaries, or to simply enjoy being young. For young women, references to their sexual purity remained amongst the most powerful ways to control female bodies and behaviors. Combined with traditional values, girls in the 1950s were often exposed to the gaze of those around them. References like, "That does not suit a lady," and the possible stigmatization of being "a loose woman" were extremely powerful in a society that held up sexual repression and patriarchy. Finally, in the 1960s, youngsters, along with many other voices, most actively used the images of *the student* and *the Gammler* to provoke and to frame an alternative narrative of events. Whereas being called a *student* or *Gammler* did not necessarily lose its stigma, the use of both constructs by protestors indicates a certain progression: the young now more actively participated in the construction of youth. Yet it was the fact that protestors organized in the 1960s that made a difference against a state still employing harsh mechanisms of social control. Ultimately, as *Coming of Age* argues, adult authorities did not merely construct deviancy and blow it out of proportion, as noted by Stanley Hall and others; they also used the existence of delinquency to control society, to follow Michel Foucault. Desires to control were grounded in historical precedents, contemporary exigencies, conflicting motives of various actors, and the unique postwar situation.

These trends regarding constructing and controlling male and female youth in Munich expose much broader dynamics, including continuities in Munich's history and beyond. Discussions around 1945 as a supposed *Stunde Null* zero hour have been questioned by scholars focusing on *Alltagsgeschichte* for quite some time. *Coming of Age* aligns with such critiques. Unlike existing studies, however, it exposes continuities in regard to the management of youth. Young people felt only

minor differences regarding their treatment after 1945, and compared
to the Nazi period: they continued to be seen as deviant if they did not
align with largely traditional norms and frameworks. That local German authorities and the U.S. Military Government worked together so
closely when it came to dealing with juvenile delinquency only hints at
even broader trends, especially since these authorities rarely agreed on
other issues. Furthermore, the protest years did not end in 1969. Instead, many authorities continued to hold on to *the student* even after
the end of broader debates and protests. For them, it was a useful tool
to continue to push their agenda. This reading challenges a top-down
approach that argues that federal dynamics—namely the chancellor-
ship of Willy Brandt—is more important when trying to understand a
sudden shift in discussions. Whereas over time broader debates within
West Germany around détente, amnesty, and more direct democracy
became noticeable in Munich, conservative state institutions in Bavaria actively questioned and challenged such an approach. The voices
of the young and others on the streets, this volume contends, are consequently significant when trying to make sense of larger historical
trends and complexities.

Conversations around youth more so than broad political shifts on
a federal level helped push Munich towards a more tolerant and open
society, an openness that had its limitations. As apparent in *Coming of
Age* and arguably for this transition period in modern German history
more broadly, authorities merely shifted towards more subtle mechanisms of social control. Direct actions in the forms of raids or invasive
health policies as apparent in the crisis years and certainly before that
increasingly lost their appeal, especially after the riots in Schwabing.
Until then, however, and in some instances beyond the early 1960s,
similarities between Munich in West Germany and the situation in city
spaces in East Germany are clearly apparent. But by the mid-1960s a
broader and organized coalition within the general public in Munich
protested directly against police brutality and invasive mechanisms
of social control—unlike in the GDR, where such protests were not
a possibility. Local officials responded to this not by rethinking their
approach overall, or even by stepping away from demonizing youth.
Constructing youth as deviant is a much too profitable framework.
Instead, adult authorities looked into more refined tactics to control
youth and society that seem to be more acceptable for a democracy:
undercover agents, surveillance, spatial planning, deescalation. All of
these frameworks were mechanisms of social control still aimed to
combat real and imagined juvenile delinquency; and all of them ultimately helped control much broader spectrums of society overall. In

this sense, coming of age for Munich and West Germany also meant growing up as a democracy by now employing more indirect and thus only outwardly tolerant mechanisms of social control.

Finally, and more globally speaking, constructions of youth as delinquent and attempts to utilize such representations to control young people and societies haunt public conversations well beyond Munich or Germany. In daily life the demonization of youth, or the war on youth as cultural critic Henry Giroux has described it,[9] takes many forms, especially in times of political and economic difficulties. A constructed distrust towards the young, grounded in the use of age as a way to frame hierarchies, is at the center of these conversations; moral panics involving gangs, rowdies, pregnant teenagers, or other concepts tied to juvenile delinquency are often the norm because these types remain lucrative setups for educators, child savers, and corporate interests alike. Historical studies must question the uncritical reliance on constructs of youth as delinquent much more broadly. As *Coming of Age* demonstrates, images of youth as deviant remain adult constructions in place due to many ulterior motives. Scholars need to be aware of this dynamic and should be extra careful when relying on such discourses in their own work. Such efforts, I hope, will more broadly affirm that talking about youth is much more than simply discussing young people.

Notes

1. See, for example: Tracey Skelton and Gill Valentine, eds., *Cool Places: Geographies of Youth Cultures* (New York, 1998); Axel Schildt and Detlef Siegfried, eds., *European Cities, Youth and the Public Sphere in the Twentieth Century* (Burlington, 2005).
2. Jarausch, *After Hitler*.
3. Dieter Rink, "Beunruhigende Normalisierung: Zum Wandel von Jugendkulturen in der Bundesrepublik Deutschland," *Aus Politik und Zeitgeschichte* 5 (2002): 3–6, here 6. See also: Krüger, "Vom Punk zum Emo," in *Inter-cool 3.0*.
4. Ross, *May '68 and Its Afterlives*.
5. Stankiewitz, *München '68*, 76.
6. Ibid., 52.
7. Holger Nehring, "'Generation' as a Political Argument in West European Protest Movements during the 1960s," in *Generations in Twentieth-Century Europe*, 57–78, here 57.
8. Jones, *Youth*, 3. See also: Bourdieu, "Youth Is Just a Word," in *Sociology in Question*.
9. Henry Giroux, *America's Education Deficit and the War on Youth* (New York, 2013).

Bibliography

Archives

Army Heritage and Education Center/U.S. Army Military Institute
Bayerisches Hauptstaatsarchiv München (BayHStAM)
    Ministerium des Inneren
    Staatskanzlei
    Pressesammlung
Bayerische Rundfunk. Historisches Archiv (BRHistAM)
    Fernseh- und Rundfunkarchiv/ Dokumentation
Bayerisches Staatsbibliothek München (BayStaBiM)
Deutsches Jugendinstitut München (DJIM)
Institut für Zeitgeschichte München (IfZM)
    Office of the Military Government (OMGUS)
Monacensia. Literatur und München Bibliothek (MonM)
Sozialpädagogische Sammlung Archiv München (SozipädAM)
Staatsarchiv München (StAM)
    Plakatsammlung
    Polizeidirektion München
    Polizeipräsidium München
    RA
    Schulämter
Stadtarchiv München (StadtAM)
    Bürgermeister & Rat
    Gesundheitswesen
    Kreisjugendring
    Polizeidirektion München
    Pressesammlung
    Ratsitzungsprotokolle
    Schulamt
    Stadtchronik
    Wohlfahrt
    Zeitungsarchiv
Universitätsbibliothek München (UniBibM)

Newspapers, Magazines, and Journals

8-Uhr Blatt
Allgemeine Deutsche Lehrerzeitung
Bayerische Staatsanzeiger/Bayerische Staatszeitung
Bravo
Caritas
Constanze
Das Steckenpferd
Der Münchner Merkur
Der Münchner Stadtanzeiger
Der Pinguin
Der Ruf
Der Simpl
Der Spiegel
Der Stern
Deutsche Jugend
Die Abendzeitung
Die Bildzeitung/Bild am Sonntag
Die Frankfurter Allgemeine Zeitung
Die Neue Zeitung
Die politische Meinung
Die Polizei
Die Süddeutsche Zeitung
Die Welt/Welt am Sonntag
Die Zeit
Europa Archiv
Frankfurter Hefte
Harlaching-Pinguin
Jugend. Münchner Illustrierte Wochenschrift für Kunst und Leben
Merkur
Mittelbayerische Zeitung
Münchner Zeitung
Neue Juristische Wochenschrift
Newsweek
profil
Quick
Ruf ins Volk
Stars and Stripes
Teen
Teenager. Zeitschrift für die Jugend
The Munich American
The New York Times
Twen
Unsere Jugend
Welt der Jugend

Primary Source Documents and Compilations of Oral Histories

Allemann, Fritz R. *Bonn ist nicht Weimar.* Cologne, 1956.

Améry, Jean. *Teenager-Stars: Idole unserer Zeit.* Rüschlikon/Zurich, 1960.

Amt des Amerikanischen Hochkommissar für Deutschland, ed. *Bericht über Deutschland. 21. September 1949–31. Juli 1952.* Frankfurt am Main, 1952.

Archiv der Jugendkulturen e.V., ed. *50 Jahre Bravo.* Berlin, 2006.

Armed Forces, ed. *GYA: Give Your Aid.* Armed Forces Assistance Program to German Youth Activities (U.S.), 1948.

B. "Musik dröhnt aus Automaten." *Ruf ins Volk* (1957): 76.

Bach, Julian. *America's Germany: An Account of the Occupation.* New York, 1946.

Bals, Christel. *Halbstarke unter sich.* Cologne/Berlin, 1962.

Barden, Judy. "Candy-Bar Romance: Women of Germany." In *This Is Germany,* ed. Arthur Settel, 161–76. New York, 1950.

Baumann, Angelika, ed. *Münchner Nachkriegsjahre 1945–1946–1947–1948–1949–1950. Lesebuch zur Geschichte des Münchner Alltags. Geschichtswettbewerb 1995/96.* Munich, 1997.

———, ed. *Verdunkeltes München: Die Nationalsozialistische Gewaltherrschaft, ihr Ende und ihre Folgen. Geschichtswettbewerb 1985/1986.* Munich, 1995.

Bayerischer Rundfunk, ed. *Hörspielsendungen, 1945–1965. Radio München, Bayerische Rundfunk. Eine Dokumentation.* Munich, 1967.

Becker, Walter. "Automatisierte Freizeit." *Unsere Jugend* 11 (1959): 407–11.

———. *Jugend in der Rauschgiftwelle.* Hamm, 1968.

———. "Rock'n-Roll: Symbol der Auflehung." *Ruf ins Volk* (1958): 27–28.

———. "Der 'Siegeszug' des Rock'n Roll." *Ruf ins Volk* (1958): 90–91.

Beckh, Daniel. "Mohren, Zigaretten und Kinderspiele." In *Münchner Nachkriegsjahre. 1945–1946–1947–1948–1949–1950. Lesebuch zur Geschichte des Münchner Alltags: Geschichtswettbewerb 1995/96,* edited by Angelika Baumann, 57–63. Munich, 1997.

Berliner Geschichtswerkstatt, ed. *Vom Lagerfeuer zur Musikbox: Jugendkulturen, 1900–1960.* Berlin, 1985.

Bilek, Franziska. *Mir gefällts in München: Ein Geständnis in Bildern und Worten.* Munich, 1958.

Bondy, Curt. *Jugendliche stören die Ordnung: Bericht und Stellungnahme zu den Halbstarkenkrawallen.* Munich, 1957.

———. "A Psychological Interpretation of Waywardness." *Journal of Criminal Law and Criminology* 36, no. 1 (1945): 3–10.

———. "The Youth Village: A Plan for the Reeducation of the Uprooted." *Journal of Criminal Law and Criminology* 37, no. 1 (1946): 49–57.

Bondy, Curt, and Klaus Eyferth. *Bindungslose Jugend: Eine sozialpädagogische Studie über Arbeits- und Heimatlosigkeit.* Munich/Düsseldorf, 1952.

Borchert, Wolfgang. "Generation Without Farewell," 39–40. In *Draußen von der Tür.* New York, 1949.

Buckel, Anton. "Der verwahrloste Großstadtjugendliche und seine Erziehung in der Arbeitserziehungsanstalt." Ph.D. diss., Ludwig-Maximilians University Munich, 1948.

Buhmann, Inga. *Ich habe mir eine Geschichte geschrieben*. Munich, 1977.

Busemann, Adolf. "Verwilderung und Verrohung." *Unsere Jugend* 8 (1956): 159–68.

Clay, Lucius D. *Entscheidung in Deutschland*. Frankfurt am Main, 1950.

———. *The Papers of General Lucius D. Clay: Germany, 1945–1949*, edited by Jean Edward Smith. Bloomington, 1974.

Dehn, Günther. *Großstadtjugend: Beobachtungen und Erfahrungen aus der Welt der großstädtischen Arbeiterjugend*. Berlin, 1919.

Dolezol, Theodor. "Die Spontanen und ihre Organisatoren." *Deutsche Jugend* 8 (1960): 470–75.

Dollinger, Hans, ed. *Revolution gegen der Staat? Die außerparlamentarische Opposition—die neue Linke*. Bern, 1968.

———. *München im 20. Jahrhundert: Eine Chronik der Stadt von 1900 bis 2000*. 2nd ed. Munich, 2001.

Dutschke-Klotz, Gretchen. *Wir hatten ein barbarisch schönes Leben. Rudi Dutschke: Eine Biographie*. Cologne, 1996.

Ehrmann, Helmut, ed. *Bravo-Leser stellen sich vor*. Munich, 1961.

Engelmann, Susanne Charlotte. *German Education and Re-education*. New York, 1945.

Enzensberger, Hans Magnus. *Europa in Ruinen: Augenzeugenberichte aus den Jahren 1944–1948*. Frankfurt am Main, 1990.

Fingerle, Anton. *München: Heimat und Weltstadt*. Munich, 1963.

———. "Zur Schulreform in Deutschland." *Europa Archiv* 1 (1946): 303–7.

Friedlaender, Ernst. *Deutsche Jugend: Fünf Reden an die Trotzenden, an die Skrupellosen, an die Müden, an die Traditionsgebundenen, an die Suchenden*. Darmstadt, 1947.

Fröhner, Rolf. *Wie stark sind die Halbstarken? Beruf und Berufsnot, politische, kulturelle und seelische Probleme der deutschen Jugend im Bundesgebiet und in Westberlin*. Bielefeld, 1956.

Gallmeier, Michael. "Freizeit: Ein Problem der Gegenwart in Sicht der Erzieher." *Welt der Schule* 11, no. 7 (1958): 289–95.

Geschichtswerkstatt Neuhausen e.V., ed. *Vom Rio zum Kolobri–Halbstark in Neuhausen: Jugendkultur in einem Münchner Stadtteil 1948–1962*. Munich, 2001.

Göbel, Edith. *Mädchen zwischen 14 und 18: Ihre Problem und Interessen, ihre Vorbilder, Leitbilder und Ideale und ihr Verhältnis zu den Erwachsenen*. Hannover, 1964.

Godal, Eric, and Rolf Italiaander, eds. *Teenagers: Mit Beiträgen von 26 Autoren*. Hamburg, 1958.

Guenter, Klaus. *Protest der Jungen: Eine kritische Würdigung aus den eigenen Reihen*. Munich, 1961.

Haensch, Dietrich. *Repressive Familienpolitik: Sexualunterdrückung als Mittel der Politik*. Reinbek bei Hamburg, 1969.

Halbinger, Josefa. *Josefa Halbinger, Jahrgang 1900: Lebensgeschichte eines Münchner Arbeiterkindes*. 2nd ed., edited by Carlamaria Heim. Munich, 1990.

Havighurst, Robert. *Report on Germany*. New York, 1947.

Hechinger, Grace, and Fred Hechinger. *Die Herrschaft der Teenager*. Gütersloh, 1965.

Heigert, Hans. "Ein neuer Typ wird produziert: der Teenager." *Deutsche Jugend* 7 (1959): 117–21.

Heigert, Hans, and Werner Wirsing. *Stätten der Jugend.* Munich, 1958.

Hollstein, Walter. "Gammler und Provos." *Frankfurter Hefte* 22 (1967): 409–18.

———. "Hippies im Wandel." *Frankfurter Hefte* 23 (1968): 637–46.

Hollweck, Ludwig, ed. *Unser München. München im 20. Jahrhundert: Erinnerungen und Berichte, Bilder und Dokumente von 1900 bis heute.* Munich, 1967.

Holm, Kurt. *Die Bekämpfung der Geschlechtskrankheiten in Hamburg: Erfahrungen seit dem Inkrafttreten des neuen Gesetzes am 1. Oktober 1927.* Berlin, 1933.

Hopker, Wolfgang. "Mehr Freizeit—aber wozu? Vierzig-Stunden-Woche und die neue deutsche Gesellschaft." *Die politische Meinung* 2, no. 12 (1957): 46.

Hürten, Heinz, ed. *Akten Kardinal Michael von Faulhabers: III 1945–1952.* Paderborn, 2002.

Kaiser, Günther. "Die Kriminalität der sogenannten Halbstarken." *Unsere Jugend* 9, no. 7 (1957): 301–9.

———. *Randalierende Jugend. Eine soziologische und kriminologische Studie über die sogenannten "Halbstarken."* Heidelberg, 1959.

Kellermann, Henry J. *The Present Status of German Youth.* Washington, DC, 1946.

Kluth, Heinz. "Die Halbstarken: Legende oder Wirklichkeit?" *Deutsche Jugend* 4 (1956): 495–503.

Kosel, Margaret. *Gammler, Beatniks, Provos: Die schleichende Revolution.* Frankfurt am Main, 1967.

Kotteder, Franz, ed. *Der Krieg ist aus: Erinnern in München nach 1945. Ausstellung im Münchner Stadtmuseum.* Munich, 2005.

Kraus, Peter. *40 Jahre Rock 'n' Roll.* Vienna, 1997.

———. "Entenschwanz & Ponyfransen." In *Bravo 1956–2006,* edited by Teddy Hoesch, 100–113. Munich, 2006.

———. *I Love Rock 'n' Roll: Keine Zeit zum alt werden.* Heidelberg, 2006.

Krebs, Diethart. "Zur Geschichte und Gestalt der deutschen Jungenschaft." *Neue Sammlung* 6 (1966): 146–70.

Kronberger, Domvikar Franz Xaver, ed. *Chronik der Erzidioezese München und Freising für die Jahre 1945–1995.* Munich, 1997.

Kunzelmann, Dieter. *Leisten Sie keinen Widerstand! Bilder aus meinem Leben.* Berlin, 1998.

Küppers, Waltraut. *Mädchentagebücher der Nachkriegszeit: Ein kritischer Beitrag zum sogenannten Wandel der Jugend.* Stuttgart, 1963.

Lamprecht, Helmut. *Teenager und Manager.* Munich, 1965.

Landeshauptstadt München, ed. *Ein Neuer Anfang im Wohlfahrts-, Jugend- und Gesundheitswesen.* Munich, 1948.

———, ed. *Jugendbilder: Kindheit und Jugend in München. Geschichtswettbewerb 1987.* Munich, 1995.

———, ed. *Zur Geschichte der Erziehung in München. Lesebuch zur Geschichte des Münchner Alltags. Geschichtswettbewerb 1997/98.* Munich, 2001.

Langer, Erich, and Wilhelm Brandt. *Geschlechts-Krankheiten bei Kinder und Jugendlichen.* Berlin, 1948.

Lauter, Edeltraut. "Krieg und Jugendkriminalität der Stadt München 1939–1946." Ph.D. diss., Ludwig-Maximilians University Munich, 1947.

Lewin, Herbert. "Problems of Re-Educating Fascist Youth." *Journal of Educational Sociology* 19, no. 7 (1946): 452–58.

Liddell, Helen, ed. *Education in Occupied Germany.* Paris, 1949.

Linhart, Paula. "Von der Teenager-Mode zur Teenager-Bewegung." *Unsere Jugend* 11 (1959): 313–16.

Loduchowski, Heinz. *Teenager und Koedukation? Jugend der freien Welt in Gefahr.* Freiburg, 1960.

Lutz, Fritz. *Über den Dächern von München.* Munich, 1966.

Mees, Günther, and Günter Graf, eds. *Pater Leppich Spricht: Journalisten hören den 'roten' Pater.* Düsseldorf, 1952.

Merkt, Hans, ed. *Dokumente zur Schulreform in Bayern.* Munich, 1952,

Merritt, Anna J., and Richard L. Merritt, eds. *Public Opinion in Occupied Germany: The OMGUS Surveys, 1945–1949.* Urbana, 1970.

Metzger, Franz. "Die Musikbox als aktuelles Freizeitangebot der Jugendpflege?" *Deutsche Jugend* 8 (1960): 124–28.

Meyer, Sybille, and Eva Schulze, eds. *Wie wir das alles geschafft haben: Alleinstehende Frauen über ihr Leben nach 1945.* Munich, 1984.

Muchow, Hans Heinrich. "Zur Psychologie und Pädagogik der 'Halbstarken,' (II)." *Unsere Jugend* 8 (1956): 442–49.

———. *Sexualreife und Sozialstruktur der Jugend.* Reinbek bei Hamburg, 1959.

———. "Zur Psychologie und Pädagogik der 'Halbstarken,' (I)." *Unsere Jugend* 8 (1956): 388–94.

Münchner Aufbaugesellschaft, ed. *Ein halbes Jahrzehnt Schuttbeseitigung und Wiederaufbau in München: Tätigkeitsbericht der Münchner Aufbaugesellschaft m.b.H. für die Zeit von Anfang 1947 bis Ende 1951.* Munich, 1952.

Münster, Ruth. *Geld in Nietenhosen.* Stuttgart, 1961.

Neubelt, Wolfgang. "Der Streit um die Freizeit." *Unsere Jugend* 11 (1959): 121–24.

Nevermann, Knut, ed. *Der 2. Juni 1967: Studenten zwischen Notstand und Demokratie. Dokumente anläßlich des Schah-Besuchs.* Cologne, 1967.

Nirumand, Bahmann. *Persien, Modell eines Entwicklungslandes oder Die Diktatur der Freien Welt.* Reinbek bei Hamburg, 1967.

Obermaier, Franz, and Josef Mauerer. *Aus Trümmern wächst das neue Leben: Eine Chronik für Stadt und Land.* Munich, 1949.

Obermaier, Uschi, and Olaf Kraemer. *High Times: Mein wildes Leben.* 4th ed. Munich, 2007.

Office of Military Government for Germany, ed. *German Book Publishing and Allied Subjects, a Report.* New York, 1948.

Office of the U.S. High Commissioner for Germany, ed. *Elections and Political Parties in Germany, 1945–1952.* Salsbury, NC, 1976.

Oppen, Beate Ruhm von, ed. *Documents on Germany under Occupation, 1945–1954.* Oxford, 1955.

Ott, Hanns. "Freizeitgestaltung oder Freizeitbildung." *Deutsche Jugend* 5, no. 3 (1957): 107–13.

Pelke, Else. *Protestformen der Jugend: Über Beatniks, Gammler, Provos und Hippies.* Donauwörth, 1969.

Pfister, Peter, ed. *Das Ende des Zweiten Weltkriegs im Erzbistum München und Freising: Die Kriegs- und Einmarschberichte im Archiv des Erzbistums München und Freising.* Regensburg, 2005.

Picht, George. *Die deutsche Bildungskatastrophe: Analyse und Dokumentation.* Olten, 1964.

Pongratz, Lieselotte, and Hans Odo Hübner. *Lebensbewährung nach öffentlicher Erziehung.* Darmstadt, 1959.

Popert, Hermann Martin. *Helmut Harringa: Eine Geschichte aus unserer Zeit.* Dresden, 1905.

Prinz, Friedrich, and Maria Krauss, eds. *Trümmerleben: Texte, Dokumente, Bilder aus den Münchner Nachkriegsjahren.* Munich, 1985.

Raschen, Günter. "Die Krawalle der 'Halbstarken' als Probleme der Erwachsenen." *Unsere Jugend* 9, no. 1 (1957): 10–15.

Reich, Andreas, ed. *Bayerisches Hochschulgesetz: Kommentar.* Bad Honnef, 1977.

Reithmeier, Gundelinde. *Verwahrlosung und Kriminalität der Jugendlichen in München in den Nachkriegsjahren 1945–1947.* Munich, 1948.

Riedel, Hermann. *Gesetz über die Verbreitung jugendgefährdender Schriften: Vom 9. Juni 1953. Kommentar.* Siegburg, 1953.

Ruhl, Hans-Jörg, ed. *Unsere verlorenen Jahre: Frauenalltag in Kriegs- und Nachkriegszeit, 1939–1949, in Berichten, Dokumenten und Bildern.* Darmstadt, 1985.

Rühmelin, Hans. "Fischer, Kurt J., US-Zone, 1947." *So lebten wir... ein Querschnitt durch 1947* (1947): 3–27.

Sagitz, Walter. "Das Problem der 'Halbstarken' in psychologischer Sicht." *Neue Juristische Wochenschrift* 18 (1959): 806–7.

Schäfer, Rudolf. "Heimstätten für die Jugend." *Frankfurter Hefte* (1948): 883.

———. "Verwahrloste Jugend." *Frankfurter Hefte* (1947): 328–31.

Schelsky, Helmut. *Die skeptische Generation: Eine Soziologie der deutschen Jugend.* Düsseldorf, 1963.

Schimetschke, Heinz. "Der jugendliche Motorradfahrer." Ph.D. diss., University of Munich, 1958.

Schmid, Josef. "Kann eine wirksame Bekämpfung der Geschlechtskrankheiten auf die Dauer ohne Meldepflicht erfolgen?" Ph.D. diss., Ludwig-Maximilians University Munich, 1945.

Schneider, Reinhold. *Stolz und Verantwortung: Von der Sendung der Jugend.* Berlin, 1947.

Schneider-Schelde, Rudolf, ed. *Die Frage der Jugend: Aufsätze, Berichte, Briefe und Reden.* Munich, 1946.

Schoeps, Hans Julius, and Christoph Dannenmann, eds. *Die rebellischen Studenten: Elite der Demokratie oder Vorhut des linken Faschismus?* Esslingen am Neckar, 1968.

Schreiber, Manfred. "Die 'Schwabinger Krawalle.'" *Die Polizei* 56 (1965): 33–37.

———. "Die 'Schwabinger Krawalle'. Versuch einer Zwischenbilanz." *Die Polizei* 55 (1964): 37–40.

———, and Ernst Krack, eds. *München und seine Polizei.* Wiesbaden, 1964.

Schröder, Friedl. "Gefahr und Not der Halbstarken." *Allgemeine Deutsche Lehrerzeitung* 8, no. 17 (1956): 326–28.

Schultz, Clemens. *Die Halbstarken.* Leipzig, 1912.

Seeberger, Kurt, and Gerhard Rauchwetter, eds. *München. 1945 bis heute: Chronik eines Aufstiegs.* Munich, 1970.

Seeliger, Rolf. *Die außerparlamentarische Opposition.* Munich, 1968.

———. *Braune Universität: Deutsche Hochschullehrer gestern und heute. Dokumentation mit Stellungnahmen III.* Munich, 1964–1965.

Selig, Wolfram, Ludwig Morenz, Helmuth Stahleder, and Michael Schattenhofer, eds. *Chronik der Stadt München, 1945–1948.* Munich, 1980.

Sonntag, Sarah. "Am Samstag fängt das Wochenende an ..." *Deutsche Jugend* 8 (1960): 226–30.

Starr, Joseph. *Fraternization with the Germans in World War II.* Frankfurt am Main, 1947.

Stouffer, Samuel Andrew. *The American Soldier.* Princeton, 1949.

Strauß, Franz-Josef. *Die Erinnerungen.* Berlin, 1989.

Sulger, Lydia. *Vom Mädchen zur Frau.* Berlin-Dahlem, 1950.

Thurnwald, Hilde. *Gegenwartsprobleme Berliner Familien: Eine soziologische Untersuchung an 498 Familien.* Berlin, 1948.

Tietgens, Hans. "Zwischen 15 und 25: Die Heranwachsenden." *Deutsche Jugend* 7 (1959): 362–67.

United States Army, ed. *German Youth Activities Army Assistance Program Guide.* [Unknown], 1948.

United States Army, Europe, ed. *The U.S. Armed Forces German Youth Activities Program 1945–1955.* United States Army, Headquarters Europe, 1956.

U.S. Department of State, ed. *Germany, 1947–1949: The Story in Documents.* Prepared by Velma Hastings Cassidy. Washington, DC, 1950.

———, ed. *Occupation of Germany: Policy and Progress 1945–46.* Washington, DC, 1947.

The Visiting Committee of American Book Publishers, eds. *German Book Publishing and Allied Subjects.* Munich/New York, 1948.

Vogel, Hans-Jochen. *Die Amtskette: Meine 12 Münchner Jahre. Ein Erlebnisbericht.* Munich, 1972.

Wanderer and Dr. Silbereisen, "Teenager-Party und Jugendschutz." *Unsere Jugend* 11 (1959): 380–81.

Wetter, Reinhard, and Frank Böckelmann. *Knast Report.* Frankfurt am Main, 1972.

Wiechert, Ernst. *Rede an die deutsche Jugend 1945.* Zurich, 1945.

Wuermeling, Franz-Josef. *Demokratie und Jugendschutz.* Cologne, 1959.

———. *Ehe und Familie Heute.* Cologne, 1958.

Zook, George Frederick, ed. *Report of the United States Education Mission to Germany.* Washington, DC, 1946.

Secondary Sources

Agazzi, Elena, and Erhard H. Schütz, eds. *Handbuch Nachkriegskultur: Literatur, Sachbuch und Film in Deutschland (1945–1962).* Berlin, 2013.

Albrecht, Willy. *Der Sozialistische Deutsche Studentenbund (SDS): Vom partei-konformen Studentenverband zum Repräsentanten der neuen Linken.* Bonn, 1994.

Andersen, Arne. *Der Traum vom guten Leben: Alltags- und Konsumgeschichte vom Wirtschaftswunder bis heute.* Frankfurt am Main, 1999.

Angermaier, Elisabeth. *München: Bewegte Zeiten: Die 50er Jahre.* Munich, 2002.

———, and Richard Bauer. *Thomas Wimmer und sein München: Eine Stadt im Aufbau 1948–1960.* Munich, 1989.

Ariès, Philippe. *Centuries of Childhood: A Social History of Family Life.* New York, 1962.

Austin, Joe, and Michael Nevin Willard. "Introduction: Angels of History, Demons of Culture." In *Generations of Youth: Youth Culture and History in Twentieth Century America,* edited by Joe Austin and Michael Nevin Willard, 1–20. New York, 1998.

Bader, Arthur, ed. *20 Jahre Kreisjugend München-Stadt 1946–1966.* Munich, 1966.

Baring, Arnulf. *Machtwechsel: Die Ära Brandt-Scheel.* Stuttgart, 1982.

Bauer, Richard, ed. *Geschichte der Stadt München.* Munich, 1992.

———. *Ruinen-Jahre: Bilder aus dem zerstörten München 1945–1949.* Munich, 1983.

Bauß, Gerhard. *Die Studentenbewegung der sechziger Jahre in der Bundesrepublik und West Berlin: Handbuch.* Cologne, 1977.

Beauvoir, Simone de. *Brigitte Bardot and the Lolita Syndrome.* New York, 1972.

Beer, Ulrich. *Geheime Miterzieher der Jugend: Macht und Wirkung der Massenmedien.* Tübingen, 1975.

Behrens, Volker. "Rebellen, Jeans und Rock 'n' Roll: Neue Formen von Jugendprotest und Sozialkritik: … denn sie wissen nicht was sie tun (Rebel Without a Cause, 1955). In *Fischer Filmgeschichte. Band 3. Auf der Suche nach Werten 1945–1960,* edited by Werner Faulstich and Helmut Korte, 252–70. Frankfurt am Main, 1990.

Belting, Isabella. "Als Mutter jung war…" In *Nylon & Caprisonne: Das fünfziger Jahre Gefühl,* edited by Isabella Belting, 14–20. Wolfratshausen, 2001.

Benninghaus, Christina, and Kerstin Kohtz, eds. *'Sag mir, wo die Mädchen sind…' Beiträge zur Geschlechtergeschichte der Jugend.* Vienna, 1999.

Benz, Ute, ed. *Frauen im Nationalsozialismus: Dokumente und Zeugnisse.* Munich, 1993.

Benz, Wolfgang, ed. *Neuanfang in Bayern, 1945–1949: Politik und Gesellschaft in der Nachkriegszeit.* Munich, 1988.

Berger, Manfred. "Bravo: 50 Jahre Pubertätserotik und Teenie-Pop." *Unsere Jugend* 58 (2006): 341–44.

Berger, Stefan. *The Search for Normality: National Identity and Historical Consciousness in Germany since 1800.* New York, 1997.

Berthold, Eva, and Norbert Matern. *München im Bombenkrieg.* Düsseldorf, 1983.

Bickerich, Wolfram. *Franz-Josef Strauß.* Düsseldorf, 1996.

Biddiscombe, Perry. "Dangerous Liaisons: The Anti-Fraternization Movement in U.S. Occupation Zones in Germany and Austria, 1945–1949." *Journal of Social History* 34, no. 3 (Spring 2001): 611–47.

Biess, Frank, Mark Roseman, and Hanna Schissler, eds. *Conflicts, Catastrophe and Continuity. Essays on Modern German History.* New York, 2007.

Bloemke, Rüdiger. *Roll Over Beethoven: Wie der Rock 'n' Roll nach Deutschland kam.* St. Andrä-Wördern, 1996.

Boehling, Rebecca L. *A Question of Priorities: Democratic Reforms and Economic Recovery in Postwar Germany: Frankfurt, Munich, and Stuttgart under U.S. Occupation, 1945–1949.* New York, 1998.

Böhnisch, Lothar. "Historische Skizzen zur offenen Jugendarbeit," (I), (II). *Deutsche Jugend* 32 (1984): 460–70 and 514–20.

Bordo, Susan. *The Male Body: A New Look at Men in Public and Private.* New York, 1999.

Borscheid, Peter. "Auto und Massenmobilität." In *Die Einflüsse der Motorisierung auf das Verkehrswesen von 1886 bis 1986,* edited by Hans Pohl, 117–41. Stuttgart, 1988.

Böttcher, Hans. *Sind Gammler Ganoven? Einige Auffälligkeiten und Anfälligkeiten der heutigen Jugend.* Gladbeck/Westfalen, 1968.

Bourdieu, Pierre. "Strukturalismus und soziologische Wissenschaftstheorie." In *Zur Soziologie der symbolischen Formen,* 7–40. Frankfurt am Main, 1974.

———. *Sociology in Question.* Translated by Richard Nice. London, 1993.

Boyer, Christoph, and Hans Woller. "Hat die deutsche Frau versagt? Die neue Freiheit der deutschen Frau in der Trümmerzeit 1945." *Journal für Geschichte* 2 (1983): 32–36.

Brandes, Volkhard. "Schwabinger Nacht '62. Über einen vergessenen Aufbruch in die Revolte." *PädExtra* 14, no. 1 (1986): 36–40.

———. *Wie der Stein ins Rollen kam: Vom Aufbruch in die Revolte der sechziger Jahre.* Frankfurt am Main, 1988.

Brandt, Allan. *No Magic Bullet: A Social History of Venereal Disease in the United States since 1880.* Oxford, 1987.

Brauerhoch, Annette. *"Fräulein" und GIs. Geschichte und Filmgeschichte.* Frankfurt am Main/Basel, 2006.

Braun, Annegret, and Norbert Göttler, eds. *Nach der 'Stunde Null' II: Historische Nahaufnahmen aus den Gemeinden des Landkreises Dachau 1945 bis 1949.* Munich, 2013.

Briesen, Detlef, and Klaus Weinhauer, eds. *Jugend, Delinquenz und gesellschaftlicher Wandel: Bundesrepublik Deutschland und USA nach dem Zweiten Weltkrieg.* Essen, 2007.

Broszat, Martin, Elke Fröhlich, and Falk Wiesemann. *Bayern in der NS-Zeit.* Munich, 1983.

Broszat, Martin, Klaus-Dietmar Henke, and Hans Woller, eds. *Von Stalingrad zur Währungsreform: Zur Sozialgeschichte des Umbruchs in Deutschland.* 3rd ed. Munich, 1990.

Brown, Timothy S. "'1968' East and West: Divided Germany as a Case Study in Transnational History." *American Historical Review* 114, no. 1 (2009): 69–96.

Bungenstab, Karl-Ernst. *Umerziehung zur Demokratie! Re-education-Politik im Bildungswesen der US-Zone 1945–1949.* Düsseldorf, 1970.

Burleigh, Michael, and Wolfgang Wippermann, eds. *The Racial State: Germany 1933–1945.* Cambridge, 1991.

Burns, Rob, and Wilfried van der Will. *Protest and Democracy in West Germany: Extra-Parliamentary Opposition and the Democratic Agenda.* London, 1988.

Burschka, Manfred H. "Re-education und Jugendöffentlichkeit: Orientierung und Selbstverständnis deutscher Nachkriegsjugend in der Jugendpresse 1945–1948: ein Beitrag zur politischen Kultur der Nachkriegszeit." Ph.D. diss., Georg-August-University Göttingen, 1987.

Campt, Tina. *Other Germans: Black Germans and the Politics of Race, Gender, and Memory in the Third Reich.* Ann Arbor, 2004.

Carter, Erica. "Alice in the Consumer Wonderland: West German Case Studies in Gender and Consumer Culture." In *Gender and Generations,* edited by Angela McRobbie and Mica Nava, 185–214. Houndmills, 1984.

———. *How German Is She? Postwar West German Reconstruction and the Consuming Woman.* Ann Arbor, 1997.

Chaussy, Ulrich. "Jugend." In *Die Geschichte der Bundesrepublik Deutschland. Gesellschaft,* edited by Wolfgang Benz, 207–42. Frankfurt am Main, 1989.

Cohen, Stanley. *Folk Devils and Moral Panics: The Creation of the Mods and Rockers.* 3rd ed. London/New York, 2002.

Crespi, Leo. "The Influence of Military Government Sponsorship in German Opinion Polling." *International Journal of Opinion and Attitude Research* 4 (1950): 151–78.

Dallinger, Peter, Christian Bode, and Fritz Dellian. *Hochschulrahmengesetz: Kommentar.* Tübingen, 1978.

Dannhäuser, Albin, ed. *Erlebte Schulgeschichte 1939–1955: Bayerische Lehrerinnen und Lehrer berichten.* Bad Heilbrunn, 1997.

Davis, Belinda, ed. *Changing the World, Changing Oneself: Political Protest and Collective Identities in West Germany and the U.S. in the 1960s and 1970s.* New York, 2010.

d'Eckardt, Bernard. *Brigitte Bardot: Ihre Filme, ihr Leben.* Munich, 1982.

Deiseroth, Dieter. "*Kontinuitätsprobleme der deutschen Staatsrechtslehre(r). Das Beispiel Theodor Maunz.*" In *Ordnungsmacht? Über das Verhältnis von Legalität, Konsens und Herrschaft. Helmut Ridder zum 60. Geburtstag gewidmet,* edited by Dieter Deiseroth, Friedhelm Hase, and Karl-Heinz Ladeur, 85–111. Frankfurt am Main, 1981.

Delille, Angela, and Andrea Grohn, eds. *Blick zurück aufs Glück: Frauenleben und Familienpolitik in den 50er Jahren.* Berlin, 1985.

———. *Perlonzeit: Wie die Frauen ihr Wirtschaftswunder erlebten.* Berlin, 1985.

Dennis, Mike, and Norman LaPorte. *State and Minorities in Communist East Germany.* New York, 2011.

Deutsches Jugendinstitut, ed. *Immer diese Jugend! Zeitgeschichtliches Mosaik 1945 bis heute.* Munich, 1985.

Dilthey, Wilhelm. "Novalis." *Preußische Jahrbücher* 15, no. 6 (1865): 596–650.

Dirke, Sabine von. '*All Power to the Imagination!': The West German Counterculture from the Student Movement to the Greens.* Lincoln, 1997.

Dittrich, Klaus, ed. *I hob a Loch im Balkon! Geschichten vom Kreisjugendring München-Stadt, 1946–1986. Ein Lesebuch zum 40jährigen Bestehen des Kreisjugendring München-Stadt.* Munich, 1986.

Doderer, Klaus, ed. *Zwischen Trümmern und Wohlstand: Literatur der Jugend 1945–1960.* Weinheim, 1988.

Dollard, Catherine. "The *alte Jungfer* as New Deviant: Representation, Sex, and the Single Woman in Imperial Germany." *German Studies Review* 29, no. 1 (Feb. 2006): 107–26.

Dolle-Weinkauff, Bernd. *Comics*. Weinheim/Basel, 1990.

Domentat, Tamara. *"Hallo Fräulein!" Deutsche Frauen und amerikanische Soldaten*. Berlin, 1998.

Dornheim, Andreas. *Forever Young? Jugendarbeit im Kreisjugendring München-Stadt von 1945–2000*. Munich, 2004.

Drasdo, Luise. "Kein Dank für Veronika Dankeschön." *Sozial Extra. Zeitschrift für soziale Arbeit* 10, no. 4 (Apr. 1986): 34–38.

Dressen, Hermann, ed. *Jugendarbeit in Bayern: Weißbuch über die Situation junger Menschen, ihr Engagement in der Jugendarbeit, über Selbstverständnis und Aufgaben der Jugendorganisationen, des Bayerischen Jugendrings und der kommunalen Jugendpflege*. Munich, 1985.

Dressen, Wolfgang, Dieter Kunzelmann, and Eckhard Siepmann. *Nilpferd des höllischen Urwalds: Spuren in eine unbekannte Stadt: Situationisten, Gruppe SPUR, Kommune 1*. Giessen, 1991.

Earmath, Michael, ed. *America and the Shaping of German Society, 1945–1955*. Providence/Oxford, 1993.

Ehrenpreis, David. "The Figure of the Backfisch: Representing Puberty in Wilhelmine Germany." *Zeitschrift für Kunstgeschichte* 67, no. 4 (2004): 479–508.

Eichhorn, Joachim. *Durch alle Klippen hindurch zum Erfolg: Die Regierungspraxis der ersten Großen Koalition (1966–1969)*. Munich, 2009.

Eichler, Antje. *Protest im Radio: Die Berichterstattung des Bayerischen Rundfunks über die Studentenbewegung 1967/1968*. Frankfurt am Main, 2005.

Eisfeld, Rainer. *Als Teenager träumten: Die magischen 50er Jahre*. Baden-Baden, 1999.

Ellinghaus, Wilhelm. "Verfassungsmässigkeit des Paragraphen 175 RsTGB." *Kriminalistik* 8, no. 3 (1954): 61–63.

Ermarth, Michael, ed. *America and the Shaping of German Society, 1945–1955*. Oxford, 1993.

Erzbischöfliches Jugendamt München und Freising, ed. *Talente. Aufbruch. Leben. Das Erzbischöfliche Jugendamt München und Freising seit 1938*. Munich, 2005.

Esser, Raingard. "'Language No Obstacle': War Brides in the German Press, 1945–1949." *Women's History Review* 4 (2003): 577–606.

Evans, Jennifer. *Life Among the Ruins: Cityscape and Sexuality in Cold War Berlin*. New York, 2011.

Fack, Dietmar. "Jugend, Motorrad und Stadterfahrung: Die Kontinuität subkultureller motorsportlicher Milieus in der modernen Industriegesellschaft." In *Jahrbuch Jugendforschung 5*, edited by Jürgen Zinnecker and Hans Merkens, 95–120. Wiesbaden, 2005.

Falter, Josef. *Chronik des Polizeipräsidiums München*. 2nd ed. Munich, 1995.

Farin, Michael, ed. *Polizeireport München 1799–1999*. Munich, 1999.

Farren, Mick. *The Black Leather Jacket*. New York, 1985.

Faulstich, Werner, ed. *Die Kultur der fünfziger Jahre*. Munich, 2002.

Fay, Jennifer. "'That's Jazz Made in Germany!': 'Hallo, Fräulein!' and the Limits of Democratic Pedagogy." *Cinema Journal* 44, no. 1 (2004): 3–24.

Fehrenbach, Heide. "Rehabilitating Father*land*: Race and German Remasculinization." *Signs: Journal of Women in Culture and Society* 24 (1998): 107–27.

Fenemore, Mark. *Sex, Thugs and Rock 'N' Roll: Teenage Rebels in Cold-War East Germany.* New York, 2007.

Fenzl, Fritz. *Münchner Stadtgeschichte.* Munich, 1994.

Ferchhoff, Wilfried. *Jugend und Jugendkulturen im 21. Jahrhundert: Lebensformen und Lebensstile.* Wiesbaden, 2007.

———. "Musik- und Jugendkulturen in den 50er und 60er Jahren: Vom Rock' n'Roll der 'Halbstarken' über den Beat zum Rock und Pop." In *Handbuch Jugend und Musik,* edited by Dieter Baacke, 217–51. Opladen, 1998.

Fichter, Tilman, and Siegward Lönnendonker. *Macht und Ohnmacht der Studenten: Kleine Geschichte des SDS.* Hamburg, 1998.

Fink, Caroline, Philipp Gassert, and Detlef Junker, eds. *1968: The World Transformed.* Cambridge, 1993.

Fischer-Kowalski, Marina. *1958—Hooligans and 1968—Students: One Generation and Two Rebellions.* Vienna, 1982.

Fisher, Jaimey. *Disciplining Germany: Youth, Reeducation, and Reconstruction after the Second World War.* Detroit, 2007.

Fleischer-Schumann, Jürgen. *Das Bildungs- und Erziehungswesen in München 1945–1976: Die Ära Anton Fingerle.* Munich, 1987.

Flügel, Rolf. *Lebendiges Schwabing.* Munich, 1958.

Foitzik, Doris. "'Sittlich verwahrlost!'—Disziplinierung und Diskriminierung geschlechtskranker Mädchen in der Nachkriegszeit am Beispiel Hamburg." *1999. Zeitschrift für Sozialgeschichte des 20. und 21. Jahrhunderts* no. 1 (1997): 68–82.

———, ed. *Vom Trümmerkind zum Teenager: Kindheit und Jugend in der Nachkriegszeit.* Bremen, 1992.

Foucault, Michel. *Discipline and Punish: The Birth of the Prison.* 2nd ed. Translated by Alan Sheridan. New York, 1995.

———. *The History of Sexuality: An Introduction.* Vol. 1. Translated by Robert Hurley. New York, 1990.

Fox, Angela. "Flüchtlinge und Vertriebene nach 1945 in München." *Xenopolis* (2005): 307–15.

France, Alan. *Understanding Youth in Late Modernity.* Buckingham, 2007.

Freund-Widder, Michaela. *Frauen unter Kontrolle: Prostitution und ihre staatliche Bekämpfung in Hamburg vom Ende des Kaiserreichs bis zu den Anfängen der Bundesrepublik.* Münster, 2003.

Frevert, Ute. "Umbruch der Geschlechterverhältnisse? Die 60er Jahre als geschlechtspolitischer Experimentierraum." In *Dynamische Zeiten: Die 60er Jahre in den beiden deutschen Gesellschaften,* edited by Axel Schildt and Siegfried Detlef, 642–60. Hamburg, 2000.

———. *Women in German History: From Bourgeois Emancipation to Sexual Liberation.* Oxford/New York, 1989.

Fricke, Florian. *München rockt: Die wilde Zeit an der Isar.* Munich, 2007.

Froese, Leonhard, and Viktor von Blumenthal. *Bildungspolitik und Bildungsreform: Amtliche Texte und Dokumente zur Bildungspolitik im Deutschland der Besatzungszonen, der Bundesrepublik Deutschland und der Deutschen Demokratischen Republik.* Munich, 1969.

Fruhstorfer, Heidi, and Georg Fruhstorfer. *Hurra, wir leben noch! München nach 1945*. Munich, 2003.

Fuchs, Margot. "'Zucker, wer hat? Öl, wer kauft?' Ernährungslage und Schwarzmarkt in München 1945–1948." In *Trümmerzeit in München: Kultur und Gesellschaft einer deutschen Großstadt im Aufbruch 1945–1949*, edited by Friedrich Prinz, 312–19. Munich, 1984.

Fürmetz, Gerhard. "Polizei, Massenprotest und öffentliche Ordnung: Großeinsätze der Münchner Polizei in den frühen fünfziger Jahren." In *Öffentliche Ordnung in der Nachkriegszeit*, edited by Christian Groh, 78–106. Ubstadt-Weiher, 2002.

———. *Protest oder 'Störung'? Studenten und Staatsmacht in München um 1968*. Munich, 1999.

———, ed. *'Schwabinger Krawalle': Protest, Polizei und Öffentlichkeit zu Beginn der 60er Jahre*. Essen, 2006.

Fürmetz, Gerhard, Herbert Reinke, and Klaus Weinhauer, eds. *Nachkriegspolizei: Sicherheit und Ordnung in Ost- und Westdeutschland 1945–1969*. Hamburg, 2001.

Füssl, Karl-Heinz. *Die Umerziehung der Deutschen: Jugend und Schule unter den Siegermächten des Zweiten Weltkriegs, 1945–1955*. Paderborn, 1994.

Gallus, Alexander. "'Der Ruf': Stimme fur ein neues Deutschland." *Aus Politik und Zeitgeschichte* 25 (2007): 23–38.

Ganser, Armin, ed. *Zwanzig Jahre Bayerischer Jugendring: Ideengeschichte und Dokumentation; ein Beitrag zur Geschichte der Jugendarbeit nach 1945*. Munich, 1966.

Gassert, Philipp, and Martin Klimke, eds. "1968: Memories and Legacies of a Global Revolt." *Bulletin of the German Historical Institute*, Supplement 6 (2009).

Gehltomholt, Eva, and Sabine Hering. *Das verwahrloste Mädchen: Diagnostik in der Jugendhilfe zwischen Kriegsende und Reform*. Opladen, 2006.

Gellately, Robert. *Backing Hitler: Consent and Coercion in Nazi Germany*. Oxford, 2001.

Gerstenberg, Günter. *Hiebe, Liebe und Proteste: München 1968*. Munich, 1991.

Gießler, H. Jürgen. *APO-Rebellion Mai 1968: Die letzten Tage vor Verabschiedung der Notstandsgesetz. Dokumentation und Presseanalyse dieser Tage vor dem 30. Mai 1968*. Munich, 1968.

Gilbert, James. *A Cycle of Outrage: America's Reaction to the Juvenile Delinquent in the 1950s*. Oxford, 1986.

Gilfoyle, Timothy. "Prostitutes in History: From Parables of Pornography to Metaphors of Modernity." *American Historical Review* 104, no. 1 (Feb. 1999): 117–41.

Gillis, John. *Youth and History: Tradition and Change in European Age Relations 1770– Present*. New York/London, 1974.

Gimbel, John. *The American Occupation of Germany: Politics and Military 1945–1949*. Stanford, 1968.

Giroux, Henry. *America's Education Deficit and the War on Youth*. New York, 2013.

Glaser, Hermann. *The Rubble Years: The Cultural Roots of Postwar Germany, 1945–1948*. New York, 1986.

Glicher-Holtey, Ingrid, ed. *1968: Vom Ereignis zum Gegenstand der Geschichtswissenschaft*. Göttingen, 1998.

Goedde, Petra. "From Villains to Victims: Fraternization and the Feminization of Germany, 1945–1947." *Diplomatic History* 23, no. 1 (1999): 1–20.

———. *GIs and Germans: Culture, Gender and Foreign Relations, 1945–1949*. New Haven, 2003.

Gordon, Beverly. "American Denim: Blue Jeans and Their Multiple Layers of Meaning." In *Dress and Popular Culture*, edited by Patricia A. Cunningham and Susan Voso Lab, 31–45. Bowling Green, 1991.

Grob, Marion. *Das Kleidungsverhalten jugendlicher Protestgruppen im 20. Jahrhundert am Beispiel des Wandervogels und der Studentenbewegung*. Münster, 1985.

Grotum, Thomas. *Die Halbstarken: Zur Geschichte einer Jugendkultur der 50er Jahre*. Frankfurt am Main/New York, 1994.

Habermas, Jürgen. *Protestbewegung und Hochschulreform*. Frankfurt am Main, 1969.

Hafeneger, Benno. *Alle Arbeit für Deutschland: Arbeit, Jugendarbeit und Erziehung in der Weimarer Republik, unter dem Nationalsozialismus und in der Nachkriegszeit*. Cologne, 1988.

———. *Jugendarbeit als Beruf: Geschichte einer Profession in Deutschland*. Opladen, 1992.

Hall, G. Stanley. *Adolescence: Its Psychology and Its Relations to Physiology, Anthropology, Sociology, Sex, Crime, Religion, and Education*. Vol. 1. New York/London, 1922.

Hall, Stuart, Chas Critcher, Tony Jefferson, John Clarke, and Brian Roberts. *Policing the Crisis: Mugging, the State, and Law and Order*. New York, 1978.

Hall, Stuart, and Tony Jefferson. *Resistance Through Rituals: Youth Subcultures in Post-War Britain*. London, 1976.

Heineman, Elizabeth D. "The Hour of the Woman: Memories of Germany's 'Crisis Years' and West German National Identity." *American Historical Review* 101, no. 2 (Apr. 1996): 354–95.

———. *What Difference Does a Husband Make? Women and Marital Status in Nazi and Postwar Germany*. Berkeley, 1999.

Hemler, Stefan. "Von Kurt Faltlhauser zu Rolf Pohle: Die Entwicklung der studentischen Unruhe an der Ludwig-Maximilians-Universität München in der zweiten Hälfte der sechziger Jahre." In *1968: 30 Jahre danach*, edited by Venanz Schubert, 209-242. St. Ottilien, 1999.

———. "Wie die 68er-Revolte eines ihrer liberalen Kinder fraß: Eine kurze Geschichte der Humanistischen Studenten-Union, erzählt am Beispiel Münchens." *Vorgänge. Zeitschrift für Bürgerrechte und Gesellschaftspolitik* 40, no. 155 (2001): 49–61.

Henke, Klaus-Dietmar. "Fraternization." In *Die amerikanische Besetzung Deutschlands*, edited by Klaus-Dietmar Henke, 185–204. Munich, 1995.

Hering, Sabine. "Verwahrloste Mädchen' als Zielgruppe öffentlicher Erziehung: Ein Rückblick auf die Jahre 1945–1965." In *Sozialpädagogik: Vom Therapeutikum zur Weltgesellschaft. Systematische und historische Beiträge*, edited by Diana Franke, 135–50. Baltmannsweiler, 2005.

Hermann, Ulrich, ed. *Jugendpolitik in der Nachkriegszeit*. Weinheim, 1993.

———, ed. *Protestierende Jugend: Jugendopposition und politischer Protest in der deutschen Nachkriegsgeschichte*. Weinheim, 2002.

Herzog, Dagmar. *Sex after Fascism: Memory and Morality in Twentieth-Century Germany*. Princeton, 2005.

Hille, Barbara, and Walter Jaide, eds. *DDR-Jugend: Politisches Bewußtsein und Lebensalltag*. Opladen, 1991.

Hillel, Marc. *Die Invasion der Be-Freier: Die GIs in Europa 1942–1947*. Hamburg, 1983.

Hoesch, Teddy, ed. *Bravo 1956–2006*. Munich, 2006.

Höhn, Maria. "Frau im Haus und Girl im *Spiegel*: Discourse on Women in the Interregnum Period of 1945–1949 and the Question of German Identity." *Central European History* 26, no. 1 (1993): 57–90.

———. *GIs and Fräuleins: The German-American Encounter in 1950s West Germany*. Chapel Hill, 2002.

Hopkins, Jerry. *Elvis: A Biography*. New York, 1971.

Hosseinzadeh, Sonja, ed. *Nur Trümmerfrauen und Ami-Liebchen? Stuttgarterinnen in der Nachkriegszeit: Ein geschichtliches Lesebuch*. Tübingen, 1998.

Jacobsen, Hans Adolf, and Werner Jochmann. *Ausgewählte Dokumente zur Geschichte des Nationalsozialismus 1933–1945*. Bielefeld, 1961.

Janssen, Philip Jost. "Jugend und Jugendbilder in der frühen Bundesrepublik: Kontexte, Diskurse, Umfragen." Ph.D. diss., Zentrum für Historische Sozialforschung Cologne, 2010.

Janssen, Wiebke. *Halbstarke in der DDR: Verfolgung und Kriminalisierung einer Jugendkultur*. Berlin, 2010.

Jarausch, Konrad. *After Hitler: Recivilizing Germans, 1945–1995*. Translated by Brandon Hunziker. Oxford, 2006.

———. *Deutsche Studenten 1800–1970*. Frankfurt am Main, 1984.

Jobs, Richard Ivan. *Riding the New Wave: Youth and the Rejuvenation of France after the Second World War*. Stanford, 2007.

Jones, Gill. *Youth*. Malden, MA, 2009.

Jost, Hermand. *Kultur im Wiederaufbau: Die Bundesrepublik Deutschland 1945–1965*. Munich, 1986.

Kain, Florian. *Das Privatfernsehen, der Axel Springer Verlag und die deutsche Presse: Die medienpolitische Debatte in den sechziger Jahren*. Münster, 2003.

Karapin, Roger. *Protest Politics in Germany: Movements on the Left and Right since the 1960s*. University Park, 2007.

Kater, Michael. *Hitler Youth*. Cambridge, 2004.

Kebbedies, Frank. *Außer Kontrolle: Jugendkriminalitätspolitik in der NS-Zeit und der frühen Nachkriegszeit*. Essen, 2000.

Kenkmann, Alfons. *Wilde Jugend: Lebenswelt großstädtischer Jugendlicher zwischen Weltwirtschaftskrise, Nationalsozialismus und Währungsreform*. Essen, 1996.

Kershaw, Ian. *The 'Hitler Myth': Image and Reality in the Third Reich*. Oxford, 1987.

Kersting, Franz-Werner. *Jugend vor einer Welt in Trümmern: Erfahrungen und*

Verhältnisse der Jugend zwischen Hitler- und Nachkriegsdeutschland. Weinheim, 1998.

Kieseritzky, Wolther von, ed. *Willy Brandt: Mehr Demokratie wagen: Innen- und Gesellschaftspolitik 1966–1974.* Bonn, 2001.

Kiesinger, Kurt Georg. *Die große Koalition 1966–1969: Reden und Erklärungen des Bundeskanzlers,* edited by Dieter Oberndörfer. Stuttgart, 1979.

Kleinschmidt, Johannes. *Do not Fraternize: Die schwierigen Anfänge deutsch-amerikanischer Freundschaft, 1944–1949.* Trier, 1997.

Klimke, Martin, and Joachim Scharloth, eds. *1968: Handbuch zur Kultur- und Mediengeschichte der Studentenbewegung.* Stuttgart, 2007.

Kniep, Jürgen. *Keine Jugendfreigabe! Filmzensur in Westdeutschland 1949–1990.* Göttingen, 2010.

Knopp, Guido, prod. *Die großen Jahre des 20. Jahrhunderts 1900–1999.* Grünwald, 2000.

———. *Unser Jahrhundert: Deutsche Schicksalstage.* Munich, 2000.

Kock, Peter Jakob, ed. *Der Bayerische Landtag: Eine Chronik.* Bamberg, 1991.

———, ed.. *Der Bayerische Landtag, 1946–1948. 2 Bände.* Bamberg, 1986.

Koeber, Thomas, Rolf-Peter Janz, and Frank Trommler, eds. *Mit uns zieht die neue Zeit: Der Mythos Jugend.* Frankfurt am Main, 1985.

Krafft, Sybille, ed. *Frauenleben in Bayern von der Jahrhundertwende bis zur Trümmerzeit.* Munich, 1993.

———. *Zucht und Unzucht: Prostitution und Sittenpolizei im München der Jahrhundertwende.* Munich, 1996.

Krauss, Marita, ed. *Nachkriegskultur in München: Münchner städtische Kulturpolitik, 1945–1954.* Munich, 1985.

———. "Sprachlose Rebellen? Zur Subkultur der 'Halbstarken' in den fünfziger Jahren." In *Autonomie und Widerstand,* edited by Wilfried Breyvogel, 78–83. Essen, 1983.

Krüger, Heinz-Hermann, ed. *'Die Elvis-Tolle, die hatte ich mir unauffällig wachsen lassen.' Lebensgeschichte und jugendliche Alltagskultur in den fünfziger Jahren.* Opladen, 1985.

Krüger, Heinz-Hermann, et al., eds. *Inter-cool 3.0: Jugend Bild Medien: Ein Kompendium zur aktuellen Jugendkulturforschung.* Munich, 2010.

Kurme, Sebastian. *Halbstarke: Jugendprotest in den 1950er Jahren in Deutschland und den USA.* Frankfurt am Main, 2006.

Lammers, Nina. "*Bravo* und die Mediennutzung von Jugendlichen." In *50 Jahre Bravo,* edited by Archiv der Jugendkulturen e.V., 265–71. Berlin, 2006.

Lanzinner, Maximilian. *Zwischen Sternenbanner und Bundesadler: Bayern im Wiederaufbau 1945–1958.* Regensburg, 1996.

Large, David Clay. "Capital of the Anti-Movement? Munich and the End of World War II." Paper presented at the conference Germany and Versailles: Seventy-Five Years After, Berkeley, CA, 28 April–1 May 1995.

Lennox, Sara. "Constructing Femininity in the Early Cold War Era." In *German Pop Culture: How 'American' Is It?* edited by Agnes C. Mueller, 66–80. Ann Arbor, 2004.

Letzke, Christel. "Die Familie gab uns immer wieder Kraft." In *Jugendbilder: Kindheit und Jugend in München. Geschichtswettbewerb 1987,* edited by Landeshauptstadt München, 108–15. Munich, 1995.

Liedtke, Max, ed. *Handbuch der Geschichte des Bayerischen Bildungswesens. Vol. 3. Geschichte der Schule in Bayern. Von 1918–1990.* Bad Heilbrunn, 1997.

Limpf, Martin. *Das Motorrad: Seine technische und geschichtliche Entwicklung, dargestellt anhand der einschlägigen Fachliteratur.* Munich, 1983.

Lindner, Werner. *Jugendprotest seit den fünfziger Jahren: Dissens und kultureller Eigensinn.* Opladen, 1996.

Link, Jürgen. *Versuch über den Normalismus: Wie Normalität produziert wird.* 3rd ed. Göttingen, 2006.

Lipitz, Georg. "Who'll Stop the Rain? Youth Culture, Rock 'n' Roll, and Social Crisis." In *The Sixties. From Memory to History,* edited by David R. Farber, 206–34. Chapel Hill, 1994.

Lombroso, Cesare, and Guglielmo Ferrero. *Das Weib als Verbrecherin und Prostituierte: Anthropologische Studien.* Hamburg, 1894.

Lönnecker, Harald. "Studenten und Gesellschaft, Studenten in der Gesellschaft. Versuch eines Überblicks seit Beginn des 19. Jahrhunderts." In *Universität im öffentlichen Raum,* edited by Rainer Christoph Schwinges, 387–438. Basel, 2008.

Lovell, Stephen, ed. *Generations in Twentieth-Century Europe.* New York, 2007.

Lüdtke, Alf, ed. *The History of Everyday Life: Reconstructing Historical Experiences and Ways of Life,* translated by William Templer. Princeton, 1995.

———, Inge Marssolek, and Adelheid von Saldern, eds. *Amerikanisierung: Traum und Albtraum im Deutschland des 20. Jahrhunderts.* Stuttgart, 1996.

Ludwig-Maximilians-Universität München, ed. *Ludwig-Maximilians-Universität München.* Neukeferloh/Munich, 2001.

Lurie, Alison. *The Language of Clothes.* New York, 1981.

Lützke, Annette. "Öffentliche Erziehung und Heimerziehung für Mädchen 1954 bis 1975: Bilder 'sittlich verwahrloster' Mädchen und junger Frauen." Ph.D. diss., University-Gesamthochschule Essen, 2002.

Maase, Kaspar. *Bravo Amerika: Erkundungen zur Jugendkultur der Bundesrepublik in den fünfziger Jahren.* Hamburg, 1992.

———. "Entblößte Brust und schwingende Hüfte. Momentaufnahme von der Jugend der fünfziger Jahre." In *Männergeschichte–Geschlechtergeschichte. Männlichkeit im Wandel der Moderne,* edited by Thomas Kühne, 193–217. Frankfurt am Main/New York, 1996.

———, Gerd Hallenberger, and Mel van Elteren, eds. *Amerikanisierung der Alltagskultur? Zur Rezeption US-amerikanischer Populärkultur in der Bundesrepublik Deutschland und in den Niederlanden.* Hamburg, 1999.

Maier, Hans. *Böse Jahre, gute Jahre: ein Leben 1931 ff.* Munich, 2011.

Mannheim, Karl. "Das Problem der Generationen." In *Wissenssoziologie: Auswahl aus dem Werk,* edited by Kurt H. Wolff, 509–65, 2nd ed. Neuwied/Darmstadt, 1970.

Martin, Elaine. *Gender, Patriarchy, and Fascism in the Third Reich: The Response of Women Writers.* Detroit, 1993.

Maynes, Mary, Brigitte Søland, and Christina Benninghaus, eds. *Secret Gardens, Satanic Mills: Placing Girls in European History, 1750–1960.* Bloomington, 2005.

McDougall, Alan. *Youth Politics in East Germany: The Free German Youth Movement, 1946–1968.* Oxford, 2004.

McRobbie, Angela, and Mica Nava, ed. *Gender and Generation*. Houndmills, 1984.

Mehr, Max Thomas, ed. *Drachen mit tausend Köpfen: Spaziergänge durch linkes und alternatives Milieu*. Darmstadt, 1982.

Mitterauer, Michael. *A History of Youth*, translated by Graeme Dunphy. Oxford/Cambridge, 1992.

Moeller, Robert G., ed. "Reconstructing the Family in Reconstruction Germany: Women and Social Policy in the Federal Republic 1949–1955." *Feminist Studies* 15, no. 1 (1989): 137–69.

———. *West Germany Under Construction: Politics, Society, and Culture in the Adenauer Era*. Ann Arbor, 1997.

Mörchen, Stefan. "'Echte Kriminelle' und 'zeitbedingte Rechtsbrecher.' Schwarzer Markt und Konstruktion des Kriminellen in der Nachkriegszeit." *Werkstatt Geschichte* (2006): 57–76.

Mrozek, Bodo. "Halbstark! Aus der Urgeschichte der Popkultur." *Merkur* (2008): 630–35.

Müller, Hans Dieter. *Press Power: A Study of Axel Springer*. London, 1969.

Müller, Winfried. *Schulpolitik in Bayern im Spannungsfeld von Kultusbürokratie und Besatzungsmacht, 1945–1949*. Munich, 1995.

Nieden, Susanne zur. "Geschichten vom 'Fräulein'." *Feministische Studien* 13, no. 2 (1995): 25–33.

Niehuss, Merith. "Kontinuität und Wandel der Familie in den 50er Jahren." In *Modernisierung im Wiederaufbau: Die westdeutsche Gesellschaft der 50er Jahre*, edited by Axel Schildt and Arnold Sywottek, 316–34. Bonn, 1993.

Niethammer, Lutz. "Privat-Wirtschaft. Erinnerungsfragmente einer anderen Umerziehung." In *"Hinterher merkt man, dass es richtig war, dass es schiefgegangen ist": Nachkriegserfahrungen im Ruhrgebiet*, edited by Lutz Niethammer, 17–105. Berlin, 1983.

Nolte, Ernst. *Sinn und Widersinn der Demokratisierung der Universität*. Freiburg, 1968.

Nussbaumer, Josef. "Wirtschaftliche und soziale Entwicklung der Stadt München, 1945–1990." *Münchner Wirtschaftschronik* (1994): I/223–I/224.

Otto, Karl. *APO: Außerparlamentarische Opposition in Quellen und Dokumenten (1960–1970)*. Cologne, 1989.

———. *Vom Ostermarsch zur APO: Geschichte der außerparlamentarischen Opposition in der Bundesrepublik 1960–1970*. Frankfurt am Main, 1977.

Pankofer, Sabine. *Freiheit hinter Mauern: Mädchen in geschlossenen Heimen*. Weinheim/München, 1997.

Panzer, Marita A. "'Volksmütter.'" In *Frauenleben in Bayern von der Jahrhundertwende bis zur Trümmerzeit*, edited by Sybille Krafft, 234–319. Munich, 1993.

Parigger, Harald, Bernhard Schoßig, and Evamaria Brockhoff, eds. *'Schön ist die Jugendzeit...?' Das Leben junger Leute in Bayern 1899–2001*. Augsburg, 1994.

Peters, Karsten, ed. *'1200 Jahre Schwabing': Geschichte und Geschichten eines berühmten Stadtviertels*. Munich-Gräfelfing, 1982.

Peukert, Detlev. *Grenzen der Sozialdisziplinierung: Aufstieg und Krise der deutschen Jugendfürsorge von 1878 bis 1932*. Cologne, 1986.

———. "Die Halbstarken: Protestverhalten von Arbeiterjugendlichen zwischen Wilhelminischem Kaiserreich und Ära Adenauer." *Zeitschrift für Pädagogik* 30 (1984): 533–48.

———. *Jugend zwischen Krieg und Krise: Lebenswelten von Arbeiterjungen in der Weimarer Republik.* Cologne, 1987.

Pfeiffer, Zara S., ed. *Auf den Barrikaden: Proteste in München seit 1945.* Munich, 2011.

Phillips, Lily. "Blue Jeans, Black Leather Jackets, and a Sneer: The Iconography of the 1950s Biker and Its Translation Abroad." *International Journal of Motorcycle Studies* 1, no. 1. (2005).

Platt, Anthony. *The Child Savers: The Invention of Delinquency.* Newark, 2009.

Poiger, Uta. *Jazz, Rock, and Rebels: Cold War Politics and American Culture in a Divided Germany.* Berkeley, 2000.

———. "Rock 'n' Roll, Female Sexuality, and the Cold War Battle over German Identities." *Journal of Modern History* 68, no. 3 (1996): 577–616.

Poovey, Mary. "Figures of Arithmetic, Figures of Speech: The Discourse of Statistics in the 1830s." *Critical Inquiry* 19, no. 2 (1993): 256–76.

Potrykus, Gerhard, ed. *Jugendwohlfahrtsgesetz nebst Ausführungsgesetzen und Ausführungsvorschriften der deutschen Länder.* Munich, 1972.

Preis, Kurt. *München unterm Hakenkreuz: Die Hauptstadt der Bewegung: Zwischen Pracht und Trümmern.* Munich, 1980.

Prinz, Friedrich, ed. *Trümmerzeit in München: Kultur und Gesellschaft einer deutschen Großstadt im Aufbruch 1945–1949.* Munich, 1984.

Reimann, Aribert. *Dieter Kunzelmann: Avantgardist, Protestler, Radikaler.* Göttingen, 2009.

Reinke, Herbert. "'Leute mit Namen': Wohlstandskriminelle, Gammler und Andere." In *Repräsentationen von Kriminalität und öffentlicher Sicherheit: Bilder, Vorstellungen und Diskurse vom 16. bis zum 20. Jahrhundert,* edited by Karl Härter, Gerhard Sälter, and Eva Wiebel, 539–53. Frankfurt am Main, 2010.

Renz, Andreas. *Die Studentenproteste von 1967/68 im Spiegel der Münchner Presse.* Munich, 1992.

Richardi, Hans-Günter. *Bomber über München: Der Luftkrieg von 1939 bis 1945 dargestellt am Beispiel der 'Hauptstadt der Bewegung.'* Munich, 1992.

Richter, Pavel. "Die Außerparlamentarische Opposition in der Bundesrepublik Deutschland 1966 bis 1968." In *1968: Vom Ereignis zum Gegenstand der Geschichtswissenschaft,* 35–55, edited by Ingrid Glicher-Holtey. Göttingen, 1998.

Rink, Dieter. "Beunruhigende Normalisierung: Zum Wandel von Jugendkulturen in der Bundesrepublik Deutschland." *Aus Politik und Zeitgeschichte* 5 (2002): 3–6.

Roberts, Mary Louise. *Civilization Without Sexes. Reconstructing Gender in Postwar France, 1917–1927.* Chicago, 1994.

———. "The Price of Discretion: Prostitution, Venereal Disease, and the American Military in France, 1944–1946." *American Historical Review* 115, no. 4 (2010): 1002–30.

Roseman, Mark, ed. *Generations in Conflict: Youth Revolt and Generation Formation in Germany, 1770–1968.* Cambridge, 1995.

Ross, Kristin. *May '68 and Its Afterlives*. Chicago, 2002.

Roth, Lutz. *Die Erfindung des Jugendlichen*. Munich, 1983.

Roth, Maren M. *'Reeducation' in Bayern: Politischer Anspruch und Schulrealität*. Ulm, 1998.

Rümelin, Hans, ed., *So lebten wir...ein Querschnitt durch 1947*. Stuttgart, 1997.

Ruff, Mark Edward. *The Wayward Flock: Catholic Youth in Postwar Germany, 1945–1965*. Chapel Hill, 2005.

Rupp, Hans Karl. *Außerparlamentarische Opposition in der Ära Adenauer: Der Kampf gegen die Atombewaffnung in den fünfziger Jahren. Eine Studie zur innenpolitischen Entwicklung der BRD*. Cologne, 1980.

Rusinek, Bernd A. "Die Auswirkungen der Niederlage von Stalingrad auf die deutsche Gesellschaft bis zum Ende des Krieges." *Sozialwissenschaftliche Informationen* 1 (1993): 30–36.

Sander, Helke, and Barbara Johr, eds. *BeFreier und Befreite: Krieg, Vergewaltigung, Kinder*. Munich, 1992.

Sander, Uwe, and Ralf Vollbrecht, eds. *Jugend im 20. Jahrhundert. Sichtweisen-Orientierungen-Risiken*. Neuwied, 2000.

Sauerteig, Lutz. "Die Herstellung des sexuellen und erotischen Körpers in der westdeutschen Jugendzeitschrift BRAVO in den 1960er und 1970er Jahren." *Medizinhistorisches Journal* 42 (2007): 142–79.

Sauter, Robert, ed. *75 Jahre Reichswohlfahrtsgesetz. Jugendhilfe zwischen Ordungsrecht und Sozialpädagogik*. Munich, 1999.

Savage, Jon. *Teenage: The Creation of Youth Culture*. New York, 2007.

Schäfer, Christine, and Christiane Wilke. *Die Neue Frauenbewegung in München 1968–1985*. Munich, 2000.

Scharinger, Karl. "Zur Reorganisation der Jugendarbeit in Bayern nach 1945." *Deutsche Jugend* 11 (1988): 491–97.

Scherl, Katja. "'Det is doch wie Kino': Marlon Brandos 'Der Wilde' als Vor- und Abbild jugenlicher Subkultur." In *Medienkultur und soziales Handeln*, edited by Tanja Thomas, 119–41. Wiesbaden, 2008.

———. "'Zeig Deine Orden, Elvis!' Banal Militarism als Normalisierungstrategie." In *Banal Militarism: Zur Veralltäglichung des Militärischen im Zivilen*, edited by Fabian Virchow and Tanja Thomas, 308–32. Bielefeld, 2006.

Schildt, Axel. *Moderne Zeiten. Freizeit, Massenmedien und 'Zeitgeist' in der Bundesrepublik der 50er Jahre*. Hamburg, 1995.

———. *Zwischen Abendland und Amerika. Studien zur westdeutschen Ideenlandschaft der 50er Jahre*. Munich, 1999.

Schildt, Axel, and Detlef Siegfried, eds. *Between Marx and Coca-Cola. Youth Cultures in Changing European Societies, 1960–1980*. New York, 2007.

———, eds. *European Cities, Youth and the Public Sphere in the Twentieth Century*. Burlington, 2005.

Schildt, Axel, and Arnold Sywottek. *Modernisierung im Wiederaufbau: Die westdeutsche Gesellschaft der 50er Jahre*. Bonn, 1993.

Schissler, Hanna, ed. *The Miracle Years: A Cultural History of West Germany, 1949–1968*. Princeton, 2001.

Schlamm, William S. *Die Grenzen des Wunders: Ein Bericht über Deutschland*. Zurich, 1959.

Schott, Herbert. "Gefahr für die Demokratie? Die Angst der Amerikaner vor Edelweisspiraten und Werwölfen in Bayern 1945/46." In *Ingolstadt im Nationalsozialismus: Eine Studie*, edited by Stadtarchiv Ingolstadt, 595–607. Ingolstadt, 1995.

Schroer, Timothy L. *Recasting Race after World War II: Germans and African Americans in American-Occupied Germany*. Boulder, 2007.

Schubert, Venanz, ed. *1968: 30 Jahre danach*. St. Ottilien, 1999.

Schulz, Kristina. *Der lange Atem der Provokation: Die Frauenbewegung in der Bundesrepublik und in Frankreich 1968–1976*. Frankfurt am Main, 2002.

Seiler, Signe. *Die GIs: Amerikanische Soldaten in Deutschland*. Reinbek bei Hamburg, 1985.

Shukert, Elfrieda, and Barbara Scibetta. *War Brides of World War II*. Novato, 1988.

Siegfried, Detlef. *Time Is on My Side: Konsum und Politik in der westdeutschen Jugendkultur der 60er Jahre*. Göttingen, 2006.

Siepmann, Eckhard, ed. *Bikini: Die Fünfziger Jahre: Kalter Krieg und Capri-Sonne: Fotos, Texte, Comics, Analysen*. Reinbek bei Hamburg, 1983.

———, ed. *CheSchahShit. Die Sechziger Jahre zwischen Cocktail und Molotow*. Berlin, 1984.

Simon, Titus. "Straßenjugendkulturen im Wandel: Brüche und Kontinuitäten im ordnungspolitischen und pädagogischen Umgang mit 'auffälligen' Jugendlichen." In *Jugendkulturen, Politik und Protest: Vom Widerstand zum Kommerz?* edited by Roland Roth and Dieter Rucht, 63–79. Opladen, 2000.

Skelton, Tracey, and Gill Valentine, eds. *Cool Places: Geographies of Youth Cultures*. New York, 1998.

Sommer, Karin. "In der 'Raubtierwelt' der Trümmerzeit: Jugendliche im Zonendeutschland." In *'Schön ist die Jugendzeit...?' Das Leben junger Leute in Bayern 1899–2001*, edited by Harald Parigger, Bernhard Schoßig, and Evamaria Brockhoff. Augsburg, 1994.

Springman, Luke. "Poisoned Hearts, Diseased Minds, and American Pimps: The Language of Censorship in the Schund und Schmutz Debates." *German Quarterly* 68, no. 4 (1995): 408–29.

Stankiewitz, Karl. *München '68: Traumstadt in Bewegung*. Munich, 2008.

Staudinger, Heinz. *Weilheimer Schulgeschichten, 1939–1952, Band 1*. Norderstedt, 2010.

Steege, Paul. *Black Market, Cold War: Everyday Life in Berlin, 1946–1949*. Cambridge, 2007.

———, Andrew Bergerson, Maureen Healy, and Pamela E. Swett. "The History of Everyday Life: A Second Chapter." *Journal of Modern History* 80, no. 2 (2008): 358–78.

Stephens, Robert P. *Germans on Drugs: The Complications of Modernization in Hamburg*. Ann Arbor, 2007.

Stern, Klaus, and Jörg Herrmann. *Andreas Baader: Das Leben eines Staatsfeindes*. Munich, 2007.

Stibbe, Matthew. *Women in the Third Reich*. Oxford, 2003.

Studentenwerk München, ed. *'Wo geht's hier zum Studentenhaus?' 75 Jahre Studentenwerk München*. Munich, 1995.

Sturm, Michael. "Tupamaros München: 'Bewaffneter Kampf', Subkultur und Polizei, 1969–1971." In *Terrorismus in der Bundesrepublik: Medien, Staat und Subkulturen in the 1970er Jahren,* edited by Klaus Weinhauer et al., 99–133. Frankfurt am Main, 2006.

———. "Zwischen Schwabing und Fürstenfeldbruck: Die Stadtpolizei München in der Reformzeit der Bundesrepublik." In *Die Geschichte des Erfolgsmodells BRD im internationalen Vergleich,* edited by Jörg Calließ, 147–72. Rehburg-Loccum, 2006.

Tast, Brigitte, and Hans-Jürgen Tast. *Brigitte Bardot: Filme 1952–1961. Anfänge des Mythos B.B.* Hildesheim, 1982.

Tempel, Helga. "Ostermärsche gegen den Atomtod." In *30 Jahre Ostermarsch: Ein Beitrag zur politischen Kultur der Bundesrepublik Deutschland und ein Stück Bremer Stadtgeschichte,* edited by Christoph Butterwegge, 11–14. Bremen, 1990.

Tent, James F. *Mission on the Rhine: Reeducation and Denazification in American-Occupied Germany.* Chicago, 1982.

Thomas, Nick. *Protest Movements in West Germany: A Social History of Dissent and Democracy.* Oxford/New York, 2003.

Thron, Hans-Joachim. "Schulreform im besiegten Deutschland: Die Bildungspolitik der amerikanischen Militärregierung nach dem Zweiten Weltkrieg." Ph.D. diss., Ludwig-Maximilians University Munich, 1972.

Timm, Annette F. "The Ambivalent Outsider: Prostitution, Promiscuity and VD Control in Nazi Berlin." In *Social Outsiders in the Third Reich,* edited by Robert Gellately and Nathan Stoltzfus. Princeton, 2001.

———. *The Politics of Fertility in Twentieth-Century Berlin.* Cambridge, 2010.

———. "Sex with a Purpose: Prostitution, Venereal Disease and Militarized Masculinity in the Third Reich." *Journal of the History of Sexuality* 11, no. 1/2 (2002): 223–55.

———. "'Think It Over!'—Soldiers, Veronikas and Venereal Diseases in Occupied Berlin." In *Es begann mit einem Kuss: Deutsch-alliierte Beziehungen nach 1945,* edited by Florian Weiss, 50–56. Berlin, 2005.

Torner, Evan. "'Das Steckenpferd' und die Jugendzeitschriften der fünfziger Jahre." In *Handbuch Nachkriegskultur: Literatur, Sachbuch und Film in Deutschland (1945–1962),* edited by Elena Agazzi and Erhard H. Schütz, 652–55. Berlin, 2013.

Trotha, Trutz von. "Zur Entshtehung von Jugend." *Kölner Zeitschrift für Soziolgie und Sozialpsychologie* 34 (1982): 254–76.

Unruh, Trude, ed. *Trümmerfrauen: Biografien einer betrogenen Generation.* Essen, 1987.

Volkmer, Ingrid. "Teenager: Ausgangspunkt medialer und ästhetischer Kommerzialisierung der Jugendphase." In *Jugend 1900–1970: Zwischen Selbstverfügung und Deutung,* edited by Dieter Baacke, Heinrich Lienker, Ralf Schmölders, and Ingrid Volkmer, 142–52. Opladen, 1991.

Wagner, Beate. *Jugendliche Lebenswelten nach 1945: Sozialistische Jugendarbeit zwischen Selbstdeutung und Reeducation.* Opladen, 1995.

Wehler, Hans-Ulrich. *Deutsche Gesellschaftsgeschichte: Vom Beginn des Ersten Weltkrieges bis zur Gründung der beiden deutschen Staaten, 1914–1949.* Munich, 2003.

———. *Gesellschaftsgeschichte: Bundesrepublik und DDR, 1949–1990.* Munich, 2008.

Weinhauer, Klaus. "Eliten, Generationen, Jugenddelinquenz und innere Sicherheit: Die 1960er Jahre und frühen 1970er Jahre in der Bundesrepublik" In *Recht und Justiz im gesellschaftlichen Aufbruch (1960–1975): Bundesrepublik Deutschland, Italien und Frankreich im Vergleich,* 33–58. Baden-Baden, 2003.

Weisbrod, Bernd. "Generation und Generationalität in der Neueren Geschichte." *Aus Politik und Zeitgeschichte* 8 (2005): 3–9.

Weiss, Florian, ed. *Es begann mit einem Kuss: Deutsch-alliierte Beziehungen nach 1945.* Berlin, 2005.

Wensierski, Peter. *Schläge im Namen des Herren: Die verdrängte Geschichte der Heimkinder in der Bundesrepublik.* 2nd ed. Munich, 2006.

Werse, Bernd. *Cannabis in Jugendkulturen. Kulturhistorische Betrachtungen zum Symbolcharakter eines Rauschmittels.* Berlin: Archiv für Jugendkulturen e.V., 2007.

Wesel, Uwe. *Die verspielte Revolution: 1968 und die Folgen.* Munich, 2002.

Whiteley, Sheila. *Too Much Too Young: Popular Music Age and Gender.* New York, 2003.

Whitney, Susan. *Mobilizing Youth: Communists and Catholics in Interwar France.* Durham, 2009.

Wickenhäuser, Silvia. "Amerikanische Reeducation und die deutsche Jugend: Mit besonderer Berücksichtigung von Radio München und AFN München." M.A. thesis., Ludwig-Maximilians University Munich, 2003.

Wierling, Dorothee. *Geboren im Jahr Eins: Der Jahrgang 1949 in der DDR: Versuch einer Kollektivbiographie.* Berlin, 2002.

Willett, Julie. "Behaving Like Brando: Transgressing Race and Gender in *The Wild One.*" *International Journal of Motorcycle Studies* 5, no. 1 (2009).

Willett, Ralph. *The Americanization of Germany, 1934–1949.* New York, 1989.

Wolff, Janet. *Kaufen Frauen mit Verstand?* Düsseldorf, 1959.

Wrage, Henning. "Neue Jugend: Einleitung." In *Handbuch Nachkriegskultur: Literatur, Sachbuch und Film in Deutschland (1945–1962),* edited by Elena Agazzi and Erhard H. Schütz, 641–65. Berlin, 2013.

Zacharias, Thomas. "Zwischen Ende der Nachkriegszeit und Anfang der Altbausanierung: Die Akademie von 1968 bis 1989." In *200 Jahre Akademie der bildenden Künste München,* edited by Nikolaus Gerhart, Walter Grasskamp, and Florian Matzner, 112–21. Munich, 2008.

Zahner, Daniela. *Jugendfürsorge in Bayern im ersten Nachkriegsjahrzehnt 1945–1955/56.* Munich, 2006.

Ziemke, Earl Frederick. *The U.S. Army in the Occupation of Germany 1944–1946.* Washington, DC, 1975.

Zierenberg, Malte. *Stadt der Schieber: Der Berliner Schwarzmarkt 1939–1950.* Göttingen, 2008.

Zimniok, Klaus. *Eine Stadt geht in den Untergrund: Die Geschichte der Münchner U- und S-Bahn im Spiegel der Zeit.* Munich, 1981.

Zinnecker, Jürgen. *Jugendkultur 1940–1985.* Opladen, 1987.

Zorn, Wolfgang. *Bayerns Geschichte seit 1960,* edited by Rolf Kießling. Regensburg, 2007.

Documentaries and Movies

Benedek, Laslo, prod. *The Wild One*. Burbank, 1953.

Brooks, Richard. prod. *Blackboard Jungle*. Culver City, 1955.

Depta, Oktavia, prod. *Wolfram Kunkel und die Schwabinger Krawalle*. Munich, 2009.

Drost, Bernd, prod. *Gestern und Heute. 'Schwabinger Krawalle.'* Munich, 1990.

Fleischmann, Peter, prod. *Herbst der Gammler*. Munich, 1967.

Forst, Willi, prod. *Die Sünderin*. Munich, 1951.

Jacobs, Werner, prod. *Conny und Peter machen Musik*. Munich, 1960.

Lévy, Raoul, prod. *Et dieu créa la femme*. Chicago, 1956.

Marischka, Ernst, prod. *Sissi; Sissi, die junge Kaiserin; Sissi, Schicksalsjahre einer Kaiserin*. Munich, 1955/1956/1957.

Ray, Nicholas, prod. *Rebel Without a Cause*. Burbank, 1955.

Stears, Fred, prod. *Rock Around the Clock*. Culver City, 1956.

Tressel, Georg, prod. *Die Halbstarken*. Berlin, 1956.

Umgelter, Fritz, prod. *Wenn die Conny mit dem Peter*. Munich, 1958.

Radio Programs

Mrozek, Bodo, prod. *Bürger, Antibürger, Intellektuelle (2): Die motorisierte Rebellion*, radio program Bayerischer Rundfunk, Munich, aired Tuesday, 10 March 2009 (8:30 P.M.–).

Prinz, Friedrich, prod. *Bayern—Land und Leute. Besatzer und Besetzte. Politik in München in den ersten Jahren nach 1945*, radio program Bayerischer Rundfunk, Munich, aired Sunday, 22 January 1984 (1:30 P.M.–2:00 P.M.).

Websites (Online Archives)

Der Bayerische Rundfunk: Digitalisierte Bestände, accessible at http://www.br.de/unternehmen/inhalt/geschichte-des-br/br-historisches-archiv-100.html.

Bayerische Staatsbibliothek München, Bildarchiv, accessible at https://www.bsb-muenchen.de/literatursuche/spezialbestaende/bilder/.

Bravo Archive, accessible at http://www.bravo-archiv.de.

Media Archive Springer, accessible at http://www.axelspringer.de/artikel/Online-Datenbank-Medienarchiv68_1086007.html.

Protest Chronicle Munich, accessible at http://protest-muenchen.sub-bavaria.de.

SZ (Süddeutsche Zeitung) Photo, accessible at http://www.sz-photo.de.

Additional Interviews

Gerstenberg, Günther. Interview by author, summer 2010. Email.

Hederer, Joseph. Interviews by author, August 2009 and July 2010. Tape re-
    cordings. Munich.
W., Gary. Interview by author, summer 2009. Email.
W., Marga. Interview by author, summer 2009. Phone.
Robinow, Wolfgang F. Interview by author, summer 2010. Mail.

Index